The Taking of American Indian
Lands in the Southeast

The Taking of American Indian Lands in the Southeast

A History of Territorial Cessions and Forced Relocations, 1607–1840

David W. Miller

McFarland & Company, Inc., Publishers
Jefferson, North Carolina, and London

LIBRARY OF CONGRESS CATALOGUING-IN-PUBLICATION DATA

Miller, David W. (David Wesley), 1926–
The taking of American Indian lands in the Southeast : a history
of territorial cessions and forced relocations, 1607–1840 / David W. Miller.
p.   cm.
Includes bibliographical references and index.

ISBN 978-0-7864-6277-3
softcover : 50# alkaline paper ∞

1. Indian land transfers — Southern States — History.   2. Indian land
transfers — Southern States — History — Sources.   3. Indians of North
America — Relocation — Southern States — History.   4. Indians of North
America — Relocation — Southern States — History — Sources.   5. Southern
States — Race relations — History.   6. Southern States — Race relations —
History — Sources.   7. United States — Territorial expansion.   8. United
States — Territorial expansion — Sources.   9. Frontier and pioneer life — Southern
States.   10. Frontier and pioneer life — Southern States — Sources.   I. Title.
E78.S65M56   2011   970.004'97 — dc22   2011000215

BRITISH LIBRARY CATALOGUING DATA ARE AVAILABLE

Front cover: "The Trail of Tears" painting by Robert Lindneux (Woolaroc
Museum, Bartlesville, Oklahoma); eagle wings © 2011 Shutterstock

Manufactured in the United States of America

*McFarland & Company, Inc., Publishers
Box 611, Jefferson, North Carolina 28640
www.mcfarlandpub.com*

Dedicated to
Nancy Guinand Miller,
bricklayer extraordinaire

Table of Contents

Preface

Two factors triggered my interest in writing this book: retirement and a vague notion of the meaning behind the words Trail of Tears. With the availability of three outstanding library systems, the Library of Congress, George Mason University, and Fairfax County, and librarians at each who could and did give advice on research, the atmosphere for research and writing was excellent.

Once the subject of Indians was to be explored a natural starting point was with Jamestown. For many years I have lived and worked in Virginia and have on occasion traveled the Colonial Parkway with Jamestown and the Yorktown battlefield on one end and Williamsburg nearby. I knew Virginia had some small Indian reservations but knew nothing of the early relationship between the English settlers and the local Powhatan Indians. From this starting point there was a natural progression from the fascinating trials, harshness, and triumphs of the Jamestown settlement to the early displacement of Native Americans from the Virginia Piedmont.

There is no shortage of books and articles on the Indian-white relations east of the Mississippi River and south of the Ohio River. But my interest was not in analyzing what had gone before; rather, I wanted to read and write about what was actually said and written from 1607 to the 1830s. Starting with the historic writing by Captain John Smith and the courting John Rolfe of the early Jamestown years, there were ample sources to meet my objective.

The spellings of rivers and places can vary depending on the source. For example, "Nolichucky" is the correct spelling for the river today, but different spellings have been retained in the text when the source being relied on spells it differently. Another example is with "St. Marks" near the Apalachee Bay which borders present-day Florida. In the text it is sometimes spelled St. Mark's or Saint Marks. Again the spelling used in the source material has been followed.

I hope the reader will find as much pleasure in the information laid out here as I have had in sorting it out.

1

Before European Intrusion and Early Patterns of Exploitation

Before Columbus made his discovery in 1492 the Americas were sparingly populated on a per acre basis with social organizations of varying degrees of sophistication. Estimates varied widely, with the population of what would become the U.S. thought to be as low as 2 million and as high as 18 million. More concentrated populations, overall perhaps between 25 to 30 million, living in more organized settings, were below the Rio Grande in present Mexico and parts of Central and South America. The West Indies, where Columbus landed, may have had 8 million people.

Estimates of population are necessarily educated guesses, and the total New World numbers have ranged from 8 to 75 million. At that time, Europe, excluding Russia, had between 60 to 70 million. There may have been as many as 3,000 different languages used in the Americas with 550 in North America. As a consequence the Indians developed sign languages. Excluding pictographs and certain mnemonic articles such as designs in belts or beadwork often exchanged as wampum to illustrate points important in meetings, there were no written languages in North America. The name "Indians" was used by Columbus when he thought he had arrived at the Indies, outposts to Asia.

East of the Mississippi River, in the Northeast, was an important combination, the Five Nations (the English name) collectively referred to by the French as the Iroquois, containing five tribes concentrated mainly in central and western New York, the Mohawks, Oneidas, Onondagas, Cayugas, and Senecas, which became the Six Nations in 1722 when the Tuscaroras came north from North Carolina. Within the same Iroquoian language family, which is one way of classifying Indian groups, were the Hurons, a confederation of four aristocratic woodland tribes, living east of Lake Huron and on the upper St. Lawrence River and the Cherokee living in what are now upper Georgia and Alabama and ranging over Kentucky and Tennessee and the western parts of the Carolinas.

Many Northeastern tribes grouped with the Algonquian language were in the same region as the Iroquoian tribes. The Algonquians extended along the Atlantic coast between Virginia and the St. Lawrence River. An important Algonquian tribe west of the Appalachian Mountains living within the Ohio Valley was the Shawnee.

In the Ohio and upper Mississippi valleys once lived Indians referred to as Mound Builders. The Mound Builders may have been active at the time of Columbus, but largely eliminated, probably by disease, at the time the French traveled down the Mississippi River from Canada in the late 1600s. In mounds with buried dead often are found ornaments and gadgets, not weapons. Evidence like this has led some to think the various tribes east of the

Mississippi River lived among themselves in a peaceful environment. Others believe, overall, the tribes were warlike. In fact it is impossible to know how the tribes interacted before the Europeans arrived. That intrusion upset all relationships. Some studies conclude that the introduction of "smallpox, bubonic plague, measles, cholera, typhoid, pleurisy, scarlet fever, diphtheria, whooping cough, influenza, gonorrhea, viral pneumonia, malaria, yellow fever, dysentery, and alcoholism" may have reduced the native population by two-thirds or more.[1]

Thomas Jefferson discussed mounds, those of lesser dimensions and referred to as "barrows," with human remains commonly found in Virginia in the 1780s. One theory explored was that when Indians settled in a town "the first person who died was placed erect, and earth put about him, so as to cover and support him; that, when another died, a narrow passage was dug to the first, the second reclined against him, and the cover of earth replaced and so on."[2] After exploring a barrow, with a diameter of about 40 feet and a height of about 12 feet, Jefferson concluded upright burial was not involved.

The argument between what is disparagingly referred to as the "noble savage myth" and the belief that the pre–Columbian Indians had their share of warlike tendencies continues. On April 15, 2002, the *Washington Post* described a study of 3,375 pre–Columbian and 1,165 post–Columbian skeletons. The "[p]re–Columbian skeletons showed an 11 percent incidence of traumatic injuries ... compared with almost 17 percent for the post–Columbians." Each side reasoned that the study supported their view of pre–Columbian Indians.

Two types of agriculture were employed. The most elemental being "extensive" which involved clearing the land by cutting trees and burning vegetation and planting a crop. When the soil was no longer sufficiently productive, the farmer would allow the land to be fallow for a number of years to permit nature to replenish it for another round of crops. This type farming required a large spread of land to provide enough for the rotation from active farming to lying fallow. Those more sophisticated, and this was mostly in the more organized societies of Mexico and South America, used "intensive" methods to take advantage of the better soils by achieving greater production per acre by irrigation and fertilization. Terracing was common in the mountainous regions.

East of the Mississippi River the skilled farmers were those in the Southeast — the Creeks, Chickasaws, Choctaws, Cherokees, Yamasees, and Seminoles. Most of these spoke a form of Muskogean.

England was slow to put a successful colony on North America at Jamestown, Virginia, in 1607. By that time there had been many European voyages to the New World, that is, regions not known to the ancestors of those living, and English ships had explored the east coast from top to bottom. Without any colonies England was nonetheless sharing in the New World bounty by fishing off the coast and by pirating some of Spain's plunder. The defeat of the Spanish armada in 1588 set the stage for it to go further and to plant settlers in America.

An observation in 1602 that the Indians were willing to trade vast quantities of valuable furs for the most trivial English products foretold the wholesale slaughter of New World animals. By the 1620s the Dutch and French were importing about 30,000 beaver skins a year and smaller amounts of marten, otter, rabbit, deer, and fox skins. The popularity of beaver hats in Paris starting about 1580 spurred on the hunters. Something between 10 to 20 million beavers were killed in the seventeenth century and by 1640 the beaver had been cleaned out of New England.

Notwithstanding the absence of lasting European settlements north of Florida until the 1600s, the relatively small amount of contact, both with the Spaniards in the southern United States, Mexico, Central and South America, and the French and English in New England and Canada, proved devastating. Some think between 50 to 90 percent of the native population died from disease in the 1500s. Diseases probably spread along the Indian trade routes. Archeological studies show that stone found in Minnesota was used by Indians for their tobacco pipes "from Texas to Canada, and from California to Maine." "[C]opper from the upper Great Lakes [has been found in] archeological sites as far south as Mexico."[3]

When Hernando de Soto traveled through the southern United States in 1540 he found, perhaps near Augusta, Georgia, a "clean and polite" people "more civilized than ... seen in ... Florida, [who wore] clothes and shoes." Their 500 houses, in what appeared to be the seat of a great lord, were "all large and of the best materials." There was a hall filled with arms — long lances "with [gleaming] blades of bronze," and clubs and "axes with copper blades." However, there were few to wield the weapons. The town itself was empty as the result of a "recent pestilence." Four "longhouses [were] filled with bodies from the plague."[4]

Disease helped the Spaniards in their conquests of Mexico (1519–1521) and the Incas of South America (1531–1537). Successive epidemics in 1520, 1531, 1545, 1564, and 1576 of smallpox, mumps, and measles may have killed 18.5 million of a 25-million population. Without a large native population to carry on its looting, Spain imported slaves from Africa to fill the void. Spain also made the indigenous Indians work the mines, and in the 1500s made forays along the lower Atlantic Coast of what was to become the United States and kidnapped Indians to use as slaves. The English were active in taking slaves from Africa to the Americas starting with a trip in 1562.

2

Jamestown

Jamestown was a business opportunity undertaken by investors in the London Company which had hopes, not fulfilled, of the colonists finding gold. Arriving late in April after a four-month voyage in 1607, in three ships, the colonists were eager to go ashore, but it was the middle of May before the place for them to settle (Jamestown) was decided upon. The 104 left at Jamestown were "verie bare and scantie of victualls [and in] danger of the Savages."[1] They were not well suited to establish a colony. They did not know how to feed themselves. Their instructions from the London Company were "not to Offend the naturals, if [they could eschew it]," and to trade with the Indians "for Corn and all Other lasting Victuals" which trading should be done before the Indians "perceive[d] [they] mean[t] to plant among them."[2]

On June 22 two of the ships left to return to England for more colonists and supplies, leaving the pinnance *Discovery*. Deaths from disease and starvation soon reduced those in Jamestown — when the ships returned in January only 38 were still alive. Times had been such "that the living were scarce able to bury the dead."[3] But for the Indians supplying "victuals, as Bread, Corne, Fish, and Flesh in great plentie"[4] others may have perished. The abundance of wildlife around them wasn't utilized — Captain John Smith, leader of Jamestown between 1608 and 1609, wrote in 1608 that the colonists were "so weake and ignorant" and the "Beasts" and "foules" so large and wild that the colonists did not "much trouble them."[5]

The common belief that the struggle to survive was caused by the incompetence of the settlers and a lack of necessary supplies was questioned in 2005. Studies of the Jamestown site are finding ample evidence that the settlers had what was needed. Also what is called the "starving time," a period in 1609–1610 when the settlers would have perished but for the help of the Indians, is thought to have been more the result of a drought than the ineptness and indolence of the settlers.

Being placed inside an area occupied by the Pamunkey Indians, a confederation of 14,000 divided into villages each with from 200 to 1,000 people, it did not take long for ill feelings to surface between the English and the Indians. The various tribes had delineated areas and the Indian families had their own plots of land for growing crops. These Indians, referred to hereafter as Powhatans, reflect their leader, Chief Powhatan, whose Indian name was Wahunsonacock, but called Powhatan by the English because of the name of one of his residences.

To be in good favor with Powhatan was important. Smith said he was "very terrible and tyrannous in punishing such as offend" him. He was like an "Emperour" and had conquered much of the territory under his authority. Within this territory, he had a number of houses and ordinarily had "40 or 50 of the tallest men [of] his Country" attending him.

At night, around his house would be "4 Sentinels" one of whom "every halfe houre," would "hollowe" and any Sentinel failing to answer would be "beateh ... extreamely."[6] The truth of the oft repeated story of Powahatan's daughter Pocahontas saving Smith's life in 1608 cannot be proved by contemporary documents. The leaders of the London Company were anxious to take control in Virginia and ordered Smith to crown Powhatan so that he would, in English minds, be a British subject and the English would own the land. Powhatan refused to be crowned.

Smith, who traveled as far north as the Susquehanna River during his years at Jamestown (1607–1609), described the land around the colony as a "coast well watred, the mountaines very barren, the vallies very fertil, but the woods extreame thicke, full of Woolves, Beares, Deare, and other wild beasts."[7] On the relative duties of men and women Smith wrote that the "men bestowe their times in fishing, hunting, wars, and such manlike exercises, scorning to be seen in any woman like exercise, which is the cause that the women be verie painefull and the men often idle. The women and children do the rest of the worke. They make mats, baskets, pots, morters, pound their corne, make their bread, prepare their victuals, plant their corne, gather their corne, beare al kind of burdens and such like."[8]

Although Jamestown's surroundings may have been attractive, its location in a marshy area with ample mosquitoes and brackish water contributed to the death of some. The London Company's answer was to drop off more people. Between 1607 and 1625 over 7,000 were brought over from England. Some of these were apprenticed children who were typically indentured for seven years and were to have land when their apprenticeship was over. A rough census in 1625 showed only 1,210 people there; either 6,000 died or fled to the Powhatans. A step to sustain Jamestown was the imposition of martial law in 1610. The prohibitions were many and violations often punished with death. Whipping was the punishment for washing clothes in public or throwing out wash water into the streets, or for daring "to doe the necessities of nature" within a quarter-mile of the fort.[9]

The Powhatans were smart enough to not live in swampy areas. Smith described the village called Powhatan as "consisting of some 12 houses pleasantly seated on a hill ... about it many of their cornefields, the place is very pleasant, and strong by nature." Furthermore their houses "were capacious and clean, made of wooden frames in a bread-loaf shape and covered with either woven mats or bark sheets that were protective in winter ... and could be pulled back on either side to let in air and light the rest of the year."[10]

Considering that Jamestown would have ceased to exist but for the food provided by the Powhatans, there was a haughty, degrading attitude in England. A 1609 pamphlet said that "in Virginia the people are savage and incredibly rude, they worship the divell, like beasts, and in manners and conditions, differ very little from beasts, having no Art, nor science, nor trade, to imploy themselves, or give themselves unto, yet by nature loving and gentle, and desirous to imbrace a better condition. Oh how happy were that man which could reduce this people from brutishness to civilitie, to religion, to Christianitie, to the saving of their souls."[11]

Ironically many whites who later, either voluntarily or involuntarily, lived with Indians found that civilization superior to that of the whites. Bil Gilbert in *God Gave Us This Country* states that whites appeared to be annoyed that Indians "seemed to bestir themselves as it pleased them, did only enough to satisfy their immediate wants, and gave the impression of enjoying themselves in the process."[12]

William Byrd, of a Virginia plantation family, described Indians as "quite idle, or at most employed only in the gentlemanly diversions of hunting and fishing."[13] Benjamin Franklin noted in the 1750s that "when white persons, of either sex, have been taken prisoners by the Indians, and lived awhile among them, though ransomed by their Friends ... in a Short time they become disgusted with [the whites'] manner of Life ... and take the first Opportunity of escaping again into the Woods, from whence there is no reclaiming them."[14] Thirty years later, as the whites continued to push the Indians off their lands, Franklin observed that "[s]avages we call them, because their manners differ from ours, which we think the perfection of civility; they think the same of theirs."[15]

In 1784 Franklin wrote "In Remarks Concerning the Savages of North America" that "Politeness of the Savages in Conversation is indeed carried to Excess, since it does not permit them to contradict or deny the Truth of what is asserted in their presence; By this means they indeed avoid Disputes, but then it becomes difficult to know their minds, or what Impression you make upon them."[16] An unusual trait of the Indian society was the absence of forms of compulsion. The Indians of Virginia considered marriage to be sacred, allowed divorces, and eschewed infidelity.

If the English had known that the Indians had occupied Virginia from at least 9,500 B.C. they may have looked at their society with more respect and found that they had agricultural practices and medicine superior to that in Europe. The civilizing English, in less than a century, were able to almost "waste" the Virginia Indians. Robert F. Berkhofer, Jr., in his book *The White Man's Indian*, summarized the European justification for their treatment of the natives in the New World: "The spread of Christianity through the conversion of the heathen, the augmentation of private and public wealth through trade, and the enhancement of national and personal prestige and glory through colonization."[17]

Jamestown, down to 60 people who had survived a 1609 famine known as "the starving time," was almost abandoned in 1610, but was saved by the arrival of Thomas West, Lord Delawarr, in June with 150 new colonists and supplies. Over the next four years, under the leadership of West and his successors Thomas Dale and Thomas Gates, the colony was put back on its feet. New public works were completed, including new forts, and a new settlement, Henrico, established at a more desirable location up the James River from Jamestown. These were years of many small "ambuscades" by the Indians who either killed or tortured those attacked, and of the English slaying Indians, destroying villages and crops, and pushing Indians off land which was then occupied by settlers. Peace came to the colonists and the Indians in 1614, helped along by the marriage of Powhatan's daughter Pocahontas to the Englishman John Rolfe that year.

This marriage was not entered into lightly. Rolfe asked permission of Dale to marry. Rolfe denied that he was motivated by an "unbridled desire of carnall affection." Rather it was for the good of the plantation and "for converting to the true knowledge of God and Jesus Christ, an unbeleeving creature, namely Pokahuntas." He saw it as a required service to Jesus Christ since Pocahontas "desire[d] to be ... instructed in the knowledge of God."[18]

In a 1611 plea for more people for Virginia, the king was asked "to banish hither all offenders condemned to die, it would be a readie way to furnish us with men, and not allwayes with the worst kinde of men either for birth, spiritts or Bodie."[19] Thomas Gates who governed the colony from 1611 to 1614 brought 300 men and supplies to Jamestown in August 1611. To attract migrants the London Company stopped hinting that gold might be found and praised the land and climate — soil "strong and lustie" and climate "most sweete and wholsome."[20] A 1612 change in policy in the colony allowing private plots of land was an effort to make the colony self-supporting. Notwithstanding, for the next few years starvation killed some. The colonists had some bargaining status vis-à-vis the Indians. Goods otherwise unavailable to them could be provided. For example, around 1614 Jamestown entered an agreement with the nearby Chickahominy Indians for an annual exchange from every fighting warrior of two bushels of corn in exchange for a like number of hatchets. "Lawes Divine, Morall and Martiall" in effect in 1611 prohibited, without lawful authority, any "barter, trucke, or trade with Indians" and anyone using force or violence to "take away any thing from any Indian coming to trade" could be put to death.[21]

The settlers' immediate future was guaranteed when, in 1613 or 1614, the first shipment of tobacco, much wanted in Europe for its narcotic effects, was made. Smoking became fashionable in England in the 1580s and tobacco was expensive. The use of tobacco by the Indians was described in the 1560s: "The Floridians ... have a kind of herb dried, which, with a cane and an earthen cup in the end, with fire, and the dried herbs put together, do suck through the cane the smoke thereof, which smoke satisfies their hunger."[22]

Tobacco was controversial from the first. King James I wrote a pamphlet in 1604 titled *A Counterblaste to Tobacco* to discourage its use, and, but for the economic importance to the colony, its importation into England would have been stopped in 1621. James said smoking was "a custome lothsome to the eye, hateful to the nose, harmfull to the braines [and] dangerous to the lungs."[23] To the colony it was the essential commodity which it could trade for "the appareling of [their] bodies and other needful supplements."[24] In 1617 nearly 50,000 pounds were sent to England.

In an effort to overcome what had been a financial failure, in 1619 the London Company was reorganized and made the availability of land the attraction of the colony. One rationale for discounting any claim of the Powhatans to the land was that "land not actually built upon was unused and therefore unowned."[25]

The year 1619 also saw the introduction of representative government for eleven settlements. Burgesses, that is, representatives from boroughs, participated in governing the colony together with a Council of State (the governor and his councillors). Immediately enacted were laws prohibiting "injury or oppression ... against the Indians," and, as for making them part of the society, the colonists were enjoined to "neither utterly ... reject them nor yet to draw them to come in." No more than "five or six" could be admitted to a settlement and those should be under "good guard in the night ... for generally ... they [were] a most treacherous people." However, steps were to be taken to educate some Indian children. Under penalty of hanging, "no man [was to] sell or give any Indians any piece, shot, or powder, or any other arms, offensive or defensive." "[N]o man [was to] go to any Indian towns, habitations, or places of resort without leave from the governor or commander of that place where he lives." Sundry laws were passed relative to the price of tobacco, idlers, swearing, "gaming at dice and cards," drunkenness, taking property from one another or the Indians by "violence or stealth," and "dishonest company-keeping with women and suchlike."[26]

New leadership came to the Powhatans on the death of Powhatan in 1618 when his brother, Opechancanough, who had a visceral dislike of the English, took over. Pocahontas was no longer in Virginia to help smooth over conflicts between the two societies. She and her husband, John Rolfe, went to England in 1616 where she was feted as the "belle sauvage" and carried herself "as the daughter of a King."[27] She became ill as she prepared to return to Virginia and expired on March 21, 1617.

In 1622 war started with a sudden attack and the killing of 347 of the 1,240 settlers then in Virginia. The aim of the attack was elimination of all whites — no prisoners were taken. An even larger number of deaths was avoided by Jamestown and some nearby settlements receiving a warning about the planned attack. The massacre caused the colonists to retrench and to build a palisade across the peninsula from the James River to the York River. This protected about 300,000 acres. Following the attack the English systematically punished the Indians. Governor Francis Wyatt, who served in the years 1621–1626 and 1639–1642, preferred to separate the races: "It is infinitely better to have no heathen among us, who were but as thornes in our sides, than to be at peace and league with them."[28] In 1623 the Virginia Council of State claimed that more Indians were killed in the preceding year than had been in all the time to 1622. When rebuked by the London Company for their actions, the colonists showed no contrition. The London Company lost title to the colony in 1624 when its charter was revoked because of rampant waste and mismanagement. The Crown assumed ownership.

For the next 10 years ongoing hostility left death and destruction on each side. Finally a truce was reached in 1632. However, it did not last. In 1644 an aged Opechancanough again organized a concerted attack along the James which killed 500 settlers. This brought on retribution by the colonists then numbering 8,000 to 10,000. Peace came after Opechancanough was captured in 1646 by an energetic 40-year-old Sir William Berkeley who was governor of Virginia, off and on, for some 30 years starting in 1641. Within two weeks of his capture Opechancanough was assassinated. Speaking of the Virginians, John Winthrop, Sr., the long-time governor of the Massachusetts Bay Colony, said they included "a multitude of rude and misgoverned persons the very scumme of the land" who were after "profit and not the propagation of religion."[29]

Following peace in 1646 the English started what was to become a pattern followed elsewhere. The defeated Indians were required to transfer land to their conquerors and a limited area was reserved for the Indians to live on. The Virginia General Assembly passed a law in March 1661 requiring Indians to carry with them metal pieces of identification.

The day of the Powhatan was over. In 1625 the Powhatan population had fallen to 5,000 from a combination of pestilence and punitive Jamestown expeditions. Among the English acts was the poisoning and death of perhaps 200 Indians at a peace conference. The poison was included in wine used to toast one another's health and good fortune at the end of a meeting. The population was down to 2,000 in 1669 embedded in a Virginia population of 35,000 located near the Chesapeake Bay between the James and Potomac rivers.

3

Pushing West from the Virginia Coastal Region (1646–1687)

In Virginia, after the Powhatans were subdued in 1646, according to the peace treaty[1] the colonists were to have the land between the York and James rivers and the Indians were free "to inhabit and hunt" to the north of the York. The Indians acknowledged that they held their land at the will of the King of England, and in return would be protected by the Virginia Assembly. For the protection the Indians were "to pay ... twenty beaver skin att the goeing away of Geese yearely." The Indians were required to turn over to the English "all ... negroes and guns" in their possession. But, by 1649, with a clamor for more land, Governor William Berkeley allowed settlers to go north of the York. A peace treaty provision excluded Indians from white settlements on pain of death. When the Assembly found abuses of this provision which resulted in the killing of innocent Indians it changed the rule — Indians could not be killed "unless ... taken in the Act of doeinge trespasse, or other harme." The "trespasse, or other harme" could be proved by "the oathe of that partie by whome the Indian shall be discovered or killed."[2]

In 1662 the Virginia Assembly recognized the friction between the settlers and Indians and put much of the blame on the English, noting that "the mutuall discontents, complaints, jealousies and ffeares of English and Indians proceed chiefly from the violent intrusions of diverse English made into their lands forcing the Indians by way of revenge to kill the cattle and hogs of the English."[3] A new law protective of the Indians was passed. If a white settlement came within three miles of an Indian town, a fence had to be erected to protect the Indian cornfields. Indians could not be enslaved. Recognizing that it was easy to "affright [Indians] to a publique as well as a private acknowledgment" of the sale of land, thereafter there would be no alienation of land "now justly claymed or actually possest by any Indian or Indians."[4] But the Indians could lease their land.

When missionaries tried to convince Indians that they should embrace Christianity, one

> inquired why [the missionary] desired the Indians to become *Christians*, seeing the Christians were so much worse than the Indians are in their present state. The Christians, he said, would lie, steal, and drink, worse than the Indians. It was *they* first taught the Indians to be drunk: and *they* stole from one another ... and he supposed that if the Indians should become Christians, they would then be as bad as these. And hereupon he said, they would live as their *fathers* lived, and go where their *fathers* were when they died.[5]

By 1671 Virginia had a population of 35,000 to 40,000. The settlements there, as throughout the colonies to the north, generally hugged the coastlines of the Chesapeake Bay or the Atlantic Ocean. Such inland expansion as there was followed the rivers so as to maintain a water connection to England. In 1646 the House of Burgesses acted to protect settlers by building Fort Henry at what is now Petersburg, Virginia. It developed into a point from which explorers of inland areas embarked and as a trading post used by the Indians. Fifty years later a buffer between the Indians and established settlers was the object of Virginia offering acreage free of quit-rents for 20 years to organizations willing to settle on the frontier. The General Assembly specified that no fewer than "twenty able fighting men"[6] were needed for such cohabitations.

In the seventeenth century there was little perception as to how extensive North America was. Thomas Wood who, starting in the 1640s, was in charge of a fort near present-day Petersburg and a man of prominence in Virginia, around 1671 arranged for an expedition deep into the West. The mission was to find "the ebbing and flowing of the waters on the other side of the Mountains in order to discover[] the South Sea."[7] The explorers thought they saw "sails on the horizon." Before turning back they reached the point where the New River breaks through Peter's Mountain in Giles County, Virginia, and then headed back. Another trip in 1673 discovered the Cumberland Gap later used extensively for settling in Kentucky.

John Lederer, who explored the Virginia back country in 1669 and 1670, viewed some of the Shenandoah Valley from the top of a Blue Ridge mountain near what is now Front Royal, Virginia. Ultimately the valley, situated between the Blue Ridge and Allegheny mountains, which is 200 miles long with widths between 20 and 70 miles, became a new frontier occupied by those pushing west in Virginia and southwest from Pennsylvania.

Lederer wrote of his experience and advised that in exploring what was in 1670 the far West not

above half a dozen, or ten at the most, to travel together; and of these the major part Indians: for the Nations in your way are prone to jealousie and mischief towards Christians in a considerable Body, and as courteous and hearty to a few, from whom they apprehend no danger.

*   *   *

The Order and Discipline to be observed in this Expedition is, that an Indian scout or two march as far before the rest of the company as they can in sight, both for the finding out provision, and discovery of Ambushes, if any should be laid by Enemies. Let your other Indians keep on the right and left hand, armed not only with Guns, but Bills and Hatchets, to build small Arbours or Cottages of boughs and bark of trees, to shelter and defend you from the injuries of the weather. At nights it is necessary to make great fires round about the place where you take up your lodging, as well to scare Wild-beasts away, as to purifie the air. Neither must you fail to go the Round at the close of the evening: for then, and betimes in the morning, the Indians put all their designes in execution: in the night they never attempt any thing.

When in the remote parts you draw near to an Indian Town, you must by your Scouts inform your self whether they hold any correspondence with the *Sasquesahanaughs*: for to such you must give notice of your approach by a gun; which amongst other Indians is to be avoided, because being ignorant of their use, it would affright and dispose them to some treacherous practice against you.

Being arrived at a Town, enter no house until you are invited; and then seem not afraid to be led in pinion'd like a prisoner: for that is a Ceremony they use to friend and enemies without distinction.

You must accept an invitation from the Seniors, before that of young men; and refuse nothing that is offered or set afore you: for they are very jealous, and sensible of the least slighting or neglect from strangers, and mindful of Revenge....

If you barely designe a Home-trade with neighbour–Indians, for skins of Deer, Beaver, Otter, Wild-Cat, Fox, Racoon, &c. your best Truck is a sort of course Trading Cloth, of which a yard and a half makes a Matchcoat or Mantle fit for their wear; as also Axes, Hoes, Knives, Sizars and all sorts of edg'd tools. Guns, Powder and Shot, &c. are Commodities they will greedily barter for: but to supply the Indians with arms and ammunition, is prohibited in all English Governments.

In dealing with the Indians, you must be positive and at a word: for if they perswade you to fall any thing in your price, they will spend time in higgling for further abatements, and seldom conclude any Bargain. Sometimes you may with Brandy or Strong liquor dispose them to an humour of giving you ten times the value of your commodity....

To the remoter Indians you must carry other kinds of Truck, as small Looking-glasses, Pictures, Beads and Bracelets of glass, Knives, Sizars, and all manner of gaudy toys and knacks for children, which are light and portable.[8]

In 1671 a group of explorers under Thomas Batts and Robert Fallam followed the Staunton River until they crossed into the Ohio Valley by reaching the New River, the headwaters of which are only about 15 miles from those of the Staunton. They supported the idea of the Pacific Ocean being close by perceiving tidal action in the New. Another crossing into the Ohio Valley occurred in 1674. From the headwaters of the Yadkin River the explorers crossed over to the headwaters of the Tennessee River. The fur traders were not far behind and by the 1690s had reached the Ohio River.

A push to settle lands to the west in Virginia in the early 1700s came from the creation of a plantation culture supported by slaves. Smaller farmers were forced to move. Their movement was stimulated by a settlement on the Rapidan River which protected settlers from Indian attacks from the north. Land acquisition by those settling the Piedmont lands were dwarfed by speculators, including government figures and Tidewater planters, who managed to assemble large tracts of land even though the Crown did not want that to occur. In Virginia the Indians in the Piedmont were placed in a reservation. Thomas Jefferson, writing in about 1787, concluded that, other than some early taking of Indian lands by conquest, most of Virginia was acquired by purchase. However, in his original draft of his *Notes on the State of Virginia* he struck out a sentence reading: "it is true that these purchases were sometimes made with the price in one hand and the sword in the other."[9] Indians to the west willingly welcomed traders that traversed the mountains with goods to exchange for furs going as far as the Ohio River.

What Jefferson did not mention, and what facilitated the transfer of land in Virginia from the Indians to the English, was the diminishment of Indian numbers from "disease, malnutrition" and other factors. Writing in 1687 the Reverend John Clayton said the surviving coastal "Indian inhabitants of Virginia are now very inconsiderable as to their members and seem insensibly to decay though they live under English protection and have no violence offered them. They are undoubtedly no great breeders."[10] In the early years of the Jamestown colony the British did not recognize any right in the Indians to land settled on by English subjects.

4

England and France Compete and Clash

In the 1600s and 1700s France expended its exploration and settlement efforts to the northern part of North America and down the Mississippi River and used the water routes of the Ottawa and St. Lawrence rivers to support a thriving fur trade. Its goal was furs not land. By contrast, during the same period England concentrated on establishing colonies along the eastern seaboard of the United States from Maine to Florida. The French developed their claims by setting up trading posts, whereas the English, who started out with the trading post model peopled by employees of the sponsors, soon made land ownership of the colonists a goal, and, as a consequence, the English colonies filled with settlers who multiplied and expanded so as to make the eastern United States essentially an English preserve.

What became clear was that the Indian life was much worse for those who stayed close to the Europeans and adopted aspects of the European life. William Byrd, a Virginian who headed a survey party in 1728–1729 laying out the boundary between Virginia and North Carolina, described a visit to an Indian town, Nottoway, of about 200 which he said was the largest group remaining in Virginia. The number of Indians in Virginia, by which he meant that part which had essentially been occupied by Europeans, had dwindled in large measure from "their ungovernable passion for rum, with which ... they [had] been too liberally supplied by the English that live near them." Rather than working, the Indian men chose to "continue in ... idleness and to suffer all the inconveniences of dirt, cold, and want, rather than to disturb their heads with care or defile their hands with labor."[1] By adopting firearms, rather than continuing to rely on bows and arrows, they came to depend entirely upon the English, not only for their trade but even for their subsistence. Many settlers set examples of deception and many other evil habits.

Byrd describes an Indian custom that must have driven the Massachusetts Bay Puritans to distraction if the same persisted with Indians in the Northeast. Single Indian girls were encouraged to have "intrigues with the men" and it was considered a "superior merit to be liked by a great number of gallants." However, once married they were "faithful to their vows."[2] Such customs were still followed in the second half of the eighteenth century when European travelers wrote that "women before marriage have a right to act with men as they please" and when "an unmarried brave passes through a village, he hires a girl for the night, and her parents find nothing wrong in this."[3] But once there was a marriage generally such freedom ended.

A Pennsylvania settler was very complimentary of the Indians. Writing around 1700 he said, "They cultivate among themselves the most scrupulous honesty, are unwavering in keeping promises, defraud and insult no one, [and] are very hospitable to strangers."[4]

When the English built a fort at future Pittsburgh, the French, with 600 troops and 18 artillery pieces, commandeered the fort and named it Fort Duquesne. After George Washington and about 170 Virginia militia, sent in 1754 to protect the British fort, surrendered to a larger French force at Fort Necessity, some 55 miles from Fort Dusquene, larger battles were to come. Major General Edward Braddock, on his way to re-take Fort Duquesne, was overwhelmed in 1755 by a force of French and Indians when he was almost in sight of Fort Duquesne. Thereafter were a number of battles and raids near the St. Lawrence River. England prevailed when Quebec surrendered in 1759 and Montreal in 1760. Until the French were forced to abandon Fort Duquesne in 1758 they orchestrated Indian raids, mostly by Delaware and Shawnee, along the English frontier as far south as the Carolinas. In 1755 the French estimated more than 700 people in the Provinces of Pennsylvania, Virginia, and Carolina, including those killed and taken prisoner, had been disposed of. Washington reported that upward of fifty miles of a rich and once thickly settled country was quite deserted from Maryland to the Carolina line.

The North American victory did not guarantee that the French would not again have Canada. That was decided after two more years of war fought in far-off places and the final English triumph expressed in the February 1763 Treaty of Paris. Officially France's North American holdings were transferred to England and Spain with England receiving all east of the Mississippi River except for New Orleans and all of Canada from ocean to ocean. Spain gave England Florida in exchange for Cuba and, in a separate secret treaty, France gave Spain New Orleans and the Louisiana Territory west of the Mississippi.

5

The Cherokee and the French and Indian War

In the 1700s the Cherokee lived on both sides of the Appalachians, including the western Carolinas, northern Georgia, and eastern Tennessee (a name derived from the Cherokee town Tanase). Kentucky was a hunting ground shared with the Shawnee, located along the Ohio River, and marauding Iroquois. The nation, made up of 50 or so towns throughout these areas had an estimated population of 20,000 to 30,000 in 1730. The Overhill Towns were along the Little Tennessee River, the Middle Towns in western North Carolina, and the Lower Towns in far western South Carolina.

The towns on the eastern side of the Appalachians were hard hit by smallpox introduced by goods brought to Charles Town in a slave ship in 1738 and sold to the Cherokee, or possibly from contact 900 Cherokee warriors had with the Spanish when they fought them in Florida in 1739. Maybe as much as one-half the population perished. At the time, according to James Adair, a 40-year trader with the Cherokee, the Cherokee "religious physicians" had another explanation for the disease; it was caused by "the adulterous intercourse of their young married people, who in the past year, had in a most notorious manner, violated their ancient laws of marriage in every thicket."[1]

In 1761 the capital was Chota located on the Little Tennessee River. Lt. Henry Timberlake visited the Overhill Cherokee villages in 1761 and described their organization: "Their government, if I may call it government, which has neither law or power to support it, is a mixed aristocracy and democracy, the chiefs being chose according to their merit in war, or policy at home."[2] He observed that their leader's "power is rather persuasive than coercive, and he is reverenced as a father, more than a feared monarch. He has no guards, no prisons, no Officers of justice." In time of peace the principal chief would be one skilled in that situation whereas, when military action was needed, a war chief would lead.

Prior to the French and Indian war, according to a Joshua Fry report in 1751,[3] Virginia "never had any war, or league of peace [with the Cherokee] but a trade [had] been carried on with them for many years to the content and advantage of both sides." In the same report Fry said what became Kentucky was "uninhabited or at most [had] only some inconsiderable Indian villages." Fry's explanation for why the area was without resident Indians was that the Iroquois frequently traversed it on the way to "the Catawbas living in North Carolina merely for the sake of killing them." Fry noted that the Iroquois were not the power they once were — perhaps "a tenth of their number ... when they first waged war with the French of Canada." At the time of Fry's report Virginia's settlers generally had reached "the Alegany Ridge [today called the Blue Ridge], that is to the head springs [of Virginias's] rivers which run into the Atlantick Ocean."[4]

The British had a true friend in Attakullakulla, known as Little Carpenter, who relished a trip to England in 1730 as a young man in the company of six other noteworthy Cherokees. The group was presented to the king and otherwise given royal treatment. At the end of their four-month stay they signed an agreement of friendship and trade. Little Carpenter, whose name has been attributed to his skill as a carpenter and to his ability as a diplomat, was spokesman for the Cherokee in many of their dealings with the British.

An English intrusion into Cherokee territory was made in 1753. When South Carolina's relations with its Indian neighbors to the west deteriorated, South Carolina wanted to build a fort which would protect its frontier settlers and applied pressure in 1751 by stopping trade with the Cherokee. The Cherokee at earlier dates, back to 1746, had proposed a fort or forts in their territory. Their gain could have been regulation of the deerskin trade, a place of refuge if their towns were attacked, and a show that the English intended to protect them from attacks by the Creeks or French-allied Indians to the west and north of them. In 1753 the Cherokee agreed to a fort to be located among the Lower Towns. The fort was constructed over a 22-day period on the Keowee River opposite the village Keowee which was near today's Clemson, South Carolina. South Carolina purchased the needed land and named it Fort Prince George.

A Cherokee nation, with a population of about 14,000, or less, which translates to about 3,000 warriors, supported the English during the early years of the French and Indian War. When warfare broke out between the French and English in 1754, each sought a commitment of Cherokee warriors to fight on their side. At a meeting at Saluda Old Town in June 1755, the Cherokee pledged allegiance to the English. At the meeting the governor of South Carolina promised to proceed with a fort in the Overhill Towns and Fort Loudoun, located on the Little Tennessee River, was in place with a garrison at the end of 1756. Forts Loudoun and Prince George were each factors in the Cherokee War, starting in 1759, which included massacres of Indians and whites.

Those Cherokee thinking Fort Loudoun was a good idea were not willing to fight on the British side without a fort that would protect their women and children. Other Cherokee thought a fort near their capital Chota was not a wise move. The French warned that the British wanted to dominate them. After the Saluda meeting one of the Cherokees great warriors, Oconostota, led an expedition against the French.

Although Little Carpenter continued to be loyal to the British there were other Cherokee, mainly Tellico chiefs, who were sympathetic to the French. Little Carpenter left in September 1757 with war parties to fight the French and was gone for four months. On his return he gathered a force to help defend Virginia and to fight the French in the Ohio country. Storm clouds gathered when Virginians killed and scalped several Cherokee warriors either by mistaking the Cherokee for Indians allied with the French or solely to get the bounty offered by the Virginia legislature for scalps of Indians fighting with the French. Ill feelings increased when Little Carpenter refused to use Cherokee warriors against Shawnee at Fort Duquesne.

A new South Carolina governor, William Henry Lyttelton, asked Little Carpenter to come to Charles Town and, when he did, Lyttelton accused him of deserting the British. The differences became irreconcilable when warriors from the Overhill town Settico battled with Virginia militia and then, to get revenge for 19 Cherokee deaths from the encounter with the militia, the Settico took 19 white scalps from those living along the North Carolina frontier. The leading Cherokee chief, Old Hop, renewed discussions with the French and the British aggravated the Cherokee by stopping any ammunition going to them.

To talk about the ammunition situation in 1759 Oconostota and several other chiefs went to Charles Town to talk to Lyttelton. Oconostota told Lyttelton, "There has been blood spilled, but I am come to clean it up. I am a warrior, but want no war with the English."[5] Lyttelton was not for any compromise. He had already mustered 1400 militiamen and forced Oconostota and about 80 Cherokee to go with the militia to Fort Prince George. To restrain these warriors was an unpardonable act to the Cherokee, who considered them ambassadors seeking peaceful relations.

Little Carpenter went to Fort Prince George to talk with Lyttelton, who had released all but 28 of the Cherokee. Oconostota was still held and Lyttelton wanted 22 warriors who he considered guilty of murder turned over to him. A treaty signed by Little Carpenter and Oconostota provided for all the captives to be released when the Cherokee turned over those guilty of murder. Prematurely Lyttelton was hailed as victor when he returned to Charles Town.

Lyttelton's terms angered the Cherokee to the point that they erupted into violence. White traders and settlers were attacked and Fort Prince George cut off from communicating with Charles Town. A change in Cherokee leadership occurred in January 1760 when Old Hop died and was replaced as overall leader of the Cherokee by Standing Turkey, who was pro–French. An effort by Oconostota to get the hostages still held at Fort Prince George released led to the killing of some whites who were lured outside the fort and the killing of all the hostages when they tried to break out of the fort. Cherokee favoring peace, such as Little Carpenter, could not stop the urge of the Cherokee for revenge. Blood-thirst was as strong on the colonists' side. When five Cherokee were killed raiding a South Carolina fort the commanding officer said, "We have the pleasure to fatten our dogs upon their carcasses, and to display their scalps, neatly ornamented, on our bastions."[6]

Fort Loudoun, with a garrison of 200, was surrounded and cut off from relief from February to August in 1760. Help arrived in the summer of 1760 when 1,200 British troops were sent from Canada under the command of Colonel Archibald Montgomery. These regulars relieved Fort Prince George and systematically burned Lower Cherokee towns and burned their crops. This style of warfare was the undoing of the Cherokee in 1760 and later. The towns destroyed were described as "agreeably situated, [the] houses neatly built, and well provided, for they were in the greatest abundance of everything."[7] The Cherokee could not defend each town or the crops needed for their livelihood. They had to choose a place where they could confront the British, and they did in this case.

As the British moved on to the Middle Towns they were challenged by Oconostota at Etchoe Pass on the Little Tennessee River, near modern Franklin, North Carolina. The British suffered a loss of 140 men and decided to declare victory. They returned to Fort Prince George, being harassed by the Cherokee as they marched and then on to Charleston.

The starving soldiers at Fort Loudoun surrendered in August and were told they could return to Fort Prince George. A condition of their release was that all of the guns and powder at the fort be left. After the British marched 45 of the 140 miles to Fort Prince George they were attacked when it was learned an effort had been made to hide ammunition left at the fort. Except for John Stuart, who Little Carpenter arranged to have turned over to him, all of the officers were killed. Also killed were 26 other soldiers and 3 women. Most of the remainder of the Fort Loudoun garrison were allowed to proceed. Stuart arrived in Charles Town, at age 30, in 1748 and in 1756 commanded the provincial troops at Fort Loudoun. Between 1756 and 1760 he and Little Carpenter became friends and he was "extreamly beloved by the Indians."[8]

Oconostota's plan to use the guns captured at Fort Loudoun to attack Fort Prince George was abandoned when a French supply boat could not reach him. The Cherokee did not have staying power in warfare, nor could they rely on the French any longer since they had been defeated in Canada. After the capture of Fort Loudoun, Oconostota and others wanted peace and Little Carpenter was given the task of approaching the British. He gained favor by returning 10 survivors of Fort Loudoun in November 1760 and 12 more in March 1761. But the British were not ready for peace. Lord Jeffrey Amherst, the English commander in chief, did not believe in coddling Indians and after the victories over the French in Canada he wanted to erase a stain on the British army. He wrote Governor William Bull of South Carolina: "I must own I am ashamed for I believe it [the battle at Etchoe Pass] is the first instance of His Majesty's troops having yielded to the Indians."[9]

Amherst ordered 2,600 troops commanded by James Grant to punish the Cherokee, which they did starting in the spring of 1761. They marched to and through the Lower Towns, destroying what had been rebuilt, and continued on to Etchoe Pass where the Cherokee were defeated. The British continued on to the Middle Towns and "their towns, amounting to fifteen in number, besides many little villages and scattered homes [were] burnt; upwards of fourteen hundred acres of corn [was] entirely destroyed,"[10] leaving 5,000 Cherokees to starve. A separate threat to the Overhill Towns was a Virginia expedition carried out in the summer of 1761.

Little Carpenter negotiated a treaty with Bull which allowed the British to build forts wherever they liked and required Cherokees murdering whites to be put to death by the Cherokee, and whites, who killed Indians, to be turned over to the British. The treaty was signed on December 30, 1761. Another treaty with a different group of Cherokee was signed in November 1761 with representatives of Virginia at the Holston River near today's Kingsport, Tennessee. In the main the Cherokee leaders accepted that they could not oppose the British military.

Part of the Little Carpenter treaty was a new boundary line with South Carolina. Although it was never laid out on the ground, it moved the old line westward to one that was 40 miles from the lowest Cherokee town, Keowee. The new land was quickly settled. In April 1763 the *South Carolina Gazette* said 1,000 families from the north had settled in that area and 400 more were expected.

After the Holston River treaty Lt. Henry Timberlake spent about six months with the Cherokee at the Overhill Towns and noted competing factions there. One led by Little Carpenter and the other by Ostenaco and that "the two leaders [were] sure to oppose one another in every measure taken."[11] Timberlake took Ostenaco and 3 others to England in May 1762 and they were presented to the king. When they returned they met with Governor Bull and the South Carolina council and expressed loyalty to the British. Their visit to England gave them insight into reality. At least one was overawed: "The number of warriors and people all of one color ... far exceeded what we thought possibly could be."[12]

6

The Carolinas, Georgia, and the Southern Tribes (1663–1763)

The tribes in the Southeast and the Old Southwest were squeezed out of their traditional lands in much the same way as were the tribes confronting the middle and northern colonies. But, because of the later dates of English colonies being established in the Carolinas and Georgia, this happened later. In the mid–1700s, using current states for reference, the large inland bodies of Indians, other than the Cherokee, were the Creek located in Georgia and Alabama with 3,500 warriors; the Choctaw, to the west of the Creek in lower Mississippi with 5,000 warriors; and the Chickasaw near the Tennessee southern border in northern Mississippi and Alabama with 500 warriors. The Catawba, with a population of 4,600 in 1682, lived along the Catawba River near the current North and South Carolina border. In a general sense, with a two-year period of civil war between pro–British and pro–French factions, during the 1700s the Choctaw were pro–French; they built a fort at modern Mobile, Alabama, in 1702 and one at New Orleans in 1718. The Chickasaw and Catawba were usually supportive of the English. The English had an important advantage over the other Europeans — they were able to give more and better presents to the tribes.

The Creek were a loose confederation of maybe 60 towns, 40 of which were the Upper Towns, that is, towns in the vicinity of the Coosa and Tallapoosa Rivers of central Alabama, and the Lower Towns to the east of the Upper Towns near the Chattahoochee, Flint, and Ocmulgee rivers of central and western Georgia. Most of the 1700s, up to and through the French and Indian War, the pro–English Upper Towns were dependent on English traders, but, at times, made war on the traders within their territory and, in 1716, let the French build Fort Toulouse near the junction of the Coosa and Tallapoosa. The Lower Towns sometimes favored the French, sometimes the Spanish who claimed East Florida (that is, from modern Pensacola eastward), and sometimes the English. And individual groups within the Creek nation on occasion had their own agenda. An example was the Upper Creek Alabamas who were located near Fort Toulouse and steadfastly maintained a pro–French attitude.

Warfare between the Cherokee, Creek, Chickasaw, and Choctaw involved different configurations in the 1700s and was a way of satisfying the egos of young warriors. Commonly warfare consisted of 20 to 30 warriors making a foray against a selected enemy that would last a short time and result in some scalps and some prisoners who could be cruelly treated or put to death. The French, English, and Spanish often urged different hostile alignments as they maneuvered for land and Indian trade. Larger forces were not unknown. In the early 1700s hundreds of Indians acted in conjunction with some European soldiers for attacks on European selected targets. An Indian vs. Indian exception was an offensive of the Creek against the Cherokee in 1750 when 500 Creek attacked and destroyed two Cherokee towns. Peace terms were agreed to by the Creek and Cherokee in 1754 which lasted for over 20 years.

The Carolinas were the first colonies to threaten these southern tribes. Land between the 31st and 36th parallels, named Carolina in honor of Charles I — Carolina being derived from Latin for Charles — was given in 1629 to Sir Robert Heath, who failed to exploit the grant. When Charles II took the crown in 1660 he took back the grant and, in 1663, granted some promoters, his friends, a proprietary charter for land extending east to west from sea to sea between Florida, which was recognized as belonging to Spain, and Virginia. Profits to the promoters were to come from the sale of land. The proprietors used a liberal head-right system to induce people to migrate, and groups of French Protestants together with Germans and Swiss came. To induce migration the proprietors heralded Carolina as having "deer and wild turkeys ... weighing many times above 50 lb. a piece, and of a more pleasant taste than in England." "The land is of diverse sorts as in all countries of the world." Settlers can have "indigo, tobacco ... and cotton wool; lime trees, orange, lemon and other fruit trees [thrive] exceedingly." Single women migrating would find themselves "in the Golden Age, when men paid a dowry for their wives; for if they be but civil, and under fifty years of age, some honest man or other will purchase them for their wives."[1] This description, published in London in 1666, went on to even higher accolades for Carolina, but, alas, the grant did not bring the hoped for profits and the proprietors sold it to the Crown, which made it into two royal provinces, North Carolina and South Carolina. In 1665 the grant was enlarged to 36 degrees and 30 minutes on the north and the 29th parallel on the south, an extension that covered Spanish claims in Florida including the settlement at St. Augustine which was established in 1565. One of the proprietors, Lord Granville, kept his interest in North Carolina and throughout the colonial period treated about half of the colony as private property. In 1677 the population was only 3,000.

When the first settlers came from Virginia to the Albemarle Sound area of North Carolina and bought land from the Indians, a few years before the grants from the Crown, there may have been 30,000 Indians in both the Carolinas in a number of small tribes. After the grants by the Crown, the proprietors forbade settlers to "hold or claim any land in Carolina, by purchase or gift, or otherwise from the natives or any other whatsoever; but merely from and under the Lords Proprietors, upon pain o[f] forfeiture of all his estate, moveable or immoveable, and perpetual banishment,"[2] and prohibited any white settlement within two-and-one-half miles of Indian towns. As early as 1675 the proprietors bought land in South Carolina from local Indians and were able to get a deed for the area between the coast to the Appalachian Mountains, most of which was not occupied nor used for hunting.

The first natives to suffer as an entity from the North Carolina settlers were the Tuscarora Indians who felt threatened by a new town at New Bern, North Carolina, some 60 miles down the coast from Albemarle Sound as the crow flies. Other possible causes of the Tuscaroras taking up the hatchet were their being cheated by traders, having tribesmen enslaved, and, in the words of a contemporary settler, being "insulted in many ways by a few rough Carolinians, more barbarous and inhuman than the Savages themselves."[3]

Cumberland R
Duck R
TENNESSEE
Tennessee R
New R
1763 Proclamation Line
Albemarle Sound
Hillsboro
Alamance Battlefield
TUSCARORA
Ft Loudon
Hiwassee R
Ft Dobbs
Catawba R
Salisbury
Yadkin R
N.
CAROLINA
Neuse R
New Bern
Muscle Shoals
Tennessee R
Great
Ft Prince George
CHEROKEE
LOWER TOWNS
CATAWBA
Reedy R
Saluda R
Wateree R
Cape Fear R
CHICKASAW
ALABAMA
GEORGIA
Long Cane
Hard Labor Cr
Santee R
Waccamaw R
Coosa R
Tallapoosa R
Black Warrior R
Augusta
Pee Dee R
UPPER
CREEK
De Vorsey
Boundary
1773
Savannah R
S.
CAROLINA
Tombigbee R
Coweta
Ocmulgee R
Oconee R
Ogeechee R
Charles Town
ATLANTIC OCEAN
Chattahoochee R
Alabama R
LOWER
CREEK
Flint R
YAMASSEE
Altamaha R
Mobile R
Mobile
Pensacola
Apalachicola R
St Mary's R
St Augustine
Appalachee Bay

Early Years in the Carolinas, Georgia, and Alabama

Ref: De Vorsey, 114, 133, 231–32; Adams, 60–61

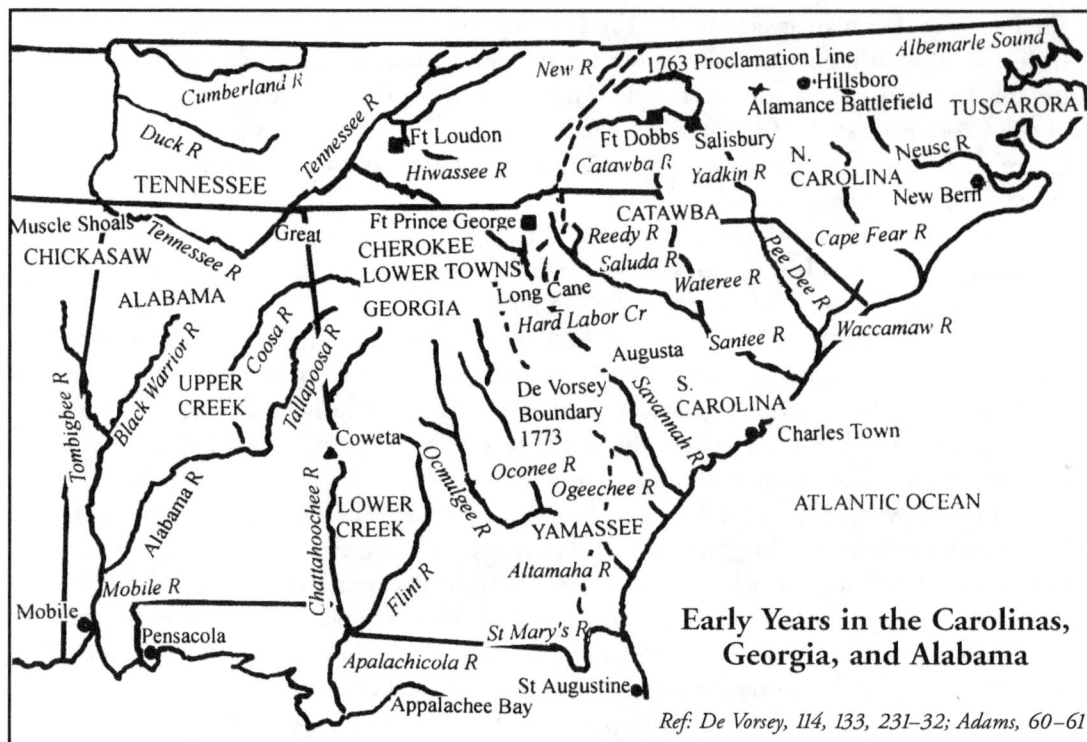

There was a market for Indian slaves in the West Indies as there was, to an extent, in New England.

Whatever the cause the Tuscaroras attacked and killed nearly 200 settlers in one day in September 1711. Descriptions of what the Indians did are harrowing. For example, women "were laid on their house-floors and great stakes run up through their bodies. Others big with child, the infants were ripped out and hung upon trees."[4] In retribution the settlers burned Indians alive. Senseless acts of anger and disdain were common in the fighting between whites and Indians in frontier areas. Scalping, done by both sides, was not a delicate surgical procedure. Often the cranium was shattered with an axe, whether or not the victim was still alive.

Attacks and counterattacks were carried on. Isolated settlements were destroyed, trade disrupted, and a blanket of fear spread over the settlers. The capture of a chief allied with the Tuscaroras who was roasted alive led to more furious attacks. Responding to a call for help, South Carolina sent a force of 30 settlers and 500 friendly Indians, mostly Yamassee, across 300 miles of unmapped forests containing veritable jungles and scarcely passable swamp land, who defeated the Tuscaroras in two battles early in 1712 and a truce was agreed to. However, the Indians resumed the war in the fall of 1712 and again South Carolina sent a force, this time of 33 whites and 1,000 Indians from the Catawba, Creek, and Cherokee tribes. The Tuscaroras were so thoroughly defeated, with casualties of 1,000, some Indians being burned in a fort, and many of the 392 captives sent off into slavery, that, except for a small number in the Albemarle Sound area who had stayed neutral, they ceased to be a factor in the Carolinas. They migrated to the north and joined the Iroquois Confederation as the sixth nation in 1722.

South Carolina had its first settlers in 1670 and by 1680 there was a fledgling settlement at Charles Town, known after 1783 as Charleston. With a good harbor Charles Town grew rapidly. In 1682 it had "about a hundred houses ... wholy built of wood."[5] It received a boost in 1685 with the introduction of rice, a crop ideally suited for the coastal area and in demand in the West Indies. It also provided a market for furs and deerskins which traders were buying from Lower Creek Indians by 1685 to the chagrin and anger of the Spanish. In the 1750s 100,000 pounds of deerskins were shipped from Charles Town per year. There was trade in Indian slaves—captives from other tribes furnished by Yamassee and Shawnee Indians living in the area. To an extent early traders, described by Louis B. Wright in his book *The Colonial Civilisation of North America, 1607–1763* as men "[f]earing neither God nor the devil ... as lawless as they were ruthless and greedy,"[6] also brought Indian slaves to Charles Town. If the indigenous Indians wanted to expel the whites from the Carolinas they should have acted before 1718 when South Carolina had a population of 6,000 whites and maybe 10,000 black slaves, and North Carolina had about 7,500 whites and 10,500 black slaves.

Traders went inland with packhorses or Indian "burdeners" who would carry loads of 50 to 60 pounds. English traders, often competing with French and Spanish traders, were well received by the Indians—as stated by a South Carolina Indian agent, Indian friendship went to "them most who sell best cheap." As trade increased, efforts were made to regularize the quid pro quos by price schedules. A 1716 schedule shows 30 buckskins for a gun, 2 for a hatchet or for a "red girdle." Prices are listed for blankets, clothing, hoes and axes, knives, rum, and other items. No price is shown for salt, gunpowder, kettles, and looking glasses— they were to be sold for "As you can." For a time the proprietors tried to keep the inland trade for themselves but the colonists persisted and trade was carried on by all comers. A 1707 South Carolina law stated that "the greater number of those persons that trade among the Indians in amity with this Government, do generally lead loose, vicious lives, to the scandal of the Christian religion, and do likewise oppress the people among whom they live, by their unjust and illegal actions, which if not prevented may in time tend to the destruction of the Province."[7]

In the early 1700s there were as many as 200 traders reaching out as far as 500 miles from Charles Town. The requirement for traders to have licenses was often violated. A law against selling arms to the Indians was ignored. Indian trade was not a major factor in the development of North Carolina. Its growth was in small farms whose products could not go directly to England since it lacked suitable ports. New England, which had small ships that could navigate its coastal waters, was its main outlet.

Charles Town had to keep an eye to the south where England and Spain disputed as to where the boundary between their colonies should be. The Spaniards supported any Indian enemies of the Carolinians. When England and Spain were at war in what was called Queen Anne's War in America (1702–1713) the Carolinians and Floridians exchanged attacks on one another but no significant change occurred. Carolinians also struck at Indian allies of the Spanish.

South Carolinians had major trouble with the Yamassee and Creek Indians in the years 1715–1717. When Charles Town was settled the Yamassee were living along the coast of what is now Georgia, but, after differences with the Spanish, they moved up the coast closer to Charles Town. Charles Town saw the Yamassee as a good buffer between themselves and

Spanish Florida, and in 1707 reserved an area for them which was to be out of bounds for the white settlers. Nonetheless whites moved onto the land. This aggravation plus the conduct of Carolina traders resulted in the Yamassee War. Traders, many of whom were not licensed to trade with the Indians, in the words of W. Stitt Robinson in his book *The Southern Colonial Frontier, 1607–1763* "beat Indian men and women, even to death, ravish[ed] Indian women, [took] supplies such as corn and poultry without adequate compensation, [and] coerc[ed] Indians to serve as burderers for very little pay."[8]

With encouragement from the Creeks, the Yamassees attacked an outlying settlement on April 15, 1715, and killed most of those there. Other southern tribes, including Creek, Choctaw, and Catawba, in different degrees, carried out attacks over the next two years. The Carolinians successfully attacked the Yamassee in June 1715 but shortly thereafter the hostile Indians penetrated a circle of garrisons protecting Charles Town and came within 12 miles of the town. But for the Cherokee supporting the settlers South Carolinians might have been forced to flee. With that support and also help from North Carolina, the Yamassee were forced to move to a Spanish-controlled area near St. Augustine and the Creeks to agree to peace in 1717. The Lower Creeks relocated from the upper Ocmulgee River westward to the Chattahoochee. Following the Yamassee War the Creeks had a policy of neutrality as to the French, Spaniards, and English. At the same time the Carolinians stayed neutral in feuds between the Creeks and Cherokee. A cynical statement of a Carolinian, maybe representing the thinking of many, was that it was difficult to "assist the [Creek and Cherokee] in cutting one another's throats without offending either. This is the game we intend to play if possible."[9] The Cherokee-Creek warfare during the Yamassee War started a long period of intermittent conflict between the two tribes into the 1750s. Discontent with the proprietors over the weak support received during the war and other factors resulted in South Carolina becoming a royal colony in 1719 and North Carolina in 1729. Particularly aggravating to the colonists was the action of the proprietors to take the former Yamassee lands for themselves rather than opening them up for settlers.

Without any major confrontations with the Southeast Indians, the Carolinas expanded their settlements. Settlers followed rivers inland. From the north, primarily Pennsylvania where the cost of land was relatively high, they came down into the valleys of Maryland and Virginia starting in the late 1720s. Ray Allen Billington, in his book *Westward Expansion: A History of the American Frontier*, noted land prices of 15 pounds per 100 acres in Pennsylvania at a time when 100 acres in western Virginia was available for 5 pounds. Many of the northern settlers, who were soon also settling the western Piedmont of the Carolinas, were Scots-Irish and Germans who had been attracted to Pennsylvania because of its religious tolerance. The route followed was the Great Wagon Road from Philadelphia through York, Pennsylvania; Frederick, Maryland; Winchester, Virginia; and to Roanoke, Virginia, where it went eastward through the Staunton River Gap to the Carolina Piedmont. Speculators, who acquired large tracts of land, encouraged emigration and made sales to those coming into the colonies. One of those speculators, William Byrd II, was not happy with the type of people migrating southward and said they "flock over thither in such numbers, that there is not elbow room for them. They swarm like the Goths and Vandals of old and will overspread our Continent soon."[10]

South Carolina saw a need to regulate purchases of land from the Indians. A 1739 law observed: "the practice of purchasing lands from the Indians may prove of very dangerous consequence to the peace and safety of this Province, such purchases being generally obtained from Indians by unfair representation, fraud and circumvention, or by making them gifts of presents of little value, by which practices, great resentments and animosities have been created amongst the Indians towards the inhabitants of this Province."[11]

Over a ten-year period (1729–1740) South Carolina doubled its population (30,000 to 59,000). North Carolina had similar growth — 30,000 to 80,000 between 1728 and 1755. In 1755 the North Carolina legislature authorized construction of a road from the western Piedmont (Hillsboro) to ports on the Cape Fear River. The Cherokee ceded all land east of the Long Cane Creek, in western South Carolina, to South Carolina in 1747.

South Carolina was pleased when a charter for a colony between the Altamaha and Savannah rivers, with an object of salvaging thousands of imprisoned debtors, was given in 1732 to James Edward Oglethorpe and others. This gave them a barrier against the Floridians. The first settlement in Georgia was at the mouth of the Savannah River in 1733 and in 1735 a settlement was made at Augusta, about a hundred miles up the Savannah, which became an important trading center used by the Cherokee Indians. Georgia quickly angered South Carolina when it required a Georgia license for anyone trading with Indians within Georgia's boundaries.

Although the charter for the colony required all laws to be approved by the British government, this restriction was substantially bypassed when the Trustees managed the colony by regulations. Georgia's relatively good relations with the Indians went back to the Trustees for Establishing the Colony of Georgia who made its first law, enacted while still in England, focus on Anglo-Indian relations. In part the law read: "the safety, welfare and preservation of the Colony of Georgia doth ... depend on the maintaining of good correspondence and regulating the trade to be carried on between your Majesty's subjects and the several nations of Indians in amity with the said colony."[12]

Oglethorpe was able to purchase land needed for the settlers. In the 1730s he negotiated a treaty with some Creeks which lifted the restriction in the South Carolina-Yamassee treaty of 1715 limiting English settlement below the Savannah River. The treaty set Georgia's limits as "all that territory south, and west of the Savannah River up to two hours walk above tide water and as far south as the St. John's River"[13] excepting specified sea islands. This southern boundary was only about 40 miles north of the Spanish bastion at St. Augustine, Florida. The treaty, however, was not agreed to by the Upper Creeks. Oglethorpe traveled in 1739 to Coweta, a Lower Creek center in Alabama, and the Treaty of Coweta was signed August 11, 1739. It stated the extent of the Creek lands, essentially from the Georgia shoreline to the mountains, as to which the "Creek nation [had] maintained possession ... against all opposers, by war, and [could] show ... heaps of bones of their enemies, slain by them in defense of the ... lands."[14]

Oglethorpe exchanged commitments with the Creek to support one another and had Georgia's ownership of settled areas confirmed as well as title to the sea coast as high as the tide flows. The tidal limit gave Georgia a relatively narrow band of land inland from the coast between the Savannah and Altamaha Rivers. Oglethorpe made a promise the Indians would often hear: the English "[would] not enlarge or take any other lands except those granted."[15]

Relations with the neighboring Spanish were not amicable. In 1739 the War of Jenkins' Ear, which pitted Georgians and South Carolinians against the Spanish of Florida, commenced after the Spaniards cut off the ears of one Jenkins, a British smuggler. Oglethorpe was able to use a large number of Indians. Most of the fighting ended in 1743 without any significant changes. Oglethorpe left for England in 1743 never to return. Georgia's population was about 1,900 whites and 400 blacks in 1751.

On June 23, 1752, the Georgia trustees surrendered their charter to the king and over the next few years there was a significant change in population — 3,442 in 1753 and 11,300 in 1762. An additional cession of certain Sea Isles was agreed to in 1757 and the "long-standing tidal limit boundary"[16] left intact. The General Assembly in 1758 prohibited private purchases from Indians, and, at the same time, without any agreement of the Indians, established parish lines extending well beyond the tidal limit boundary.

King George's War (1744–1748), which brought England and France into conflict, did not engender any active fighting in the southern colonies. But the status of the French in the South was weakened when a British blockade reduced their ability to supply goods to Indians relying on them. However, during the French and Indian War (1755–1763), starting with General Braddock's defeat near Fort Duquesne in July 1755, the frontiers from Nova Scotia to Georgia were attacked. For many Indians the choice between the French and English was easy — only the English were after the land. On learning of Braddock's defeat Governor Dobbs of North Carolina, anticipating Indian attacks, spoke to his Assembly:

> The flame has already reached our Border and God Almighty has extended his correcting arm and made a Breach upon us, upon account of our wantoness, luxury and neglect of the practice of our religious duties and moral virtue, and we are now to fight *pro aris et facis*, and it requires the united forces of all the Colonies notwithstanding our great superiority to withstand their arms supported by the whole power of France.[17]

Dobbs decided on a frontier fort, appropriately named Fort Dobbs, to be built west of modern Statesville on the South Yadkin River. The location was one "fixed upon ... as most central to assist the back settlers and [to] be a retreat to them as it was beyond the well settled Country, [with] only straggling settlements behind them."[18]

The French, relying primarily on Indian surrogates, spread death and destruction along the colonies' western frontier in 1755. The raids continued in 1756 and in 1757 extended into Georgia. After Fort Duquesne, from which the French supplied western Indians and directed war parties, fell to the British in 1758, the attacks abated. The western Indians abandoned the French, who were no longer able to give them supplies. In 1756 most Creeks did not want to make war on either the English or French and the Choctaw wanted English trade to match the deficiencies in that of the French. There was general opposition to the planned Fort Loudoun in the Overhill Cherokee area. It was argued that an English fort was a projection of English expansionism. When it came to presents, the Creek were willing to accept them from any of the European powers.

When cumulative French losses of Louisbourg on Cape Breton Island, Fort Frontenac on Lake Ontario, and Fort Duquesne at the forks of the Ohio were followed by capture of Quebec in 1759, and Montreal in 1760, the war was over in America for practical purposes. The southern nation suffering the most during the French and Indian War was the Cherokee. It killed many whites but in the end was overcome by the British army. In the early 1760s an omen of the future was an invasion of whites on to Creek lands. In April 1763 the Creek wanted illegal settlers removed and complained of Virginians who had settled all over the woods with people cattle and horses, which had prevented [the Creeks] for some time from being able to supply their women and children with provisions as they could formerly, their buffalo, deer and bear being drove off the land and killed [with the result that] Creeks kill cattle wandering in these lands to fill their bellies.[19]

As for rumors that the French were going to cede lands of Georgia to the English, Governor Wright of Georgia was told "[t]he red people are poor and dependent upon the whites but the white appear to believe that the red people have no lands" whereas the lands belong to the Creeks who had lent it to the French and Spanish "and they [were] surprised how people can give away land that does not belong to them."[20] Unfortunately for the Creek the Europeans saw their rights as overriding those of the Indians and that when it came to ownership "might made right" was a controlling principle.

In the Treaty of Paris in 1763 France relinquished all of its claims in North America and Spain, which had joined France in the war against England, traded Florida to England for Cuba and received New Orleans from France. Great Britain needed a policy on how it would handle this large area between the colonies and the Mississippi River inhabited mainly by Indians. Before the peace treaty was completed, Lord Egremont, Secretary of State for the Southern Department, in January 1763 observed that the king had "it much at heart to conciliate the affection of the Indian nations" and to protect them "from any encroachment on the lands they have reserved to themselves, for their hunting grounds, & for their own support & habitation."[21] Egremont passed on to the Board of Trade a suggestion that a western boundary "beyond which our people should not at present be permitted to settle" would result in a filling-in of the present colonies rather than a "planting [of settlers] in the heart of America out of the reach of governments and where from the great difficulty of procuring European commodities they would be compelled to commence manufactures to the infinite prejudice of Britain."[22] Supporters of this approach were those engaged in the fur trade who preferred to retain a huge reservoir for furs rather than a country divided into small farms. Also the idea of restricting the area to which settlers could go satisfied those concerned about Americans with "notions of independency [from] their mother Kingdom"[23] which were most often held by those furthest from harbors and navigable streams of the coastline.

The Proclamation of 1763[24] announced on October 7 set a western boundary beyond which the colonists would not "for the present" be permitted to settle. The boundary was defined by a line reflecting the divide of waters that emptied into the Atlantic Ocean and those emptying into the western lands. Pursuant to the proclamation, warrants of survey or patents for land west of the line were forbidden and only the Crown should purchase land from the Indians. Recognizing that some may have already settled west of the line, the proclamation directed that they should "forthwith ... remove themselves." Virginians in the Holston and New River valleys were in that category.

7

Southern Tribes after the Proclamation of 1763 (1763–1775)

The proclamation of 1763 left for resolution the boundaries of Indian lands located to the east of the proclamation line. To face this a Southern Indian District Congress was held at Augusta, Georgia, on November 5, 1763. Governors from Virginia, North and South Carolina, and Georgia, together with John Stuart, who had recently been made superintendent of Indians in the Southern District, were there, as were about 600 representatives from the Chickasaw, Choctaw, Cherokee, Creek, and Catawba tribes. A boundary for Georgia was agreed to as was one for the Catawba.

Except for a lapse during the Yamassee War (1715–16) the English had no better ally than the Catawba. The lapse was explained by a missionary in 1715 as the result of settlers "abus[in]g the Indians with drink and then cheat[ing] them in Trading ... and Stealing Even their Child[re]n ... and [selling] them for slaves." They were known as fierce warriors and the anger between them and the northern Indians was persistent. When rampages against both the Catawba and settlers occurred over the years 1745–1750 the colonies made special efforts to make peace between the northern Indians, the Catawba, and other southern tribes who were being overwhelmed by the attacks. Peace between Indians of both regions had the advantage for the colonies of creating a combined force for use against the French and their allies. There was limited success in creating peaceful relations between the two regions. By 1760 the continuous aggressive attacks by northern Indians, deaths from smallpox, and losses of warriors who fought for the English in the French and Indian War and against the Cherokee in the Cherokee War, reduced the number of young and able-bodied Catawba men to between 60 and 150.[1] Another cause for a weakened Catawba tribe was the subject of a 1754 message to North Carolina commissioners by Catawba chief "King Hagler" who was assassinated by Shawnees in 1763:

> You Rot Your grain ... and make Strong Spirits You sell it to our young men and give it [to] them, many times; they get very drunk [and] oftentimes Commit those Crimes that is offencive to You and us ... it is also very bad for our people, for it Rots their guts and causes our men to get very sick and many of our people has Lately Died by the effects of that strong drink....[2]

With their depleted numbers the Catawba were willing at Augusta to accept for their use a 15-mile square of land (144,000 acres). The English promised, once a survey was made, to remove any settlers within the land and the Catawbas were not to "be molested by any of the King's subjects."[3] South Carolina, which included the Catawba land located along its northern border where the boundary line was raised so as to include all of it in South Carolina, was appreciative of the Catawbas' loyalty and tried to treat them fairly. In addition to the 144,000 acres they had the right to hunt throughout the state. Despite the state's effort, the lack of business acumen by the Catawba and the acquisitiveness of whites left the Catawba with little of the 144,000 acres for their own use. Most was leased to whites by the Catawba. After 1763 the Catawba were not a threat to anyone, but the few warriors left fought with the revolutionists during the Revolutionary War.

After the peace treaty of 1763 the Creek could no longer look to Spain and France for support in its relations with the English. One result was the decision of the Creek at the Southern Indian District Conference to cede additional land to Georgia bounded on the north by the Savannah River of approximately twice the acreage to that previously ceded. The treaty purported to explain why the Creek acted: "to prevent any mistakes, doubts, or disputes for the future, and in consideration of the great marks of clemency and friendship extended to us the said Creek Indians, we ... have consented and agreed ... [to] the boundary between the English settlements and our lands and hunting grounds."[4] The additional land was mainly between the Ogeechee and Savannah rivers from Augusta southeast toward the ocean.

A provision in the treaty, and a similar one in later ones, created the grounds for numerous future disputes. It was agreed that "Indians who killed whites would in turn be killed by Indians in the presence of whites, while whites who killed Indians would be tried under colony law and punished in the presence of Indians."[5] Only rarely did the Creek put to death those the whites saw as murderers, and the English did not often respond satisfactorily to Creek complaints about murders of Indians. An English weapon in cases of what they saw as Indian non-compliance was to cut off trade or to threaten to do so.

Neither side was able to adequately control those theoretically subject to their command and each, for a period, were inclined to let the Indians and whites on the frontier settle their own disputes. A British Indian agent in 1767 told Stuart "their young men are become so boistrous and wanton that without a hearty drubbing such as the Cherokees had they will never be a tractable people."[6] Another cause of friction was the theft of settlers' horses. When Stuart complained a Creek response was that the Creeks

> learned to be thieves and rogues from these back settlers — the Virginians are very bad people. They pay no regard to your laws. Yet you expect that we who have no laws can govern our young men. They are corrupted and made rogues by the example of these back settlers who give them rum for stolen horses, I and my warriors present have had many horses stolen by white people....[7]

In contrast the Quakers who settled near the boundary line were "good and peaceable and [did] not take a pride in riding about with rifle guns in their hands, drinking and swearing like the Virginians."[8] The Indians called all new settlers "Virginians."[9] During these years the English took pleasure in an ongoing war between the Choctaw, Chickasaw, and Creek. British concern was that if they were to stop fighting they would form an anti–English coalition.

A flaw in the new boundary was that the Upper Creek chiefs deliberately avoided the congress and were not satisfied with the cession made by the Lower Creek. It was another five years before the boundary, with some changes, was marked and ratified by a treaty signed at Augusta. In 1763 the Crown enlarged the colony by making its bottom line the St. Mary's River instead of the Altamaha, and a commission in 1764 said Georgia's western boundary was the Mississippi River.

South Carolina's border with the Cherokee in 1763 was agreed to after the Cherokee War of 1760–1761, before which it had never been marked. The land between the 1747 Long Cane boundary and the 1761 one, which was considerably closer to the Cherokee Lower Towns, was a magnet for settlers. A story in the April 2, 1763, *South Carolina Gazette* spoke of 1,000 families moving to the Long Cane region in 1762 with 400 more expected. This was the situation at the time of the Southern Indian Congress at which the Cherokee leader Little Carpenter was willing to accept the new settlements but said the settlers "must proceed no farther."[10] No resolution was reached at the Congress and in August 1764 the governor had a complaint of settlers being within 12 or 15 miles of the Cherokee Lower Towns. In this instance an order was given to remove the settlers and to burn their huts. However, the commanding officer at Fort Prince George was reprimanded for arresting men hunting and poaching on the Indian land.

To avoid conflicts the Cherokee asked South Carolina to have the boundary marked and the governor agreed. Showing some dissatisfaction with South Carolina the Cherokee sent the governor a talk:

> We know that the white people are very troublesome to you for land & that they tell you that their boundary is Broadies Plantation; and if it [the boundary] is not soon run out, the white people will say next that twelve Mile River is the boundary. We desire therefore since you was not at the Treaty at Augusta that you will stop your white people from settling on our ground until our beloved brother [Stuart] comes home.[11]

Stuart wasn't pleased with the manner in which South Carolina was handling the boundary question. He wrote to the Board of Trade on August 24, 1765, saying the governor was carrying on negotiations without help from him and if anything less than "all the Nation" agreed to a boundary there would be "perpetual Grumbling and Disputes" and the superintendent should be involved. His idea on the proper boundary was that one "too near the Indian Nations, will expose us to perpetual Broils." Broils were likely since the "Inhabitants of those back Countries are in general the lowest and worst Part of the People, and as they and the Indians live in perpetual Jealously and Dread of each other, so their rooted Hatred for each other is reciprocal."[12]

At Fort Prince George on October 19, 1765, the Cherokee made a new cession which established a straight line boundary from a point on the Savannah River to one on the Reedy River, a line eastward from the unmarked 1761 line, thereby in theory establishing more space between the settlers and the Lower Towns. As for the Indian land to the west of the line the whites were told by the Indians to "remember all our dependence for the necessaries of life is upon Hunting — that we shall Hunt nowhere but on our own land, and that we expect to reserve it for ourselves unfrequented by white hunters."[13] South Carolina accepted the new boundary on December 10, 1765, and the next year it was marked by blazing trees. South Carolina's governor published a proclamation on June 2, 1766, telling any settlers to the northwest of the line to remove themselves and "all surveyors, hunters and other [of] His Majesty's subjects are hereby forbidden to pass beyond said boundary line [and do so] at their peril."[14]

As with other cessions there was a rapid movement to settle lands near the boundary. The settlements were not a continuation of those moving inland from the coast. In 1768 Stuart visited the line and wrote[15]: "The country near the Line is very full of Inhabitants mostly emigrants from the Northern Colonies it is remarkable that in going hence to the

Frontiers I rode at times 30 & 40 miles without seeing any house or hut yet near the Boundary that Country is full of Inhabitants which in my memory was considered by the Indians as their best hunting grounds." Relations were not good between the Indians and these settlers. Continuing he wrote:

> The people Inhabiting the Frontiers of this Province carry on a trade with the Indians by bartering rum for Horses, the Chief complained of this as the source of many disorders their young men being thereby encouraged to steal horses from the neighbouring Provinces besides the danger of committing outrages when intoxicated which may involve their Nation in trouble. These back settlers pay little or no regard to Law or Government.... The Indians detest the back Inhabitants ... which will account for the reluctancy with which they give up any part of their lands being anxious to keep such neighbors at a distance.

After the Cherokee finished marking the South Carolina boundary in 1766 they were anxious to have a boundary agreed upon for North Carolina and Virginia. To delay was to disregard the Virginians and North Carolinians hunting on their land which was east of the 1763 Proclamation line. North Carolina's governor, William Tryon, saw a need for the boundary since "last autumn [1765] and winter, upwards of one thousand wagons passed thro' Salisbury with families from the northward, to settle in this province chiefly."[16] In a letter dated September 13, 1766, the governor was told by the Secretary of State that the intentions of the Proclamation were to be enforced.

A meeting with the Cherokee scheduled for the fall of 1766 had to be postponed when disease struck them. The catastrophic effect of disease is described in a talk the Cherokee sent: "When [we] got up this morning [we] could hear nothing but the cries of women and children for the loss of their relations, in the evenings there are nothing to be seen but smoak and houses on fire, the dwellings of the deceased; [we] never remember to see any sickness like the present, except the smallpox, and if we should attempt to go to run the line we might have been taken sick in the woods and die, as several ... who attempted to escape this devil of a disorder."[17]

In the main a boundary line agreed to in 1767 was a straight line starting near the present boundary of North Carolina and South Carolina at Reedy River to Chiswell's Mine in Virginia. This line and the 1765 South Carolina line were agreed to in a treaty at Hard Labor, South Carolina, on October 14, 1768. A line for Virginia was also adopted.

Cherokee chief Oconostota told Stuart that the "white men [would have] enough land to live on."[18] Despite commitments by the North Carolina governor to protect the Indians in their land in 1768 or 1769 the line was pierced by settlers going to what is now northeastern Tennessee and settling on the Watauga River and other nearby areas. They crossed over not only the 1767 line ratified at Hard Labor but also the 1763 Proclamation line. Settlers reached the Nollichucky area by 1772.

Stuart was dismayed in 1768 when London took control of the Indian trade away from him and put it in the hands of the colonies. He saw the lack of control of the frontier to be a consequence of this. His orders prior to 1768 had been to "restrain the Traders and other loose and irregular People so instrumental in Debauching the minds of the Indians."[19] He was idealistic — in 1764 he wrote to the Board of Trade:

> Fixing the British Empire in the Hearts of the Indians, by Justice, and moderation; to soften & Humanize their Manners, & sentiments, by an Intercourse with Good people; and from Savage Barbarians, to render them rational people, industrious & Good Subjects: Ends never to be

obtained by Force & restraint. Trading with them under the mouths of our cannon will nourish mutual Distrust & Jealousy; and be the sure means of their continuing in their present state of Barbarity. By which, His Majesty's Desire of becoming their Father and Benefactor must prove abortive, and the British Empire, be deprived of an acquisition of 80,000 Subjects.[20]

In the back-country of North Carolina the settlers proposed to look after themselves. Associations called "Regulators" were formed in the late 1760s which wanted to stop paying taxes and outrageous legal fees until such time as the frontier was treated fairly. North Carolina's militia, led by Governor William Tryon, beat down the Regulator movement by defeating about 2,000 Regulators at the Battle of the Alamance, near today's Burlington, North Carolina, on May 16, 1771. There were few deaths in the battle, perhaps as little as eighteen, but of fifteen prisoners tried, six were hanged. Back-country males were required to take an oath of allegiance. Many didn't and went further west and settled in the headwaters of the Tennessee River and were later to seek independence by forming the State of Franklin.

The history of pre–1775 boundaries in Virginia is discussed in the next chapter. When it came time to negotiate a boundary for what was East and West Florida, Stuart had to deal with the Creek and Choctaw tribes. It wasn't until governors were appointed for each colony that negotiations were undertaken. Since the French had not made significant settlements in West Florida, other than at Mobile, nor had the Spanish in East Florida except for Pensacola and at the coastal fort in St. Augustine, there was no immediate pressure on Indian lands. English settlers came to both Floridas but not before boundary lines were negotiated.

Having in mind the strength of the Creek nation, with near 4,000 men, and his lack of troops (only 197), East Florida governor James Grant emphasized at the congress he convened on November 15, 1765, that he was "ordered by the Great King not to take any lands which are of use to [the Creek] even if [they] should agree to give them up." However, he stressed the symbiotic relationship between the Indians and the English:

> Your profession is hunting, you therefore must have a large tract of country, but it is [in] your interest to have your brothers the English near you, as they only can supply you, in exchange for your skins, with clothes to cover you, your wives & children, with guns, powder & ball for your hunting & a number of other things which you cannot make for yourselves tho' you cannot exist without them.[21]

Despite such blandishments the Creek stuck, with some deviation, to a coastal boundary limited to tidal waters. As for the presents given to them at the congress, the official Creek reply noted that they "may last for a year but will afterwards rot and become of no value but the land which we now give you will last forever."[22] The Creek never viewed the land handed over by the Spanish to the British in 1763 as anything other than land they had lent to the Spanish.

The Indians in and near West Florida were the most numerous in the Southeast and the Choctaw and Creek in the area were hostile. Negotiations became serious after the arrival of the colony's first governor, George Johnstone, in October 1764. Without sufficient soldiers he proposed to deal with them with "fair Promises, Presents, [and] entering into the Policy of their Nations, creating Jealousies amongst themselves, and using these Engines in the best manner."[23] Stuart endeavored to find the root of the hostility of the Creek and met with them when they drank freely and became convinced their uneasiness proceeds from jealousy on account of their lands.

Johnstone's first congress was in March 1765 at Mobile with the Choctaw and Chickasaw. The Choctaw were willing to give the British land to plant and stressed that to replace the French the British "must act the part of a father in supplying [the Choctaw] wants by proper presents and also by furnishing a plentiful trade."[24] A significant cession was made by the Choctaw and Chickasaw. Two months later a congress was held with the Creek at Pensacola and a boundary agreed upon. Although the boundary went back about 15 miles from the shore it did not include any but infertile soils. In return the Creek had expectations expressed by a Creek chief called The Mortar:

> The King of England knows his Red Children are very Numerous & must be cloathed, they are all indigent & I hope the King, the governor, and superintendent & all other White people are sensible that they are so, & as I have this day considered the conveniency of the English in granting them land to plant, so I expect they will in return consider me and my people, this land was formerly part of our hunting ground, but now many of us are grown old and incapable to kill deer enough to purchase cloathing ... [and] as deer skins are become scarce, the trade may be reduced in proportion so that we may be enabled to clothe & maintain our families.[25]

To encourage the English to act appropriately The Mortar said that if "peace and friendship ... between white and red people continued for four years, then there will be an addition made to the lands already granted." However, if the whites crossed the boundary there would be "great disturbances in the Nations" as shown by the fact that Spaniards had been "killed who attempted to settle on the Indian territories without permission."[26]

Johnstone had a view shared by Stuart that the Indians "are a much more moral & virtuous people than ourselves & ... most of their Vices are of our Importing: Every Evil Seems to Spring Cheifly from the corrupt Conduct of the Traders & the little Power which Government has over them."[27] Stuart wanted courtroom rules which allowed Indians to testify. Also he wanted to see Indian headmen in a judicial role in settling disputes between traders and Indians. These approaches were rejected by Georgia's governor.

Another significant pre-revolution cession was made by the Creek and Cherokee in June 1773 to eliminate their debts to traders. About 2.1 million acres were ceded which gave Georgia control of most of the west bank of the Savannah River and a 30- or 40-mile strip to the west of the river. On the eve of the Revolutionary War the Southern Indian Boundary Line was as shown on the map titled "Early Years in the Carolinas, Georgia, and Alabama" according to the conclusion of Louis De Vorsey, Jr., in his book *The Indian Boundary in the Southern Colonies 1763–1775*.

The manner the 1773 cession was achieved was anathema to Stuart. It originated in 1770 when trader creditors of the Cherokee proposed it as a way of paying off debts. The land was to be transferred directly to the traders. The Cherokee were willing and signed a deed in 1771— the land was remote from their towns. Stuart and the governor of Georgia did not approve the deed, and the traders took another tact. The Indians should deed the land to the Crown for the express purpose of paying off their debts and in this way skirt the prohibition against private land transfers. Another problem was that the Creek also claimed the land.

The traders had an ally in Governor James Wright who had a vision of expanding Georgia's boundary to the west and attracting to Georgia "something better than the common sort of Back Country People" by charging six pence per acre for the land. The land was represented to be "upwards of three Millions of Acres of as fine Lands ... as any in America."[28]

Stuart particularly objected to the traders essentially negotiating for land — negotiations should be carried on by Stuart who would weigh the advantages and disadvantages to each side.

The Upper Creeks opposed a cession which would allow more cattle to be brought among them and for traders to make new plantations. Creek headman Emistisiguo opposed the land-for-debts swap; it would only be a temporary solution. He said the Creek would pay their debts with "Skins & dont mean to give up their Lands at all as the Skins is the produce of the Land."[29] Augusta merchants brought pressure on the Creeks by threatening to stop sending them goods.

Stuart was ordered to promote the cession and the reluctant Creek at the last minute agreed to most of what was wanted. Although the traders prevailed in getting the cession it was a Pyrrhic victory. The debts of the Cherokee and Creek to "over forty merchants and principal traders and many more local traders at Augusta" were canceled but the traders never got any of the proceeds from the sale of the land by Georgia. Wright refused to sell the land in other than small tracts and as the money came in he spent it on "public works projects and a troop of rangers." Sales were halted in 1774 when the Creek complained of violations of the terms of the cession and "violent conflict erupted between certain Creeks and settlers in the ceded lands." When the Creeks defeated the Augusta militia settlers fled. Stuart explained the Creek acts: "[the whites'] incessant requisition for land, affords Matter of Discontent and Jealousy to all the Indian Tribes, and ... they cannot see our advances into the heart of their most valuable hunting Grounds with pleasure."[30]

8

Virginia and the Cherokee Agree on a Boundary (1768–1771)

After France gave up its claims in North America and Spain traded England Florida for Cuba at the Treaty of Paris in 1763, the Crown formulated policies vis-à-vis the Indians in the vast areas east of the Mississippi River. The Proclamation of 1763 established a western line beyond which Indian claims were to be protected but modifications were required respecting the Cherokee since some settlements were already in place west of the line, principally in the watersheds of the New and Holston rivers. John Stuart, who became superintendent of Indian affairs for the land below the Ohio River in 1762, was given the task of negotiating a Southern Indian boundary and reached agreement with the Cherokee at Hard Labor, South Carolina, in October 1768. In the main the Virginia boundary was a line from Chiswell's Mine on the New River in southwest Virginia to the mouth of the Kanawha River on the Ohio. This ceded a large area west of the Proclamation line since the waters of the New and Kanawha rivers flowed into the Ohio River, not the Atlantic Ocean.

Out of the Cherokee capture of Fort Loudoun in 1760 came a special relationship between Little Carpenter and John Stuart. One of the prisoners at Fort Loudoun was Stuart and Little Carpenter arranged for his release. When a peace treaty was signed with South Carolina in the fall of 1761 the *Carolina Gazette* reported that Little Carpenter asked that Stuart "be made chief man (Indian agent) in their nation," and said "[a]ll the Indians love him and there will never be any uneasiness if he is there."[1] Stuart, called Bushyhead by the Cherokee, was married to a Cherokee and always had warm relations with them. According to Woodward, he left a legacy of mixed-blood descendants.

In a letter summarizing relations with the Cherokee up to 1765 Stuart described the attitude of the Cherokee as to murders and encroachments on their land: "The Indians can comprehend that the wicked actions of a few individuals ought not to be considered as a proof of the intentions of the whole community.... But grants of land claimed by [encroachers], they know to be the acts of whole Provinces which alarms them and they consider as incontestable proofs of our bad intentions and want of faith."[2] Getting commitments from the Cherokee as to land matters was complicated by their concept of ownership. Stuart explained this: "Each individual has a right to, and looks upon himself as proprietor of all the lands claimed by the whole nation"; consequently, "no Indian whatsoever, let his influence or power in his own country be ever so great, can give away any more than his own right in any piece of land."[3] Be that as it may, the relative strengths of the parties left the Cherokee in no position to enforce their concepts of ownership. Furthermore, as Stuart clearly stated in a report of 1764: "A modern Indian cannot subsist without Europeans; and would handle a flint ax or any other rude utensil used by his ancestors very awkwardly; so what was only conveniency at first is now become necessity."[4]

The Treaty of Hard Labor demonstrates misleading language often found in cession treaties. In the treaty the Cherokee accepted a boundary line giving up Indian lands well west of the 1763 Proclamation line. The treaty statement that the Cherokee were agreeing to give up these lands because "of his Majesty's generosity and paternal Goodness, so often Demonstrated to them"[5] glosses over the relative bargaining positions. The Cherokee were well aware of what was happening. In 1767 Cherokee chief Oconostota observed to Stuart that the "[l]ands [being given up would] last long, but the Cloath & other necessaries [given to the Cherokee would] soon wear out."[6]

The Hard Labor line was not acceptable to Virginia. Basic to its position was a denial that the Cherokee had any claim to the New River area. Furthermore, Virginia's leaders wanted London to open up all of what became Kentucky to settlement. Legal arguments aside, settlers were in the New River area and were not removing themselves and used the uncertainty of their title as a ground for refusing to pay quit rents. Settlers west of the New River based their claims on large grants of land to Colonel James Patten in 1744 from which he sold parcels that were then settled. Patten, an old sea captain who had weathered many voyages bringing redemptioners to America and returning with furs and tobacco, was killed in the French and Indian War after spending 20 years on the frontier. Stuart, in negotiations with the Cherokee, pointed out that they, the Cherokee, had "acquiesced [to the settlements] without complaint to [1764], as they [were] a great distance from [the Cherokee] country."[7] Joshua Fry's "Report on the Back Settlements of Virginia," written in 1751, noted that there were "about one hundred families" on the New River and its branches. A landmark settlement on the upper New River was that of John Chiswell, the owner of the Raleigh Tavern in

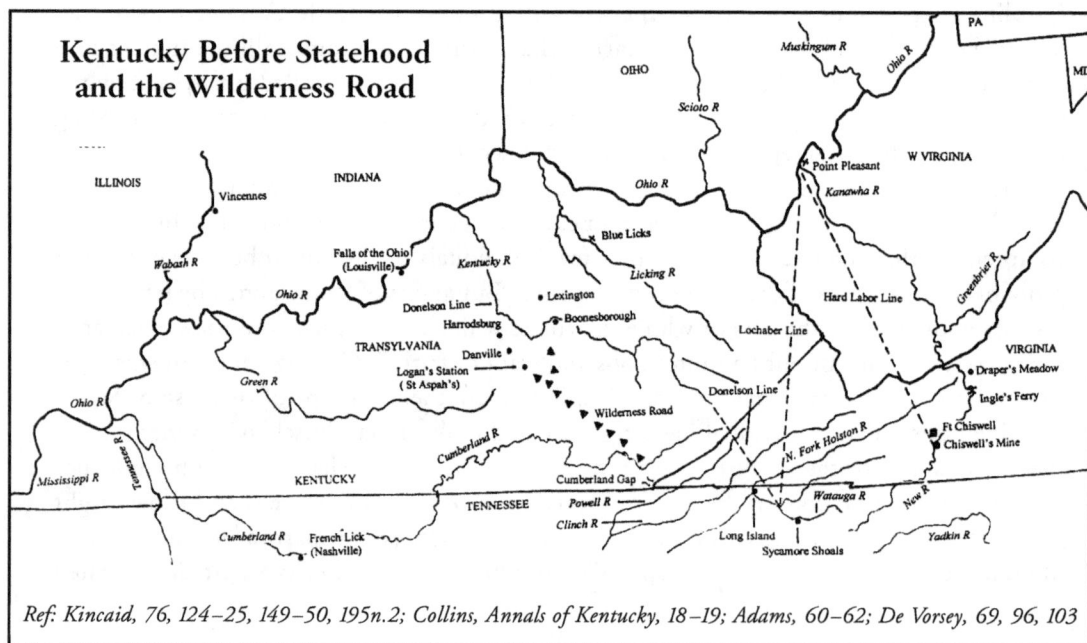

Ref: Kincaid, 76, 124–25, 149–50, 195n.2; Collins, Annals of Kentucky, 18–19; Adams, 60–62; De Vorsey, 69, 96, 103

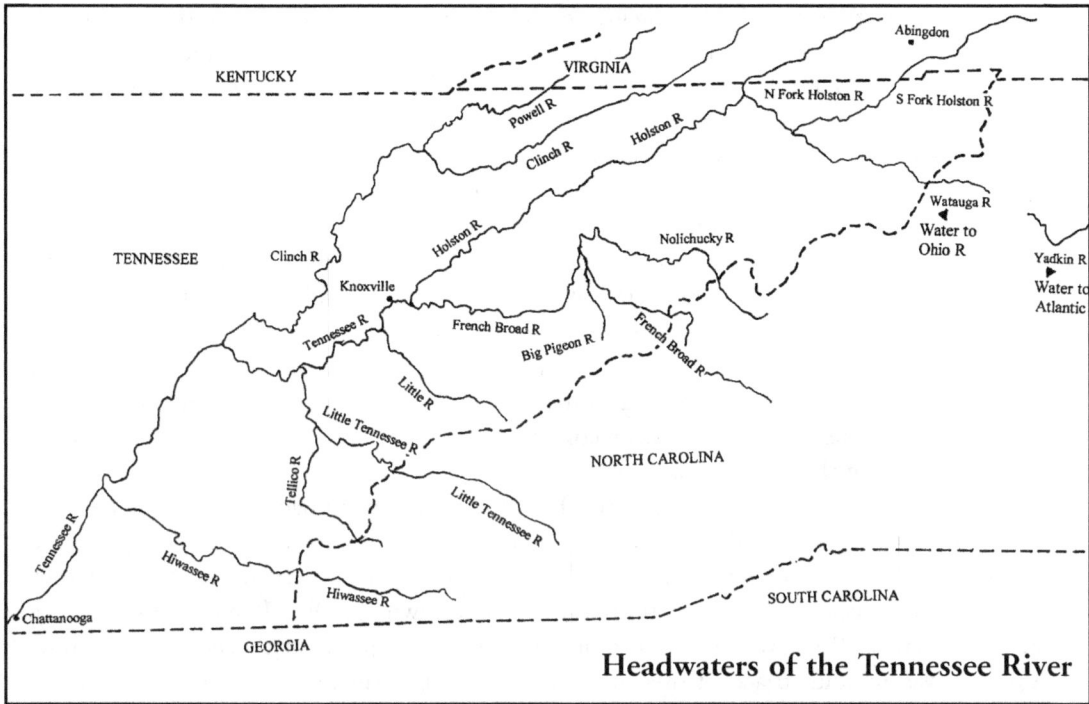

Headwaters of the Tennessee River

Williamsburg, who was granted 1,000 acres on each side of the river and had a lead mine on the property starting in the 1750s; a fort was built nearby in 1758.

Instructions of the Board of Trade in April 1768 to the Indian superintendents that the "colonies [be] required to inact the most effectual laws for preventing all settlement beyond [the 1768 Hard Labor] line"[8] did not reflect reality. The superintendents did not have the power to make the colonies pass laws. In 1769, when the Cherokee complained of hunters and of settlers west of the Hard Labor line, the best Stuart could do was to suggest the Cherokee require the intruders to pay rent.

The Hard Labor line was undone by the actions of the northern Indian superintendent, William Johnson, who was negotiating for Indian boundaries north of the Ohio River. In his negotiations with the Iroquois they agreed, and, according to Johnson, persuaded him to include country south of the Ohio River in the cession of land made at Fort Stanwix in November 1768. In the Iroquois deed it is recited that the true boundary between the Iroquois and the Cherokee was the Cherokee, now the Tennessee, River. Virginia seized upon this cession to press their desire to have a line further to the west than the Hard Labor line. To buttress its request the Virginians took two Cherokee chiefs to Charles Town and met with Stuart. The chiefs indicated the Cherokee were willing to have a line to the westward of Hard Labor so as to exclude white settlements on the upper Holston River from the Indian lands. Ignored in these dealings were the Indians living west of the Allegheny Mountains north of the Ohio River who hunted in what became Kentucky and Tennessee, primarily the Shawnee and Delaware.

When news of the Iroquois cession became public knowledge, seekers of land reacted quickly. The *Virginia Gazette* of December 1, 1768, reported that the "Six Nations and their tributaries have granted a vast extent of country to His Majesty, and settled an advantageous boundary line between their hunting grounds and this and other colonies to the southwards as far as the Cherokee [now the Tennessee] River."[9] A group of frontiersmen who passed through the upper Holston area in 1769, only to decide on a rapid retreat after meeting a large party of Indians, found only three families in the upper Holston when they first went through the area, but, six weeks later, as they returned cabins were on every suitable spot.

After receiving permission from London to renew negotiations, Stuart met with the Cherokee at Lochaber, South Carolina, in October 1770. Virginia provided funds for gifts to be given to the Indians. Gifts were a necessity for a successful conclusion. Oconostota said in March 1769, "We shall give no part of our land away unless we are paid for it and indeed we want to keep the Virginians at as great a distance as possible, as they are generally bad men and love to steal horses and hunt for deer."[10] The Cherokee agreed to move the division line further west since it was recognized that "His Majesty's Subjects" were inhabiting land west of the Hard Labor line.

Virginia was even more pleased with what happened next. As background, the Cherokee in the negotiations insisted that the boundary line in the south start "about six miles eastward of Long Island on Holston River"[11] now Kingsport, Tennessee. In return for that they were willing to move the northern termination point down the Ohio River from the mouth of the Kanawha River which was the northern terminal point of the Hard Labor line. Virginia was anxious to accept this western movement of the northern termination point which would add "a great tract of country"[12] to the cession, but Stuart refused to make that change as it would conflict with his instructions from London. In forwarding the Lochaber line to London, Stuart recited this facet of the negotiations and, when approval came back from London in the summer of 1771, the King agreed with how Stuart had handled it.

The Crown's rejection of the offered movement of the northern terminal point was not known to Colonel John Donelson, who later helped establish Nashville, Tennessee, and was the father of Andrew Jackson's wife, who left in May 1771 to survey the Lochaber line. He was accompanied by Alexander Cameron, deputy Indian superintendent, and the Cherokee chief, Little Carpenter. A decision was made by the surveyors to have the line on the northern end terminate at the mouth of the Kentucky River (then called the Louisa River) some 150 miles down the Ohio River from the mouth of the Kanawha, measured on a straight line basis. This boundary, known as the Donelson Line, in Donelson's estimation added 10 million acres to the Cherokee cession, and was reluctantly ratified by the Crown. In submitting the line to London, Governor Dunmore of Virginia justified the change as being necessary to avoid a terrain "so mountainous rugged and difficult of access, that they could not have accomplished [the survey] in many months, nor without an expense that would have been enormous."[13] It was, Dunmore said, a change consistent with the Indians' "earnest desire." Dunmore also stressed what had happened since the Lochaber line was agreed to: "by this [Donelson] line are taken in a great number of families who had settled without the intended line, and who, if that had been adopted, would be excluded from the government and protection of the colony, to their great detriment if not utter ruin."[14] Reluctantly London approved the Donelson Line.

Little Carpenter, aware that a major shift had been made in the line, gave Donelson a message:

As we are now going to part ... I beg that you will carry a short talk from me to the new governor.... When you met us with our father [Stuart] at Long Cane [Lochaber] it was then agreed that the line should run to the mouth of the New River [Kanawha] but we have altered that course a little and I hope [Stuart] as well as my people will approve of it.[15]

Louis De Vorsey, Jr., in his book *The Indian Boundary in the Southern Colonies, 1763–1775*, carefully analyzed what went on in arriving at the Donelson Line and suggested several reasons why Little Carpenter was willing to make the change:

1. The desire to establish a "natural" boundary....
2. ...[C]ession of lands to the northeast of the Kentucky [River] would act as a "safety valve" and divert ... settlements away from the Cherokee coreland farther south.
3. ...[T]he Cherokee claim to the lands south of the Ohio River was at best tenuous....
4. ...[W]hite settlements in the area [would] protect the Cherokee flank from northern enemies.
5. The desire for personal gain from the sale of lands to which his tribe held a debatable claim.[16]

The Lochaber treaty contained a guarantee to the Cherokee: "His Majestys white Subjects Inhabiting the Province of Virginia shall not upon any pretence whatsoever settle beyond the said Line."[17] It is questionable if Cherokee Chief Oconostota gave much credence to this provision. After the Hard Labor treaty of 1768 he said: "The land is now divided for the use of the red and white people and I hope the white inhabitants of the Frontiers will pay great attention to the line marked and agreed upon."[18] This hope was no sooner expressed than it was shattered.

Settlers were not the only plague suffered by the Cherokee. Scofflaws of a different nature were the traders. Alexander Cameron, a Scot living with the Cherokee as a Crown agent, said, "No nation was ever infested with such a set of villains and horse thieves.[19] A trader [is] indefatigable in stirring up trouble against all other white persons that he judges his rivals 'in trade.'"[20] With much exposure in the New York, Pennsylvania, and Ohio country, William Johnson described traders in 1770 as a "[s]ett of very worthless fellows."[21] Efforts to regulate those trading with Indians during these years failed. Walter H. Mohr's book on *Federal Indian Relations 1774–1778* sums it up: "The English traders made themselves obnoxious to the Indians by cheating them in trade, by selling rum illegally, and by defrauding them of their lands."[22]

There was no stopping the whites. In these years frontiersmen, mostly with impunity, attacked and sometimes murdered Cherokees. In a show of disdain the English failed to compensate the Cherokee with 500 Indian-dressed deerskins' value in goods for every person murdered. This refers to Indians killed in Virginia for whom promises had been repeatedly made that either the perpetrators would be executed or compensation made. When the Indians achieved their own justice by murdering five Virginia emigrants going to Mississippi, Stuart wrote to the acting governor, John Blair, and said the Indians were acting in accord with the custom of their country when they had not been given any satisfaction by the English.

9

Land Grabbers and Early
Kentucky Settlements

The cession of the Iroquois in 1768 and the Cherokee agreement to the Lochaber line in 1771 cleared the way, in the minds of expansionists, to what became the state of West Virginia and the eastern half of Kentucky for settlement. Ignoring opposition of the Indians living north of the Ohio River, especially the Shawnee and Delaware, who hunted in those areas, the remaining challenge was to get permission from the Crown to settle in those areas.

George III's 1763 proclamation prohibiting settlement of land "beyond the ... sources of any of the rivers which fall into the Atlantic Ocean"[1] had a mercantile objective. The Secretary of State (Lord Egremont) wanted to keep settlers from "planting themselves in the Heart of America, out of reach of Government where from the great difficulty of procuring European commodities, they would be compelled to commerce and manufactures, to the infinite prejudice of Britain."[2]

In terms of fairness and truthfulness the 1763 proclamation is an outstanding document. It admitted "great frauds and abuses [had] been committed in the purchasing lands of the Indians," and directed that "all persons whatever, who [had] either wilfully or inadvertently seated themselves upon any lands ... which [had] not ... been ceded to or purchased by [the Crown should] forthwith ... remove themselves from such settlements."[3]

If the population of the colonies had remained static, the Indians might have been secure behind the wall of mountains, but it didn't. In the southern colonies (Maryland, Virginia, the Carolinas, and Georgia) between 1760 and 1780 the numbers almost doubled: the whites (432,000 to 780,000) and blacks (284,000 to 510,000). The increase in New England (Maine, New Hampshire, Massachusetts, Rhode Island, and Connecticut) was not as great: 450,000 to 665,000. The Middle Colonies (New York, New Jersey, Pennsylvania and Delaware) went from 428,000 to 723,000. Looked at as an entirety, the colonies had 1.3 million whites and 0.3 million blacks in 1760 and 2.1 million whites and 0.6 million blacks in 1780. Of serious concern in England was the rate at which its population was going to America. Between 1760 and 1775 those leaving the British Isles numbered 125,000. To slow this transfer, which the English landlords feared would depopulate their estates, the British government in 1767 refused to approve a Georgia act subsidizing immigration.

Even though the 1763 proclamation asserted an intention to protect the "hunting-grounds" of Indians living under British protection, the protection was "for the present" and could be avoided by "purchases or settlements" made under the Crown's "special leave and license."[4] The 1763 line was an interim measure and during the period of uncertainty as to how rights to land west of the 1763 Proclamation line would be acquired, the land hungry were exploring it to locate desirable tracts. George Washington told his agent, William Crawford, to go into what would be the "King's part" between the Proclamation line of 1763 and any negotiated Indian boundary line and to "hunt[] out good Lands and in some measure mark[] and distinguish[] them for their own (in order to keep others from settling them)." This was to be done "snugly under pretence of hunting other Game." As for the Proclamation line, he looked upon it "as a temporary expedient to quiet the Minds of the Indians [which] must fall ... in a few years especially when those Indians are consenting to our Occupying the Lands."[5]

Many in England weren't worried about Egremont's mercantile concern. The Indian trader George Croghan, deputy superintendent of Indian affairs north of the Ohio River since 1756, wrote to his superintendent in 1766, Sir William Johnson, that "one half of England is Now Land Mad & Every body there has thire Eys fixt on this Cuntry."[6] He was disappointed in 1764, when in England about controlling trade with the Indians, to find those striving for power to be concentrating more on serving themselves and their friends than the public.

The situation in what became Kentucky was unique. There were no Indian villages. A University of Kentucky archaeologist, A. Gwynn Henderson, has concluded that in 1775 the Cherokee and "other native groups, used portions of the region with permission of the Shawnee, who claimed much of it." Most Indian villages had moved "north of the Ohio River for safety, and ... returned in small groups ... to hunt and camp during the winter." This pattern of usage differs from archaeological evidence which shows that "Kentucky ... was inhabited by native peoples for over twelve thousand years." During the period 1000–1750 Indians "lived in large, fortified towns [with] over one thousand people [and] in smaller villages, and in single-family hamlets." Henderson believes "it is possible that many of the villages [were] abandoned shortly before the settlers arrived" and this change was the result of "fear of reprisals from the British (after the fall of Fort Duquesne in 1758)." The lives of the Indians were probably changed by exposure to diseases brought by the whites. She writes of "multiple graves of from four to thirty individuals, [and of] mass graves estimated to contain the remains of over one hundred individuals densely packed into a small space."[7]

Fertile minds were at work. Various proposals were made to the Crown as to settlement of what became Kentucky. A promising scheme before the start of the Revolutionary War was that of the Grand Ohio Company with supporters on both sides of the Atlantic. It called for a grant of 20 million acres for a new colony which encompassed an earlier Indiana cession. Between 1769 and 1773 the possibility of getting the grant waxed and waned in London but it was not to be. Near the end of the proposal's life, the company was called the Vandalia Company because the colony was to be named Vandalia to recognize that Queen Charlotte was "descended from the Vandals."[8]

As Vandalia stalled, the governor of Virginia, Lord Dunmore, was encouraged to think the Ohio Valley land below the Ohio River would stay within Virginia's jurisdiction. Virginia's claim to the forks of the Ohio (Fort Pitt) and nearby land was based on the 1609 charter given the London Company. The charter, without precision, established an eastern boundary along the Atlantic coast from which the north and south boundaries would go from "sea to sea, west and northwest."[9] Although the 1609 charter was revoked in 1624 and the land reverted to the Crown, Virginia asserted its jurisdiction was only reduced as the Crown later made grants to others.

Future
OHIO

Future
INDIANA

Muskingum R

Steubenville •

Allegheny R
■Ft Dunmore
(Ft Pitt)

PA

Monongahela R

Youghiogheny R

Redstone Cr

Ohio R

Scioto R

MD

*Great
Miami R*

Chillicothe ▲ • Camp Charlotte

*Little
Kanawha R*

Indiana
Cession

Cheat R

VANDALIA

Ohio R

Ohio R

Licking R

i Point Pleasant

*Great
Kanawha R*

Falls of the Ohio
(Louisville)

Kentucky R

•
Harrodsburg

Future
KENTUCKY

VANDALIA

New R

Greenbrier R

Fincastle County

New R

VIRGINIA

Cumberland R

Cumberland Gap

Dunmore's War and Vandalia
Ref: Adams, Maps 61, 63; Royce, Plate CLX

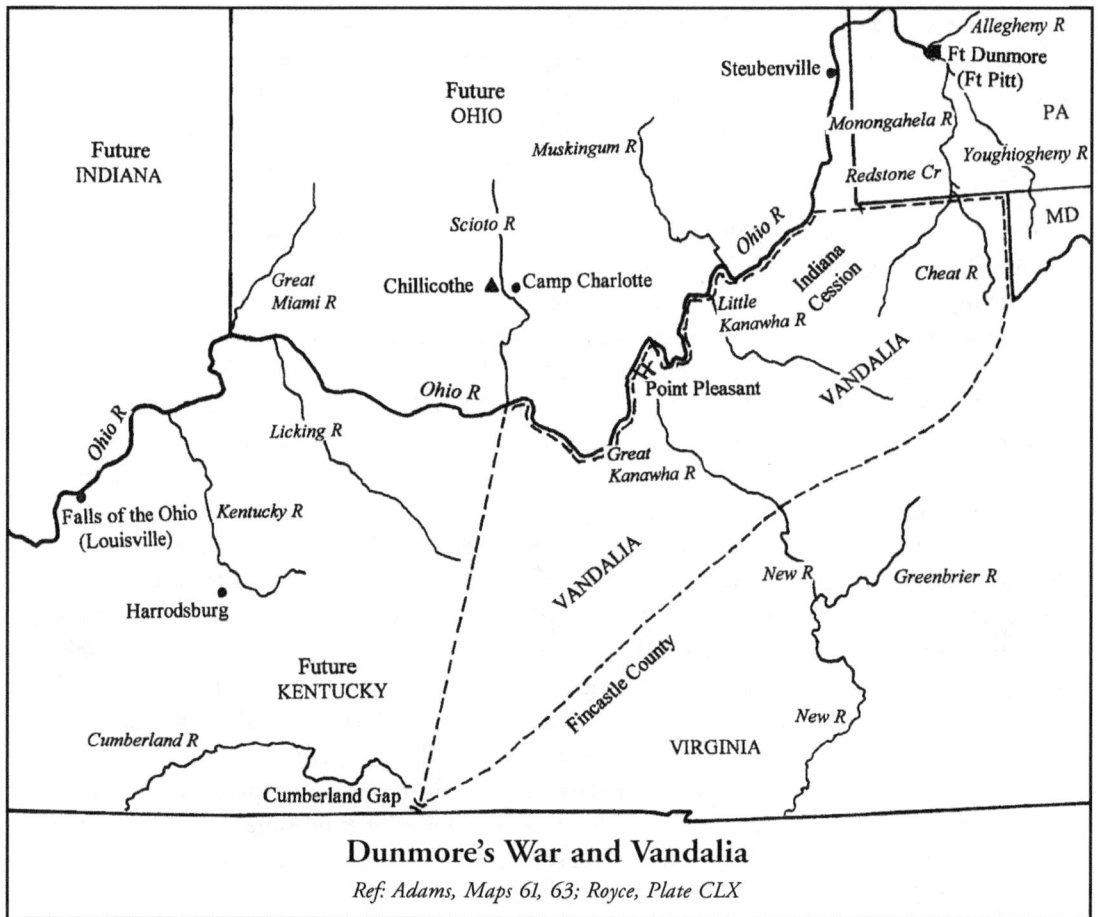

When Dunmore was told by London in October 1773 that he could proceed with grants in future Kentucky it set off a race of surveyors and jobbers into Kentucky. The Shawnee were not ready to concede that what was to become West Virginia and Kentucky were available for white settlers and understood the consequences of surveyors, who they called Red Flag men, coming on to their land. Settlers were apt to follow. Thomas Jefferson in his *Notes on the State of Virginia* described another bellwether: "The [honey]bees have generally extended themselves into the country, a little in advance of the white settlers. The Indians therefore call them the white man's fly, and consider their approach as indicating the approach of the settlements of the whites."[10] The Shawnee could not stop the honeybees, but they could and did act out against those exploring along the Ohio River. Early in 1774 they killed some of the whites in what they considered their land and tried to enlist other tribes north of the Ohio River (Miami, Wyandot, and Ottawa) to join with them for, otherwise, in time the whites would be after their land. These tribes saw the problem as being remote from their areas and refused to join in.

The area was ripe for an explosion. It was described as of 1772–1773 by a Moravian missionary:

The whole country on the Ohio river, had ... drawn the attention of many persons from the neighbouring provinces; who generally forming themselves into parties, would rove through the country in search of land, either to settle on, or for speculation; and some, careless of watching over their conduct, or destitute of both honour and humanity, would join a rabble (a class of people generally met with on the frontiers) who maintained, that to kill an Indian, was the same as killing a bear or a buffalo, and would fire on Indians that came across them by the way;— nay, more, would decoy such as lived across the river [that is, north of the Ohio River], to come over, for the purpose of joining them in hilarity; and when these complied, they fell on them and murdered them.[11]

Activities were curtailed when news circulated that "Indians had robbed some of the land jobbers."[12] The Indians went on the warpath, essentially stopping efforts to settle along the Ohio River downstream from Pittsburgh. Although it is not clear as to who was responsible, the Indians were reacting to murders by whites. Among those killed were members of the family of John Logan, the son of a Cayuga chief, who, with others, was camped on the north side of the Ohio at the mouth of Yellow Creek near present-day Steubenville, Ohio. When Logan and other warriors were absent, a drunken party killed thirteen Indian women and children, including all of Logan's immediate family. Logan and eight warriors exacted their own brand of justice by crossing the river and scalping thirteen Virginians. War parties went out and took scalps and prisoners. "[G]reat numbers of innocent men, women and children, fell victims to the tomahawk and scalping knife."[13]

The Indians' action gave Dunmore an excuse for what he may have wanted to do. Patrick Henry thought he wanted a war so that Indians could be driven off land he coveted. He declared war against the Shawnee and over the summer of 1774 raised 3,000 militiamen to invade and destroy Shawnee communities on the Scioto River north of the Ohio. At a June 1774 confrontation at Point Pleasant, Kentucky, an Indian force of about 700, led by Shawnee war chief Cornstalk, attacked about 1,000 Virginians but was unable to annihilate them or force a surrender. Even though the loss to the Indians was about half of the 222 men killed or seriously wounded on the white side, it was a serious loss in view of the limited maximum force they could muster. The Virginians at Point Pleasant were under the command of Colonel Andrew Lewis, who was proceeding up the Kanawha River to join a force led by Dunmore headed from Pittsburgh to Chillicothe and other Shawnee towns on the Scioto River.

After Point Pleasant Cornstalk's warriors were reluctant to continue the war. Consequently, Cornstalk met with Dunmore, who was positioned at Camp Charlotte, a fortified position near Chillicothe, to make peace. Although it is disputed as to what was agreed to, that is, if the Shawnees agreed to give up hunting lands south of the Ohio and if Dunmore recognized that the Indians should have lands north and west of the Ohio River, a truce was reached and Dunmore took his men back to Virginia and the Shawnee over the next few years migrated westward to the two Miami Rivers in the western part of the present state of Ohio.

Dunmore's report to the Earl of Dartmouth dated December 24, 1774, described, in part, what was agreed to: "[The Indians] [s]hould not hunt on *our Side the Ohio*, nor molest Boats passing thereupon.... In return he [gave] them every promise of protection and good treatment *on our Side*" (emphasis supplied).[14] He exuded optimism in the report: "this affair, which undoubtedly was attended with circumstances of Shocking inhumanity, may be the means of producing happy effects; for it has impressed an Idea of the power of the White People, upon the minds of the Indians, which they did not before entertain; and, there is reason to believe, it has extinguished the rancour which raged so violently in our People against the Indians: and I think there is a greater probability that these Scenes of distress will never be renewed, than ever was before."[15]

An opportunist in 1775 was Richard Henderson, who had a grandiose plan of establishing an inland empire within Kentucky to be called Transylvania. Henderson and several others organized the Transylvania Company with the object of "rent[ing] or purchas[ing] a certain Territory lying on the west side of the mountains ... from the Indian tribes now in possession thereof."[16]

With the Shawnees supposedly eliminated after the battle at Point Pleasant, Henderson was ready to act. He wasn't deterred by the Crown's injunction against white settlements in that area. Nor did the laws of Virginia and North Carolina prohibiting individuals from dealing with Indian nations stop him. To Henderson the *sine qua non* was an agreement with the Cherokee who had a limited claim over Kentucky. This would give the appearance of legality sufficient to induce "Emigrants or Adventurers" to pay twenty shillings per hundred acres so as to be able to settle on, as advertised, "Land purchased by Rch'd Henderson & Co."[17] Neither Dunmore nor the governor of North Carolina, Josiah Martin, thought well of Henderson. Dunmore described him as an "evill disposed and disorderly Person," and Martin declared any sale would be "null and void."[18]

Disparaging remarks did not stop Henderson once he had a tentative agreement with the Cherokee. Daniel Boone, who Henderson hired, invited the Cherokee to meet in March 1775 to negotiate a sale of land. Boone was also "to mark out a road in the best passage from the settlement through the wilderness to Kentucke"[19] and to select and fortify a town site. For this service Boone was to receive 2,000 prime acres.

Over a thousand Cherokee men and women, including Little Carpenter and other chiefs, met with Henderson, known to them as Carolina Dick, and his associates at Sycamore Shoals (near present Elizabethtown, Tennessee, and on the Watauga River) and the sale and purchase of 20,000,000 acres between the Kentucky and Cumberland rivers was completed. This land was west of the Donelson Line. Since the sale included waterways flowing into the Cumberland River a large amount of what became the state of Tennessee was also included. Although the Cherokee claim of ownership of all these lands might be questioned, the treaty making the transfer asserts they were the Aborigines and sole owners by occupancy from the beginning of time.

Little Carpenter and other chiefs probably thought the land would be taken in any event and they might as well get something for it. In fact they got very little. The overall price was 10,000 pounds, which, when divided among 1,000 or more Indians, left some with a single shirt. Rum, in "discreet" amount, was passed out after the sale.

Not all the Cherokee were agreeable to the sale. Under the leadership of Little Carpenter's son, Tsiyu Gansini, known as Dragging Canoe, operating from new towns near what is now Chattanooga, Tennessee, the dissidents, called Chickamaugans, carried on war against settlers and hunters for the next 20 years. At the time of the cession, Dragging Canoe observed that the whites had passed over the mountains and "settled upon Cherokee land."[20] He did not think this would satisfy them, and that future cessions would be sought and "'The Real People,' once so great and formidable, will be compelled to seek refuge in some distant wilderness" where they would "be permitted to stay only a short while, until they again behold the advancing banners of the same greedy host." Eventually, when no further retreat is possible, "the extinction of the whole [Cherokee] race will be proclaimed." Neither he nor his young warriors would accept this—they would "have [their] lands."[21] Dragging Canoe told Boone: "You have bought a fair land, but there is a cloud hanging over it. You will find its settlement dark and bloody."[22]

A separate sale included a path grant which became the Wilderness Road. Boone assembled thirty to thirty-five men at present-day Kingsport, Tennessee, located on the Holston River, to cut a path for settlers. Over two weeks the Warriors Path, which was only a rough trace through the mountains, was cleared and widened to the Cumberland Gap. Wagons could not quite make it to the Gap nor be used beyond that point. Before reaching the Gap, wagons were taken apart and carried. From the Gap to the northwest the road deviated from the Warrior's Path but often followed "buffalo roads" until they reached the rolling country.

An official reaction to what Henderson was doing came in a proclamation of Dunmore. It denounced "the unwarrantable and illegal designs of ... Henderson and his abettors" who were described as "disorderly persons."[23] George Washington was also negative: "There is something in that affair which I neither understand, nor like, and I wish I may not have cause to dislike it worse as the mystery unfolds."[24] North Carolina's governor was equally outraged: Henderson was "a famous invader," associated with "an infamous Company of land Pyrates."[25]

Undeterred, Henderson, Boone, and others established a settlement at Boonesborough, located west of the Kentucky River in April 1775. Other early settlements were at Harrodsburg, Logan's Station (sometimes called St. Aspah's Station), and Boiling Spring. However, the person with a vision for the future was Henderson.

Henderson was probably encouraged when Virginia, which was acting independent of the Crown, did not object to his settlement in Kentucky. Word of the splendors of Kentucky and its open spaces spread rapidly in southwestern Virginia. Writing to his father-in-law, Colonel William Preston of Draper's Meadow (now Blacksburg, Virginia), the official surveyor of Fincastle County, on May 5, 1775, a Lexington, Virginia, minister said:

> What a buzzel is amongst people about Kentuck! To hear people speak of it one would think it was a new found paradise; and I doubt not if it be such a place as represented but ministers will have thin congregations, but why need I fear that? Ministers are moveable goods as well as others and stand in need of good land as others do, for they are bad farmers.[26]

For a time the Revolutionary War (1776–1783) shut down much of the westward migration. By supporting the British the Indians were able to strike out at the settlers encroaching on their historic lands. John Stuart's deputy among the Cherokee, Alexander Cameron, around 1775 spoke ill of the adventurers and settlers: "If the Indians committed half the irregularities the Virginians did since the conclusion of the last war [i.e., since 1763], they would have been at war with them long ere now."[27] During the war three fortified communities, Logan's fort, Harrodsburg, and Boonsborough withstood Indian attacks.

10

The Southern Frontier during
the War Years (1775–1783)

During the war years (1775–1783) there was little settlement west or north of the Ohio River. In contrast, significant migration and entrenching went on in modern day Kentucky, Tennessee, and southwest Virginia. At the start of the war the Indians were courted by both sides. However, their predisposition was toward the British, who could convincingly point out that it was the Americans who were threatening to move ever deeper into Indian country and it was the king who could provide them with what had become the necessaries of life. Up to the peace treaty, under which all the Indians lost, the big losers during the war were the Cherokee in the South and the Iroquois in the North.

When the Second Continental Congress provided for commissioners to deal with Indians in the South, the commissioners decided to talk with the Cherokee and Creek in the spring of 1776. Ominously, none of the Overhill Cherokee attended a meeting at Fort Charlotte designed for the Cherokee. The Cherokee, with a population of about 13,000, were spread over a large area in "three settlements known as the Lower Towns, the Middle or Valley [T]owns, and the Overhill [T]owns."[1] The major towns were upon the headwaters of the Savannah, Hiwassee, and Tuckasegee rivers and upon the whole course of the Little Tennessee. These towns were roughly within the area where the boundaries of Georgia, Tennessee, and North Carolina meet, and some in northwest South Carolina.

The British had an early policy with respect to the southern Indians. Their Indian superintendent, John Stuart, was told by General Thomas Gage in a letter of September 1775 that "when opportunity offers" he should "make [the Indians] take arms against His Majesty's enemies." Stuart, who had to leave Charles Town when rebels took control there, was in St. Augustine, Florida, in 1776. He urged both Loyalists and Patriots living along the Holston, Watauga, Nolichucky, and French Broad rivers, all of which fed into the Tennessee River in present-day northeastern Tennessee and southwestern Virginia, to withdraw so as to avoid a conflict with the Indians. These settlers are referred to here as the Wataugans. At the same time Stuart sent thirty horse-loads of ammunition to the Cherokee which could be used against a rebel invasion. Stuart instructed his brother, Henry, who took the ammunition to the Overhill Cherokee in 1776 to obtain Indian support in "distressing the Rebels" but to do so in a manner not to provoke "an indiscriminate attack"[2] that would anger the Loyalists.

In May 1776 General Henry Clinton, who later in 1776 led an unsuccessful attack on Charles Town, told Stuart to delay military cooperation between Indians and frontier Loyalists. This may have been a recognition that in supporting the Indians the British would make Rebels of settlers who would suffer from Indian acts of war.

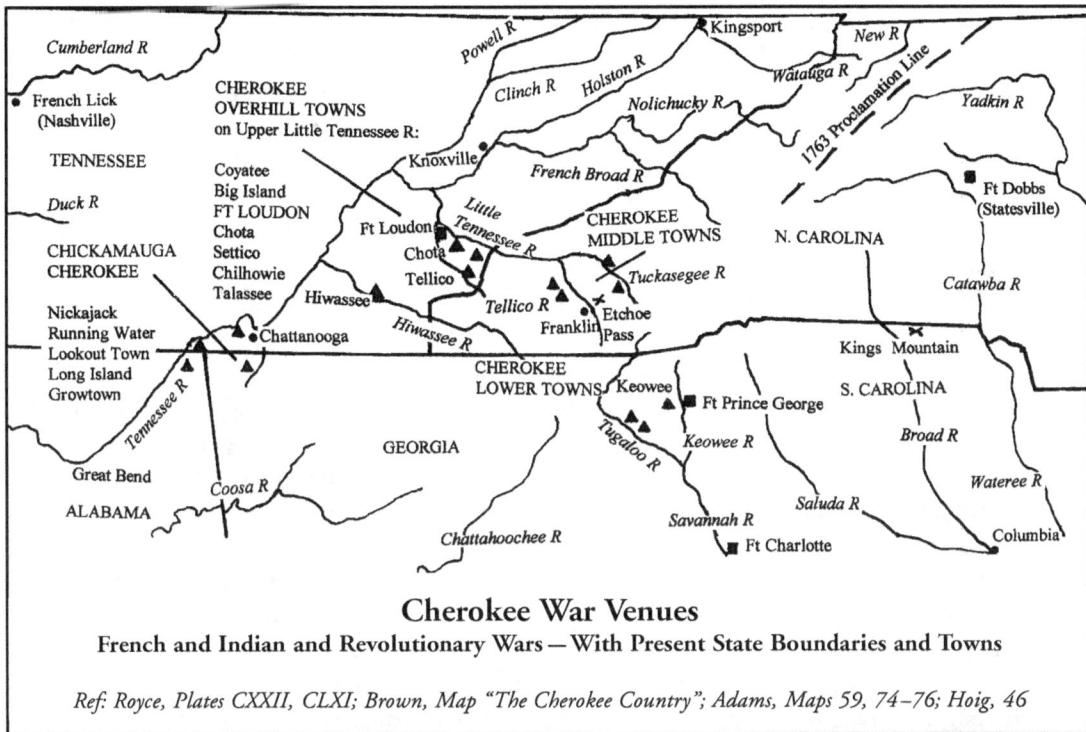

Cherokee War Venues

French and Indian and Revolutionary Wars — With Present State Boundaries and Towns

Ref: Royce, Plates CXXII, CLXI; Brown, Map "The Cherokee Country"; Adams, Maps 59, 74–76; Hoig, 46

The Wataugans did not withdraw. At least in the eyes of the whites, the Wataugans had some legal standing to hold their ground. In 1772 they leased some of the occupied land from the Cherokee and made purchases in 1773 and March 1775. The Cherokee were "chafed" at the presence of the Wataugans who acquired land by taking advantage of the Indians' poverty and wants.[3]

Dragging Canoe, who fumed over the 1775 sale of Kentucky land to Richard Henderson, was not in a mood to sit quietly on the sidelines. When, in 1776, a group of northern tribe representatives, probably encouraged by the British, asked the Cherokee to join with a united Indian force to rid America of whites, Dragging Canoe and his followers accepted the tendered war belts. Among those agreeing with Dragging Canoe were Double Head and John Watts, brother and nephew of the revered Cherokee chief Old Tassel, also referred to as Corn Tassel. The northern tribe members may have also encouraged the Lower Town Cherokee who attacked South Carolina settlers before Dragging Canoe took action. During the summer of 1776 attacks were carried out along the frontiers of Georgia and Virginia.

Henry Stuart tried to keep warfare from occurring. He addressed the following to the northern Indians trying to proselytize the Cherokee:

> You northern Indians have proper white men to direct you, but the Cherokees have not. If they go over the border and kill women and children, and fall on the King's friends as well as his enemies, they will draw against themselves all the forces that were intended to be used against the King's troops; and will rouse the resentment of those who otherwise might have been their friends.[4]

An effort to get the Wataugans to peacefully remove themselves from what the Cherokee considered to be their land did not have any significant positive results.

Dragging Canoe's first attack in July 1776 failed when his force was ambushed by settlers who had been warned. Dragging Canoe was wounded and 13 warriors were killed. The defeat only goaded Dragging Canoe and his followers into small raids in the Clinch, Powell, and Holston valleys with a resulting 18 killings. Then the words of Henry Stuart became reality. Cherokee towns on the Chattahoochee and Tugaloo rivers were eliminated by 200 Georgians in July 1776, the Lower Towns were attacked by 1,000 Carolinians in August and September and a combined force of 3,800 Carolinians and Virginians destroyed and punished Middle, Valley, and Overhill Towns. Loyalists and Rebels joined in these attacks of retribution.

In August 1776 Thomas Jefferson, a member of the Continental Congress' standing committee on Indian affairs, hoped an example would be made of the Cherokees and that they would be "driven beyond the Missisipi and that this ... future will be declared to the Indians the invariable consequence of their beginning a war."[5] Writing in 1813 about the fight with the Cherokee, Jefferson said they had been "seduced by the agents of the British government to take up the hatchet against us, had committed great havoc on our southern frontier, by murdering and scalping helpless women and children according to their cruel and cowardly principles of warfare. The chastisement they then received closed the history of their wars, prepared them for receiving the elements of civilization, which, zealously inculcated by the present government of the United States, have rendered them an industrious, peaceable and happy people."[6] Jefferson's recollections in 1813 were flawed. Dragging Canoe did not need encouragement from the British, who he hated as much as he did the settlers. The Dragging Canoe Cherokee did not cease to attack settlers, and the rosy picture of the Cherokee adopting the white man's ways was correct but the white man ultimately forced their removal to the West. Jefferson's attitude respecting Indians was often a reflection of a particular situation. In a philosophical sense he said that "the Indian ... in body and mind [was] equal to the white man."[7]

The older Cherokee chiefs entered into negotiations with the colonies and, in 1777, gave up more than five million acres to restore peace. The treaty moved the Cherokee eastern boundary west of the Cumberland Gap. The Treaty of Long Island (July 20, 1777) ceded to Virginia everything east of the Blue Ridge. Virginia received the Cumberland Gap, which fit in with Governor Patrick Henry's plan for a road to the West. South Carolina, by the Treaty of DeWitt's Corner (May 20, 1777), received most of the Indian land still within its boundaries (the modern-day counties of Greenville, Anderson, Pickens and Oconee). North Carolina received land north of the Nolichucky River, except for Great Island. Some 17 Cherokee agreed to act as scouts for Washington's army. Not all Cherokee were parties to the treaties.

Those signing the treaty were not well supplied with necessities by the Americans who had little wherewithal to do so if so inclined. Dragging Canoe's followers were taken care of by the British who hoped to use them at a later date in conjunction with the Creeks, Shawnees, and Chickasaws. In October 1777 Stuart told the Lower Creek that in the event of a Rebel victory the Rebels would "immediately endeavour to possess themselves of all [the Creek] lands and extirpate [them.]"[8]

The treaties of 1777 did little to stop further incursions into Cherokee land. A Cherokee protest to North Carolina shows what was happening:

> Brother: I am now going to speak to you. We are a poor distressed people, that is in great trouble.... Your people from Nolichucky are daily pushing us out of our lands. We have no place to hunt

on. Your people have built houses within one day's walk of our towns. We don't want to quarrel with our elder brother; we therefore hope our elder brother will not take our lands from us, that the Great Man above gave us. He made you and he made us; we are all his children.... We are the first people that ever lived on this land; it is ours.[9]

There were no bended knees in Dragging Canoe's people. They continued to raid. Virginia's governor, Patrick Henry, wanted them stopped. He was particularly concerned about this group since they could block a route to posts on the Mississippi and Ohio and prevent much desired trade with New Orleans. He sent a force of 600 Virginians and North Carolinians under Colonel Evan Shelby in April 1779 to "totally destroy"[10] the homes of Dragging Canoe's followers. They did this with ease since the warriors were away fighting for the British along the South Carolina and Georgia borders. Dragging Canoe's people did not rebuild. They were given land by the Creek and settled near modern Chattanooga in the towns of Nickajack, Running Water, Lookout Town, Long Island, and Crowtown from which in the 1780s and 1790s they made war on white settlers. They became known as Chickamaugan Cherokees.

A British plan to have Indians from the North and South join in a pincer movement so as to control the West was scuttled when George Rogers Clark captured Kaskaskia and Fort Vincennes in the North and sent Henry Hamilton, the British governor of the Northwest Territory headquartered in Detroit, to Virginia as a captive in 1778–1779.

Dragging Canoe was talked into making a costly move against the frontier settlers in 1780. British Indian agent Alexander Cameron persuaded him to act by pointing out that the presence of Cornwallis in Georgia and South Carolina had pulled frontier militia out of their home territory. Cornwallis also wanted the Indians on the warpath, thinking that would draw militiamen back from the American forces he was facing. Cameron was correct but had not anticipated the militia victory over the British at Kings Mountain, South Carolina, in October 1780. Returning from that win, Lieutenant Colonel John Sevier, at the head of a North Carolina force of about 250 Wataugans and others, struck at the Cherokee before they had accomplished much from going on the warpath. Sevier was later joined by 400 Virginians led by Colonel Arthur Campbell and punitive action was taken against the Cherokee. Human casualties were few — three Americans and twenty-nine Indians. However, life-threatening destruction was substantial. Chota and ten other towns were destroyed as were large quantities of food. Campbell wrote to Thomas Jefferson, Virginia's governor as of 1779, that his objective was "to distress the whole, as much as possible, by destroying their habitations and Provisions."[11]

Ironically the punishment wasn't administered to Dragging Canoe. The Americans did not go far enough west to reach him and those attacked were the friendly Cherokee in the Overhill area. The leaders reported to Jefferson that no place in the Overhill Country remained unvisited. The Treaty of Long Island on the Holston River of July 20, 1781, made peace. Under the treaty the Cherokee gave up land in the upper eastern part of modern Tennessee and in western North Carolina. New leadership in the Cherokee nation was required when Little Carpenter died around 1781. Corn Tassel and Raven spoke for the Cherokee at Long Island.

Corn Tassel was against the cession but there was no sensible alternative. His talk to the Americans denounced what was occurring:

It is a little surprising, that when we entered into treaties with our brothers, their whole cry is *more land*! Indeed, formerly it seemed to be a matter of formality with them to demand what they knew we durst not refuse. But on the principles of fairness, of which we have received assurances during the conducting of the present treaty, and in the name of free will and equality, I must reject your demands.

Indeed, much as been advanced on the want of what you term civilization among the Indians; and many proposals have been made to us to adopt your laws, your religion, your manners and your customs. But we confess that we do not yet see the propriety, or practicability of such a reformation, and should be better pleased with beholding the good effect of these doctrines in your own practices than with hearing you talk about them, or reading your papers upon such subjects.[12]

The Cherokee were forced to cede land at Long Island and virtually nothing was paid for it.

The rough treatment accorded the Cherokee had a significant impact on the Creek. They tried to avoid angering either the Loyalists or Patriots during the Revolutionary War. The Americans wanted them to stay neutral and the Loyalists wanted them to actively help bring down the revolution. The challenge for the Creek was to keep each side sufficiently satisfied with their conduct so that trade would continue. To have goods from the whites was essential. South Carolina appointed three commissioners of Indian affairs one of whom, George Galphin, informed the Creek that he would be taking John Stuart's place. A message sent in September 1775 to the English and Americans expresses the overall attitude of the Creek during the first years of the war: "We hope the path between us and you will remain white and clear, and as we are a poor people we hope you will help us with as much ammunition as you possibly can and we are determined to lye quiet and not meddle with the quarrel."[13]

Within the Creek nation there were strong advocates for each side and at times a civil war was a possibility. A coalescing of both factions within the Creek nation occurred in the winter of 1777–1778 when the Americans did not supply the needed goods for the tribes. But, by the summer of 1778, some support for the Americans revived. The British put pressure on the pro–American towns by refusing to give them goods. A decisive event was the capture of Savannah by the British in December 1778. Stuart called upon the Creek to supply warriors and they mobilized to fight the Americans but accomplished little; however, the neutralist policy essentially vanished. After Stuart's death in March 1779, Colonel Thomas Brown, who was then superintendent of the Creek, with a mixed force of Loyalists and 250 Creeks captured Augusta in the summer of 1780. Then, when an American force of 600 attacked Augusta in the fall, the Creek fought valiantly and repelled the Americans but, in doing so, suffered great losses.

As the war went badly for the English, the needs of the Creek were no longer being met. Spain, which declared war on England in June 1779 and captured Pensacola in May 1781, cut off trade from there. When Creeks were not able to force their way through an American siege of Savannah in 1782, they were essentially on their own. Rumors that England would turn Florida over to Spain caused great consternation and on May 1, 1783, a Creek told the English at St. Augustine:

The old beloved men informed me that the warriors of my town first joined the English as men and friends — that they gave them lands and became one flesh — that they considered their enemies as our own — that in all the wars either against Indians, Spaniards or Virginians, they assisted them.... Do the English mean to abandon their own children [that is, Indian children fathered by Englishmen] with their friends? Why will they turn their backs on us and forsake us? We never expected that men and warriors our friends would throw us into the hands of our enemies — Is it the great king's talk that we [be] left in distress? I hope he will inform us — If the English mean to abandon the land we will accompany them — We cannot take a Virginian or Spaniard by the hand — we cannot look upon them in the face.[14]

As with the other Indian allies of the British, no provision was made in the Treaty of Paris for them.

Another area of conflict between settlers and the Indians was the Cumberland River Valley around what was to become Nashville. A settlement was founded through the efforts of John Donelson, a Virginia surveyor and land speculator, and John Robertson, who had connections with both Virginia and North Carolina. They arrived at the Nashville area in different ways. Robertson came by land in the fall and winter of 1779, arriving at French Lick, an earlier name for Nashville, in December. His was a small group of men. Donelson brought the makings of a settlement by a six-month journey starting on the Holston River then to the Tennessee and Cumberland rivers, arriving at French Lick in May 1780. In addition to his own family, which included 13-year-old Rachel who was to become the wife of Andrew Jackson, there were 50 other families, slaves, and livestock on 30 flatboats 100 feet in length. They were not the first settlers in that area. Kaspar Mansker, a Virginian, already had settled within 12 miles of Nashville and had a fortified structure which gave cover for the new arrivals during Indian skirmishes in their first year. The Cherokee killed many and stole what they could. Indians were also killed. The area was so hazardous in 1781 that Donelson moved his family to a Kentucky settlement.

An unanticipated result of the war was the continued dominance of the Indian trade by Loyalists. During the war William Panton, a Scottish merchant, controlled all Indian trade coming from East Florida, and after the war, operating from Spanish East and West Florida, his business, Panton, Leslie, and Company, was given a monopoly by Spain to supply the Choctaws and Chickasaws. The Creeks were loyal to Panton who established, during the war at a Creek request, a store at St. Mark's, Florida. The Cherokee were less dependent on Panton.

11

The Creek and a Vacillating Partner (1783–1789)

A different Creek nation emerged after the Revolutionary War. Rather than being splintered in its approach to outsiders, it spoke with one voice, that of Alexander McGillivray. His capable voice worked to preserve the Creek nation as it had been in the past. McGillivray was a leader not because of any warrior traits but as a skillful administrator and diplomat. He was born in 1759, the son of a Scotsman, Lachlan McGillivray, who accumulated a reasonable estate by trading with the Creeks. Lachlan conducted his business from a plantation at Little Tallassee in Upper Creek territory. Alexander's mother, a Creek, Sehoy Marchand, whose French father was dead at the time Lachlan arrived in the Upper Creek area, was a member of a family with considerable power in the Creek nation. Since Creeks trace family lines through mothers the nationality of fathers was of small importance. Alexander's father probably had little to do with his youthful upbringing but when he reached age 14 he was sent to Charles Town for schooling. Charles Town, with a population of maybe 15,000, was the only large community south of the Potomac.

When the Revolutionary War started his father, in danger because of his loyalist views, headed back to Scotland and Alexander went back to the Creek. Alexander was immediately made a lesser chief in recognition of his mother's position in the Wind clan and the British soon made him a colonel with a function of keeping the Creek loyal to England.

After the war the Creek nation had alternative sources for goods. There were Spaniards in Florida and Americans on its other borders. The choice was easy. The Americans wanted Creek land and the Spaniards didn't. Another factor was McGillivray's anger over his father's treatment by the revolutionists. Explaining his decision to New Orleans' governor, Esteban Miro, he wrote on March 28, 1784: "For the good of my Country I have Sacrificed my all & it is a duty incumbent on me in this Critical Situation to exert myself for their Interest. The protection of a great Monarch is to be preferred to that of a distracted Republic."[1] Above all the Indians were pragmatists — in 1784 McGillivray said the "Indians will attach themselves to & Serve them best who Supply their Necessities."[2]

Spain declared war on England in 1779, captured West Florida in 1780–1781, and acquired all of Florida and gulf land east of the Mississippi below the 31st parallel and west of the Apalachicola River from England after the Revolutionary War. England had control of all this land for the 20 years after the conclusion of the French and Indian War (1763) to the end of the Revolutionary War (1783) and in 1764 created the East and West Floridas with a common boundary at the Chattahoochee and Apalachicola rivers. Spain's ownership of both sides of the Mississippi River as it emptied into the Gulf of Mexico threatened Ohio

Valley settlers who needed navigation of the Ohio and Mississippi rivers to market their produce.

Spain and the United States argued over the boundary between the two countries. Spain claimed land between the 31st parallel and 32 degrees, 28 minutes, west of the Chattahoochee River based on its interpretation of its 1783 acquisition of West Florida from England. Spain also had a weaker claim to most of the land south of the Tennessee River and west of the Flint River. In short it claimed sovereignty over all of the Chickasaw and Choctaw land and about half of what was claimed by the Creek.

Wanting to establish "a barrier state by means of a trading alliance with the Creeks, Chickasaws, and Choctaws," Spain entered into a trade agreement with each in the summer of 1784. The Indians "agreed to exclude all traders not able to show Spanish licenses."[3] McGillivray wanted more than a trade agreement. In a letter of July 10, 1785, to Spanish Governor Arturo O'Neill at Pensacola, McGillivray set out why the "Creek Chickasaw and Cherokee Nations" should receive from "His most Gracious Majesty [the King of Spain] ... assurances of protection to us, our respective propertys and Hunting Grounds":

> ... [H]is Brittannick Majesty was never possessed either by session purchase or by right of Conquest of our Territorys and which the Said treaty [the Paris Treaty of 1783] gives away. On the contrary it is well known that from the first Settlement of the English colonys of Carolina and Georgia up to the date of the Said treaty no [title] has ever been or pretended to be made by his Brittanic Majesty to our lands except what was obtained by free Gift or by purchase for good and valuable Considerations.
>
> ... [N]or did we the Nations of Creeks, Chickesaws and Cherokees do any act to forfeit our Independence and natural Rights to the Said King of Great Brittain that could invest him with the power of giving our property away unless fighting by the side of his soldiers in the day of battle and Spilling our best blood in the Service of his Nation can be deemed so.

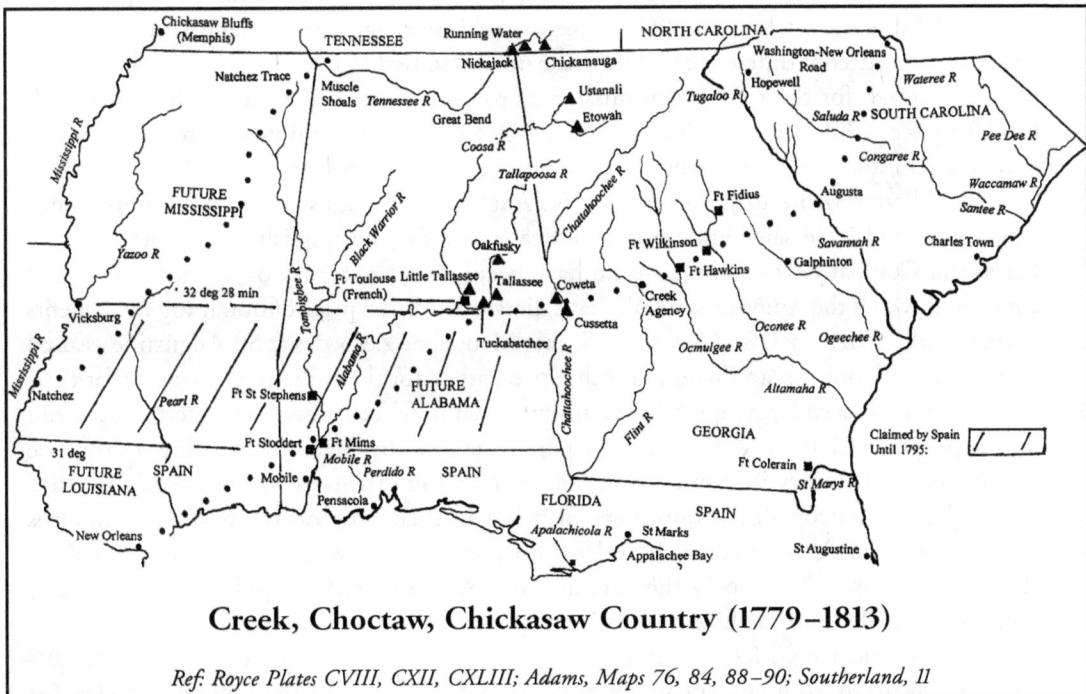

Creek, Choctaw, Chickasaw Country (1779–1813)

Ref: Royce Plates CVIII, CXII, CXLIII; Adams, Maps 76, 84, 88–90; Southerland, 11

The Americans altho' sensible of the Injustice done to us on this occasion in consequence of this pretended claim have divided our territorys into countys and Sate themselves down on our land, as if they were their own. Witness the Large Settlement called Cumberland [Nashville] and others on the Mississippi which [with] the Late attempts on the Occonnee Lands are all encroachments on our hunting Grounds.

We have repeatedly warned the States of Carolina and Georgia to desist from these Encroachments and to confine themselves within the Land [granted] to Britain in the Year 1773. To these remonstrances we have received friendly talks and replys it is true but while they are addressing us by the flattering appellations of Friends and Brothers they are Stripping us of our natural rights by depriving us of that inheritance which belonged to our ancestors and hath descended from them to us Since the beginning of time.[4]

Even though McGillivray was disappointed with the Spanish, who would only guarantee Creek land to the extent it was within Spanish territory, he rebuffed American overtures. Under the Articles of Confederation it was not clear the extent to which states could make treaties with Indian nations, and Georgians, relying on what the Creek nation regarded as bogus treaties, were moving on to disputed land. Between 1783 and 1786 the Georgians entered into three treaties. The first at Augusta in 1783 was, according to McGillivray, signed by "two chiefs of the Second rank" [Tame King and Fat King] who went to Augusta to talk of peace and were "threaten[ed] ... with Instant Death" and "surrounded by armed men for five days" before agreeing to the treaty.[5] When settlers moved into the land covered by the treaty, that is, land between the Tugaloo River and the Upper Oconee, conflicts arose. Georgia used the land to pay war veterans.

A second treaty was signed in the fall of 1785 when federal commissioners tried to meet with the Creek at Galphinton on the Ogeechee River, in Georgia. Only "two chiefs and a handful of warriors" came. McGillivray wrote to one of the commissioners, Andrew Pickens, that the Creek nation wanted "nothing ... but justice. We want our hunting grounds preserved from encroachments. [The Creek would meet with the federal commissioners when] every matter of difference will be made up and settled."[6] Deciding the Creek presence was not enough for the federal commissioners to deal with, they went north to talk with the Cherokee, Choctaw, and Chickasaw, but Georgians at Galphinton were not deterred and entered into a treaty with the small number of Creeks present.

McGillivray wrote to John Leslie at St. Augustine in August 1785 of the importance of getting goods. He said, but for "the active efforts of [the English merchants] Panton, Leslie and Company [the Creeks would have been] under necessity of admitting the hard conditions which the Americans would have dictated ... as the price of obtaining the benefits of their trade."[7] In May 1786 Governor Vicente Manuel de Zespedes at St. Augustine assured McGillivray of "powder and balls and other presents ... for the Indians as formerly for their hunting, and an even larger quantity of ammunition to whoever gives me a letter from you for the purpose."[8] Earlier McGillivray told Zespedes that the Creeks were going to "traverse all parts of the Country in dispute & whenever they found any American Settlers to drive them off & to destroy all the buildings on it but in their progress to conduct themselves with moderation & to shed no blood on no pretense but where Self defense made it absolutely necessary."[9] Miro in the summer of 1786 "promised a supply of five thousand pounds of powder with balls and flints in proportion."[10]

With ample arms McGillivray gave an ultimatum to the governor of Georgia: "We warn you again to keep your people within the natural limits of the Ogeechee River, for we are resolved not to permit your people to enjoy the usurpations that they have made on our land."[11] An answer was to be given by the end of September. Georgia wanted to avoid war and sent a conciliatory invitation to meet at the mouth of Shoulderbone Creek, on the Oconee river, on October 15. McGillivray declined but Tame King and Fat King and a few others went and were seized and confined in forts. Taking hostages had no effect on McGillivray, who thought these chiefs had professed friendship for Americans and was not willing to make any accommodation for their release. From the seized Indians the Georgians got the last treaty of this period which affirmed the earlier treaties of Augusta and Galphinton and provided for trade between the Creeks and Georgians. This only made conditions between the Creeks and Georgia worse.

Although McGillivray told the Spaniards that the Creek were not embarking on "Hostilities with the whole American States," and had a limited objective of freeing their "Hunting Grounds Fronting the Georgians,"[12] in 1786 and 1787 settlers at Cumberland and Muscle Shoals were attacked.

Spain granted a monopoly in 1783 to the English firm Panton, Leslie and Company to trade with the southern Indians. McGillivray developed a close relationship with William Panton, who headed the firm. When Panton insisted on McGillivray associating with the company before he would open a store at St. Marks near the Appalachee Bay in East Florida, McGillivray became a partner. After Panton died in 1801 the business was carried on by John Forbes under the same name and later in 1804 as John Forbes and Company.

A United States commissioner, James White, was well received by the Creek in the spring of 1787 but was unable to resolve the Georgia-Creek differences. The Creek were an imposing threat. White estimated they "had 6000 well-armed men who had the Spanish resources and territories to fall back upon."[13] Recognizing that Washington had 5,700 Continentals and 3,100 militia at the siege of Yorktown in 1781, and that, over strong opposition, a U.S. Army of only 1,216 enlisted was authorized in 1790, this was an armed body that had to be respected. White was able to get the Creek to agree to an armistice until August 1787.

Early in 1787 McGillivray found the Spanish less resolute than in the past. In February Zespedes suggested the King would likely support the Indians "without prejudice to the good harmony that exists ... between Spain and the United States."[14] A month later New Orleans Governor Miro wrote Governor O'Neill at Pensacola that McGillivray should be told "not to make another attack while the United States does not harm them" for to do so might result in "all the states to make common cause" with the Georgians. However, if an "American army form[ed]" O'Neill was authorized to supply "ammunition and military stores."[15]

In the Continental Congress Georgia proposed in August 1787 that a treaty be held by the southern superintendent with the object of confirming the Georgia treaties. A committee report noted that the Indians had reasons to complain of those on the frontier and that the government should enforce impartial justice. However, a question existed as to which governments were to act. The committee proposed that North Carolina and Georgia should give the power to the federal government.

The Creek were not idle during the last months of 1787. Writing to Zespedes in early 1788 McGillivray said his "Warriors [were] victorious in every quarter over the americans, the people of Cumberland are drove over the Ohio river & the State of Georgia now lays at [the Creeks'] Mercy." But there was a hitch in making future plans. The Indians were short of ammunition which was needed both for fighting and for the Indians to "subsist [themselves] upon game when on an expedition."[16] A complication for the Creeks was a Spanish interest in the possibility of white settlers breaking off from the United States.

The sine qua non for many frontier settlers and land speculators was free navigation of the Mississippi River of which the last 150 miles or so flowed through land controlled by Spain. When Spain closed the river to American shipping in 1784 settlers and speculators wanted a solution. The danger of settlers west of the Appalachians separating from the United States was recognized by Washington in 1784 when he wrote after traveling in the back country that the "western settlers stand as it were upon a pivot. The touch of feather would turn them any way." Not much had changed by 1787 when Benjamin Hawkins wrote to Thomas Jefferson that Westerners must have the right to Mississippi navigation or they would "be disposed to carve for themselves."[17] Notions of separation were entertained by John Sevier, a leader in what was to be eastern Tennessee, and James Robertson, an early founder of the Cumberland settlements (in the present Nashville area). James Wilkinson and others in Kentucky, which lacked the support of Virginia for separate statehood, unsuccessfully tested the idea of separation at a Kentucky convention. As a tribute to Spanish Governor Miro, the Cumberland settlements were organized as the Mero District.

At negotiations between John Jay, secretary for foreign affairs of the Continental Congress, and the Spanish envoy, Don Diego de Gardoqui, in New York in 1785–1786 Spain refused free passage to Americans, and, to the dismay of Westerners, Jay proposed to Congress that the United States forbear "the right to navigate the Mississippi for twenty-five or thirty years in return for a commercial treaty with Spain."[18] Virginian Patrick Henry, who had interests in western lands, said he "would rather part with the confederation than relinquish the navigation of the Mississippi."[19] Jay was burned in effigy in the West. The seven northern states which relied heavily on foreign trade were agreeable to this arrangement, but the other states did not support it. With nine votes needed to ratify a treaty it went no further. Spain defused the river controversy in 1788 by granting passage for the payment of duties. In disputes with the United States over the river and who had sovereignty over land south of the Tennessee River, the Creek were a force the Spanish could influence by conditioning their supplies of goods.

Rather than going to war with the Creek, Georgia and the Carolinas acted to implement a Continental Congress resolution of October 26, 1787, to join with the southern superintendent to negotiate with the Creek. James White was replaced as southern superintendent of Indian affairs by Richard Winne in February 1788. White went off to support a Spanish effort to colonize the Mississippi Valley. As early as 1786 he discussed a possible western Spanish alliance.

Negotiations brought no agreement. An impasse on the Georgia-Creek differences existed when Georgia insisted on its earlier treaties and McGillivray wanted Georgia to repudiate them. In June 1788 McGillivray wrote to Miro that he went "down amongst these Americans who are a set of crafty, cunning, republicans."[20] Georgia's hope was to keep the differences with the Creek at a peaceful level until the United States assumed the responsibility of Creek relations. Georgia assured the Creek of its friendly disposition in January 1789 and of an expected treaty with the new federal government.

McGillivray's relationship with the Spanish deteriorated in 1788. Miro pressed him to make peace with the Georgians, and McGillivray told him if making peace required "the

Sacrifice of all those lands which was the principal object of the War, [the Creek would] consider [them]selves as a Ruined Nation, to Shift for [them]selves."[21] In 1788 McGillivray found it difficult to get arms. Then, on December 13, 1788, Miro assured him that he would have the supplies he wanted. McGillivray wrote to Zespedes on February 6, 1789, that since "the Americans Seem resolved to persist in their Encroachments, a Continuance of the War appears to be inevitable."[22]

12

The Creek Deal with the Federal Government and Spain (1789–1795)

When George Washington and a new government were installed in 1789, South Carolina's governor, Thomas Pinckney, wrote to the Creek on April 20, 1789: "We are now governed by a President who is like the old King over the great water.... He Commands all the Warriors of the thirteen great fires."[1] Steps were taken to thwart plots for a western separation. Washington involved leaders in the West with the federal government. William Blount, known as the Dirt King by the Creek because of his gigantic participation in land speculation, was made governor of the Southwestern Territory which was established in 1790. There is evidence suggesting Blount was thinking treasonous thoughts when he was made governor. Sevier and James Robertson were made brigadier-generals in the western army, and Wilkinson was commissioned as a lieutenant-colonel in the federal army.

In 1789 the new Congress wanted federal commissioners to meet with the Creek and to persuade them to accept Georgia's treaties. Secretary of War Henry Knox directed the commissioners "to guarantee the Creeks that their remaining territory would be protected by a line of federal military posts ... [and that] '[t]he United States [did] not want Creek lands.'"[2] In September 1789 McGillivray snubbed the commissioners, but left open the possibility of future talks. The angry commissioners wanted the Creeks punished for killing 82, capturing 140, and either killing or stealing 2,000 head of livestock.

Over the winter of 1789–1790 nothing happened but the next summer McGillivray accepted Washington's invitation to come to New York where success came from pandering to his vanity, indulgence in drink, sexual pleasure, and greed. McGillivray came to New York after a warning of the "direful consequences of a rupture with the United States,"[3] and after traveling to Creek towns to have approval for his trip. He was joined by 23 other chiefs in signing a treaty. The treaty, dated August 7, 1790, contained secret provisions including those making McGillivray a brigadier with a salary of $1,200 per year. In the treaty the Creek accepted American sovereignty over those lands within the United States' boundaries, and agreed to a boundary for Indian country that surrendered land Georgians had already settled on. In general the surrender was of land between the Oconee and Ogeechee rivers.

The treaty had important provisions which could, if enforced, have curtailed intrusions on Indian lands. If the Creek acted under Article VI white settlers would have been careful to stay on their side of the boundary. Article VI gave the "Creeks [the right to] punish ... or not, as they please" intruders attempting to settle on their land. Article VII restricted

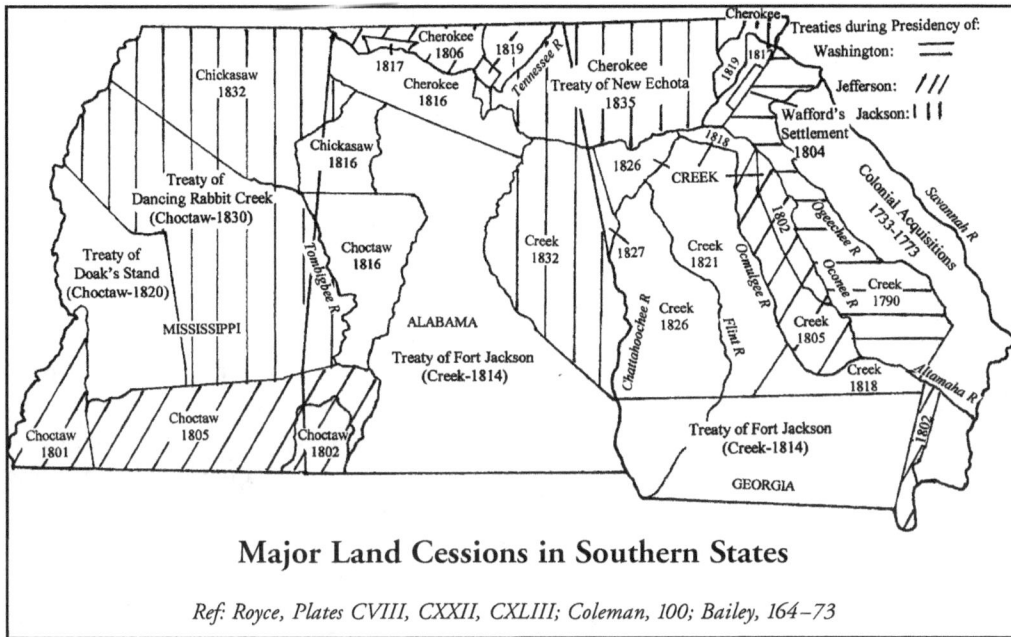

Major Land Cessions in Southern States

Ref: Royce, Plates CVIII, CXXII, CXLIII; Coleman, 100; Bailey, 164–73

entry into "Creek country, without a passport," and forbade "attempt[s] to hunt or destroy the game on the Creek lands." Article XII stated a policy of leading the Creek "to a greater degree of civilization, and to become herdsmen and cultivators."[4] An important secret article guaranteed the use of American ports to get supplies to the Creek if the use of Spanish ports was cut off by the Spaniards or by war.

The Georgians felt betrayed — the United States, they thought, had no right to be dealing with the Creek and by the treaty had given up three million acres of land belonging to Georgia, that is, land lying to the west of the Oconee River which was purportedly ceded to Georgia at Galphinton in 1785.

The Creek were far from being in the American camp. In a letter explaining the 1790 treaty to the Spanish dated August 11, 1790,[5] McGillivray noted that Spanish aid lent him was done "scantily and with reluctance" and stressed that a peace treaty with the United States was one encouraged by New Orleans Governor Miro. Furthermore, he feared that failing to come to New York to negotiate would have resulted in the United States declaring war against the Creek and had not thought "Spain would go into a war in order to sustain [the Creek] claims." The letter ended with a plea for a definite understanding between Spain and the Creek. Many Georgians bristled at the treaty and on November 10, 1790, McGillivray wrote to Governor Quesada of East Florida that Georgians were "taking measures to frustrate the good Consequences of the late treaty of Peace with their government."[6] Not all Creeks accepted the treaty. At a June 1791 meeting of chiefs from all the towns, McGillivray could not get agreement to the Georgia boundary specified in the treaty; he wrote to Knox asking for a revision — Knox replied that the treaty was "sacred, and must be complied with, in all its parts."[7]

A destabilizing element in the Creek nation during the years 1788–1792 was William Augustus Bowles, an American who fought against the patriots in the Revolutionary War and had lived with the Creek off and on as a young man. In the Revolutionary War he demonstrated "reckless courage"[8] in fighting with Creek guerrillas against frontier Georgians and gained the respect of the Creek and Cherokee. During a sojourn on New Providence Island (Nassau) he formed an understanding with Lord Dunmore, formerly of Virginia and then governor of the Bahamas, who, together with a wealthy merchant, John Miller, wanted the trading rights being exercised by Panton, Leslie and Company. Bowles had a grandiose plan for driving Spain out of Florida and replacing it with England.

The Creek nation, sometimes referred to as the Creek Confederacy, was not a homogenous collection. They were "scattered over a wild country of at least three hundred miles square."[9] Its members had very different backgrounds. Geographically the Upper Creeks lived south of the Cherokee and mostly in modern Alabama, on the waters of Tallapoosa, Coosa, and Alabama rivers. The Lower Creeks were more in Georgia and south and east of the Upper Creeks on the waters of the Flint and Chattahoochee rivers. In Florida were the Seminoles, mostly émigrés from Creek tribes together with many runaway slaves, considered wild people who acted within the Creek Confederation. The "wild" appellation stems from their settlement in wild country.[10] Creek warriors were formidable.

When Spain cut back on war supplies for the Creeks in 1788, Bowles stepped in with promises of supplies from the English firm of Miller, Bonnamy and Company. McGillivray used this offer to convince the Spaniards to again supply arms. Bowles had a flair for the theatrical. When visiting London he dressed as an Indian and at times identified himself as the "Director General of the Creek Nation" or "Ambassador from the United Nation of Creeks and Cherokees."[11] An opportunist, following the treaty of 1790, he worked to make the Creeks angry with the result and with McGillivray. When McGillivray had assassins searching for him in October 1791, Bowles told the United States: "We have retreated from the plain to the woods, from thence to the mountains, but no limits established by nature or compact have stayed the ambition, or satisfied the avarice of your people."[12] The way to end warfare was to make a true agreement "not a Clandestine bargain with an unconnected individual." Included was a warning: "KNOW that we have enough WARRIORS to stain your land with blood." The sender was "Genl Wm a Bowles, Director of Affairs Ck Nn. By order of the Supreme Council."

In January 1792 Bowles mounted a raid on the Panton store and Spanish fort at Saint Marks, Florida, which he easily controlled. At the same time he made peace overtures to Spanish Governor Baron de Carondelet at New Orleans, who replaced Miro at the start of 1792, and was offered safe conduct to come to New Orleans. Foolishly Bowles went and ended up as a prisoner. For a time the Spanish considered making use of Bowles as a substitute for McGillivray, but, in the end, he was a prisoner in the Philippines, where he remained until 1796.

A Bowles legacy was doubts created in Carondelet's mind as to what McGillivray wanted to do. Carondelet feared that McGillivray and Panton planned a Creek-American alliance to move against the Spanish territory. A letter of March 30, 1792,[13] outlined the Spanish policy Carondelet intended to pursue. The Creeks should "draw near to Spain [which was] ready to defend them if they [would] conclude a defensive alliance with the Cherokee, Choctaw, and Chickasaw nations." If the Americans "declare[d] war on the Creek nation for the purpose of taking possession of the vast territory which they so unjustly claim, the King is ready to sustain the nation, to such an extent that orders are already given to furnish its warriors with arms and ammunition in abundance at Pensacola." An effort should be made to win over McGillivray.

A factor undoubtedly influencing Carondelet was the threat posed by Georgia in the so-called Yazoo land grants made in December 1789. These grants to land speculators included most of modern Mississippi and land around Muscle Shoals. Among the speculators were men active in state and federal politics: Patrick Henry, Joseph Martin, John Sevier, and William Blount. These grants were later canceled by Georgia, but, in 1795, new grants were made covering much of the same area and a large part of what became Alabama. Georgia's action conflicted with claims of the Spanish and of the Choctaw, Chickasaw, and Creek Indians. Carondelet was undoubtedly encouraged in his plans by the victory of the Northwest Indians over the American armies under generals Harmar and St. Clair in October 1790 and November 1791.

McGillivray was easily convinced to support the new Spanish policy and, after he met Carondelet at New Orleans for the first time in the summer of 1792, Carondelet became convinced that McGillivray was loyal to Spain. A treaty signed by each of them on July 6, 1792, continued in force the treaty of 1784 giving exclusive trading rights to Spain and included an important provision critical to the Creeks: "His Catholic Majesty ... will fully and sufficiently furnish [the Creek] Indians and allies with arms and ammunition, not only to defend their territories but also to recover the usurped lands, in the event that the Americans shall refuse to retire voluntarily and peacefully within the fixed time, or in case the Creek nation finds itself attacked unjustly by any other, without having provoked the war."[14]

Carondelet also intended to cooperate with the northern Indians against the United States. He anticipated that negotiations between Spain and the United States would establish boundary lines and, he told McGillivray, Spain would "act vigorously to preserve for [its] Indian allies the lands possessed by their ancestors."[15]

On August 5, 1792, Washington wrote to his Secretary of War: "the difficulty of deciding between lawless settlers and greedy (land) Speculators on one side, and the jealousies of the Indian Nations and their banditti on the other, becomes more and more obvious every day; and these, from the interference of the Spaniards ... and other causes ... add not a little to our embarrassment."[16]

The Creek nation lost much of its coherence when its leader, McGillivray, died on February 17, 1793, from a lingering illness. Turbulence was not limited to that between the whites and Indians. The Upper Creeks were kept from going to war against the Chickasaw by an ultimatum of William Panton that "he would stop all supplies for them"[17] if they proceeded. Provocative conduct by Georgians invited Indian action. At this time the United States agent to the Creek was James Seagrove who had two assistant agents for the Lower Creeks, James Holmes and Timothy Barnard. In February Barnard warned of Georgians pasturing stock on Indian land: "if those cattle are not removed soon, the owners will lose them all, and some of them their lives too."[18]

Florette Henri's book *The Southern Indians and Benjamin Hawkins 1796–1816* evaluated what was happening: "[M]ost of the serious crimes were committed by whites, not Indians, and ... most of these were unprovoked except by the circumstance that the Indians were where whites wished to be. Indians killed almost entirely for revenge, if not in self-defense; in both cases, bloodily." "One purpose of the white violence on the frontier was to provoke Indian retaliation, in the hope of persuading the federal government to declare full-scale war against the southern tribes."[19] Acts of violence often brought retaliation which led to more violence.

In one instance the Georgians were kept from proceeding with a war from a lack of competence; on June 9, 1793, a militia force of 600 crossed the Oconee only to be back four days later having accomplished nothing. They were an undisciplined force troubled by mutiny. Georgia's preference was to have the United States go to war or at least to pay for Georgians doing so. The United States definitely did not want Georgia to act aggressively. The governor was told in June: "a general ... Creek War, in the present crisis of European affairs, would be a complicated evil of great magnitude, the President of the United States is anxiously desirous of avoiding such an event."[20] In September the Secretary of War was even more emphatic. The governor was told of ongoing negotiations in Madrid about Spain's treaty with the Creeks and the danger of "a general confederacy of all the southern tribes"[21] being formed.

Notwithstanding Washington's admonitions, in the fall of 1793 Georgians in small numbers attacked Indian towns, at times with the governor's approval. This was during a period when the Spanish wanted the Creeks to avoid conflict with Americans and, in general, they restrained their young warriors. Carondelet made progress in forming a southern confederacy of the Chickasaws, Choctaws, Cherokees, and Creeks with a treaty of alliance signed on October 28, 1793, near present-day Vicksburg. Although named as a party to the treaty no Creek chiefs were present. In a productive meeting with Creeks in the fall of 1793, also attended by a Spanish agent, Seagrove reached an agreement for peace between the Creek and the whites. Missing was the agreement of the Georgians.

The peace agreement was violated almost immediately. The Bird Tail King of Cusseta, while hunting on Indian land with eight others, was attacked by a party of whites — two Indians were killed. Bird Tail took his complaint to Fort Fidius located on the U.S. side of the Oconee River. Reporting on the incident the War Department agent in Georgia said he was "seriously alarmed for the safety of the Bird-tail king and his men.... It seem[ed] to be the determination of some people in [Georgia] to prevent all reconcillation with the Creeks."[22]

After news in May 1794 of Indians killing two people on the upper Georgia frontier, Georgia militia attacked a small group of Indians camping opposite to Fort Fidius. This caused the Creeks to send a delegation to New Orleans to see if the Spaniards would give them a supply of ammunition. A similar request was made of the Spanish in East Florida. At best they got an offer of friendship. Another crisis arose in September when Elijah Clarke placed an establishment on Indian land near the Oconee River. The governor of East Florida was willing in this case to supply ammunition for the Creeks to defend themselves but not to support offensive action which is what the Creeks planned. As to the invasion of their land they said, "The injustice will be apparent to anyone who understands that our life is dependent upon the woods; for if they deprive us of our lands how can we clothe our women and children? Where shall we find game? We cannot clothe ourselves in any other way."[23]

Relief came from an unexpected source. The Secretary of War wanted Clarke and his party removed and the Georgia militia did so. Creek chiefs advocating for peace with the whites seized the moment and tried to unite the nation behind a peace effort. Creek leaders supporting this step were Mad Dog of Tuckabatchee, White Lieutenant of Oakfusky, and the Bird Tail King of Cusseta. Each had been in New York for the 1790 treaty and were given great medals. Mad Dog addressed the Lower Creeks asking that they "restrain [their Young People] from doing any Mischief."[24] He wanted to meet with them in November and to have agreement on returning prisoners and stolen property, including black slaves, to the whites. The Lower Creek chiefs agreed but when Mad Dog went to Georgia he only had one white prisoner and one black.

Georgia was not interested in returning any land to the Creeks and in the Yazoo Act dated December 28, 1794, intended to appropriate and sell Indian lands. Georgia wanted the president to negotiate the needed treaty with the Creeks. The Yazoo grants made in 1789 were rescinded in 1790 but these new grants were of an even larger amount of land in the modern states of Mississippi and Alabama which Georgia claimed were within its boundaries. Application to the president was not made until just before Congress adjourned in March 1795. When Congress returned in June it was told by Washington[25] that a treaty would be held but any cession should "be made in the general terms of the treaty of New York." The commissioners were to "inquire into the causes of ... hostilities [since the New York treaty] and to enter into such reasonable stipulations as [would] remove them." In 1795 Washington told his new Secretary of War, Timothy Pickering, that "scarcely any thing short of a Chinese Wall, or a line of Troops will restrain land Jobbers, and the Incroachment of Settlers, upon the Indian Territory."[26]

The Creek position vis-à-vis the United States changed markedly in the last six months of 1794. In August 1794 the northern Indians were conclusively defeated by an army under General Anthony Wayne. Relations between the United States and England had improved significantly when the Jay Treaty was signed on November 19, 1794, and ratified by the Senate on June 24, 1795. Then, on October 27, 1795, the Treaty of San Lorenzo (Pinckney Treaty) settled the United States boundary with Spain — Spain agreed that what is the northern five-sixths of the modern states of Mississippi and Alabama was within the United States. Each of the nations agreed to have peace with the Indians on their sides of the boundary. The San Lorenzo treaty removed a long festering problem — free navigation of the Mississippi River was agreed to. The Creeks could no longer look to Spain for the supplies it required to assert its independence from the United States.

13

The Chickasaw and Choctaw
(1783–1795)

The Chickasaw and Choctaw were not threatened by white settlers to the degree that the Creek were. But they were not immune from efforts to take their land. Virginia's governor for the years 1782–1784, Benjamin Harrison, a man with both national and Virginia credentials whose youngest son, William Henry Harrison, was destined to be the ninth president of the United States, proposed joint action by the southern states saying that without established boundaries "there [was] too much reason to apprehend that continued encroachments [would] be made on [the Indians'] land and, of course, the frontiers of each state laid waste in its turn in revenge for the injuries."[1]

Virginia wanted to purchase Chickasaw land between the Mississippi, Tennessee, and Ohio rivers. Harrison told his commissioners to be careful that no language was put into the treaty "from which a plea may be made of our quitting the claim we have to the land laying [sic] within our charter and resting it on the Indian purchase, which purchase is only intended to quiet the minds of the Indians and give them a mark of our friendship and esteem, your utmost caution is necessary in this lest you give some force to the strange plea the northern states have set up to a large tract of our country as being contained in a purchase from the Six Nations."[2]

The Chickasaw were the least populous of the southern Indian nations — 3,500 to 4,500 whereas the neighboring Choctaw had 20,000. They were organized into self-governing clans and towns with a principal chief (High Minko). Similar to other tribes their system of justice was for the injured to exact retribution. For a time, in the early 1700s, they engaged in slave raids on other tribes and sold the enslaved Indians to English traders from Charles Town who usually sent them to the West Indies. At the same time the Chickasaw purchased black slaves from the English traders.

Virginia representatives, Joseph Martin and John Donelson, met with Chickasaw delegates in November 1783 at French Lick (Nashville). No land was ceded but an eastern boundary of the Chickasaw nation was agreed to as was peace between the Chickasaw and Virginia. Virginia obligated itself to assist in ejecting intruders from Chickasaw land.

During the revolution the Chickasaw were defiant when the colonists threatened them with destruction if they continued to support the British. In 1779 the Chickasaw spoke to the Americans:

> We desire no other friendship of you but only desire you will inform us when you are Coming and we will meet you half Way, for we have heard so much of it that it makes our heads Ach[e]. Take care that we dont serve you as we have served the French before with all their Indians, send

you back without your heads. We are a Nation that fears or Values no Nation as long as our Great Father King George stands by us for you may depend as long as life lasts with us we will hold him fast by the hand.... This is our Talk to you and we desire that you may not keep it hid but have it printed in your News Papers that all your people may see it and know who it was from; We are men & Warriors and dont want our Talks hidden.[3]

When "Great Father King George" abandoned them in the peace treaty of 1783, the Chickasaw sent a message to the "President of the Honorable Congress of the United American States":

Brother,
   ... The Spaniards are sending talks amongst us, and inviting our young Men to trade with them. We also receive talks from the Governor of Georgia to the same effect—We have had Speeches from the Illinois inviting us to a Trade and Intercourse with them—Our Brothers, the Virginians Call upon us to a Treaty, and want part of our land, and we expect our Neighbors who live on Cumberland River, will in a Little time Demand, if not forcibly take part of it from us, also as we are informed they have been marking Lines through our hunting grounds: we are daily receiving Talks from one Place or other, and from People we Know nothing about. We Know not who to mind or who to neglect. We are told that the Americans have 13 Councils Compos'd of Chiefs and Warriors. We Know not which of them we are to Listen to, or if we are to hear some, and Reject others, we are at a loss to Distinguish those we are to hear. We are told that you are the head Chief of the Grand Council, which is above these 13 Councils: if so why have we not had Talks from you,—... [W]e wish to Speak with you and your Council, or if you Do not approve of our so Doing, as you are wise, you will tell us who shall speak with us, in behalf of all our Brothers the Americans, and *from whare and whome we are to be supplyed with necessaries in the manner our great father supplied us*—we hope you will also put a stop to any encroachments on our lands, without our consent, and silence all those People who sends us Such Talks as inflame & exasperate our Young Men, as it is our earnest desire to remain in peace and friendship with our Br: the Americans for ever.

*   *   *

   Brothers, *we are very poor for necessaries, for Ammunition particularly.* We can supply ourselves from the Spaniards but we are averse to hold any intercourse with them, as our hearts are always with our Brothers the Americans. [Emphasis supplied.][4]

In 1784 the Indians described to Spanish Governor Cruzat, who was in St. Louis, what was happening: "The Americans, a great deal more ambitious and numerous than the English, put us out of our lands, forming therein great settlements, extending themselves like a plague of locusts in the territories of the Ohio River which we inhabit."[5]

The Chickasaw met with the Spanish at Mobile in June 1784 and pledged "fidelity to the king of Spain" and agreed "to accept no traders except those sent by Spain."[6] An immediate consequence was Panton-Leslie agents making trade goods available in the nation.

The Chickasaw did not cede any large amount of its land to the United States until 1805. However, in a treaty of January 10, 1786,[7] at Hopewell, boundary lines were agreed to consistent with lines established for the Choctaw and Cherokee a few days earlier "and the lands at [that time] in the possession of the Creeks." Land was reserved for a United States trading post at Muscle Shoals. The valuable right for the Chickasaw to "punish [trespassers] or not as they please" was included. Far-reaching provisions which the Chickasaw may not have understood gave the United States "the sole and exclusive right of regulating the trade with the Indians" and the right to manage "all their affairs" for the benefit and comfort of the Indians. The "hatchet" was to be forever buried. Federal commissioners signing the treaty were Benjamin Hawkins, Andrew Pickens, and Joseph Martin. An important witness was William Blount of North Carolina.

The struggle for Chickasaw loyalty was not over. Spain continued to be a source of "ammunition & other necessarys" and the Creeks tried to forcefully cut them off from American trade and to create a schism in the Chickasaw leadership, hoping for the same result. By 1792 the Americans had a good avenue for goods for the Chickasaw. By way of the Ohio and Mississippi rivers American goods could reach Chickasaw Bluffs (Memphis today) for distribution. To increase the bonds of the United States with the southern tribes, in August 1792 William Blount, then governor of the territory south of the Ohio and superintendent of Indians affairs for the region, held a council with the four nations. A treaty was agreed to which committed each tribe to peace and amity with the United States. To allay the Spanish warning that the United States was only after their land, Blount told them: "we wish you to enjoy your lands and be as happy as we ourselves are; nor do we want the land of any red people; the United States have land enough."[8]

The Spanish remained aggressive. Early in 1795 a Spanish fort was built on one of the Chickasaw Bluffs and the Panton firm opened a store at the fort. Although Spain, in the Treaty of San Lorenzo, acknowledged the Chickasaw land was all within the United States, it did not give up its desire to work with the Chickasaw. A new Spanish post was built across the Mississippi opposite Chickasaw Bluffs. The Panton store closed in 1797 but the Chickasaw continued to trade with a Panton store in Mobile. It wasn't until 1802 that the United States placed a trading house at Chickasaw Bluffs.

The Choctaw Indians were essentially a French dependency from 1750 until the end of the French and Indian War and then, with little difficulty, converted over to an English dependency until the start of the Revolutionary War when they switched with ease to the Americans. A Choctaw treaty with the United States at Hopewell, South Carolina, in 1786,[9] at the same time treaties were made with the Cherokee and Chickasaw, agreed to boundaries for the Choctaw nation. Three tracts, each six miles square, to be chosen by the United States, were reserved for trading posts. As in the 1785 and 1786 treaties with the Cherokee and Chickasaw, the Choctaw could "punish [trespassers] or not as they please" and the United States had the exclusive right to regulate trade with them. The "hatchet [was to] be forever buried" and was, essentially, until the United States Civil War. To arrive at Hopewell the Choctaw made "a fatiguing journey of seventy-seven days" and, on arrival, "the whole of them almost naked." They had, according to Benjamin Hawkins, "a particular aversion to the Spaniards and the Creeks and [were] determined to put themselves under the protection of the United States."[10]

Peace was not always the case between the Choctaw and neighboring tribes. Under prodding by the French it helped to almost exterminate the Natchez Indians in the 1730s and went to battle with the Chickasaw who had been urged to assist the Natchez by English traders. When the Choctaw and the Chickasaw were on the verge of settling their differences in 1744 the French blocked a settlement. After the French were deposed, by the French and Indian War, the Choctaw became a pawn in a British policy of inciting the Choctaw, Chickasaw, and Cherokee to make war against the Creek.

After the Revolutionary War, the Spanish returned to Florida and set out to create a barrier between Florida and the Americans by becoming a trading partner with the Choctaw, Chickasaw, and Creek. In a treaty of 1784 these tribes agreed to exclude traders who did not have Spanish licenses. The Spanish continued to enhance their relations with the southern tribes by a treaty of friendship dated May 14, 1792, with the Choctaw, Chickasaw, Creek, and Cherokee.

The Choctaw were in the unenviable situation of occupying land claimed by both Spain and the United States from the end of the Revolutionary War, until the Treaty of San Lorenzo in 1795 placed most of their land within the United States.

14

Benjamin Hawkins Leads

With the changed conditions of 1795 — that is, the defeat of the northern Indians and the smoother relations between the United States and both England and Spain — the effort to have a Creek treaty, as sought by Georgia, was given to Benjamin Hawkins, a United States senator, and other federal commissioners. The Creek were asked to meet with them at Fort Colerain on Saint Mary's River in southern Georgia. The Creeks were slow in coming to the fort but Hawkins was patient and set up rules to keep Georgians, who were there as observers with presents and some armed militia, from taking advantage of the Creeks. When the meeting started 435 Indians were present, including 22 kings, 75 principal chiefs, and 152 warriors.

Speaking for the Creek were Bird Tail King and a half blooded Creek, Oche Haujo, known to whites as Alexander Cornells, who was later Hawkins' deputy. The Creek were willing to abide with the boundary agreed to in 1790 but refused to surrender any more land; however, Cornells recognized the realities of the parties: "If you are determined to take the land, to drive us off, and make us poor, it must be so. If the sharp weapons of defence are to be taken from us, and as our dependence is on the white people, we must be driven from our lands, and made poor. We must, we suppose, submit."[1] His complaint against the Georgians was that "the woods are constantly full of white men, hunters, even going about in the night, hunting deer with fire light" and the cane swamps where Indian hunters "look for a bear, which is part of their support, is near eat out with stocks put over [the boundary line] by the citizens of Georgia."[2]

The Creek agreed on June 29, 1796, to having trading posts built on their land but rejected an offer of schools for their children. To them "Indians, when educated, turned out very worthless; became mischievous and troublesome."[3] They accepted boundary lines of the Choctaw, Chickasaw, and Cherokee established in earlier treaties between the United States and those tribes at Hopewell and Holston. A payment of $6,000 was promised to the Creek. The Georgians were upset with the treaty — the state as a whole did not accept it. The Senate ratified the treaty with the proviso that no violation of the rights of Georgia was contemplated. When John Adams proclaimed the treaty, he emphasized that the treaty did not give the United States "without the consent of [Georgia] any right to soil or the exclusive legislation over the same."[4]

Establishment of trading posts was an approach favored by Washington; he saw this as a way to protect the Indians from "the continual pressure of land speculators and settlers on one hand; and ... the impositions of unauthorized, and unprincipled traders (who rob them in a manner of their hunting) on the other."[5] Hawkins told the Indians at Colerain that at federal stores "every item of goods would have a fixed price, which would be posted in every town; that weights and measures would be introduced so that a hunter would get accurate value for his deerskins at the store; and that the stores would stock a full assortment of goods at reasonable, nonprofit prices."[6]

Shortly after the treaty at Colerain Hawkins was appointed by Washington as "Principal Temporary Agent for Indians Affairs South of the Ohio"[7] — a position with responsibilities exercised by territorial governor Blount before Tennessee became a state in 1796. After Colerain he told Washington that the Creek Indians could be kept at peace by an Indian agent who would live with them. At Colerain the chiefs asked repeatedly that a "beloved man" of the United States be sent to their towns. Washington, thinking that approach worth a try, asked Hawkins to sacrifice a few years of his life to test the thesis. Hawkins accepted and spent the next 20 years living with the Creek as their agent while also having, for some years, oversight obligations as to the other southern tribes.

From November 1796 to March 1797 he traveled through Cherokee and Creek lands becoming acquainted and telling the Indians about the policy of the government. He wanted to "introduce [the Indians] to the benefits of civilization and to influence them to produce agricultural commodities."[8] Ample evidence was observed to see that the Cherokees in Georgia were being driven to new hunting grounds. This was necessary because of white settlers moving on to their land and the result of more deer being destroyed than were needed to clothe and feed them, that is, killing so as to have deerskins to be sold. In talking with the Cherokees he found them willing to adapt to agriculture. The women told him they were healthy and that "even when they bore children they were their own midwives and would most of them turn out the next day after delivering themselves and pursue their ordinary occupations."[9]

On reaching Creek country his first reaction was that they were poorer than the Cherokee. But, as he advanced into the Upper Creek area he found "[m]ore land was cultivated, stock was better and more numerous, houses cleaner and more comfortable" and a receptive attitude "to cooperate with the government in a program of farming and handicrafts."[10] In a conversation with an elderly chief he was told that in the past the Indians "were strangers to, cloathing, comfortable houses, and plenty of bread" and that they had advanced to the point of having "hoes, axes, knives, guns and other necessaries."[11] When Hawkins mentioned to some Lower Creeks plans for "raising and spinning of cotton" the men objected, saying "that if the women can cloathe themselves, they will be proud and not obedient to their husbands."[12] Hawkins related the experience of white husbands: "the women have much of the temper of the mule, except when they are amorous, and then they exhibit all the amiable and gentle qualities of the cat."[13]

The need for the Creeks to change was apparent to Hawkins. He wrote that the "traveller, in passing through a country as extensive and wild as this, and so much in a state of nature, expects to see game in abundance. The whole of the Creek claims, the Seminoles inclusive, cover 300 miles square; and it is difficult for a good hunter, in passing through it, in any direction, to obtain enough for his support."[14]

So long as Hawkins had the final say, he insisted that the trading stores, referred to as factories since the government agents in charge were called factors, not sell goods on credit. To him to force the Indians to produce something of equal value to what they took from the store was a step towards their civilization. Factories were established in Cherokee country at Tellicoe Blockhouse and in Creek country at Colerain. The Colerain factory moved to

Fort Wilkinson in 1797. Early factories were established for the Choctaw at Saint Stephens, in present-day Alabama, and for the Chickasaw at Chickasaw Bluffs (Memphis). The factories did not have a monopoly of the Indian trade. Private traders continued to have licenses and were present in most Indian towns. Hawkins' journal covering his travel through Cherokee and Creek lands "listed forty-six traders ... and classified them as to honesty, sobriety, and whether they owned property or were in debt to Panton, Leslie & Company. About a fourth of them were addicted to drunkenness and a similar proportion in debt to Panton, Leslie & Company, and dishonest in their relations with the Indians."[15] Hawkins wrote to William Panton in February 1797 offering to assist his firm if a need should arise. The War Department wanted Hawkins to discourage trade with the Spanish.

Hawkins opposed giving *presents* to Indians. He thought the Indians were inclined to oppose changes in their lifestyle "as long as there is hope to obtain *presents*, the infallible mode heretofore in use, to gain a point."[16] He "detested a system that made beggars of capable people."[17] To the Indians, "[a]ccepting help brought no loss of face, because in the Indian economy there was no charity, only hospitality and sharing."[18] In 1798 Hawkins wrote to a friend, Colonel David Henley, that Indians "demand anything they want from a white man, and feel themselves insulted, when refused. [They] think they confer a favour on the donor if they accept of clothes from him [when] naked, or provisions when hungry."[19]

White attacks on Indian settlements were often attributed to horse stealing. But, the whites had to share the blame since they bought the stolen horses. In March 1797 there was little stealing considering that the woods on the Indian side of the boundary were "swarmed with hogs horses and cattle"[20] put out to range by their white owners.

To give cohesion to the Creek nation, Hawkins relied on annual meetings of all chiefs, also called miccos, in the spring. The national council did not vote on propositions, rather they sought a consensus. A record of decisions was kept by chosen rememberers who could later recite what happened. At the national council on one day all whites were to attend and differences between them decided, and differences between whites and Indians resolved by Hawkins. Efforts were made to change the Indian practice of personal retaliation by including provisions in treaties — in the 1785 and 1786 treaties negotiated by Hawkins with the Cherokee, Chickasaw, and Choctaw the language was: "punishment of the innocent under the idea of retaliation, is unjust, and shall not be practiced on either side."[21] Notwithstanding this provision the Choctaw still practiced retaliation in 1812. An innocent white man was killed in retaliation for white hunters murdering a peaceful Choctaw. Under pressure from the Indian agent the Choctaw gave up the murderer of the white man, being careful not to do so until the guilty whites were punished. At this time the Choctaw and Western Cherokee agreed to only punish the guilty in their relations, and the Chickasaw joined in the agreement.

During Hawkins' first years with the Creek he met resistance to the idea of civilizing them by turning them into farmers. On June 24, 1798, he wrote to the Secretary of War that the Indians told him "[t]hey could not work, they did not want ploughs, it did not comport with the ways of the red people, who were determined to persevere in the ways of their ancestors."[22] Keeping peace between Indian and white was difficult when the young on each side were bent on stealing horses and murdering. Another cause for friction was the Creeks encouraging slaves to flee to their country.

In a report to Congress in December 1801 Hawkins recited positive results from his efforts:

Raising of stock. — This is more relished by the Creeks than any part of the plan devised for their civilization.... [S]ince the failure of supplies from hunting, they are resorted to, as the substitute, and bear a pretty good price.

Agriculture. — The improvements in this are slowly progressive.... There has been a demand this season for plows.... Wheat, barley, rye, and oats, have been introduced, and fairly tried.... Apple trees, grapevines, raspberries, and the roots, Herbs, and vegetables, usually cultivated in good gardens, have been lately introduced, and they all thrive well.

Manufactures.–The present spring, the agent has delivered to Indian women, one hundred pair cotton cards, and eighty spinning wheels. There are eight looms in the nation....[23]

15

The Cherokee, State of Franklin, and North Carolina

Before and following Virginia's cession of land above the Ohio River to the Confederation in December 1783 other states claiming western lands were pressed to do likewise. North Carolina's governor, Alexander Martin, was willing provided the cession did not include "any land worthy of acceptance."[1] To that end North Carolina's "Land Grab Act" of 1783 was enacted at the suasion of speculators and a land office opened relating to lands between the Appalachian Mountains and the Mississippi River. In general, North Carolina claimed that the Indians forfeited their claims to what was to become Tennessee by supporting the British in the war. Excepted from the Act were a military reservation in the Cumberland Valley to be used to compensate war veterans and land occupied by the Cherokee east of the Tennessee River. To avoid conflicts with the Chickasaw who claimed much of the western land, a peace treaty was negotiated in November 1783.

Many thousands of acres, perhaps four million, were sold over a seven-month period. Among those filing for land were "speculators and leading politicians of North Carolina,"[2] including General Richard Caswell, who was soon to become governor, and John Donelson, the co-founder of Nashville in 1780. Alexander Martin explained the reluctance to cede western land without first extracting some value:

> ... To insist that the State should cede her vacant lands which are daily settling up with numerous inhabitants and from which she expects to derive considerable advantage ... is the same as to urge an individual to give up to a stranger without compensation part of his land he is daily improving with husbandmen and husbandry to his own enrichment and that of his family.[3]

The Land Grab Act was a bonanza for speculators. By the use of money at face value, instead of its depreciated value, land could be bought for as little as $5 per 100 acres. Although each entry was limited to 5,000 acres, entries could be joined together for large de-facto entries. If a speculator was short of cash, sales were made on credit. Speculators were more interested in getting the land than in how it was acquired. A master speculator, William Blount, told associates in May 1784 to "enter as much [land] as you can and make use of any Names fictitious ones will do I suppose."[4]

Settlers in what was to become East Tennessee, the Wataugans, faced a dilemma in June 1784 when North Carolina ceded its western lands to the Confederation with important conditions. They anticipated a vacuum in government during the one year which North Carolina provided for the Confederation to decide if the conditional cession would be accepted. This group had a history of being their own masters; for example:

1. An order of Alexander Cameron, deputy to the southern superintendent for Indian affairs, for them to move behind a boundary line that had been agreed to with the Cherokee in 1771 was ignored.

2. The Watauga Association, formed in 1772, was characterized by Lord Dunmore as "a separate state."[5]

3. They fought at Point Pleasant in Dunmore's War of 1774, and, in 1780 at Kings Mountain to quell Loyalists in the Carolinas, and often punished Indians objecting to their settlements.

A convention made up of representatives from militia companies of the Holston River area met at Jonesboro on August 23, 1784, and unanimously "declare[d] the three western counties independent of North Carolina."[6] Another convention in December 1784 stated they were a "separate and distinct State, at this time."[7] John Sevier was appointed the governor of the State of Franklin. The boundary of Franklin went far beyond the headwaters of the Tennessee River, it included land on both sides of the river as it flowed southwest through the great bend of the river to and slightly beyond Muscle Shoals.

The Muscle Shoals area was recognized as very valuable land for future settlements. It connected the point of maximum navigation from the mouth of the river and the point to which navigation was practical from the upper reaches of the river. Land in the Muscle Shoals area was excellent for farming.

Sevier, who first married at 16 and after 10 children and the death of his wife married again and fathered another 8 children, first settled in the Holston River area in 1773, moved to the Watauga River in 1776, and then two years later moved south to the Nolichucky River. All locations were close to or over the Cherokee boundary. It wasn't until 1791, and the treaty at Holston, that most of the Holston and Nolichucky rivers were ceded to the United States by the Cherokee.

During the Revolutionary War Sevier fought against the British and the Cherokee. In 1780 he commanded troops at the important battle against Loyalists, under British command, at Kings Mountain near the border between the two Carolinas. The British commander called upon Patriots to lay down their arms or have their country laid to waste by fire and sword. In raising a Loyalist army the British commander warned against being "pissed upon by a set of mongrels."[8] Loyalists, who were surprised by the Patriots' attack, surrendered after about an hour.

The Franklinites justified their organization of a new state in a letter of March 22, 1785, to Governor Martin:

> ... [At the spring session of the General Assembly of North Carolina of the preceding year] when the members from the Western Country were supplicating to be continued a part of your State [were there not] epithets: "The inhabitants of the Western Country are the off-scourings of the earth, fugitives from justice, and we will be rid of them at any rate." ... [Then] on passing the act of cession, [the Assembly] enter[ed] into a resolve to stop the goods that they ... had promised to give the Indians for the lands they had taken from them and sold for the use of the State.... In short, the Western Country found themselves taxed to support government, while they were deprived of all the blessing of it-not to mention the injustice done them in taxing their lands, which lie five hundred miles from trade, equal to the land of the same quality of the sea shore. The frequent murders committed by the Indians on our frontiers have compelled us to think on some plan for our defense. How far North Carolina has been accessory to these murders we will not pretend to say.[9]

Heated exchanges took place between North Carolina and Franklin. When North Carolina changed governors, Richard Caswell for Martin, Sevier wrote on May 14, 1785, that the new state was formed out of "a real necessity to prevent anarchy, promote [their] own happiness, and provide against the common enemy." He said that since the cession to the Confederation bill passed "[n]early forty people [had] been murdered ... some of which lived in [Franklin] and the remainder on the Kentucky Path."[10] In May 1785 Franklin petitioned the Continental Congress to be received "into the federal union."[11] The status of North Carolina's western lands changed when it retroceded its western lands in 1784, just six months after the conditional cession.

Franklin was busy during this period in its dealings with the Cherokee. At a treaty of "Dumplin Creek on the French Broad river"[12] in June 1785 it was given the right to land "lying ... south [of the] Holston and French Broad rivers [and north of the watershed which] divides the waters of Little river" from the waters of the Little Tennessee River, an area in which many white families had already settled and one in which many more settled after the treaty. As with many Indian treaties this one was only signed by "one faction of the Overhill Cherokees."

Sevier was not troubled about how land was obtained from the Indians. Throughout his life he abided by the belief stated when he was governor of Tennessee in 1798 that "[b]y the law of nations, it is agreed that no people shall be entitled to more land than they can cultivate. Of course, no people will sit and starve for want of land to work, when a neighboring nation has much more than they can make use of."[13] More land was needed for settlers. Between 1771 and 1790 North Carolina's population went from 250,000 to 393,751.

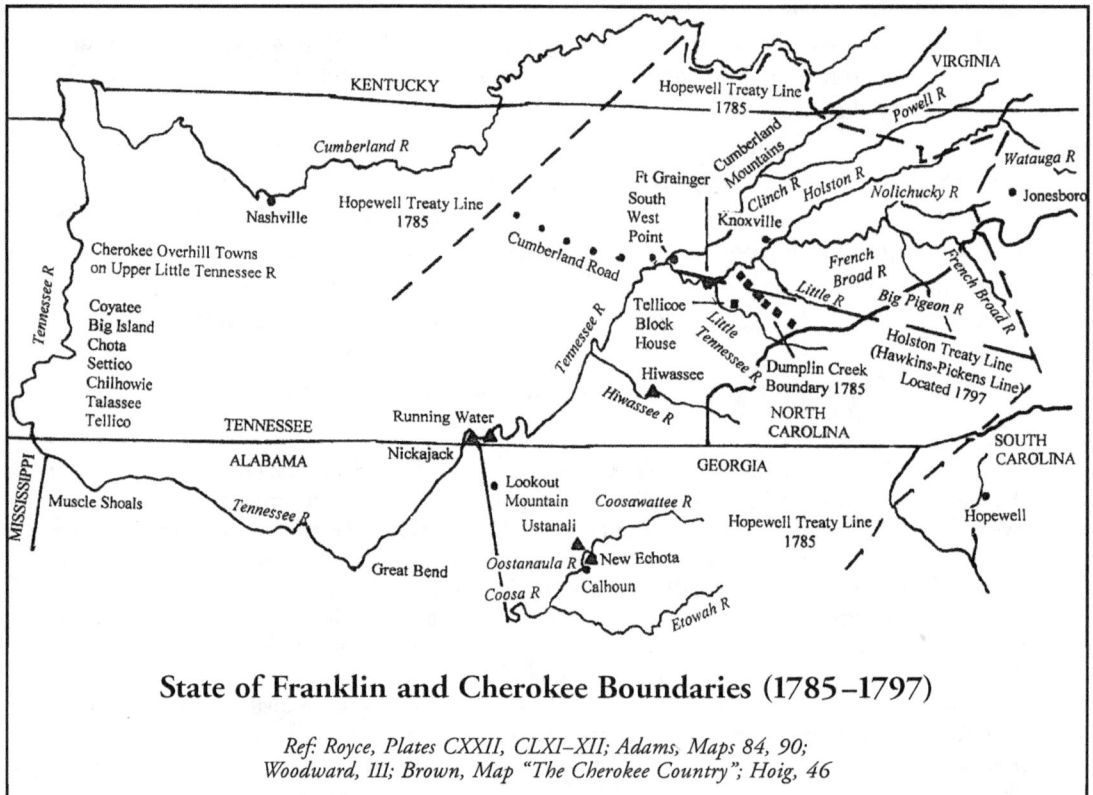

State of Franklin and Cherokee Boundaries (1785–1797)

Ref: Royce, Plates CXXII, CLXI–XII; Adams, Maps 84, 90;
Woodward, III; Brown, Map "The Cherokee Country"; Hoig, 46

A letter of November 1785 spoke of "not less than one thousand families cross[ing] the Appalachian mountains to settle in [the Nashville area] and in Kentucky [that] fall."[14] About the same time Patrick Henry, then governor of Virginia, was told of "great confusion in the [Cherokee] nation [the result of] rapid encroachment of the whites on the Indians' lands."[15] The Holston area settlers did not restrict themselves to land covered by the Dumplin Creek treaty. They went further south and also west to what was to become Knoxville.

Americans' threatening actions, such as the Land Grab Act and the formation of the State of Franklin, propelled the Creek's Alexander McGillivray to propose a Spanish-Indian alliance against the Americans. Congress decided to calm affairs by appointing a commission to negotiate treaties with the southern Indians.

Franklin came into conflict with the Confederation when the Treaty of Hopewell with the Cherokee was negotiated in November 1785. Hopewell was General Andrew Pickens' plantation about 120 miles above Augusta, Georgia. The treaty moved the Cherokee boundary line far to the north of the French Broad and Holston rivers, placing most of Franklin within Cherokee lands. The treaty withdrew protection of the United States from any settler within Cherokee land, of whom there were many, according to the Hopewell boundary, and specified that "the [Cherokees] may punish him or not as they please."[16] Hopewell disregarded the boundary agreed to at Dumplin Creek. In a gain for the settlers the Cherokee released claims to the Cumberland River purchase made by Richard Henderson which included Nashville, formerly known as French Lick or Nashboro.

At the Hopewell negotiations there were 918 Indians, men, women, and children, even though only the headmen had been invited. The North Carolina representative at the treaty, William Blount, pointed out to the Confederation commissioners, Benjamin Hawkins of North Carolina, Andrew Pickens of South Carolina, Joseph Martin of North Carolina, and Lachlan McIntosh of Georgia, before the treaty was signed that North Carolina had established a military reserve and sold "tens of thousands of grants ... all the way to the Mississippi."[17] He warned that to fix a boundary within North Carolina contrary to boundaries fixed by the state would violate the state's "legislative rights."[18]

Blount had a personal interest. He and his brothers as well as the then governor, Richard Caswell, had titles from North Carolina for land which was declared to be that of the Cherokee. North Carolina was still objecting in 1787 when Blount and another North Carolina representative unsuccessfully proposed in the Continental Congress that treaties could not override state's policies.

Hopewell retained protection for settlers, perhaps 3,000 in number, between the French Broad and Holston rivers with their situation being referred to Congress. In the spring of 1786 the Cherokee made war "upon the settlers on the waters of the Holston"[19] perhaps acting under their punishment right in the Hopewell treaty. In July 1786 Caswell wrote to Sevier that "Congress itself will be persuaded that the result is so repugnant to the rights of the State that they will not consider [North Carolina] by any means bound to abide by that treaty."[20]

Blount and other speculators paid little attention to the Hopewell treaties made with the Cherokee, Chickasaw, and Choctaw at the end of 1785 and the start of 1786. A settlement was tried at Muscle Shoals, many miles to the west of the Hopewell boundary. A private purchase of land at the shoals from the Cherokee by Joseph Martin and John Donelson in 1783 was the basis for a claim of right to settle the area, and Georgia cooperated by creating a county for the area and making a large grant of land to those seeking to develop it. In

1784 Blount suggested partnering with gentlemen of Georgia by creating in them a "thirst for back lands."[21] However, it wasn't such partnering that was difficult–the tough challenge was convincing the Indians that white settlers should be accepted on Indian land.

Hostile Indians scuttled settlement efforts for the time being. A principal claimant of land around the Tennessee River passing through present Alabama, the Creek, were at war with Georgia in early 1786. A victim of efforts to settle around Muscle Shoals was Donelson who moved there from Kentucky to do survey work in 1784 and 1785. His family returned to Nashville in March 1785 and, on his way to join them in April 1786, he was attacked on the road and died.[22]

In 1787 the Choctaw and Chickamauga wanted a trading post at Muscle Shoals and complained that the Americans only seemed interested in "jockey[ing] [them] out of [their] lands."[23] They had to have goods and said the "Spaniards are often sending talks to us, but we want to have nothing to say to them if we can help it, but must have Trade from some place.... Necessity will oblige us to look for new friends if we cannot get Friends otherwise."[24]

The Continental Congress tried to satisfy both the federalists and the state righters. A special Indian Ordinance of August 7, 1786, asserted the exclusive right of the Confederation to deal with Indian tribes, but at the same time told the Indian superintendent and frontier military commanders that "the legislative right of any state within its own limits"[25] was not to be disturbed. The ordinance established two Indian districts, each with a superintendent. James White was made the superintendent for the Southern District. In the spring of 1787 old Corn Tassel of the Cherokee, who signed the Hopewell treaty, complained to Joseph Martin, who was acting as an agent for North Carolina, that "the Franklin people are settling all our Lands."[26] Corn Tassel was aware of what was happening to the Cherokee saying: "I observe in every treaty we Have had that a bound is fixt, but we always find that your people settle much faster shortly after a Treaty than Before. It is well known that you have taken almost all our Country from us without our consent.... Truth is, if we had no Land we should have Fewer Enemies."[27]

Historian Francis Paul Prucha concluded the United States was not a true protector of Indian land:

> The federal government was sincerely interested in preventing settlement on Indian lands only up to a point, and it readily acquiesced in illegal settlements when they had gone so far as to be irremediable. The basic policy of the United States intended that white settlement should advance and the Indians withdraw. Its interest was primarily that this process should be as free of disorder and injustice as possible. The government meant to restrain and govern the advance of whites, not to prevent it forever.[28]

Benjamin Hawkins sent a copy of the Hopewell treaty made with the Cherokee to Thomas Jefferson and exuded pessimism. He wrote: "You will see by the Treat[y] ... how attentive I have been to the rights of these people; and I can assure you there is nothing I have more at heart than the preservation of them.... [However, the] interposition of Congress without the co-opperation of the southern States is ineffectual, and Georgia and North Carolina have refused by protesting against their authority."[29] Jefferson, who was in Paris, replied:

> The attention which you pay to their rights, also, does you great honor, as the want of that is a principal source of dishonour to the American character. The two principles on which our conduct towards the Indians should be founded, are justice and fear. After the injuries we have done

them, they cannot love us, which leaves us no alternative but that of fear to keep them from attacking us. But justice is what we should never lose sight of, and in time it may recover their esteem.[30]

Commissioners Hawkins and Pickens were truly after just treatment of the Indians, but the agreement of Joseph Martin, who fought against the Cherokee in 1780–1781, may have been motivated by a desire to direct settlers from the French Broad and Tennessee rivers to the Great Bend, which he wanted developed.

As the Cherokee probably knew from the past, agreements on paper didn't control those in the area. In retaliation for Cherokee attacks on settlers on the Holston River, Sevier, in the spring of 1786, raised a force that destroyed the valley towns of the North Carolina Cherokees on the Hiwassee river. In 1787 Franklin decided that land north of the Little Tennessee River-that is, south of the Dumplin Creek treaty line which was between the Little and Little Tennessee rivers-should be settled and established a land office for that purpose. Franklin had a semblance of right to do this through a Treaty of Coyatee which was negotiated in July 1786 with a small group of Indians, including headmen Corn Tassel and Hanging Maw, who were clearly under duress. The whites negotiating the treaty, a force of 250 that burned the council house at Coyatee and destroyed corn, reported that the Indians "seemed friendly and well satisfied [that Franklinites] should settle the country, and [said] they [would] sell ... the country on the south of the Tennessee ... if [the Franklinites would] keep the Creeks from killing them; or they [would] leave the country entirely, [if the Franklinites would] give them goods for it."[31] For the Cherokee Overhill Towns this was a severely invasive treaty since most of their towns were along the Little Tennessee River as was their capital, Chota.

North Carolina reached out to settlers in Franklin in January 1786 by offering to forgive taxes not paid since 1784 and to pardon those guilty of offenses against the sovereignty of North Carolina. Amnesty was not extended to Sevier and other leaders of Franklin, and, even more divisive, North Carolina intended to remove settlers who were on Cherokee land according to a 1783 boundary line accepted by North Carolina.

On the ground within Franklin most of the support for a separate state vanished in the parts north of the French Broad River. At the start of 1788 Sevier, whose term as governor of Franklin expired March 1, 1788, was ready to accede to North Carolina's demands but did not want to abandon the stalwart Franklin settlers below the French Broad who, according to North Carolina, were occupying Indian land.

For those on the frontier of Franklin the main problem in the summer of 1788 was with Indians. A Moravian brother who traveled in the French Broad area in the winter of 1783–1784 observed that the settlers "would ... like to extirpate [the Indians] altogether and take their land themselves. They scarce look upon them as human creatures."[32] A Methodist preacher making the Nolachucky circuit in 1787–1788 wrote of having his path "infested with savage men, the deadly foe of white men who had but too justly incurred their resentment; and more subtle and terrible enemies among human beings could not be imagined than were the native red men, incensed at the wrongs inflicted upon them by the whites."[33]

The fury of the Cherokee was fed in the summer of 1788 when the principal chief of the Upper Cherokee, Corn Tassel, was killed while under a flag of truce. Corn Tassel was a man of peace who had appealed to the governors of North Carolina and Virginia in a letter of September 19, 1787, "to remove the disorderly whites that had settled within sight of Cherokee towns."[34] He was a victim of the tit-for-tat mentality of the frontier. The starting event may have been an unprovoked murder of an old Cherokee woman, the wounding of two children, and the plundering of a nearby Cherokee town by whites. Or the start could have been the slaying of a white family within nine miles of Chota. A slaughter of all members of the Kirk family but one son in May 1788 led to a serious escalation in the white response.

Sevier, referred to as "Nolichucky Jack" by the whites and "Little John" by the Cherokee, and 150 mounted horsemen, wanting to drive Cherokees east of the Cumberland Mountains out of their settlements, in May and June 1788 went south eventually to the Hiwassee River about 40 miles south of the Cherokee towns on the Little Tennessee River. Without any losses to themselves they killed Indians, drove Indians into the mountains, and cleared out or burned the following towns: Tallassee, Hiwassee, Chilhowie, Settico, Chota, Tellico, Big Island, and Coyatee. They went beyond the morality of the frontier when the leaders of the militia, in Sevier's absence, under a white flag convinced Corn Tassel and four or five others to come to a house where they were executed by the surviving Kirk son by tomahawk blows to the head. This action was condemned by the Continental Congress.

Kirk showed no contrition. On October 17, 1788, he wrote to John Watts, the chief warrior of the Cherokee nation, warning that if the Cherokee shed more white blood the Cherokee would "feel something more to keep up remembrance of [him.]" He signed as "Captain of the Bloody Rangers."[35] The Cherokee struck back. Most warrior-age Cherokees in the Upper Towns joined Dragging Canoe's warriors and in October there were 28 people killed at one settlement. The leaders in the Upper Towns tried to stop the bloodshed. They wrote to Brigadier General Joseph Martin, who had been an agent to the Cherokee for both Virginia and North Carolina and in the militia of both states, stating that his "people provoked [them] to war ...; however, [they had] laid by the hatchet, and [were] strongly for peace."[36] Notwithstanding that Martin led about 500 men down the Tennessee River in the summer of 1788 and made an unsuccessful attack on the Chickamaugans in their area around Lookout Mountain he generally had the confidence of the Cherokees who gave him the name Glugu. This was a time when the Chickamaugans were being supplied with guns and ammunition by the Spanish and were supported by the Creeks.

Sevier was not ready for peace. Leading 450 militiamen he attacked the winter camp of Watts and other Cherokee leaders on January 10, 1789, and had a decisive victory over a force of Creeks and Cherokees in January 1789. His description of the fighting shows the vicious nature of frontier combat:

> Our artillery soon roused the Indians from their huts; and, finding themselve pretty near surrounded on all sides, they only tried to save themselves by flight, from which they were prevented by our riflemen posted behind the trees.... Our ammunition being much damaged by the snow ... I found it necessary to abandon that mode of attack, and trust the event to the sword and the tomahawk.... 100 horsemen, charged the Indians with sword in hand, and the rest of the corps followed with their tomahawks.[37]

How the Americans acted in battle can be judged by his report on the wound of Gen. M'Carter who "while taking off the scalp of an Indian, was tomahawked by another whom he afterward killed with his own hand."[38] M'Carter was characterized as a "brave and good man." Sevier reported on a shortage of supplies and that they "suffer[ed] most for the want of whiskey."[39] Taking scalps could interfere in the flow of battle. Even a skilled scalper used about two minutes.

Nolichucky Jack's retribution was so devastating that the Cherokee in the Overhill Towns moved their capital from Chota southward to Ustanali or Oostanaula (now Calhoun, Georgia), roughly 120 miles southwest from its former location.

In 1788 angry Indians ranged as far as to the north of the Cumberland River where they ran off surveyors and broke abandoned compasses which the Cherokee called "land stealers."[40] A flash point for violence during the years 1788–1791 was the Muscle Shoals area. The Georgia legislature gave over 3.5 million acres to a Tennessee land company. Washington issued a proclamation warning those looking to settle that area that the Indians under the Hopewell treaty were free to deal with settlers. Dragging Canoe did this. He laid a siege on settlers from Franklin and chased them back up the river.

Recognizing their unique situation settlers "inhabiting south of [the] Holston, French Broad and Big Pigeon Rivers"[41] formed an association in 1789 which asked North Carolina to extend protection to them. Sevier took an oath of allegiance to North Carolina around February 1789 and in August 1789 was elected to, and seated in, the North Carolina Senate. After North Carolina ratified the United States Constitution on November 19, 1789, he went to Congress.

All those living in the Holston area had to focus on the federal government when North Carolina ratified the Constitution about seven months after Washington was inaugurated as president, and, in December, ceded its western lands to the federal government. Congress accepted the cession on April 2, 1790. Much of what had been Franklin escaped from North Carolina's clutches when the North Carolina Assembly put the eastern boundary of the ceded land west of the Allegheny Mountains instead of west of the Cumberland Mountains. Many in eastern North Carolina did not want to be saddled with the costs involved in protecting western settlers.

Conditions in the cession left the federal government with only a small amount of desirable land to dispose of. Secretary of State Jefferson estimated the acreage which had "been entered or passed to grant under North Carolina's authority ... to be 8,177,598 acres, which naturally was of the best lands."[42] North Carolina came into conflict with the new State of Tennessee, which was accepted into the United States on June 1, 1796, when it tried to control land entries within Tennessee, relying on conditions attached to the cession. In those controversies North Carolina was up against an old adversary — John Sevier was the first governor of the State of Tennessee and served for 12 years in that capacity. During his years as governor (1796–1809) Tennessee's population went from 85,000 to 250,000.

16

The Cherokee, the Creek, the Chickamauga, and the New Federal Government (1789–1796)

After Washington was sworn in as president, April 30, 1789, his Secretary of War, Henry Knox, expressed his dismay over what was happening in Cherokee country:

> The disgraceful violation of the Treaty of Hopewell with the Cherokees requires the serious consideration of Congress. If so direct and manifest contempt of the authority of the United States be suffered with impunity, it will be vain to attempt to extend the arm of government to the frontiers. Indian tribes can have no faith in such imbecile promises, and the lawless whites will ridicule a government which shall, on paper only, make Indian treaties and regulate Indian boundaries.[1]

Washington knew the importance of achieving boundary agreements with the Indians. In 1783 he wrote that "the Settlemt. Of the Western Country and making a Peace with the Indians are so analogous that there can be no definition of the one without involving considerations of the other."[2] In August 1790 Washington told the Senate that 500 families had settled on Cherokee lands on the French Broad and Holston rivers and asked for, and was given, authority to enforce existing treaties and to make new ones.

Early in 1789 the federal government lacked any authority in North Carolina, including its land running to the Mississippi River. This changed when North Carolina ratified the United States Constitution on November 21, 1789, and ceded its western lands to the United States on December 12, 1789. Although the cession was conditioned so as to protect land sales made by the state and its military reservation, North Carolina had no agreement with the Cherokee and Chickasaw as to either. Someone still had to resolve the white-Indian ownership question, otherwise Indian warfare on the frontier would continue. Congress accepted the cession on April 2, 1790.

The Cherokee may have worried about the future when Congress, on May 26, 1790, formed, out of the ceded North Carolina land, The Territory of the United States South of the River Ohio and speculator William Blount became governor on June 8, 1790. He was also appointed superintendent of Indian affairs for the southern department. The Cherokee weren't likely to share the reasoning of Blount's fellow speculator and North Carolina congressman, Hugh Williamson, who supported the appointment and gave his rationale to Washington: "[i]t is true that Mr. Blount has a considerable Quantity of Land within the ceded Territory, but he has none to the Southward of it, and he must be the more deeply interested in the Peace and Prosperity of the new Government."[3]

As governor he oversaw what essentially became Tennessee, about 43,000 square miles, but as Indian superintendent he acted in relation to all Indian affairs in the Southwest. Settlers in the future Tennessee were in two areas. In the upper tributaries of the Tennessee River were about 28,000 — the former State of Franklin people, and along some 30 miles of the Cumberland River, the Nashville area, another 6,000 to 7,000. Defensive-minded settlers around Nashville lived in stations which were half-forted houses. The settlers were far removed from the markets "for their wheat, corn, hemp, pork, beef, or tobacco"[4] — those in the east used the Shenandoah Valley as an export route, and those along the Cumberland used the rivers to get to either Natchez or New Orleans.

When Blount took office the Creek, Chickasaw, and Choctaw were not particularly threatening to the settlers. But there was ample trouble with the combative band of Cherokee, the Chickamauga, located in five towns about 100 miles below the mouth of the Holston (near present-day Chattanooga). Their attacks "had been fierce and incessant since 1782."[5] The other Cherokee were not threatening but were agitated by the incursions across the Hopewell boundary, the State of Franklin treaties, and the activities of the North Carolina land office. An atmosphere of rebellion was fueled by the defeat in the Northwest of General Harmar's army in October 1790.

Blount acted to quiet the Cherokee. He asked for a meeting on May 31, 1791, at the mouth of the French Broad. He wanted additional cessions to be paid for by an annual annuity. He had his eye on the Muscle Shoals area. Others wanted to legalize "three hundred squatter families south of the French Broad" and to obtain land for "routes between Cumberland and East Tennessee." His official duties did not stop his buying more land. General Pickens, who had helped negotiate the Hopewell treaties and had often fought the Cherokee during the Revolutionary War, warned the Cherokee about Blount and said "he loved land, and would have all their lands."[6] Although outraged over the violations of the Hopewell line, Knox did not think it practical to remove those settlers west of the Hopewell line.

At the same time Benjamin Hawkins was warning Blount:

> If you should but attempt so enormous a grasp in the present situation of affairs as all the lands on the North side of the Tennessee, you will rouse the resentment of the Cherokees, give serious alarm to the Chickasaws and risk cause of suspicion to the Creeks and Choctaws, a part of those lands are considered as a sort of common property among the hunters of all these nations.[7]

With much ceremony, in an atmosphere of Blount's claim to all "disputed lands by right of conquest in the Revolution," and with hard bargaining the Treaty of Holston dated July 2, 1791, was agreed to.[8] Twelve hundred Cherokee and forty chiefs were at the bank of the Holston, near the mouth of the French Broad River, when the treaty was negotiated. The boundary line was moved some 45 miles westward and about 4,000 square miles surrendered, including land claimed by Blount.

The Indians refused to sell Muscle Shoals land which was "the common hunting grounds of four nations"[9] and gave in on land for a road to the Nashville area, the Cumberland Road. The Holston treaty hoped to establish a "permanent peace" by "remov[ing] the causes of war." The price for the ceded land was delivery of "certain valuable goods" immediately and an annual payment of $1,000 thereafter. Included was a common promise never honored in the past: "The United States solemnly guarantee to the Cherokee nation,

Unmarked grantees
are the United States.

Ohio R

1772
Virginia

Kanawha R

1770
British

WEST
VIRGINIA

New R

Ohio R

Kentucky R

1775
Richard Henderson

1770
British

KENTUCKY

VIRGINIA

1768
British

Chickasaw
Land

Cumberland R

1798

1768
British

1777
North Carolina
Virginia

Tennessee R

TENNESSEE

1791

1785   1805

1798

NORTH CAROLINA

Duck R
1806

1817   1819

1819

1798

1785

Catawba R

1819

1819
1819

1817

Tennessee R

GEORGIA

1798

1819

1777
Georgia
South Carolina

1755
South Carolina

Wateree R

1816

1835
Last Cession
Before Trail of Tears

1783

Georgia

SOUTH CAROLINA

1773
British

1721
South Carolina

ALABAMA

1817

Wafford's
Settlement
1804

Savannah R

S. Fork
Edisto R

Santee R

Cherokee Make Major Land Cessions — Dates

*Ref: Royce, Plates XCVIII, CXXII, CLXI–XIII; Royce, Map of the
Former Territorial Limits of the Cherokee "Nation of" Indians, 1884*

all their lands not hereby ceded." Whites were not to "attempt to hunt or destroy the game on the lands of the Cherokees" nor to go "into the Cherokee country, without a passport." Repeated was the carte blanche right of the Cherokee to punish illegal settlers as was in the Hopewell treaty. However, a significant limitation was included as to the United States prosecuting white crimes against the person or property of a Cherokee. Such miscreants could be punished only if the act was against "peaceable and friendly Indian or Indians." Retaliation or reprisal was to be delayed "until satisfaction shall have been demanded of the party of which the aggressor is, and shall have been refused."

The policy and hope of the United States was expressed in Article XIV: so that "the Cherokee nation may be led to a greater degree of civilization, and ... become herdsmen and cultivators, instead of remaining in a state of hunters, the United States will from time to time furnish gratuitously the said nation with useful implements of husbandry, and further ... assist the said nation in so desirable a pursuit." To facilitate this change the United States would send a person or persons to reside in the nation "to act as interpreters" and the Cherokee would provide land for their cultivation. Some Cherokee were receptive to adopting the ways of the white man. The Secretary of War was reminded of the commitment for ploughs and the like and a desire for them by the Cherokee: "this is what we want; game is going fast away from among us. We must plant corn and raise cattle, and we desire you to assist us.... In former times we bought of the traders goods cheap; we could then clothe our women and children; but now game is scarce and goods dear, we cannot live comfortably."[10]

Other Cherokee were dissatisfied and accused the Americans of deceit — a boundary line described in the Hopewell treaty was not as agreed to and instead of providing for a $2,000 annuity in the Holston treaty, as agreed to, the amount of $1,000 was inserted in the treaty as was a provision for free navigation of the Tennessee which was not agreed to. Bloody Fellow, a Chickamauga leader who signed the Holston treaty, met with Washington and Knox in Philadelphia in February 1792 and an article was added to the Holston treaty increasing the annuity to $1,500. Undoubtedly it was a heady experience for the Cherokee to receive money without the quid pro quo of exchanging land. In a conciliatory step Bloody Fellow made a mark as "Isagua, or Clear Sky" instead of as Bloody Fellow.

The degree to which Dragging Canoe signed on to the idyllic view of Article XIV is uncertain, he died of natural causes in 1792, and the Chickamauga continued to make raids in the Nashville area and frightened and attacked those traveling the Wilderness Road.

Federal officials were concerned when the government was unable to live up to its treaty promise to keep white settlers from intruding on Indian country. Thomas Jefferson, Washington's Secretary of State, in March 1792, expressed a practical position for the government:

I hope ... admonitions against encroachments on the Indian lands will have a beneficial effect — the U.S. find an Indian war too serious a thing, to risk incurring one merely to gratify a few intruders with settlements which are to cost the other inhabitants of the U.S. a thousand times their value in taxes for carrying on the war they produce. I am satisfied it will ever be preferred to send armed force and make war against the intruders as being more just & less expensive.[11]

However, this wasn't the course followed.

Hawkins expressed his displeasure with how the Indians were being treated in a letter to Washington on February 10, 1792:

During the war we acknowledged the Indians as brothers ... assured them of our disposition [to care for them], urged them to be patient and declared that when success crowned our efforts, they should be partakers of our good fortune, they were then acknowledged to be possessors of the soil on which they lived.

At the close of the war ... we seem to have Forgotten altogether the rights of the Indians.[12]

As Hawkins saw it, Blount was for war with the Indians. After the Holston treaty Blount located his capital at White's Fort within the ceded land. The area was named Knox-Ville in honor of the Secretary of War.

Conditions beyond Blount's control made the territory a dangerous place to live. In 1791 the Spanish were concerned about the Americans trying to locate at Muscle Shoals and built a fort at the future Memphis. During the summer of 1791 attacks were carried out by the Chickamauga, Creeks, and some Cherokee against Cumberland River settlers. When St. Clair was soundly defeated in the Northwest in November 1791 even the friendly Chickasaw and Choctaw showed signs of discontent with the increasing number of white settlers.

The Creek were urged to confront the Americans by the English adventurer William Augustus Bowles and by a new Spanish "governor and intendant of Louisiana and West Florida" when Baron Hector Carondelet replaced Esteban Miro on December 31, 1791.

April 1792 was a violent month, filled with murders, ambush, and attacks by both Indians and whites. A festering problem in the to-be East Tennessee (the Washington District) was the theft of horses — corrupt traders were organizing the stealing. Trying to improve relations with the Cherokee, Blount, at the invitation of half-blooded Chickamauga John Watts, who was elected head war chief of the Chickamauga following Dragging Canoe's death, met with 2,000 Cherokee at the Indian village Coyatee in May 1792. Even though the meeting seemed to go well, a short time later Watts cast his lot with the Spanish at Pensacola. With a Spanish offer of arms, ammunition, and supplies, he decided on an open war against the Americans which began with harassment in August and September 1792. When the Cherokee national council, without either Watts or Bloody Fellow present, met around July 1792, there was continuing dissatisfaction with the Holston treaty and white encroachments. On the first day of the national council a devastating attack was made in the Nashville area (the Mero District)—five whites killed and 25 captured.[13]

Bloody Fellow attempted to talk Watts out of his decision to attack the Americans. When the proposed action was under discussion, he said, "Look at that [American] flag; don't you see the stars in it? They are not towns, they are nations; there are thirteen of them. These are people who are very strong, and are the same as one man; and if you know when you are well, you had better stay at home and mind your women and children."[14] Nonetheless after Watts made his decision Bloody Fellow joined in the effort and went to Pensacola to get promised supplies. The Spanish refused to give him canons, saying that to do so would bring a Creek request for the same.

Blount, without success, tried to convince the federal government then in Philadelphia to send soldiers to the South. He was given a free hand to deal with the Indians but told to keep costs down and that a general Indian war was an "insupportable evil."[15] Federal attention and resources during this period were focused on preparing for further Indian warfare in the Northwest and in trying to avoid any serious conflict with the Spanish in the hope that agreement could be reached on a Florida boundary and use of the Mississippi River.

Blount had to confront the knowledge that the Chickamauga and Creeks had decided to go to war. Panic set in with settlers fleeing to stations for protection. Militia were ordered out but the response was not good. Then Blount was lulled into complacency by deceiving messages from the Chickamauga that a reported Indian army of 300 to 500 was in fact nothing more than a marauding party that the chiefs had been able to stop. He relaxed some of the requirements for militia, but, fortunately for the settlers, James Robertson in the Nashville area remained alert.

The Indians attacked a lightly manned Buchanan's Station, four miles south of Nashville, on the night of September 30, 1792. A stalwart few held the Station and news of their success encouraged men to join the militia and for plans of a counterattack to punish the Indians. Blount wrote Knox about 119 persons killed, wounded, or made captives of the Indians since January 1791 but was not able to get approval for a punitive action against the Creeks and Chickamauga. Knox told him only Congress, which would not meet until March 1793, could authorize a war and Blount should only take steps to defend against further Indian attacks. Knox also advised on conciliatory steps that could be taken to suppress Indian dissatisfaction.

To try to calm the Indians, Blount took steps to mark the Holston treaty line and when the Indians did not appear to participate, an "experimental line"[16] was completed in 1792. The line was not marked earlier to avoid irritating the Indians who were upset with the treaty. When the Cherokee saw how far south the line was and the amount of land ceded by only 41 chiefs "they rejected the treaty ... [and] a surge of Cherokee hostilities and Tennessee reprisals"[17] occurred.

Discontent among the settlers grew as did political opposition to a defensive posture — they wanted offensive action. Nonetheless, Blount refused to go against Knox's directions to stay on the defensive. When attacks continued in the first half of 1793, Blount with difficulty, against public opinion in the West, kept the settlers from going on the offensive. In February 1793 Knox wanted Blount to bring chiefs from the Chickamauga and Cherokee to Philadelphia to meet with the president. Blount met with Watts and others on February 6 and Watts declined the invitation, saying such a meeting would have to be approved by the Cherokee council.

A barrier to getting agreement with the Indians was the pro–American, pro–Spanish splits within the Cherokee and Creek nations and the inability of older chiefs to control younger warriors who were for plunder and attacks. Instability within the Creek nation was exacerbated with the death of McGillivray in February 1793. Blount made some progress at a meeting with Cherokee and Chickamauga leaders in April 1793 near Knoxville. Despite some indication that the chiefs would go to Philadelphia, the Creeks and Chickamauga continued with repeated attacks throughout the territory and settlers on the frontiers were huddling within stations. The Knoxville *Gazette*'s message was that "The Creek Nation must be destroyed."[18] The situation was further inflamed when ambushes of friendly Indians occurred.

The desire for a bloody solution is illustrated by a massacre of Cherokees meeting at the house of Chief Hanging Maw of the Upper Towns in June 1793 who were considering, at Blount's request, a trip to Philadelphia. Captain John Beard of the United States Mounted Infantry, who claimed he was after horse thieves, attacked the house. Maw was wounded and 10 or 11 others murdered. The acting territorial governor denied that the attack was authorized and Beard was court-martialed with the bizarre conclusion of being promoted and, in August, was commended for his work in patrolling the Cumberland frontier.

At the time of the attack on Hanging Maw, Blount was in Philadelphia intent on getting approval for "a vigorous *national* war" to "bring the Indians to act as they ought."[19] He and Andrew Pickens, who shared his goals, were frustrated. They wanted a war against the Creek and a military post near Muscle Shoals to stop any alliance between Northern and Southern tribes and to give protection to the Nashville area. Possible interference with Spanish negotiations, other international considerations, and anti-war sentiment in Congress blocked such steps. Also it was a time when the government was concentrating on its ongoing war in the Northwest.

Knox told Blount in August 1793 that continued violations of land guaranteed to the Indians by treaty would destroy the treaty approach to Indian dealings and "violence and injustice [would] be the Arbiters of all future disputes between the whites and neighbouring tribes of indians; and of consequence much innocent blood [would] be shed, and the frontiers depopulated."[20]

In the fall of 1793 attacks and retribution were rampant. On the Indian side were Creeks, Chickamauga, and small Cherokee bands. When Blount arrived back in the territory in October 1793, Sevier and several hundred men were at war in Indian lands repaying an Indian raid by nearly 1,000 Cherokees and Creeks led by Watts, which threatened Knoxville. Sevier followed the Indian army into northwestern Georgia, routed it, and destroyed several towns and 300 cattle. Thereafter, the Indian raids declined.

In 1794 Knox tried to buy peace with the Cherokee. Delegations from the Cherokee and Chickasaw went to Philadelphia and the Cherokee bargained for an increase in payments under the Holston treaty. The Chickasaw were given gifts and encouraged in their confrontations with the Creek. The Creek and Chickamauga were still harassing settlers. A treaty of June 26 stated there was public recognition that the Holston treaty had "not been fully carried into execution by reason of some misunderstandings."[21] The new treaty restated the need for the boundary to be marked, and rather than $1,500 per year the Cherokee were to be furnished "goods suitable for their use, to the amount of five thousand dollars yearly." Also in the 1794 treaty was a one-sided Article IV: "to evince the sincerity of [the Cherokee] to prevent the practice of stealing horses ... for every horse which shall be stolen from the white inhabitants by any Cherokee Indians, and not returned within three months, ... the sum of fifty dollars shall be deducted from the said annuity of five thousand dollars."

When Blount's first territorial legislature met in August 1794, a petition to the United States Congress was fashioned which wanted steps taken to "punish those two faithless and bloodthirsty nations, the Creeks and Cherokees" and advocated that "fear, not love, is the only means by which Indians can be governed."[22] The petition listed what had happened between February and September 1794: 67 killed, 10 wounded, 25 captured, and 374 horses stolen.

James Robertson, Nashville's founder, often Blount's agent or co-speculator, and a general in the militia, proposed to the governor an expedition against Chickamauga towns. Unofficially Blount agreed and asked Knox for approval, which was unequivocally denied. Blount was no longer willing to faithfully follow the federal policy of non-action. He and Robertson came to an understanding. Robertson, without the governor's sanction, would proceed and, after the fact, would resign his official position. On August 6, 1794, Robertson ordered troops to attack two Chickamauga towns (Nickajack and Running Water) and about a week later they were completely destroyed. Blount feigned disapproval and accepted Robertson's resignation when it was tendered but no action on the resignation was taken in Philadelphia. Robertson threatened John Watts with further action against the Chickamauga.

Other 1794 events influenced the Chickamauga to seek peace. Anthony Wayne defeated the Indians in the Northwest on August 20, 1794, and federal troops were stationed at three locations in the South (South West Point, Fort Grainger, and Tellico Block House). Only the Creeks continued with raids. A change in the Spanish objective from one of aggressive anti–Americanism promoted by Carondelet to one of protective treaties with the Indians of Governor Gayoso made a difference. Spain, for global reasons, did not want to make an enemy of the United States. At the end of 1794 Watts and other Cherokee chiefs and the Chickamauga met with Blount at Tellico Block House, near old Fort Loudoun, and exchanged assurances of peace. Blount declared that "[p]eace with the Indians exists now not only in name or upon paper in form of treaty but in fact."[23] Bloody Fellow, who participated in the treaty, said, "I want peace, that we may ... sleep in our houses, and rise in peace on both sides."[24] In the future Watts gave up his leadership position and Double Head became the Chickamaugan leader. And by 1798, after Hanging Maw's death, Bloody Fellow became the principal chief of the Cherokee.

Blount turned his attention to the Creek. He told Knox the only alternative with the Creeks was "to kill or be killed."[25] Knox might have agreed but he gave up his office on December 31, 1794. As of January 2, 1795, Blount was dealing with a new Secretary of War, Timothy Pickering, a New Englander who did not have a high opinion of the governor, in fact, considered him a "self-seeking swindler."[26] In March 1795 Pickering advised Blount that Congress would not support a war against the Creek nor would it support urging other tribes to fight the Creek.

Pickering saw events in the West much differently than did those living there. Blount was told Forts Grainger and Tellico Block would be removed unless the Indians approved of them. Trespassing settlers should be forcefully removed if necessary. As for horse stealing, it resulted from illegal entry on Indian land and a market created by whites who would buy stolen horses. Additionally he thought murders at times might be attributed to illegal hunting of game essential to the Indians. In December 1791 Pickering wrote about how the Indians would grow into the white world "when ... they acquire property, laws will be necessary to secure its enjoyment."[27] To be effective, laws must appear to be necessary.

During 1795 Blount was anticipating that the territory's population would reach the necessary 60,000 so that steps toward statehood could go forward. The taking of a census began in September 1795. When the total was shown to be 77,262 a constitutional convention was scheduled for Knoxville on January 11, 1796. A draft constitution was sent to Congress which was in session and Tennessee was admitted as a state on June 1, 1796. Blount was elected as one of its senators and Sevier was voted in as governor. Hawkins was appointed Principal Temporary Agent for Indian Affairs South of the Ohio River when Blount ceased to be governor.

17

Blount's Downfall and a 1797 Treaty Line

Blount's political life was a success but he strained his fiscal resources by committing himself to buy at least 1,000,000 acres in 1796. His timing was bad. The market for selling large holdings to others vanished and he, with his associates, faced the prospect of financial disaster. Blount was hounded by creditors and his paper wealth, based on claims to land, fell as the price for western land plummeted to 10 cents per acre. Always a schemer willing to take chances, Blount became involved in a plan to join with the British in a takeover of Spanish possessions in the Floridas and possibly Louisiana which he calculated would be a trove of unsettled lands. This would be done by the use of Indians of the South in conjunction with the British navy. The roster of those involved to some degree in the discussions is lengthy and contained the names of many in high places from England, France, Spain, and Canada who were looking to speculate on western land; e.g., the British foreign secretary and minister to the United States and the governor of Canada. The actual steps to be taken were in flux when its existence was disclosed in the United States Congress.

Blount made a colossal error in a letter of April 21, 1797, to Indian interpreter James Carey who would be dealing with the Creek and Cherokee. Carey was told to be careful not to enhance the position of Benjamin Hawkins with the Indians since "[a]ny power [of] consequence [Hawkins got would] be against [the] plan" and Carey was to consider a way "to get the Creeks to desire the President to take Hawkins out of the nation ... for, if he stays in the Creek nation, and gets the good will of the nation, he can and will do great injury to our plan."[1]

In the letter Blount was concerned about the fact that Congress had appointed commissioners to run a new boundary line as provided for in the Holston treaty of 1791. He anticipated the new line would differ significantly from the "experiment line" which had been run earlier. If so, he wanted to be cleared of any responsibility for the earlier line: "though [he] made the treaty, [he] made it by the instructions of the President, and, in fact, it may with truth be said, that [he] was by the President instructed to purchase much more land than the Indians would agree to sell. This sort of talk will be throwing all the blame off me upon the late President, and as he is now out of office, it will be of no consequence how much the Indians blame him." Furthermore, he "was not at the running of the line, and [if he] had been, it would have been more to their satisfaction."[2]

Carey was told to "read [the] letter over three times, then burn it." He didn't burn it and it ended in the hands of a Blount enemy, David Henley, who passed it on to Hawkins who saw that it got to Philadelphia where it reached the hands of President John Adams.

Blount learned of this after it was read aloud on the floor of the Senate. Former President Washington was furious. Abigail Adams bemoaned the lack of a guillotine in Philadelphia. Hawkins wrote on June 4, 1797, to the Secretary of War extolling the "exposure of those dirty intriguers and their villanous attempts to involve the government in difficulties and distress."[3] On July 5 Blount wrote to the Senate committee investigating the matter that he did "not recollect" writing the letter but in any case nothing he had ever written was designed "to injure the United States."[4] An attempt to return to Carolina was frustrated and the Senate committee "seized [Blount's] clothes, trunks, and papers."[5] The House of Representatives passed a charge of impeachment and wanted his seat sequestered. By a vote of 25 to 1 Blount was expelled from the Senate and set out by horseback to Carolina rather than staying in Philadelphia for an impeachment trial. He was fleeing not only from the Senate but also from creditors.

His reputation in Philadelphia suffered but his supporters in the West were not phased and wanted him to run for the Senate again. He was welcomed in Knoxville when he returned but decided to not seek re-election to the Senate. Ever the entrepreneur, he publically tried to drive the price of Nashville area land down (declaiming "threatened Indian hostilities, bad titles, and lack of water") so he could acquire it cheaply. These assertions were designed to "raise the *Horrors* with timid land Holders"[6] in North Carolina.

Blount's concern about the consequences of a new boundary line under the Holston treaty was well founded. Not only was Hawkins not removed from his position as Agent for Indians Affairs, he and Andrew Pickens ran a new treaty line in 1797 determined to follow the treaty as written. John Sevier, as governor of Tennessee, opposed their doing something so important to the state of Tennessee. Nonetheless they proceeded.

The concern in Tennessee was the fact that since the Holston treaty "many white men had encroached upon Cherokee lands." Furthermore, the settlers admitted the "experiment line" was not laid out for accuracy but rather "to see how the citizens could be covered, as they were then settled on the frontier."[7] Settlers were told by Hawkins they could expect "indulgence" if the settlement was "doubtful ... for want of the line," but none if there were "manifest violations of the Treaty of Holston."[8] Writing about his months of labor in locating the line Hawkins told a friend about "the anxiety ... at seeing a number of [his] fellow citizens certain victims of their own folly by intruding on the rights of the Indians."[9] There was acrimony aplenty about marking the line. Hawkins wrote:

> A something crept into the State of Tennessee, which leaped over the bounds of decency and law, and determined to put the government to defiance; it had already taken such a growth when I arrived there as to be alarming in a high degree, and nothing but the prudent precaution of the President in sending Colonel Butler there with a respectable force checked it.[10]

The Tennessee legislature denounced the Hawkins-Pickens line. Angry Tennesseans ran a revised line claiming the Hawkins-Pickens line to be wrong. It took federal troops, arriving in November, to remove complaining settlers.

Hawkins misjudged the extent to which Blount's debasement in the United States Senate translated into a curtailment of pressure on Cherokee lands. In November 1797 he wrote a friend: "I have ... witnessed the downfall of a character I highly valued, ... and seen a check given, I hope an effectual one, to a base system for the destruction of the four nations by [people greedily grasping after all their lands], and I have the happiness to know that I have contributed much to the establishment of the well grounded confidence which the four nations have in the justice of the U.S."[11] Blount's attitude, not Hawkins, prevailed in the West.

Indian-white relations changed significantly after the northern Indians were defeated by Anthony Wayne in 1794 and the Treaty of Greenville in 1795. The Cherokee were probably less assertive in 1798 when the federal government proposed that there be a treaty to deal with what the ultimate treaty of October 2, 1798,[12] described as "divers settlements ... made, by divers citizens of the United States, upon the Indian lands." A Blount-type solution was the cession of 1,539 square miles in the upper Tennessee River watershed in Tennessee and North Carolina. The quid pro quo was $5,000 of "goods, wares and merchandise" and "other goods [annually] to the amount of one thousand dollars" thereafter in addition to pre-existing obligations.

Noting that settlers were removed "for the purpose of doing justice to the Cherokee nation of Indians" a new boundary was adopted to "remedy[] inconveniences arising to citizens of the United States from the [1797] adjustment of the boundary line." A federal negotiator named in the treaty was the officer "commanding the troops of the United States, in the state of Tennessee." Another intimidating presence was that of John Sevier. Hawkins was not appointed a commissioner for the treaty but could have attended as an observer if orders from the War Department had arrived in time.

A significant provision was due notice to be given to "the principal towns of the Cherokees" as to delivery of the annual stipends and the obligation of the United States "to subsist such reasonable number that may be sent, or shall attend to receive them during a reasonable time." It was common knowledge that Double Head, spokesman for the Cherokee, profited from the treaty.

The price for stolen horses not returned in 90 days was $60 and payment was to be made by both Indians and whites. As to: "all [past] animosities, aggressions, thefts and plunderings ... [they] shall cease, and be no longer remembered or demanded on either side." A view of the future is presented in Article VII: "until settlements make it improper, the Cherokee hunters shall be at liberty to hunt and take game upon the lands relinquished and ceded by this treaty." And a degree of hypocrisy is found in the United States "guarantee of the remainder of [the Cherokee] country for ever." The changing nature of Tennessee is reflected in the agreement for "open and free road[s]" going through Indian land. The "for ever" guarantee for Cherokee land lasted until 1805.

Blount regained a leadership role in Tennessee when he was elected to the Tennessee assembly in 1798 and became speaker. At the same time impeachment proceedings against him were carried out in the United States Senate which ended with a dismissal of the proceedings for lack of jurisdiction, Blount no longer being a member of the Senate. When Sevier showed no inclination to relinquish his position as governor, Blount dropped out of the political picture and struggled with his money problems. All this ceased to be important when he died suddenly on March 21, 1800, at the age of 50 years.

When Hawkins, in his capacity as Agent for Indian Affairs South of the Ohio River, visited Cherokee country in 1796 he was able to make encouraging reports to the new Secretary of War, James McHenry. Women were found driving fat cattle to sell to white settlers, and were learning to spin and weave cotton into cloth. Certain sections of the country had "fenced farms, orchards, plowed fields, sizable stocks of cattle and hogs, and comfortable dwellings, and a goodly number of fine horses."[13] He also observed many mixed-blooded members of the Cherokee population.

Another advance toward the American view of what the Cherokee should be was the assignment of Silas Dinsmoor in 1797–1798 by President John Adams to live with the Cherokee and to instruct them "in raising of stock, the cultivation of land, and the arts."[14] Unfortunately, the whites did not all act as the Cherokee were led to believe they would. Andrew Jackson of Tennessee in 1795 was in Philadelphia trying to sell land which was within the Indian boundaries. A co-owner told him to be "canded and unreserved with the purchasers ... [a]nd particularly inform them that the 'fifty thousand' acres are situate[d] without the [the boundaries of land open to white settlement as fixed by the] treaty of Holston."[15]

18

Jefferson and the Southern Nations (1801–1809)

As president in 1801 Jefferson was positive in his first annual message to Congress on Indian relations. Progress was being made in "introduc[ing] ... them [to] the implements and the practice of husbandry and of the household arts" which they were finding more satisfactory than relying on "the precarious resources of hunting and fishing."[1] This view was consistent with his desire to increase "settlement of the extensive country remaining vacant within"[2] the United States. In January 1802 Jefferson told a delegation of Indians, "We shall, with great pleasure, see your people become disposed to cultivate the earth, to raise herds of the useful animals, and to spin and weave, for their food and clothing."[3]

One of Jefferson's earliest decisions as president was to send commissioners to the southern nations to seek agreement for roads through their land. Roads were necessary for both commerce and national defense. Brigadier General James Wilkinson, senior general in the United States Army, Hawkins, and Andrew Pickens, a general in the South Carolina militia who had fought against the Cherokee for forty years, were selected and, although roads were an objective, the possibility of cessions was also to be considered. Jefferson gave the commissioners special instructions respecting the Cherokee. Tell them "that the United States [had] no desire to purchase any of their land, unless they [were] quite willing to sell" but that roads were "necessary to keep up a communication with all parts of the United States, without trespassing on the lands of the red people."[4]

The first meeting was with the Cherokee in August and September 1801 and the Indians were in no mood to cede any rights. They saw roads as an invitation to undesirable people and wanted no roads in addition to those previously agreed to, that is, between the Clinch and Cumberland rivers and the Natchez Trace which ran from the Cumberland River (Nashville) to Natchez. The Trace was the last leg of the post riders' long route from Washington City to New Orleans, a route through Abingdon, Virginia, and Knoxville, Tennessee. Progress in the civilization program surfaced when the Upper Cherokee chiefs told of an envy of the other Cherokee over their acquisition of the implements of civilization, that is, of ploughs, wheels, cotton cards and looms.

The commissioners were well received by the Chickasaw with whom they met at Chickasaw Bluffs (later Memphis) in October. They found that the Chickasaw were making "considerable progress in agriculture, and in stocking their farms, and [were] desirous to increase their domestic manufactures."[5] Agreement was reached for the United States to make a wagon road from the Nashville area to Natchez, but not for roadside rest houses. The Chickasaw received $700 in goods, control of any necessary ferries, and a commitment of the president to help them "preserve ... their rights against the encroachments of unjust neighbours, of which [the president should] be the judge."[6]

The Natchez Trace was not much of a road in 1797 when traveled by an Englishman. Starting from Natchez the first "three sleeps"[7] or days took his party to the outer edge of the Natchez district settlements. From there another five days passed them through the Choctaw nation to the Chickasaw. Recurring obstacles were watercourses that had to be waded or bridged in some fashion. It was easy to lose the pathway. If not careful, horses could be stolen and the Chickasaws were inclined to treat petty theft from travelers' baggage as a game. Poison ivy was a danger to be avoided if possible as one proceeded along narrow trails. It took the group 18 days to reach the Tennessee River which was about three-fourths of the entire distance from Natchez to Nashville. The Tennessee, being a large river, required the travelers to build rafts. It took this party another week to travel the remaining 100-plus miles to Nashville. As they came closer to Nashville the path widened from "the narrow single track it had been for hundreds of miles."[8]

The Trace was an important part of trade coming down the Mississippi to Natchez. It was relatively easy to use a flatboat to haul goods for sale to Natchez, and to dismantle the boat and sell the lumber, but to get back required a trip over the Trace of about 450 miles. The difficulty of bringing goods to Natchez and New Orleans didn't stop 486 boats from making the trip in the first six months of 1801. Using the Trace as a post road for mail, barring unusual circumstances two riders, one for the upper half and one for the lower half, could deliver letters from Nashville to Natchez and vice versa in two weeks. When the Chickasaw and Choctaw agreed to a road through their territory in 1801, steps were taken to improve the Trace, but it wasn't until 1809 that it was finally considered a wagon road.

At a meeting with the Choctaw in December 1801 permission was given for a "durable wagon way," without roadside accommodations. They also agreed to have an old British boundary "retraced and plainly marked, in such way and manner as the President may direct." This seemingly innocuous agreement[9] ended up costing the Choctaw about a million acres. The retraced line, which went from the 31st degree of north latitude, the United States boundary with Spain under the 1795 Treaty of San Lorenzo, to the Yazoo River (near modern Vicksburg), was supposed to be eastward of the Mississippi River and "in a parallel direction with" the river. For this they received $2,000 in goods and "three sets of blacksmith's tools." The commissioners thought an interest shown by young Choctaws in farm implements, a blacksmith, and wheels and looms for Choctaw women was a good omen of a future which could save the United States "the pain and expense of expelling or destroying them."[10]

The Choctaw were swindled when the retraced line was not parallel to the river — it was more of a north-south line whereas the river course was in a northeast-southwest direction. The north-south line increased the amount of land between the line and the river; hence, more land was ceded.

The trickery was an affront considering the Secretary of War's instruction to the commissioners to "impress [on the Indians] that the United States have no desire to purchase any of their land, unless they are quite willing to sell"[11] and that Wilkinson told the Choctaw that the commissioners came "not to ask lands from [them,] nor shall [they] ever ask for any unless [the Choctaw were] disposed to sell."[12]

H. B. Cushman, born in 1822, lived among and near the Choctaw in Mississippi and later when they moved into the Indian Territory west of the Mississippi. In his book *History of the Choctaw, Chickasaw and Natchez Indians,* he described the Choctaw warrior in his Mississippi setting to be as fine a specimen of manly perfection as he had ever beheld. He observed admirable traits in the Choctaws — they "never forgot an act of kindness," had an "innate politeness," and "unfeigned hospitality."[13]

Negotiations with the Creek were complicated during the years 1799–1803 by the presence of William Augustus Bowles, who escaped from the Spanish around 1797, was cordially received in England, and returned to Florida "by His Majesty's schooner *Fox*" in the fall of 1799. A mystery is how he came to be on a ship taking him from imprisonment in the Philippines to Spain and how he escaped from the ship. Florette Henri's book *The Southern Indians and Benjamin Hawkins 1796–1816* suggests that William Blount, who was possibly plotting an Indian uprising against United States' authority, "through Spanish connections and bribery procured Bowles's escape."[14]

Bowles' hold in the Indians was that he alone among white leaders insisted upon "Indian title to the lands of their nations."[15] In July 1801 Hawkins advised the Secretary of War against trying for further cessions "until Bowles [was] effectually removed and the ferment he [had] occasioned subsided."[16]

Calling himself "Director General of Muskogee,"[17] Muskogee being another name used for the Creek, Bowles robbed a Panton store and on May 19, 1800, captured the fort at Saint Marks, which the Spanish took back a few weeks later. He was not a threat on a large scale and continued to live at Miccosukee (inland from Apalachee Bay) with about sixty followers, who, said Hawkins, were "more attentive to frolicking than fighting."[18] However, Bowles' influence on the Creeks was such that it interfered with efforts to get additional cessions and his assaults against Spain resulted in friction between Spain and the United States.

Hawkins planned a trap for Bowles at the 1803 spring meeting of the four southern tribes, which Bowles was expected to attend and to challenge the old chiefs. Bowles attended with "Semanole" chiefs and spoke of being made "King of the Four Nations."[19] Rather, he was taken away in manacles and turned over to the Spaniards at Pensacola. He died two years later at Morro Castle in Cuba.

In 1802 the older Creek leaders risked an insurrection of the younger Creeks if they did not act carefully. Unfortunately for the Creek, the commissioners were no longer just after roads. The Jefferson administration made a bargain in April 1802 that brought on major confrontations between the Cherokee and Creek with the state of Georgia. In return for its western land, which was to become Alabama and Mississippi, Georgia was paid $1,250,000 and the United States agreed to "extingiuish the Indian titles within the borders of the state as then drawn."[20] Important Cherokee towns in 1802 were located in northern Georgia.

From the Creek the three commissioners wanted cessions within Georgia of two areas, already settled, and the large area between the Ocmulgee and Oconee Rivers. On May 23, 1802, a large gathering of Creeks met with the commissioners at Fort Wilkinson. Bowing to what seemed inevitable, the Creeks proposed a cession of some land west of the Oconee for $2 per acre, a price justified by white conduct — whites did "not spare in their charges for things that are not lasting, and therefore [the Creek] ask[ed] a price for that which is lasting."[21] Wilkinson, wanting a bigger cession, cajoled the Creeks and made a dubious promise: "if you make [the Ocmulgee River] the line, it shall be guarded by troops from one end to the other ... and stock, *sent into your land,* shall be killed."[22] Viewing past unfulfilled promises of whites this one had to be something less than a good faith assertion by Wilkinson and surely one doubted by the Indians. The Creek were not persuaded but agreed on June 16[23] to a smaller cession for which they only received 2 cents per acre. Hawkins made the point to the Creek negotiator, Efau Haujo, that with the scarcity of game and the outlawing of begging, the Creek options were limited to "sell[ing], steal[ing], or starv[ing]."[24]

Of $25,000 to be paid immediately, $10,000 were for Creek creditors and $5,000 to pay for property the Creek had taken. Another surrender of sovereignty was to allow garrisons possibly needed to protect the frontier to be established "upon the land of the Indians, at such place or places" as the president would determine. Pickens refused to act as commissioner after this treaty since he thought "undue pressure for a land cession was exerted against the Creek."[25]

The commissioners reported to the Secretary of War on June 17, 1802:

> [W]e had to combat, not only the jealousies, distrusts, and fears, natural to the Indians, but also, an apprehension, serious and alarming to the old chiefs, that, if they ceded any part of their country, their young warriors might resist it, and joining the partizans of Bowles, divide the nation, wrest the government from those who at present administer it, and, by some hasty and imprudent act, involve their country in ruin.[26]

Rumors that Spain had ceded Louisiana and the Floridas to France concentrated Jefferson's attention on the Mississippi River. Under the First Consulship of Napoleon, France was "the most rapacious and aggressive of the Powers."[27] Jefferson received some confirmation of the rumors in a letter from Rufus King, the minister to Great Britain, dated November 20, 1801, but France did not officially admit it. In fact, a secret Treaty of San Ildefonso between Spain and France, signed in October 1800, agreed to the transfer, but only to Louisiana, which included New Orleans.

Before Jefferson's Minister to France, Robert E. Livingston, sailed in September 1801 he was advised that if the transfer had not been made "he was to try to dissuade the French" but if it had been made he should "avoid irritating the French" and explore a possible cession from France of the Floridas.[28] A fear that France would aggressively reestablish itself on America's mainland was fueled by a King letter of June 1801 to the effect that influential French saw "a natural separation between the American people on the two sides of the mountains."[29]

A crisis developed in the fall of 1802. In violation of the San Lorenzo treaty, the Intendant of New Orleans closed the deposit at New Orleans. Use of the river was not restricted but no longer could goods be placed ashore for later trans-shipment to other destinations. Westerners demanded action to remove this barrier to their trade. In January 1803 Jefferson dispatched James Monroe to Europe to talk with the French and Spanish about purchasing "the island of New Orleans and the provinces of East and West Florida."[30]

Anticipating possible trouble with his European neighbors, Jefferson told his Secretary of War, Henry Dearborn, on December 29, 1802, that "Indian land should be acquired on the southern and western frontiers, particularly along the Mississippi, so as to provide a well-defended border with France in Louisiana and Spain in Florida."[31] To him the sooner the Indians could be convinced of the wisdom of farming instead of hunting the better. His vision expressed to Dearborn was of future Indian cessions closing the Indians "in between strong settled countries on the Mississippi & Atlantic" and forcing them "for want of game ... to agriculture" and to find "that small portions of land well improved, [are] worth more to them than extensive forests unemployed."[32]

In correspondence with Andrew Jackson in February 1803 Jefferson said the reasons for "keeping agents among the Indians [were] principally ... 1. The preservation of peace; 2. The obtaining lands." As for doubts about the dedication of Hawkins to get land, Jackson was told that Hawkins would be "placed under ... strong ... pressure from the executive" and would be "made sensible that his value will be estimated in proportion to the benefits he can obtain."[33]

During the unsettled period of late 1802 Wilkinson met with the Choctaw, as a sole commissioner, signing on October 17, 1802,[34] "A Provisional Convention," agreeing to re-marking another British boundary. Involved was land along the present borderline between Mississippi and Alabama, above the 31st parallel, eastward to the Tombigbee and Mobile rivers. Aspects of the "Provisional Convention" make it appear to be an instrument never agreed to by the Choctaw nation as a whole. First, only 10 Choctaw signed, only 3 of whom also signed the 1801 treaty, meaning that 13 of those signing in 1801 did not sign in 1802. Second is the statement that the only consideration for the Choctaw was "one dollar, to them in hand paid." This was an un–Indian-like provision.

When, in 1803, Wilkinson started to run the old British boundary, which dated back to 1765, the Choctaw learned that Wilkinson had a different idea of where the line was to be drawn than they did. Wilkinson was not interested in hearing complaints from the Choctaw and told them they would be in danger if they opposed the line as he drew it; "he would positively throw them away and they would soon become a lost people."[35] A statement like this by the commander of the United States Army in the West had to be taken seriously, and they did. Wilkinson told the Secretary of War, in October 1803, that "he had run the boundary far beyond the old British line." He justified this as being "zealous attention to the Interests and accommodations of our fellow Citizens and of our Country."[36]

A document dated August 31, 1803,[37] describes the re-marked line. Of those signing this document only one had signed the 1801 and 1803 documents. The others are identified as chiefs residing on the Tombigbee. For confirming the concession of land within the new boundary which had "not been [previously] ceded by the ... Choctaw nation," Wilkinson gave to those present on August 31 "fifteen pieces of strouds, three rifles, one hundred and fifty blankets, two hundred and fifty pounds of powder, two hundred and fifty pounds of lead, one bridle, one man's saddle, and one black silk handkerchief." The cost of the land acquired was $179 in gifts.

Wilkinson, sometimes described as a "fat, deceitful general" and a "mammoth of iniquity"[38] was a schemer with little if any concern for the rights of others. In 1787 he was a merchant in Kentucky and, when Spain closed the Mississippi River, was able to convince Spanish governor Miro that he could help Spain get Kentucky. In return he received trading rights and an annual pension of $2,000 from Miro. Back in Kentucky he was striving for statehood, not separation from the United States. He was able to get a commission as lieutenant colonel in 1791, joined Anthony Wayne's army as second in command with a rank of brigadier general, fought in the battle of Fallen Timbers, and, on Wayne's death in 1796, took his place as head of the army. All this time he stayed in the pay of Spain and passed it intelligence. Whatever his shortcomings, he stayed in favor with Jefferson and was appointed governor of the Louisiana Territory in 1804.

Jefferson saw the trading houses, commonly called factories, in Indian territory as important to the Indians and the government. The idea of having factories was voiced by

George Washington and Congress provided money for a trial run in 1795. The original factory was for the Creeks at Colerain on the St. Mary's River in Georgia. Congress was satisfied with the result and continued the concept in 1796. A second factory was established at Tellico Blockhouse in eastern Tennessee.

There were no additional factories during the John Adams presidency. When Jefferson became president he wanted and got Congressional support for additional factories. In the South: Fort St. Stephens (Choctaw) and Chickasaw Bluffs. In a letter to William Henry Harrison, governor of the Indiana Territory, Jefferson outlined his overall approach to the Indians:

> Our system is to live in perpetual peace with the Indians, to cultivate an affectionate attachment for them [and to] protect [them] against wrongs from our own people. [He wanted] to draw them to agriculture [with a result of their being willing to sell land to whites.]
>
> To promote this disposition to exchange lands, which they have to spare and we want, for necessaries, which we have to spare and they want.... [Trading houses had a function:] good and influential individuals among them run in debt, because we observe that when these debts get beyond what the individuals can pay, they become willing to lop them off by a cession of lands.[39]

Typical of the items stocked were "cloth, thread, looking glasses, ivory combs, wool hats, saddles, rifles, padlocks, small brass bells, brass kettles, iron spoons, scissors, Barlow penknives, and fish hooks."[40]

Indians resented traders trying to charge interest on their debts, a procedure totally foreign to the Indian culture. H. B. Cushman's book *History of the Choctaw, Chickasaw and Natchez Indians* describes a contempt of whites which has a ring of truth: "The white people [except for missionaries] have ever and everywhere assumed an air of superiority over them, which the Indians have ever justly denied; and which justly created in their minds pity for the foolish self-conceit and egotism of the Whites, which seemed to them a lamentable weakness."[41]

Cherokee entreaties to Adams and Jefferson to eliminate the federal factory system were refused. Adams was content with the two existing factories and Jefferson wanted more. In both the North and South, factories competed with British traders, and private traders licensed under the Trade and Intercourse Act. Jefferson's message to Congress on January 18, 1803, reported on what was happening:

> The Indian tribes ... have, for a considerable time, been growing more and more uneasy, at the constant deminution of the territory they occupy ... and the policy has long been gaining strength with them, of refusing, absolutely, all further sale, on any conditions.... In order, peaceably, to counteract this policy ... and to provide an extension of territory, which the rapid increase of our numbers will call for, two measures are deemed expedient: First, to encourage them to abandon hunting.... Secondly, to multiply trading houses among them....[42]

By 1809 fourteen trading houses were operating.

Although Jefferson's approach to the tribes was different from that preferred by Hawkins, he stayed on with the Creek and the word "temporary" was removed from his title. With the change Hawkins decided to make a permanent location for his office and home. He selected the Flint River in Lower Creeks territory reasonably close to the Upper Creeks and white settlers in Georgia. In his December 1801 message to Congress Jefferson credited Hawkins with introducing sheep to the Creeks, settling them in villages, fencing fields, and using plows. Throughout his presidency Jefferson was complimentary of the progress being made by the southern tribes.

19

Jefferson after the Louisiana Purchase and Anarchy in 1810

Developments unrelated to a muted bellicosity towards France as a new neighbor solved Jefferson's problems. Spain, having on October 15, 1802, ordered that Louisiana be delivered to the French, was not interested in creating a confrontation over the deposit in New Orleans at a time when they were handing over New Orleans to France. On March 1, 1803, Spain's foreign secretary ordered that the deposit be restored. Then, as a complete surprise, before Monroe reached Paris, on April 11, France's foreign minister, Talleyrand, asked Minister Livingston if the United States would be interested in buying all of Louisiana. Livingston and Monroe ignored the limits of their authority, which only went to buying land east of the Mississippi, and agreed on May 2 to buy Louisiana for about 15 million dollars. On December 20 the United States took possession.

Various reasons have been attributed to Bonaparte's desire to sell Louisiana. One explanation is a need for money to carry out a war in Europe which started shortly after the Louisiana Purchase and a belief that Louisiana would be a military liability. Although the purchase may have exceeded the president's authority under the Constitution, in the main, the addition of some 828,000 square miles was eagerly embraced. The failure of the purchase agreement to define the boundaries of Louisiana led to a controversy with Spain. The United States believed that Louisiana included part of West Florida, that is, the land east of the Mississippi to the Perdido River which is slightly west of Pensacola. Spain said no.

At the time of the Louisiana Purchase Jefferson stated an honorable objective for the Indians. Congress was told in 1803 that "[i]n leading [Indians] to agriculture, to manufactures, and civilization ... we are acting for their greatest good."[1] The same year that Jefferson told Hawkins the "ultimate point of rest and happiness for [the Indians] is to let our settlements and theirs meet and blend together, to intermix, and become one people,"[2] he told Indiana Territory governor William Henry Harrison an alternative — removal west of the Mississippi. In March 1804 Congress authorized the president to agree with "Indian tribes owning lands on the east side of the Mississippi [to] exchange [such] lands [for] property of the United States, on the west side of the Mississippi."[3]

In the South the lever of Indian debts was used to the maximum. A deal was made with John Forbes, who headed Panton, Leslie, and Company after the death of William Panton in 1801, to pay off Indian debts if he would encourage them to make cessions. In 1804 the name of the firm was changed to John Forbes and Company. Jefferson showed anger in March 1803 when the Indians did not warmly embrace offers to buy their land; he found them adhering to "habits of their bodies, prejudices of their minds, ignorance, pride" and criticized tribal leaders for trying to "inculcate a sanctimonious reverence for the customs of their ancestors" as a way to retain their leadership.[4]

Jefferson had a vision as to Louisiana. In private correspondence, he predicted that land north of New Orleans would "be locked up from American settlement, and under the self-government of the native occupants."[5] He told an economist friend, DuPont de Nemours, the policy would be for the land above New Orleans to be a place "to transplant our Indians into it, constituting them a Marechausee [that is, a constabulary] to prevent emigrants crossing the river, until we have filled up all the vacant country on [the east side of the Mississippi],"[6] which he thought would take fifty years.

Once agreement was reached with France to buy Louisiana, Jefferson worried about the constitutional authority to make the purchase. In July 1803 he drafted a constitutional amendment, which was not approved by Congress, that reflected his thinking as to how Louisiana would be treated. In part the draft provided "that lands purchased by the United States on the west side of the Mississippi could be exchanged by act of Congress for Indian lands wanted by the United States on the east side of the river, and that whites on the west side might be removed to the thus-acquired lands on the east side."[7] Not deterred by Congress not approving the draft, Jefferson explored such exchanges, but neither the whites on the west side of the river nor most of the Indians on the east side were interested. About 1,000 Cherokee moved into present northeastern Arkansas in 1805 and some Delaware and Shawnees settled in the Camp Girardeau area of to-be-Missouri starting in 1789. But relocation was not easy since the resident Osage Indians often made war on any outside Indians coming west of the Mississippi. The Osage barrier was greatly reduced by treaties negotiated and completed before and shortly after Jefferson's presidency ended. The Great and Little Osage gave up virtually all of the current state of Missouri and the part of current Arkansas north of the Arkansas River. The Osage were put under the protection of United States troops at Fort Clark, which was located along the Missouri River about 300 miles from the river's mouth. The treaty was ratified in March 1810.

The usually optimistic Hawkins wrote to James Madison, then Secretary of State, in July 1803 that "Labour is no longer a disgrace in our land, and our men lend a hand. Hunting has become insufficient to clothe and subsist us, and will soon be resorted to as an amusement for our young men. We shall in future rely on stockraising, agriculture and household manufactures."[8] All this was well, but Jefferson had another job in mind for Hawkins. He had to deliver on his promise to Georgia to eliminate Indian land within its state boundaries. On February 18, 1803, he ordered Hawkins to negotiate for a Creek cession of their remaining land between the Oconee and Ocmulgee rivers. Jefferson explained that "it is for [the Creeks'] interest to cede lands at times to the United States, and for us thus to procure gratifications to our citizens from time to time, by new acquisitions of land."[9]

When Hawkins and Georgia congressman David Meriwether wanted to talk with the Creek in 1804, the Lower Creeks were not even willing to meet, an understandable attitude since the target land was in their area, not that of the Upper Creeks. Hawkins, in a threatening move, told an Upper Creeks spokesman that a failure to give up the land could lead to a swap of land for some in "the wilds in the west."[10] Further pressure was put on the Creeks by the presence of Georgians who said they intended to enforce the old Georgia treaties. An impasse was reached and several months were allowed for the Creeks to confer. To induce a favorable atmosphere Hawkins was "ordered to drive intruders from Creek lands by military force, if necessary, until after the treaty in the fall."[11]

When the Creek met with the commissioners in the fall of 1804, representatives from both the Upper and Lower Creeks were present and a bargain struck. Hawkins gave up asking for a road and agreed to a payment of $200,000—about half of which would go to John Forbes—for about 2 million acres. Hawkins was skeptical of the Senate agreeing to these terms and it didn't. Hawkins was not appointed to negotiate any further treaties. It may have been that doubts "entertained by some whether ... he [was] more attached to the interests of the Indians than of the United States" prevailed in Washington.[12]

Jefferson was insistent on a treaty for both the land and a road and directed that talks be held in Washington. Hawkins took six Creek chiefs to Washington at the end of 1805, two of whom were half-blooded Creeks, where they received flattering attention. Jefferson met with them on November 2, 1805, and gave a mixed message. They were told "the civilization program ... would enable [them] to sell useless lands" and that "Your lands are your own, my children, we will protect your right in them not only against others, but against our own people."[13] Negotiations were handled by Dearborn, the Secretary of War, and for $206,000 he got a cession of land and agreement for a road.[14] Since the $206,000 was to be paid over an 18-year period the capital outlay was only $130,000 which at 6 percent interest would cover the annual payments. The Senate approved.

Dearborn thought that with the Ocmulgee as a boundary he would "not live long enough to hear any contention for any other boundary line between Georgia and the Creek Nation."[15] What he did not anticipate was a Creek uprising starting in 1811 with the objective of removing all white presence from Creek lands. The 1805 treaty accomplished a Jefferson priority. He wanted a post road to New Orleans through Creek land. Needed was a road four to six feet wide with "trees to be fallen across the water courses so as to enable the mail carrier to pass the waters upon them carrying the mail secure from the water and swimming his horse by his side."[16] The 1805 treaty[17] gave the United States "a right to a horse path, through the Creek country, from the Ocmulgee to the Mobile [with a right] to clear out the same, and lay logs over the creeks." The Creek were to "have boats kept at the several rivers for the conveyance of men and horses, and houses of entertainment established at suitable places on said path." Charges were to be controlled by the Indian agent.

The need for more land was triggered by an increasing population in the South. During Jefferson's years in office (1801 to 1809) "Tennessee's population grew more than 100 percent, Georgia's about 55 percent, Kentucky's almost 85 percent, and Mississippi's 312 percent."[18] Commissioners chosen to negotiate for land differed depending on the tribes involved. Although Hawkins was the agent for all the southern tribes when appointed in 1796, over time his position became essentially as an agent for the Creek and different agents were appointed for the other southern tribes—for most of the Jefferson years, Return Jonathan Meigs for the Cherokee, Silas Dinsmoor for the Choctaw, and Samuel Mitchell for the Chickasaw. Meigs replaced Silas Dinsmoor as Cherokee agent in 1802 when Dinsmoor was made agent to the Choctaw. In 1804 Meigs and Daniel Smith eliminated an affront to the Cherokee of several thousand acres settled by whites in northeast Georgia just inside the Cherokee-Georgia boundary, Wafford's Settlement. For $5,000 and an indefinite $1,000 annuity the Cherokee ceded the land to the United States.[19]

In 1804 Meigs and Smith were directed by Dearborn to get all the Cherokee land they could in Kentucky and Tennessee. They were told to deal with Double Head and they delivered 8,118 square miles in the middle of Tennessee and some slightly into southern Kentucky by a treaty of October 25, 1805. The Cherokee received $3,000 in "valuable merchandize," and $11,000 to be in cash or, at the Cherokee's option, for "useful articles [for] agriculture and manufactures."[20] In addition there was to be an annual payment of $3,000. Accepting the fact that an annuity to be paid 10 or 25 years later has a relatively small present worth value, for present purposes the annuity will be given a 1805 value of $30,000. Using that number the overall consideration to the Cherokee in 1805 was $44,000. When this is applied against the 8,118 square miles ceded, the payment was less than 1 cent per acre.

Many Cherokee were outraged at the cession of the "best hunting grounds in the Cherokee domain." The anger focused on Double Head when it became known that in a secret agreement he was reserved two tracts, and that his kinsman, Tahlonteskee, had a similar reserve. Although not the principal chief of the Cherokee, Double Head was the "spokesman for the Cherokees in talks with the Federal Government."[21]

On October 27, 1805, Meigs and Smith agreed, in a separate treaty, to pay the Cherokee $1,600 for small tracts of land near Kingston which were thought desirable for use by the Tennessee assembly. In each of the October 1805 treaties concessions were made for roads through Cherokee land. The treaty recites that the Cherokee were "possessed of a spirit of conciliation."[22]

Another 7,000 square miles were ceded in a treaty negotiated with Dearborn in Washington in January 1806.[23] With this cession the Cherokee gave up all the land they still had in mid–Tennessee and were left only with land in southeast Tennessee, northwest Georgia, and northern present-day Alabama. Also surrendered was some land in Alabama north of the Tennessee River. The price was low—$10,000 in cash. It was about 5 acres for 1 cent plus a grist mill and a machine for cleansing cotton. Those instrumental in the treaty, including Double Head's brother and Double Head's close associate John Chisholm, received tracts of land at Muscle Shoals. Secret awards were also given. The Upper Towns Cherokee were angry and accused the Chickamaugans of violating "the ancient Cherokee law prohibiting the cession of lands without the National council's consent."[24] Also disputing the cession were the Upper Creeks who "said time out of mind they had claimed to the hunting grounds of the Tenesee, that their old camps were to be seen there long before the white man crossed the mountains."[25]

Double Head's gain was completely negated with his murder in June 1807 by a fatal blow administered by hatchet. He was disliked for many reasons. The book written by Thomas L. McKenney and James Hall, *History of the Indian Tribes of North America*, states he "made himself odious by his arbitrary conduct. He not only executed the laws according to his own pleasure, [he] caused innocent men to be put to death who thwarted his views. The chiefs and the people began alike to fear him." McKenney as superintendent of Indian trade from 1816 to 1822 and superintendent of Indian affairs from 1824 to 1830, is a credible authority. Thurman Wilkins, in his book *Cherokee Tragedy*, says the tomahawk was driven into Double Head's "forehead with such force that it took two hands and a foot against the cloven skull to pry it loose."[26]

Another possibly bribed, Tahlonteskee, fearing for his life, in 1809 led a group estimated at from 300 to 1,130 Chickamaugans to land in the present state of Arkansas. There was no treaty delineating the land they were to occupy in the West nor any cession of land in the East. However, a swap was contemplated in Tahlonteskee's statement that an exchange did not depend on the consent of the Cherokee nation. In 1811 Tahlonteskee wrote to Meigs that he wanted to trade his "half of the Cherokee Nation" for land on the Arkansas River.[27] It wasn't until treaties of 1817 and 1819 that the exchange received some definition.

Tahlonteskee's followers, and others relocated west of the Mississippi River, became known as the Western Cherokee. Meigs estimated in 1816 that they numbered over 2,000 but another estimate was over 3,000. It was not unusual for the Cherokee, Choctaw, and Chickasaw to hunt west of the Mississippi, and some Cherokee families settled there around 1800. By 1813 there were enough Cherokee in Arkansas for a United States' agent to be assigned to them. The agent, William L. Lovely, described his situation to President Madison in 1815: "I may say with propriety that I am entirely secluded from the land of the living surrounded on all sides by Indians together with the Worst of White settlers living just below me betwix whom there are daily disturbances arising & against whom there are no possible means in my power of enforcing any laws...."[28]

An "Elucidation"[29] of the 1806 treaty was signed on September 11, 1807, by Black Fox, and four other Indians. Black Fox was described in the 1806 treaty as "the old Cherokee chief" who was to receive $100 per year for life. In the 1807 "Elucidation" Black Fox is described as "the king or head chief of said Cherokee nation." The "Elucidation" defined the eastern limit of the land ceded in 1806 and provided that on the ceded land "Cherokee hunters ... may hunt ... untill by the fullness of settlers it shall become improper."

It may not be fair to criticize those negotiating the 1805 and 1806 treaties for the United States for the small amounts paid. The earlier treaty at Hopewell negotiated in 1785 by Hawkins and others considered sympathetic to the Cherokee made no payment for 6,381 square miles, over 4 million acres. However, if it had been complied with, the Wautaugans would have removed themselves from the headwaters of the Tennessee River. The growing importance of mixed-blooded members of the Cherokee nation is reflected in the treaty of 1805 making the large cession. Eight of the thirty-three signatures are of men with English names.

Jefferson hoped to have cessions along the eastern border of the Mississippi River to advance his concept of surrounding the Indians and forcing them into smaller and smaller areas with expansions of the settlers' territory surrounding them. Neither the Chickasaw or the Choctaw were willing to do this. However, they both had large debts with John Forbes and were willing to explore ways to lift their obligations, particularly when Forbes threatened to stop providing them with supplies.

On July 23, 1805, James Robertson, a land speculator, and agent Dinsmoor completed a treaty in which the Chickasaw ceded a band of land north of the Duck River and a large area in south-central Tennessee and some in northern to-be-Alabama, roughly 3 million acres for about 1 cent per acre, which was the average price being paid for Indian land. The treaty starts with the statement: "Whereas the Chickasaw nation of Indians have been for some time embarrassed by heavy debts due to their merchants and traders, and being destitute of funds to effect important improvements in their country have agreed and do hereby agree to cede to the United States...."[30] The United States established a factory for the Chickasaw at Chickasaw Bluffs in 1802. In about three years the Chickasaw ran up a debt of $12,000. Out of the $20,000 paid to the Chickasaw, half ended up with Forbes. Separate sums totaling $5,000 were paid to tribal leaders. In addition to the $20,000, payments of $1,000 were made to George Colbert and Chief O'Koy "for services rendered their nation" and a $100 annuity for life for "Chinubbee Mingo, the king of the nation."

The same negotiators reached agreement with the Choctaw on November 16, 1805. Ceded was a large tract, of over 4 million acres, along the Spanish boundary in the future states of Mississippi and Alabama. Other than paying off what was owed to Forbes, none of the immediate payment of $50,500 went to the nation, but the nation did receive a commitment of $3,000 per year for an indefinite period. The Choctaw agreed to having houses of accommodation along roads through their country. The cession included land east of the Tombigbee claimed by the Creeks. Jefferson, who thought the price paid was not enough, delayed presenting the treaty to the Senate and it was not proclaimed until 1808. After it was proclaimed, Big Warrior of the Creeks sent the Choctaw a talk: "You Choctaws have done thro with our land and we have now found you out.... I desire you will let me know why you gave land to the white people this side [of the Tombigbee River]."[31] Similar complaints to the United States were fruitless.

In a show of rancor Jefferson did not submit the treaty to the Senate until 1808. The negotiators were supposed to get land along the Mississippi River. When relations with Great Britain and Spain deteriorated Jefferson justified the treaty with the desirability of "obtain[ing a] footing for a strong settlement of militia along our southern frontier, eastward of the Mississippi."[32] Another Jefferson concern was information supplied by General Wilkinson about "Aaron Burr and other American adventurers' plans ... to invade Mexico or possibly Florida" and "to persuade the west to secede."[33]

Jefferson was not necessarily against the West breaking off from the rest of the union, but only under circumstances meriting such action. During the Adams administration he urged the Kentucky legislature to pass the Kentucky Resolutions, which claimed the right to declare federal laws unconstitutional. This was shortly after Senator William Blount, the former territorial governor over what became Tennessee, was accused of conspiring to establish an independent western federation and was expelled from the Senate over Jefferson's objections. In the face of opposition to the Louisiana Purchase by eastern Federalists, he was willing to see a new nation in the West. In August 1803 he wrote extolling the virtue of adding land mass and said if the acquisition resulted in some in the West wanting to separate, "why should the Atlantic States dread it."[34] They would have friendly instead of hostile neighbors on their Western waters.

Although Jefferson contemplated a policy aimed at removing the Indians west of the Mississippi after the Louisiana Purchase, he remained true, to a degree, with his concept of Indian sovereignty stated in 1792 in responding to questions from Washington: "I consider[] our right of pre-emption of the Indian lands not as amounting to any dominion, or jurisdiction, or paramountship whatever ... but of preventing other nations from taking possession, and ... that the Indians [had] the full, undivided and independent sovereignty as long as they choose to keep it, and that this might be forever."[35] In outlining his conversation with a British representative concerning the implementation of the peace treaty ending the Revolutionary War, Jefferson denied any intent "to exterminate the Indians and take the land." In fact, to the contrary, the policy was "to protect them, even against [U.S.] citizens." The Indians were considered as a "police, for scouring the woods on [the] borders, and preventing their being a cover for rovers and robbers."[36]

After the Louisiana Purchase Jefferson put a large part of what was to become Missouri and Arkansas, that is, land west of the Mississippi River, in the hands of the United States by a treaty in 1808 with the Great and Little Osage tribes with 2,200 warriors. Dearborn told Cherokee Indian agent Meigs to test the idea of a move to the West with the Eastern Cherokee. Nothing significant came of this. Hawkins admired Meigs but didn't like the fact that he speculated in Indian lands.

Meigs, at age 68, in 1808 had an illustrious career behind him as a Revolutionary War hero, a member of the settlers founding Marietta, Ohio, in 1788, a Northwest Territory judge, commissary of clothing in Anthony Wayne's army in 1795, and a member of Ohio's territorial legislature. Following the Cherokee treaty of 1806 many settlers moved into what became an Alabama area north of the Tennessee River. Those who relied on the Cherokee treaty soon found that the land was also claimed by the Chickasaw. In March 1809 the acting Secretary of War, John Smith, told Meigs to remove trespassers on Indian land, and Meigs, with a military detachment, proceeded to move families from Cherokee and Chickasaw land. The families left on request and Meigs told the secretary that "many of them [were] reputable well informed, & rich in Cattle & horses — no hunting[;] agriculture their sole pursuit."[37]

Meigs was not enthusiastic about removing families. He wrote to James Robertson in June 1809: "I removed 201 families off the Chickasaw lands, and 83 families off the Cherokee lands.... These people bear the appellation of intruders but they are Americans ... in our new country every man is an acquisition — we ought not to lose a single man for the want of land to work on."[38] The removal was not much considering that the territorial governor estimated 5,000 families might be on Indian land.

When either the same or other settlers moved back in as the year progressed, Meigs issued new warnings to settlers on the formerly cleared land. He sent a discouraging report to the secretary:

> The great length of this frontier, & the few troops in this quarter, puts it in the power of the people of the character mentioned to impose on the Indians & to put the U States on considerable expence. Should this disposition to make intrusions on Indian lands increase, they will perhaps at last put the few troops here at defiance. These intruders are always well armed, some of them shrewd & of desperate character, have nothing to lose & hold barbarous sentiments towards Indians. They see extensive tracts of forest exceedingly disproportioned to the present or expected population of the tribes who hold them. They take hold of these lands, some of them in hopes the land will be purchased, when they will plead a right of preemption, making a merit of their crimes. With these people remonstrance has no effect, nothing but force can prevent their violation of Indian rights.[39]

Meigs was relieved of any responsibility for clearing Chickasaw land when James Neelly was appointed Chickasaw agent. Neelly pressed the War Department and the governor of the Mississippi Territory, formed in April 1798, for help from the military. Governor David Holmes told the War Department that there were between four and five thousand whites on Indian land and troops were needed. In June 1810 Madison's Secretary of War responded. Notice was to be given for the trespassers to move in the fall and, if they didn't, soldiers would be sent to burn cabins and fences. The settlers sent a petition to Congress and the president, reading in part: "if you could have A true representation of our carractor the industry we have made and the purity of our intentions in settling here together With the Justice of our cause you would say in the name of God let them stay on and eat their well earned bread."[40] The size of the problem was represented as "2250 souls on what is called chickasaw land" all of whom "could live tollarable comfortable if [they] Could remain on [their] improvements."

Anarchy was afoot. The petition said the settlers could not agree to move and thereby "bring many women and children to a state of starvation mearly to gratify a heathan nation Who have no better right to this land than we have ourselves and they have by estemation nearly 100,000 acres of land to each man Of their nation and of no more use to government or society than to saunter about upon like so many wolves or bares whilst they who would be a supporte to government and improve the country must be forsed even to rent poor stoney ridges to make a support or rase their famelies on whilst there is fine fertile countrys lying uncultivated and we must be debared even from inJoying a small Corner of this land."[41]

20

The Creek War (1813–1814)

The Creeks were not pressed by the United States into ceding any more land between 1805 and 1814, but there were several instances of lethal clashes between whites and Indians preceding the start of a Creek civil war. Incursions by whites on Indian lands was common, as were instances of Indians stealing horses, hogs and cows. In 1809, when the Indians complained to Jefferson, they were told:

> Your land is your own. Nobody can make it smaller without your consent. The trees and game and every thing which your land produces is also your own. Nobody can touch them without your leave. The President will not allow them to do it. [Then, in a recognition of reality:] But you know there are some bad men every where....
>
> *   *   *
>
> You say you are poor ... Turn your ear to [the President] and believe what he says.
> Fence in your lands, plow as much land as you can, raise corn & hogs & cattle. Learn your young women to card & spin.... You will then have food and clothing and live comfortably.[1]

A rift with the United States occurred when, in 1810, the Secretary of War directed a military party to explore paths through the Creek nation without advising Hawkins. Learning of this Hawkins wrote the secretary that the "compass and chain is always dreaded by Indians and will be stopped."[2] Nonetheless, Hawkins saw the need for whites to use roads and watercourses within the Indian boundaries. The Federal Road authorized by the Creek in 1805 was in use. In January 1811 Hawkins said it was "crowded with travellers moving westward, for the safety of whose property at times [he had] some anxiety; yet [he had] but two complaints during the fall and winter; two horses and some bells were stolen."[3] Tame King wrote to the president that for whites to use roads and watercourses through Creek land could result in mischief and promised to assemble the Creek chiefs in the spring of 1811 to consider the president's response.

President James Madison was resolute on the need for transportation routes. On June 27, 1811, the Secretary of War told Hawkins: "It would give the president pain to do any acts which imply injustice to the Creek Nation, but the white inhabitants have their rights ... as well as the Indians.... [I]t remains for the Creeks to reconsider ... and to conclude whether it will not be to their interest to meet the good will which exists towards them, and to give their consent, rather than compel the government to the use of means which it is desirous to avoid."[4] At a general meeting of the Indians in September 1811, Hawkins told them the commander of United States' forces in the South had "received orders from the President to make [the needed roads] with the troops under his command."[5] Ferries and toll bridges were to remain the property of the Indians. A road from Fort Hawkins (near modern Macon, Georgia) to Fort Stoddert on the Mobile River was completed by November 30, 1811. Between October 1811 and March 1812, many vehicles (2,323) and people (3,726) passed Hawkins' agency. On a single day, April 6, 1812, twenty-two vehicles and 90 persons passed the agency.

It was at this September 1811 meeting that Tecumseh, in Hawkins' words, "encourage[d] the acceptance of the War pipe."[6] Tecumseh, a Shawnee living north of the Ohio River whose mother was a Creek and whose Shawnee father was killed during Pontiac's rebellion, traveled in the South in 1811 looking for allies to fight the whites. He claimed to have magical powers through the Master of Breath. To the Choctaws and Chickasaws, asking rhetorically what had become of the Narragansetts and Mohawk, he delivered a warning: "They have vanished before the avarice and oppression of the white man.... Sleep not longer, O Choctaws and Chickasaws, in false security and delusive hopes.... Are we not being stripped day by day of the little that remains of our ancient liberty?"[7] Neither nation was convinced to act.

A sample of his oration contains some truthful assertions:

> The white race is a wicked race. Since the day when the white race had first come in contact with the red men, there had been a continual series of aggressions. Their hunting grounds were fast disappearing, and they were driving the red men farther and farther to the west. Such had been the fate of the Shawnees, and surely would be the fate of ... [all tribes] if the power of the whites was not forever crushed.... His whiskey was destroying the bravery of their warriors.... The only hope for the red men was a war of extermination against the paleface. Would not the ... [warriors of] the ... southern tribes unite with the warriors of the Lakes.[8]

Then, traveling with "an impressive escort of twenty-four dignified and powerful warriors dressed in buckskin shirts and leggings, heavily hung with silver ornaments [wearing] red and black face paint and carr[ying] rifles, tomahawks, and war clubs,"[9] he went to the general meeting of the Creek National Council in the fall of 1811. He was intent on changing the relatively peaceful relations between the whites and Creeks of the years 1806–1810. Waiting until Hawkins left, he harangued the Creeks with a cry of "Let the white race perish!"[10] but was unable to convince Creek chief Big Warrior. However, he instilled a rebellious spirit in a number of Creeks. His claim of magical powers had special significance to the Creeks who "believed devoutly in the Master of Breath and in his priests, the Prophets, who could predict the result of a battle, foretell flood or drought, and even assume the power of directing thunder and lightning."[11] Tecumseh, who may have visited the Creeks again in 1812, was assessed by Hawkins as spreading "fanaticism."[12]

Tecumseh's speech to the National Council in 1811 had a spiritual context. Reportedly he vowed to leave prophets with the Creeks who would "stand between [the Creeks] and the bullets of [their] enemies. When the white men approach [the Creeks] the yawning earth shall swallow them up."[13] Tecumseh told of the future: "Soon shall you see my arm of fire stretched athwart the sky. I will stamp my foot at Tippecanoe [Indiana], and the very earth shall quake."[14] Legend is that Tecumseh left a bundle of "red-painted sticks ... one to be broken for each day until the last, the time set for an uprising synchronized with a British attack."[15] When an earthquake shook Creek lands in January 1812 shortly after Tecumseh left, other converts were made.

All Creeks were roiled when a representative of the Forbes company came to the Upper Creek town of Tuckabatchee in the fall of 1812 to arrange for payment of what was claimed to be a debt of $40,000. The Creeks refused to pay any interest, which was half of the

$40,000 claimed. The chiefs said the Creeks "were poor ... they knew nothing about interest, about what it meant, it might be a custom, a law among ... white people, but poor Indians did not understand it, there was no word for it in their language."[16] The best the Forbes' representative could get was a payment of $22,000 over three years, but such a commitment by the Creeks was the equivalent of all the money they were to receive for land ceded in the past over that three-year period.

Other events in 1812 and 1813 caused turmoil in the Creek nation — before it was over some Creeks declared war on whites and on those Creeks not willing to throw out the whites. Willing to do this were those, mostly Upper Creeks, who accepted Tecumseh's message and were known as either Red Clubs or Red Sticks. A series of murders leading to a showdown between whites and Creeks started in the spring of 1812 with the murder of two families on the Duck River in Tennessee and the imprisonment of a Mrs. Cawley, who was later rescued. In the same period "a respectable old man, travelling [the new road] with his family to the Mississippi territory"[17] in March 1812 was killed. Another murder in May was of a man near the home of Alexander Cornells.

Hawkins demanded that the Creek Council punish those Creeks responsible, and was able in September to tell the Secretary of War that the Creeks had "executed eight for murder, and seven were cropped and whipped for theft."[18] This action blunted a retaliatory campaign against the Creeks which Governor Willie Blount of Tennessee was urging on the United States. Ready to move with or without orders was Andrew Jackson, who spoke of "beloved wives and little prattling infants, butchered, mangled, murdered, and torn to pieces ... we are ready and pant for vengeance."[19] A Nashville paper asserted the Creeks had "supplied us with a *pretext* for the dismemberment of their country."[20] Jackson wrote Blount on July 3 that the "safety of [Tennessee's] whole frontier require[d], a speedy stroke against the Creeks." In August Blount was told by the Secretary of War that "he hoped the prompt manner in which the Indians ... administered justice on the offenders, [would] supersede the necessity of making a campaign against [the Creek]."[21]

The spark that led to the Creek civil war was ignited early in 1813. A group of Upper Creeks, returning from the Great Lakes where they had seen Tecumseh and were carrying talks to the "four Southern nations ... to take up the hatchet against the United States," murdered seven families near the mouth of the Ohio River. Hawkins told Big Warrior and other Creek chiefs that the "murderous outrage must be settled immediately."[22] Hawkins reported to the Secretary of War on April 6 that there had been a murder on the post road and that he had told the Upper Creeks "to call out their warriors immediately, and, if not sufficient, to call out the warriors of the Lower Creeks."[23]

Retribution followed swiftly. Between April 16 and 26 eleven "were executed for murders near the Ohio, on Duck River, and on the Federal Road."[24] Big Warrior, mistakenly, told Hawkins that the Creeks had no intention of following Tecumseh. When the chiefs who ordered the capture of the Red Stick murderers sent a message to Hopohielthle Micco of Tallassee (Tame King), an old Upper Creek chief who had joined the Red Sticks, saying they were willing to listen to what the Great Spirit had told him, the messenger, a warrior who was one of those who had killed the eight murderers, was slain. The Red Sticks also attacked and killed two more warriors who had been in the party punishing the Red Sticks, and said they would destroy the Upper Creeks town Tuckabatchee and the Lower Creeks town of Coweta and every person in them and kill Hawkins and the old chiefs taking "his talks" and all half-blooded Indians. Then they would be ready to destroy the white people.

General Wilkinson traveled east on the Federal Road through Creek country and described the situation in a letter dated June 29, 1813: "[Big Warrior] has been entrenched against the war party a week ... and lives in fear of his life. [His] antagonists are daily making converts and increasing [their] strength, with the avowed intention to destroy him and all who have been concerned in the execution of the murderers; after which, they expect to intimidate the rest of the nation to join them, and then... to make war on the whites."[25] In short order the Red Sticks took control of many Upper Creek towns.

It was a time to take sides. A majority of the Creek nation chose the Red Sticks, most of them being from the Upper towns. In June 1813 "one hundred and ninety friendly chiefs and warriors of Upper and Lower towns were gathered at Tuckabatchee, awaiting the threatened Red [Stick] attack."[26] Two hundred warriors came from Lower Creek towns, Cusseta and Coweta, and escorted those in danger from Tuckabatchee to Coweta. The Red Sticks were mindlessly advancing their vision. They ranged over the country killing cattle, hogs, fowls, and destroying other foods associated with civilization. They vowed to destroy everything received from the Americans. The Upper Creeks were incensed at roads being built to bring white settlers into the Creek nation.

The Cherokee sent help to the beleaguered at Coweta and warriors came from other towns not dedicated to the Red Sticks. Forays from Coweta damaged Red Stick towns. The scope of the rebellion escalated when Red Sticks under the leadership of Peter McQueen and William Weatherford, a nephew of Alexander McGillivray known as Chief Red Eagle, attacked Fort Mims on the Alabama River near the Florida boundary on August 30. Within the fort were perhaps 500 people, about half of whom were settlers, black and white, who had come into the fort for protection from the Red Sticks. Around 250 were slaughtered. The Red Sticks "behaved like demons, killing, dismembering, disemboweling, throwing living bodies into burning buildings, sparing neither women nor children."[27]

Writing about the savagery at Fort Mims, Hawkins said the Red Stick mystics were convinced of "the boasted power of the Prophet to take American forts with bows and arrows [and] to know the secrets of their enemies [and that the] Master of Breath [had] permitted a conquering spirit to arise among them [which would] ravage like a storm." Hawkins warned the Red Sticks, telling them that "war with the white people [would be their] ruin."[28] Although the die was cast after the Fort Mims massacre, one must wonder if the Red Sticks would have acted differently if they had had foreknowledge of Tecumseh's death on October 5, 1813, from wounds received in the Battle of the Thames in Canada at which William Henry Harrison decisively defeated a British army. Tecumseh was loyal to the British in the War of 1812, which was proclaimed to exist by Madison on June 19, 1812.

Those living in West Tennessee, afraid that the Upper Creeks would attack them, urged Jackson, head of the West Tennessee militia, to go on the offensive. The War Department devised a large-scale operation against the Creeks. In addition to a force under Jackson, one from East Tennessee and others from Georgia and the Mississippi Territory under the overall command of Major General Thomas Pinckney would "kill the Red Sticks, burn their villages, and destroy their crops."[29] Tennessee's governor Willie Blount, William Blount's half-brother, saw this as a golden opportunity for the people of the South and

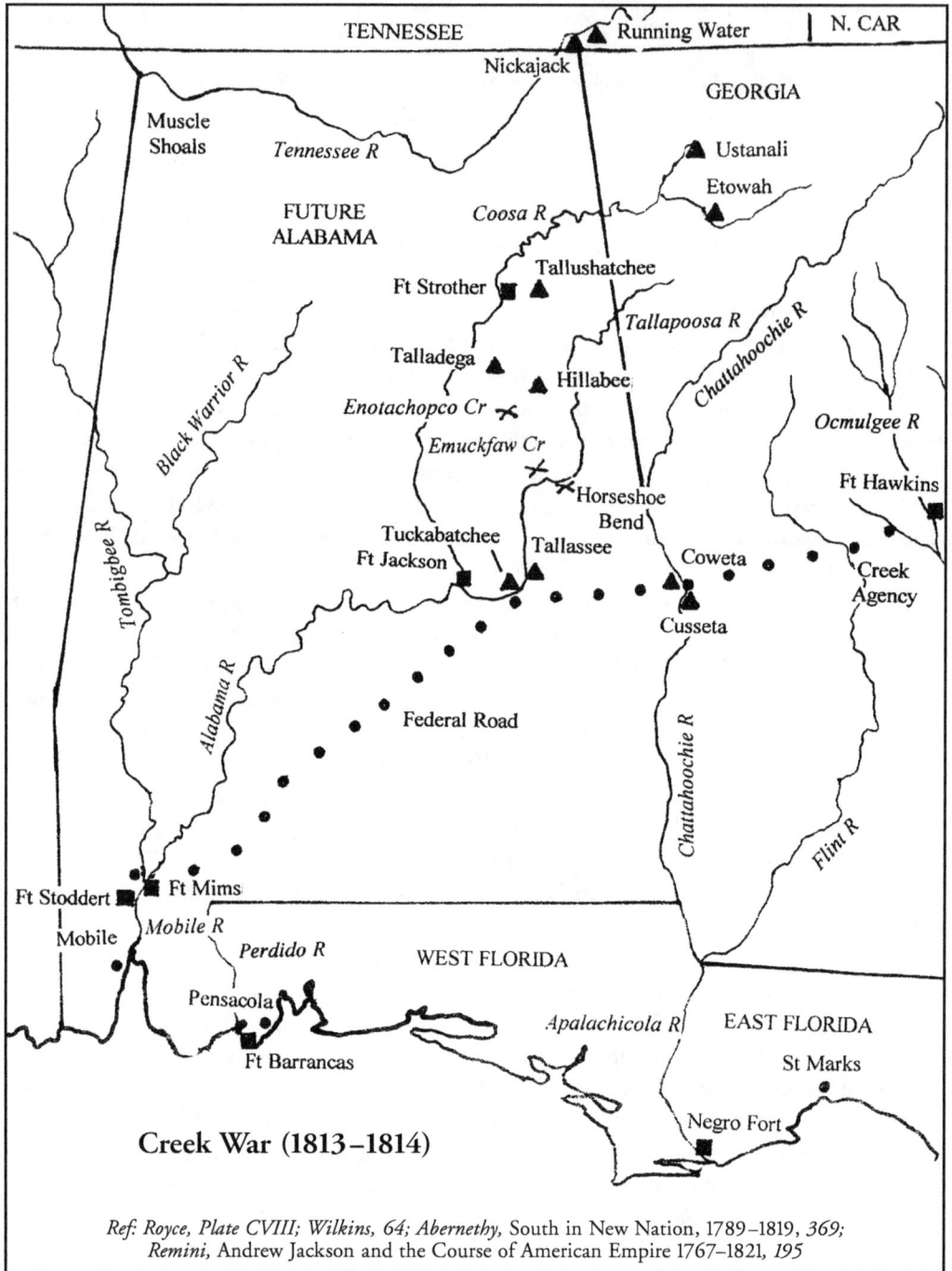

TENNESSEE   N. CAR
                          ▲ Running Water
              Nickajack
                                        GEORGIA

Muscle
Shoals   *Tennessee R*
                                        ▲ Ustanali
                                        Etowah
FUTURE   *Coosa R*   ▲
ALABAMA
                          Tallushatchee
              Ft Strother ■ ▲
                                        Tallapoosa R   *Chattahoochie R*
              Talladega ▲
                      ▲ Hillabee
        Enotachopco Cr
          Emuckfaw Cr   *Ocmulgee R*

                          Horseshoe
                          Bend   Ft Hawkins
              Tuckabatchee Tallassee   ■
              Ft Jackson ■ ▲ ▲   Coweta
                                      ▲
                                      Cusseta   Creek
                                                            Agency

                  Federal Road

Tombigbee R   *Alabama R*   *Chattahoochie R*   *Flint R*

Ft Stoddert ■ ■ Ft Mims
Mobile *Mobile R*
            Perdido R   WEST FLORIDA
        Pensacola
                                      Apalachicola R   EAST FLORIDA
          Ft Barrancas   St Marks

Creek War (1813–1814)   Negro Fort ■

Ref: Royce, Plate CVIII; Wilkins, 64; Abernethy, South in New Nation, 1789–1819, *369;*
Remini, Andrew Jackson and the Course of American Empire 1767–1821, *195*

West to "become the cultivators of the rich soil, which they may ... soon become possessed of by their valor."[30]

Andrew Jackson was a primary force in stripping the Creeks of about one-half their land. Once described as "an angry young man who became an angry old man,"[31] Jackson carried proof of how his anger could carry him to extreme measures. During his life he had in his body a bullet from a duel, in which his opponent, who fired first but not with deadly consequences, was shot and killed by Jackson with unhurried deliberation. Born in South Carolina in 1767, of Scotch-Irish parents, as a thirteen-year-old he participated in the Revolutionary War Battle of Hanging Rock and was later captured by the British.

He was orphaned at fourteen and lived with relatives for a few years before moving to North Carolina in 1784. After qualifying to practice law in North Carolina, he moved to Tennessee and ended up in Nashville, where he successfully practiced law and served as a public prosecutor. He married the daughter of one of Nashville's founders, John Donelson, under circumstances that caused bitter words in later years. Rachel had been married and was not divorced at the time she and Andrew married in 1791; her first husband was granted a divorce in 1794 on grounds of desertion and "adultery with another man."[32] To besmirch Rachel's name was like asking for a challenge to duel — later, in the political arena, Jackson struck out at anyone doing so.

Indian attacks along the Cumberland River in the 1790s were common. Young Jackson loathed Indians and the British and Spanish, who often supplied Indians with gunpowder and bullets, and the federal government which entered into the Jay Treaty. At age 29 he was elected to represent Tennessee in the House. His political career was nourished by William Blount, the governor of the Territory of the South, which became the state of Tennessee on June 1, 1796. He immediately showed his independence by joining with a few others refusing to vote for the lavish praise of George Washington contained in a congressional response to Washington's Farewell Address. He was unforgiving of Washington's support of the Jay Treaty, which Jackson saw as a show of national weakness.

After his term in the House, Blount pushed him to be elected to the Senate, which he was, but it was a position he did not relish. He resigned that office in 1798 and, shortly thereafter, was elected to serve as a judge on Tennessee's highest court, a position he held for six years. When Blount died in March 1800, Jackson became a leading political figure in western Tennessee. A heated contest with John Sevier, the first Tennessee governor, over who would be the major general of the Tennessee militia escalated in 1803 into a public square confrontation in Knoxville at which first words and then bullets were exchanged. Sevier committed the greatest of sins when he spoke of Jackson "taking a trip to Natchez with another man's wife." Neither man was struck but Jackson challenged Sevier to a duel, referring to Sevier's "gasgonading conduct." Sevier accepted the challenge, speaking of Jackson's "scurilous and paltroon language."[33] When the two men, each with supporters, confronted one another, curses and verbal exchanges seemingly satisfied each and the challenge was not renewed. Sevier, after being out of office, was again elected governor and what had been personal animosity became a split in political leadership between East and West Tennessee.

In the West of the early 1800s "[a]ny scheme was a good one — indeed a patriotic one — if it advanced western land and trading interests. Any scheme was a good one if it expelled the Indians and Spanish."[34] Such would have been Jackson's mind set as he prepared to fight the Creeks in 1813.

Although the Red Sticks were attacked in October 1813 by a force of Mississippians which moved up the Alabama River and by the Georgia militia which crossed the Chattahoochee and struck a Red Stick village on November 29, only Jackson's army inflicted substantial harm in the fall of 1813. On November 3 he sent about 1,000 cavalry and mounted riflemen to destroy the village of Tallushatchee near the Coosa River in what is now northeast Alabama. Most of the 200 warriors there were killed, as were women and children. Davy Crockett said they were "shot ... like dogs."[35] Eighty women and children who survived were taken prisoner, and Jackson took responsibility for an infant taken from a dead mother who he sent home and raised as one of his family. Six days later, at the village of Talladega where friendly Indians were surrounded by Red Eagle, Jackson struck with about 2,000 men, twice those with Red Eagle. About 300 Red Sticks were slain but 700 were able to escape. In the two battles Jackson's army only had 20 dead.

In November, Hillabee, a town offering to surrender was attacked by a thousand East Tennessee militia. General James White, nominally under Jackson's command, moved without Jackson's knowledge, and perhaps being unaware of the offer to surrender. White reported that the militia "lost not a drop of blood, and Fort Mims was again avenged."[36]

A shortage of supplies and expiration of the enlistments of most of his army left Jackson virtually army-less at the end of December. This would have happened earlier except for Jackson, almost singlehandedly, facing down military units preparing to return to Tennessee. To make matters worse, Jackson received orders from Willie Blount to return to the Tennessee frontier. Blount, a Jackson supporter, received a scorching Jackson letter written on December 29 couched in language leaving no doubt as to Jackson's reaction:

> Is the campaign ended? Is protection afforded to the frontiers of the Territory ... is the creek nation exterminated or conqueored? ... The answer is plain, is it not? ... And are you my Dear friend sitting with yr. arms folded under the present situation of the campaign recommending me to retrograde to please the whims of the populace and waiting for further orders from the Secy war. Let me tell you it imperiously lies upon both you and me to do our duty regardless of consequences or the opinions of these fireside patriots, those fawning sycophants or cowardly paltroons who after all their boasted ardor, would rush home or remain [at the] fireside and let thousands fall victims to my retrograde.[37]

The letter seemed to have an effect. Blount ordered a new levy of men, and on January 14, 800 new recruits reached Fort Strother near Tallushatchee, where Jackson was located. Seven days later he had the new recruits, along with 400 additional men and some friendly Creeks, on the march toward a Red Stick fortress at Horseshoe Bend. Red Eagle attacked him at his campsite on Emuckfaw Creek, just three miles from Horseshoe Bend. But for a decision of a Red Stick tribe to break off from the battle and return to its village, Jackson might have been routed. He headed back to Fort Strother and was again attacked as he crossed Enotachopco Creek; he was able to fight off the Red Sticks and leave them with 200 dead, compared to an American loss of 20 dead and 75 wounded.

Back at Fort Strother new troops arrived and by March he had 5,000 men who he turned into a disciplined force, and on March 14 started back to the Bend. The Red Sticks had about 1,000 braves at the Bend together with 300 women and children. The Bend was "a 100-acre wooded peninsula almost completely surrounded by water and with a stout breastwork running across its 350-yard neck."[38] To attack the Bend Jackson had between 2,000 to 3,000 troops, including some friendly Cherokees. Later Jackson wrote to General Thomas Pinckney, his next level of command, that "[it was] impossible to conceive a situation more eligible for defence than the one [chosen by the Red Sticks and that] the skill which they manifested in their breastwork, was really astonishing."[39]

Nonetheless, on March 27 Jackson sent a force across the river which partially surrounded the Bend to block any Creek retreat and directed that a diversion be made from that direction. A two-hour artillery barrage at the breastworks did little damage but the diversion to the Red Sticks' rear created the opportunity for the main force to rush the breastworks. One of those going over the wall was Ensign Sam Houston, who was struck by an arrow but continued to fight. In his autobiography Houston described the scene: "Arrows, and spears, and balls were flying; swords and tomahawks were gleaming in the sun; and the whole Peninsula rang with the yell of the savage, and the groans of the dying."[40] Once the breastwork was overcome, Jackson reported the "carnage was dreadful."[41] Notwithstanding, the Indians refused to surrender, and most of the warriors were killed. However, missing was Chief Red Eagle who was not in the compound. Jackson had 47 army dead and 23 friendly Creeks and Cherokees were killed.

In the main what is called the Creek Civil War was over but severe retribution was yet to come. Many Red Sticks surrendered, including Red Eagle, many fled to Florida, and many unbowed were spread over the Lower Creek lands. Although earlier Jackson would possibly have been severe with Red Eagle as payment for the slaughter at Fort Mims, he was impressed with the dignity and courage displayed in his surrender. Red Eagle made no apology for the war and said "I have done the white people all the harm I could; I have fought them, and fought them bravely: if I had an army, I would yet fight, and contend to the last: but I have none; my people are all gone. I can now do no more than weep over the misfortunes of my nation."[42] He was released after agreeing to use his influence to bring others to the peace table. Later he became an Alabama planter and on occasion visited Jackson's home, the Hermitage, near Nashville. Tame King was surrendered by his former followers and died, maybe at age 95, on June 12, 1814.

Hawkins commented on the futility of the Red Sticks warfare in August 1814: "cattle were killed, the gins smashed, and the axes, hoes, and ploughs flung into the rivers to rust. Theirs was a starvation course, win or lose, because natural resources were by then so depleted that the Creeks could not feed themselves in their traditional ways, and by destroying the tools and domesticated animals of the new way they lost their only means of survival."[43]

21

Andrew Jackson's 20 Million Acres and the Battle of New Orleans (1814–1815)

Jackson rebuilt the French Fort Toulouse at the confluence of the Coosa and Tallapoosa rivers and named it Fort Jackson. There he dictated a treaty titled Articles of Agreement and Capitulation, signed on August 9, 1814. Historian John F. Doster, who wrote *The Creek Indians and Their Florida Lands 1740–1823*, after a detailed review of the background to the agreement, called it "an instrument of robbery."[1] Out of 20 million acres ceded to the United States he considers the 8 million acres of Lower Creek land to have been stolen. The crux of Doster's conclusion is that of the 35 chiefs signing, only one was a Red Stick chief. The chiefs who had not made war on the United States, and had contributed warriors in battles against the Red Sticks, were forced to agree to this huge cession of land. Treaty language reflects why they were willing to do so: "The Creek nation being reduced to extreme want, and not at present having the means of subsistance, the United States ... will continue to furnish gratuitously the necessaries of life."[2]

A sequence of events after the battle of Horseshoe Bend put the friendly Creeks at Jackson's mercy. Absent knowledge of Jackson's victory the Secretary of War gave General Pinckney guidelines for peace with the hostile Indians. "[I]ndemnification (for expenses incurred by the United States in prosecuting the war)"[3] should be made by cessions of land. In early April the secretary said "the proposed treaty with the Creeks should take a form altogether military, and be in the nature of a *capitulation*" and the authority to make and set terms would rest "exclusively [with the] Commanding General."[4] Pinckney understood this approach would leave the decision as to "the quantum and location of the lands to be ceded as indemnity ... [to] Commissioners to be appointed by the President."[5] When Pinckney and Hawkins were appointed as commissioners, there was an outcry from Tennessee — Tennessee wanted a presence.

Pinckney, with the responsibility of preparing for a possible attack by the British, left it up to Hawkins to tell the Indians the terms of surrender. Hawkins, following Pinckney's instructions in a letter of April 23, 1814, communicated to the Indians terms much different from those included in the Articles of Agreement and Capitulation later signed on August 9. Pinckney had said retribution was to be made "for the injuries sustained by [whites] and by the friendly Creek Indians." As to the friendly Indians "the United States [would] not forget their fidelity; ... in the arrangements ... made of the lands to be retained as indemnity, their claims will be respected."[6] Any friendly Creek understanding these terms did not expect to come out of the war worse off in a land sense than they were before.

The landscape changed entirely when Jackson was appointed a brigadier general of the line in the regular army with a brevet of major general on May 22. And then, a few days later, when William Henry Harrison, angry with the administration, gave up his commission, Jackson was appointed major general in charge the Seventh Military District which covered Louisiana, Tennessee, and the Mississippi Territory. Unfortunately for the friendly Creeks Jackson was directed to "consummate the arrangements committed to Major General Pinckney in relation to the hostile Creeks."[7] If Jackson had his way it would have been bad news for others; in a May 18 letter to Pinckney he said, "Now is the time ... to extinguish the cherokee and chikesaws claims with the state of T."[8]

Jackson, referred to by the Indians as Sharp Knife or Pointed Arrow, arrived at Fort Jackson on July 10 and immediately told Hawkins the first day of August was set for "chiefs of the hostile creeks" to meet with him.[9] Hawkins described what happened:

> ... General Jackson as sole commissioner ... addressed a speech to the chiefs, among whom there was but a single hostile one.... [He] marked his line [and was asked by the chiefs why, since] his powers extended only to retaining as much land conquered from the hostiles as would indemnify the United States ... he took the lands eastwardly to Georgia, belonging obviously to the friendly Indians.... [He] answered, he did it from political motives — to prevent an intercourse between the Indians and the Spaniards and English in the Floridas.[10]

The friendly Creeks signed the treaty with reservations stated in a document they called "their part of the treaty" which never reached the president or Senate, even though Jackson agreed to send it. Consequently, it was not considered when the Articles were studied for ratification. It stated: "We have adhered faithfully, in peace and war, to our treaty stipulations with the United States.... [W]e rely on the ... United States to cause justice to be done us ... [and] request that General Pinckney's letter of the 23d April to Colonel Hawkins ... be sent on with the treaty, which we will sign after delivering this instrument."[11]

Strange as it seems, 8 million acres of Lower Creek land were taken from friendly Indians who had acted as allies, nine-tenths of whom "had left their old towns and formed new settlements on creeks and rivers, where lands and stock ranges were good." Their efforts to become civilized were not respected nor were their wartime efforts. The total cession was the southern fifth of both Georgia and the present state of Alabama and a core part of Alabama. The Creek were left with land in eastern Alabama and western Georgia. Jackson, in his words, took "20 million acres of the cream of the Creek Country, opening a communication from Georgia to Mobile."[12] Jackson's concept of strong frontiers was land occupied by "thick and wealthy inhabitants, unmixed by Indians."[13]

The introductory language of the treaty justified taking land from the hostile Indians but not the friendly: "Whereas an unprovoked, inhuman and sanguinary war, waged by the hostile Creeks against the United States, hath been repelled, prosecuted and determined, successfully, on the part of the said States ... [t]he United States demand an equivalent [in land] for all expences incurred in prosecuting the war."[14]

On its side the United States guaranteed "to the Creek nation, the integrity of all their [remaining] territory [in modern eastern Alabama and Georgia]"; however, it was subject to the United States "establish[ing] military posts and trading houses, and [opening] roads" in it and free navigation of its waters. Important to Jackson was the demand that the Creeks "abandon all communication, and cease to hold any intercourse with any British or Spanish post, garrison, or town."[15]

A defense of this land grab, which went to the borders between Florida and Georgia and the to-be-Alabama, was a danger known to Jackson as early as June 27. The British were establishing bases in Spanish Florida. In the early years of the War of 1812 England was battling Napoleon in Europe and did not give the attention to America that it did after Napoleon was overthrown in April 1814. A discouraging result of the increased British presence was the capture and burning of Washington on August 24–25.

Anticipating a British advance starting at either Mobile or Pensacola, Jackson first moved to occupy Mobile, which was 400 miles through a wilderness from Fort Jackson. His force covered that distance in 11 days and arrived on August 22.

An irony is Hawkins' reliance on friendly Creeks after Jackson took 8 million acres of their land. On October 5, 1814, he reported to the Secretary of War[16] that Major William McIntosh, a half-breed Coweta chief, was marching with 300 to 400 warriors "to seize the British arms and ammunition on the lower Apalachicola River." They did this while at the same time complaining against the United States for "withholding their annuity for 1812, '13, and '14." Hawkins painfully described the injustice being shown to these friendly Indians: "They are called on for warriors, for runners, and other purposes, without receiving any pay for the services they have often willingly performed. They are now in a manner naked, their hunting done, their resources destroyed by their civil war, and they are without the means of clothing their helpless people and themselves, and winter is approaching."

On October 10 James Monroe, made Secretary of War while retaining his position as Secretary of State, warned Jackson of a large expedition coming from England to take New Orleans. The outlook for protecting New Orleans was grim. Jackson left Mobile on November 22, 1814, with 2,000 men whereas British Vice Admiral Sir Alexander Cochrane had 60 ships and 14,000 men *en route* to capture New Orleans. The stage was set for Jackson to make himself a national hero of Washingtonian proportions. At 47 years of age he arrived in New Orleans on December 1 and on December 13 the British flotilla arrived. Over the days before December 13 Jackson stayed flexible as to how his forces should be positioned. That could only be decided after he knew what route the British would take to come to the city. A valuable ally, the pirate Jean Lafitte, who was also courted by the British, agreed, on terms, to provide 1,000 men to help in defense of the city, and the help of free blacks was also sought.

A series of fortuitous circumstances came together to give Jackson an amazing victory. Timely arrival of troops from Tennessee and Mississippi, a daring escape of Major Gabriel Villere permitting Jackson to be warned of the path being taken by the British, and a decision of the British advance force to wait on the main body rather than advancing on a relatively undefended New Orleans were early breaks for the Americans.

On December 24 Jackson decided to put his men in a ditch about four feet deep and ten feet wide which barred the British path to the city. Work was undertaken to make the ditch a more formidable barrier. Then another fortunate event occurred. A new British general arrived to take charge — Lieutenant General Edward Michael Pakenham. He proved to have valor but not good judgment. On December 26 a British advance against the ditch failed and Pakenham brought in heavy cannons. The three days he took to do this were used by Jackson to make his ditch more protective of his soldiers and to position more artillery. On January 1 another artillery exchange caused a small number of deaths on each side but left the parties still facing one another. Pakenham decided to wait for more troops and during the next few days Jackson also received more men. The final showdown came on January 8.

At 4 A.M. on that date the British tried to storm the 4,000 men Jackson had in the ditch. Their losses were substantial and included Pakenham. The battle was over by 10 o'clock in the morning. Jackson only had 13 killed. It is uncertain as to how many English were killed on January 8 but during the whole campaign they had 291 deaths. Following the battle Pakenham's body was placed in a hogshead of rum and returned to England. Jackson credited his victory to "the unerring hand of providence [which] shielded [his] men from the showers of Balls, bombs and Rocketts, when every [American] Ball and Bomb ... carried with them the mission of death."[17]

If the war had continued there were still 6,000 English soldiers available in the area. This became unimportant — news of the Treaty of Ghent, signed on December 24, 1814, ending the war reached New York on February 11. News of Jackson's victory at New Orleans reached Washington on February 4 and made Jackson a national hero. On February 14 the *Niles Weekly Register* exclaimed: "Glory be to God that the barbarians have been defeated ... Glory to Jackson ... Glory to the militia.... Sons of freedom ... benefactors of your country ... all hail!"[18]

22

Exploiting the Mississippi Territory (1815–1816)

As stated by Robert V. Remini in his book *Andrew Jackson and the Course of American Empire 1767–1821,* the War of 1812 "triggered the ruination of the American Indian and the spoliation of his property."[1] The British provided for their Indian allies in words but not in deeds. Article 9 of the Treaty of Ghent specified hostile tribes should have "all the possessions ... which they may have enjoyed or been entitled to in [1811] previous to such hostilities." The Creeks wanted back the 20 million acres ceded at Fort Jackson in August 1814 and removal of settlers from that land. The Secretary of War told Jackson to comply with Article 9 and he did according to his own sense of what was required. He reasoned that the Creeks were already out of the war as a result of the treaty at Fort Jackson and therefore Article 9 did not apply to them. This ignored all of the Creeks that did not sign the Fort Jackson treaty, but there was no way Jackson was going to give the land back. The Madison administration wasn't in a position to tell the war hero, who was doing what most of those living in the West wanted, to act differently, and the British did not insist on another interpretation. And the truth of the matter was that the administration approved of the outcome of Jackson's actions.

Following the Treaty of Ghent Jackson was given command of the southern division of the army — that is, the force south of the Ohio River — and made his headquarters at his home, the Hermitage, near Nashville. There was plenty of activity in 1815. Lieutenant-Colonel Edward Nicholls, who had organized the Creeks to fight against the United States as British allies, was still in Florida and encouraged the Creeks to rely on Article 9 of the treaty and dispute the boundaries set in the Fort Jackson treaty. After the Fort Jackson treaty was proclaimed on February 16, 1815, opposition to it came from several sources. The angry, formerly friendly Indians, being dispossessed, clashed with whites moving onto the ceded land and opposed the Fort Jackson boundaries. Raids from untamed Red Sticks and Seminoles continued.

To take advantage of the ceded land the United States appointed Commissioners of Limits to lay out the boundary lines. When one of the commissioners, Captain William Barnett, stationed at Fort Stoddert, did not go through Hawkins in asking for a meeting with the chiefs, Big Warrior told him "he knew him not and not go one step."[2] The chiefs complained to Hawkins: "This treaty called Jacksons which took almost the whole of the lands of the Hostiles and a very large part of that belonging to the Indians who had always been friendly to the United States was made different from all other treaties. It had but one side to it. The side belonging to the friendly Indians [who opposed the treaty] was loped off and the whole to be concluded without their participating in it."[3]

In June 1815 Hawkins advised the Secretary of War that some friendly chiefs were becoming "lukewarm toward [the United States since] their annuity for 1812, 13, 14 & 15 is withheld from them without [telling] then any cause for it."[4] When the president asked Hawkins about the friendly Indians' objections to the boundary, Hawkins said, "Justice is on the side of the [Creek Indians]"[5] and they may refuse to ratify the treaty. At the same time Hawkins asked Jackson about the Indians' "part of the treaty" and predicted if it was not considered there would be "much more trouble in perfecting [Jackson's] capitulation than [Jackson] had in making it."[6]

On June 29 Governor David Holmes of the Mississippi Territory extended the territorial laws to the ceded land west of Georgia. This prompted Hawkins to ask the Secretary of War if the United States intended to proceed to mark the Fort Jackson boundaries whether or not the Creeks ratified the treaty. The Commissioners of Limits, Barnett and John Sevier, were at Ft. Jackson when Hawkins, also a commissioner, wrote them, on August 19, that he would try to get the Creeks to ratify the treaty. The reply was blunt: "We know of no ratification the Creeks have yet to make of any capitulation ... nor do we know of any preliminaries."[7] Sevier's attitude should not have been a surprise — he had been taking Indian lands for decades. In this case it was consistent with the fact that the United States proclaimed the treaty on February 16, 1815. Jackson sent a talk from Nashville on September 4 advising the Creeks they had no options: "Listen I now tell you that line must and will be run, and the least opposition brings down instant destruction on the heads of the opposers."[8]

Land grabbers introduced another dimension. The Secretary of War wrote Hawkins on October 16: "I understand that the land lately ceded ... is rapidly settling by whites. This must not be permitted.... [Pre-emptors] deprive the government of the profitability of receiving more than two dollars per acre."[9] By December 1815 the Creeks were reconciled to the line being run by a force of 800 but not to settlers — they told Hawkins "an attempt to run out and settle the lands [would] be resisted with all their force."[10]

The whites were not satisfied to march into the ceded land; Hawkins reported in January 1816 that they settled across the Ocmulgee River, the eastern boundary of land in Georgia which the Creeks retained by the Fort Jackson treaty, and that "numerous herds of cattle [were] driven over to winter on the Indian lands."[11] When a party of Indians murdered two white men in the ceded territory, Jackson "instantly gave orders that all Indians on the ceded Territory should remove from it, with the exception of those friendly Indians secured in possession of their improvements by the late treaty of Fort Jackson."[12] Very few Creeks fit into this exception.

A calming force in white–Indian relations was lost when Hawkins died at the Creek Agency on June 6, 1816. His even-handed approach, with a tilt to whites, is evidenced in the names of seven children born to his wife Lavinia, who he married in 1812: Georgia, Muscogee, Cherokee, Carolina, Virginia, Jeffersonia, and Madison. Compared to the opportunities he had to profit from land deals, his estate of $65,990 was modest. His replacement, David B. Mitchell, who resigned as governor of Georgia, was more supportive of the Indians than would have been expected from a Georgian, but he was not the steadfast friend to the Creeks that Hawkins had been. Mitchell was appointed on March 1, 1817.

A partial accommodation with the friendly Creeks was reached when Chief William McIntosh of Coweta and others went to Washington early in 1817 and came away with $85,000 to compensate friendly Creeks for property destroyed by hostile Creeks. While in

Washington a land cession was proposed which McIntosh said should be presented to the Creek head men. McIntosh, who is described as "[b]rave, sly, smart, avaricious, and calculating,"[13] was a major force in the Creek nation until he was executed by Creeks in April 1825 for violating Creek law. He was a literate half-blooded Creek who acted courageously as a war chief in the Creek War and had a cousin who for a time was governor of Georgia — George Troup.

Jackson, on March 4, 1817, let the newly installed president, James Monroe, know his attitude toward Indians: "I have long viewed treaties with the Indians an absurdity not to be reconciled to the principles of our Government. The Indians are the subjects of the United States, inhabiting its territory and acknowledging its soverignty, then is it not absurd for the soverign to negotiate by treaty with the subject.... Congress [has] as much right to regulate by act of Legislation, all Indian concerns as they [can for the] Territories."[14] Monroe's Secretary of War, John C. Calhoun, agreed.

Indicative of improved relations between the Creek nation and the United States was a cession of roughly one million acres of land within Georgia on January 22, 1818. One parcel was south of the Ocmulgee River and a lesser amount along the Ocmulgee near present-day Atlanta. A total payment of $120,000 was made, spread over ten years; this was close to 8 cents per acre. The "kings, chiefs, head men, and warriors of the Creek nation" signing, 18 in number, met at the Creek Agency on the Flint River. One signatory was McIntosh, who soon was made a brigadier general by Jackson and placed in command of about 1500 Indians recruited to accompany Jackson on a move against the Seminole Indians in Florida. A cooperative attitude was easy to achieve when the Creeks could only look to the United States for the necessities their lifestyle required. As noted hereafter later statements of McIntosh indicated that bribes played a part in getting the cession.

A part of Jackson's character was displayed in his treatment of the Cherokee. On August 5, 1814, at Fort Jackson he recognized that the Cherokee had fought with him in the Creek War and told a group of Cherokee that "in battle you have been brave [and] I am charged by your father President of the United States to say to you, Chiefs and Warriors, that your conduct has met with his entire approbation."[15] But when the Cherokee, through their agent Meigs, asked for and received payment "for losses suffered by the wanton maraudings and depredations of the Tennessee levies on their marches and counter marches though the Cherokee country,"[16] which Meigs had recorded as events happened, Jackson, in July 1816, told the Secretary of War the claims were a "complete tissue of groundless falsehood."[17] This must have astounded the Cherokee, who had shared their limited food with Jackson after the drought of 1813 when his army needed it.

Jackson's anger was directed even more to the effort of the Cherokee to preserve their land. The treaty at Fort Jackson in 1814 did not take a position on a dispute between the Creek and Cherokee over the northern boundary of the Creek cession in the to-be-state of Alabama. At the time of the treaty Jackson told them to settle it themselves, which they were unable to do. A suggestion of Creek agent Hawkins that "each nation should establish the distance they had carried their tomahawk into each other's country and between the extreams [sic] should be the line,"[18] although considered by each tribe, was rejected by the Creek. This left the decision to the commissioners appointed by the president to lay out the boundary lines of the cession, Hawkins, Barnett, and Sevier.

Two of the boundary line commissioners, Hawkins and Barnett, met with the two nations in September 1815 but no agreement was reached. Fearful that the commissioners would include some Cherokee land in the Creek cession, the Cherokee decided to take their case to the president and were given permission to come to Washington. The delegation was led by John Lowrey, a member of the National Committee established in 1809 to speak for the Cherokee nation. The delegation was authorized to make a cession of land to South Carolina which Madison had requested "for a valuable consideration." Of the delegation the *National Intelligencer* said it was "men of cultivation and understanding ... entitle[d] ... to respect and attention."[19]

When the delegation arrived in Washington in February 1816, Jackson was also there. According to Thurman Wilkins' book *Cherokee Tragedy*, which relies on an extraordinary number of primary sources, Jackson "knew the purpose of the delegation and had no intention of allowing them to repossess land he had assigned to the Creeks so that, in turn, he could squeeze more land for the United States [into] the Creek cession."[20] When Jackson left Washington he thought he had accomplished that end, but he underestimated the Cherokee delegation.

In a show of diplomacy the delegation did not include in presentations to the president and others this passage in a memorandum prepared to support their boundary claim: "Father, you have with you, as with us red children, those who make crooked talks; they, like the serpent, speak with a split tongue. Believe not their talks, for they are false.... The spirit of gain urges them, the laurel of popularity prompts them, and we, your faithful children of the Cherokee nation, ... are to fall a sacrifice to their rapaciousness."[21] The Cherokee were not ignorant of what was going on and were wise enough to not make it the core of their meetings.

Jackson was incensed with the Madison administration when a treaty, signed on March 22, 1816,[22] recognized a Cherokee claim to near 1.3 million acres, in northern present-day Alabama south of the Tennessee River, which Jackson thought the Creeks ceded in the Fort Jackson treaty. The Cherokee claim was based on a treaty dated January 7, 1806. The 1806 treaty specifically stated that the Cherokee claimed land "southward of the Tennessee river" and enlisted the aid of the United States to get the Chickasaw to agree to a boundary with the Cherokee in that area.

The 1816 treaty provided for a $25,000 payment to the Cherokee for damage caused within the nation "as a consequence of the march of the militia and other troops in the service of the United States through that nation," the claim Jackson had labeled a "tissue of ... falsehood." A valuable provision in the treaty gave the United States "the right to lay off, open, and have the free use of, such road or roads, through any part of the Cherokee nation, lying north of the boundary line [being] established, as may be deemed necessary for the free intercourse between the States of Tennessee and Georgia and the Mississippi Territory. And the citizens of the United States shall freely navigate and use as a highway, all the rivers and waters within the Cherokee nation." On the same date the Cherokee made a cession to South Carolina of roughly 100,000 acres for $5,000.

Jackson felt the March 1816 treaty was a personal humiliation. He may have given little attention to Madison's statement to the Cherokee delegation that the United States "wish[ed] to do everything for the promotion of civilization."[23] The "civilization" policy was taken seriously by the Cherokee. In May 1797 Benjamin Hawkins told the Secretary of War that "[t]he Cherokees are giving proof of their approximation to the customs of well regulated societies; they did in full council, in my presence, pronounce, after solemn deliberation, as law, that any person who should kill another accidentally should not suffer for it, but be acquitted; that to constitute it a crime, there should be malice and an intention to kill."[24] An expansion of this policy was adopted in 1808 after Double Head had been killed. Thereafter "the infliction of punishment [was to be] a governmental transaction."[25] An object of this extension was to relieve members of the Double Head clan of a duty to seek revenge for his death.

In this change the Cherokee were going against a "blood debt" tradition embraced by most Indians. Any killing, accidental or otherwise, called for revenge on the killer's people by the deceased's relations. If the killer was from another tribe the revenge would be taken against someone in that tribe. Revenge need not be against the person responsible for the death. This tradition played well in the desire of young Indians to succeed in war to enhance their position in their society. When applied on a larger scale "blood debt" could justify continuous warfare between different tribes — such was the case between the Cherokee and Creek from 1715 to 1753.

The Cherokee did more than adopt a policy of tribal punishment in the place of individual retribution. A Lighthorse Guard of two "regulating companies" of six men each was established. The Guard took "cognisance of all crimes and breaches of law, and [decided] all controversies between individuals."[26] One job of the Guard was to remove white trespassers on Cherokee land. To be sure they didn't come back, often homes and crops were burned. Another advance toward the white man's civilization was adoption of a constitution in 1810.

To Jackson those agreeing with the Cherokee in 1816 did a "wanton, hasty, useless thing" and the "hight of [his] diplomatic ambition" was to undo it.[27] Jackson's rage and that of other westerners caused Madison's Secretary of War to appoint commissioners, including Jackson, to negotiate boundary lines with the Cherokee, Choctaw, and Chickasaw. Considering Jackson's belief that the United States had the right to "occupy and possess [any Indian territory] whenever the safety, interest or defence of the country"[28] required it, this did not bode well for the tribes.

In essence Jackson was given a chance to buy back from the Cherokee what had been conceded to be their property in northern Alabama. His approach was signaled in a letter to his friend General John Coffee who replaced an ill Hawkins on the boundary commission. Coffee was to contact important Cherokee leaders, including Lowrey, and "obtain [a resignation of all claims] for a very small sum [since they knew] they never had any rights and they will be glad, as I believe to swindle the U. States out of a few thousand dollars, and bury the claim, which they know, [if persisted in] might bury them and there nation."[29] Such a statement coming from Jackson, who had recently buried the Creek nation, had to be taken seriously.

Jackson met with the Cherokee and Chickasaw at the Chickasaw Council House in September 1816. Harassed by threats and soothed by bribes, the Cherokee, on September 14, 1816,[30] gave up the 1.3 million acres it was conceded to have in the treaty of March 22, 1816. This action contravened the instructions to the Cherokee delegation to sell no land. Included was the much coveted Muscle Shoals area. A treaty provision provided that the Cherokee nation would meet with Jackson and the other two commissioners two weeks later at Turkey Town "to express their approbation, or not, of [the] ... treaty." Then followed

a lawyer-type provision: if the nation did not assemble that would be taken as "a tacit ratification ... of the Cherokee nation, of [the] treaty."

At the later meeting on October 4, 1816, nine chiefs ratified the treaty.[31] Fourteen
Cherokee had signed the September treaty. Only one Cherokee signed both. None of those
signing the March 22 treaty signed the ratification on October 4, 1816. Later Cherokee
complaints were ignored that at the ratification all debate on the treaty had occurred at a
forced meeting late at night, when attendance was scant, and that only four of the eight
chiefs who signed had actually voted for the treaty.

Under the ratified September treaty the Cherokee were promised $6,000 per year for 10
years, and an immediate payment of $5,000 "as compensation for any improvements [the
Cherokee] may have had on the lands surrendered." A meager payment to receive for 1.3
million acres, even if no consideration is made for improvements. It wasn't consistent with
Jackson's position that this was Creek land to pay so much for Cherokee improvements on
land said to be that of the Creeks. Considering that the Cherokee were paid $5,000 by South
Carolina for about 100,000 acres six months earlier, regardless of how this payment for improvements is perceived, the Cherokee had 1.3 million acres of prime land wrested from them for
virtually nothing. Jackson felt vindicated. He wrote to his wife on September 18 that he had
"regain[ed] with tribute what [he had] fairly & hardly purchased with the sword."[32]

The Chickasaw were given the same rough treatment. By 1800 "mixed bloods had
completely taken over the management of [Chickasaw] affairs."[33] At the summit of the leaders were the Colberts, descendants of a Scotsman, James Logan Colbert, who lived in the
Chickasaw nation for 40 years and married three Chickasaw women. A Colbert was a principal spokesman for the Chickasaw for about a hundred years.

With a combination of warnings and bribes the Chickasaw were impelled to sign a
treaty on September 20, 1816,[34] surrendering claims to millions of acres above and below
the Tennessee River. This eliminated any Chickasaw claims to the Muscle Shoals area. Their
treaty extended to some of the same Muscle Shoals lands covered in the Cherokee treaty of
September 14. In addition to cash payments of either $100 or $150 to every signatory of the
treaty, the Chickasaw nation was to be paid $4,500 immediately and $12,000 per year for
10 years. In secret Jackson made payments to influential Chickasaw. Jackson said secrecy
was necessary "or the influence of the chiefs would be destroyed."[35] Article 7 of the treaty,
giving the appearance of concern for the Indians' welfare, complained of "the crowd of ped-
lars ... constantly traversing [the Chickasaw Nation] ... [with instances of] frauds ... often
practised on the ignorant and uninformed of the nation" and included an agreement that
the United States would not grant any "more licenses ... to entitle any person or persons to
trade or traffic merchandise" in the nation.

A restriction on licenses to traders plus agreement, in 1819, of the United States to
move the trading post at Chickasaw Bluffs (near modern Memphis) to the Arkansas Territory
left most trade in control of the Chickasaw.

During this same period Coffee and two other commissioners, operating under instructions from Jackson, negotiated with the Choctaw at the Choctaw Trading House. For an
initial payment of $10,000 and annual payments for 20 years of $6,000 the Choctaw signed
over about 2 million acres east of the Tombigbee River on October 24, 1816.[36] This may
not have been a bad treaty for the Choctaw. Earlier the Creek complained that land ceded
east of the Tombigbee was really theirs and not that of the Choctaw.

Washington was satisfied with the results Jackson achieved. In December 1816 the Secretary of War told Jackson that by eliminating questions of title, surveys could be made and "the lands in the Mississippi Territory [brought] to market." A new road being built from Tennessee to Louisiana should "effect ... the price of the land contiguous to the road."[37] Former Creek land was valuable in 1815: "bottom lands bordering the Tombigbee brought $10 an acre ... and desirable farms were worth $30 an acre."[38] Settlers were numerous enough that Mississippi became a state in 1817 and Alabama in 1819. These were states that as late as 1814 were virtually all considered Indian land.

23

The Cherokee of the East and West (1817–1828)

Andrew Jackson's letter to the new president, James Monroe, in March 1817 said "all Indians within the Territorial limits of the United States, are considered subject to its sovereignty, and have only a possessory right to the soil, for the purpose of hunting and not the right of domaine, hence ... Congress [has] full power, by law, to regulate all the concerns of the Indians."[1] Territorial limits should be that necessary to "feed, clothe, and house the tribe."[2]

The letter reasoned that "[a]lthough it may be said that we have sufficient Territory already, and that our settlements ought not to be extended too far, yet every thing should be done to ... consolidate our settlements." His justification was national defense. A "wedge [should be placed] between the Northern and Southern tribes, [to make] secure commerce on the Ohio and Mississippi, and afford a strong defense within striking distance of the settlements on the Mississippi and Missouri rivers."[3]

Monroe and his Secretary of War, John C. Calhoun, were of the same mind as to the desirability of acquiring more Indian land. Monroe wrote Jackson in October 1817 that "the hunter or savage state requires a greater extent of territory to sustain it, than is compatible with the progress and just claims of civilized life, and must yield to it."[4] In his December 1817 message to Congress Monroe thought the solution was to move the Indians west of the Mississippi by making liberal offers. Monroe opined that "the earth was given to mankind to support the greatest number of which it is capable, and no tribe or people have a right to withhold from the wants of others more than is necessary for their support and comfort."[5] During the Monroe presidency 40 treaties were signed with Indians from the North and South, about 30 of which covered cessions of land.

Consistent with these attitudes Jackson was told to talk to the Eastern Cherokee about their moving west of the Mississippi. The Cherokee refused to move but under pressure, and after being reminded of what had happened to the Creeks, agreed on July 8, 1817,[6] to give up roughly 1 million acres in 4 separate parcels in Tennessee, Georgia, and Alabama, with the understanding that more would be ceded after a census was made of the Cherokee in the West or planning to go to the West and those remaining in the East. The Western Cherokee were guaranteed "acre for acre"[7] on the Arkansas and White rivers land matching what was ceded in the East. As discussed in Ch. 19 the Western Cherokee migrated to present-day Arkansas in 1809.

According to the 1817 treaty, in 1808 the Cherokee went to Washington and asked that a division line be established between the Upper and Lower Cherokee Towns. The Upper

Towns were "anxious ... to engage in the pursuits of agriculture and civilized life" whereas the Lower Towns wanted "to continue the hunter life" and because of a scarcity of game wanted "to remove across the Mississippi river, on some vacant lands of the United States." The United States agreed in 1809 to exchange land on the Arkansas and White rivers for land east of the Mississippi proportioned to the numbers of those moving. The 1817 treaty purported to implement this 1808–1809 understanding. Many at the talks with Jackson disputed the version of what happened in 1808 and 1809 recited in the treaty but, after intimidating acts, agreed to the treaty. When the rationale for the 1817 treaty was first presented to the Eastern Cherokee leaders they said the solution was for Tahlonteskee to return to the East. There was no willingness to pay with eastern land for those Cherokees who moved to Arkansas in 1808 or 1809 to escape the wrath of the Cherokee who never approved of the 1806 cession made by the Chickamaugans.

The 1817 treaty was ratified even though the Secretary of War recognized that it had "not received the unbiased sanction of a majority of the [Cherokee] residing ... east of the Mississippi."[8] To get approval in the West, Jackson paid John D. Chisholm, a white leader of the Western Cherokees in Arkansas, $1,000 "to stop his mouth and obtain his consent."[9]

Chisholm, who worked for Blount at the time of the Treaty of Holston in 1791, was influential in Cherokee circles. In 1802 he wrote letters for Double Head and was given land under the Cherokee's 1806 cession treaty. He worked with Cherokee agent Meigs to get the Lower Towns Cherokee to move west and wrote to Meigs in 1809 on behalf of Tahlonteskee's decision to move. Tahlonteskee became the Lower Towns leading chief after the deaths of Double Head, in 1807, and John Watts, a war chief, in 1808. Chisholm relocated with Tahlonteskee in 1809. Each played important roles with the Western Cherokee until their deaths in 1818 and 1819, respectively.

The Western Cherokee, numbering about 2,000, had reasons for pressing for a new treaty. In December 1813 the Missouri Territory established the county of Arkansas which covered two-thirds of the modern state. This extension of civil authority embraced the land which the Western Cherokee considered to be theirs. Also of great importance was the fact that they were not receiving any of the annuities being paid the Cherokee under earlier treaties. Another problem was warfare with the Osage, which they thought could be countered by a military post on the Arkansas River.

Critical to deciding how much additional land in the East would be ceded was completion of the census. Since the census was to include those enrolling to go to the West, more was involved than just counting heads of those in each area at a particular time. The 1817 treaty encouraged migration by promising to "poor warriors" who went west "one rifle gun and ammunition, one blanket, and one brass kettle, or, in lieu of the brass kettle, a beaver trap." For those desiring to move, the United States would provide "flat bottomed boats and provisions sufficient for that purpose."[10] If emigrants left land with improvements, they would be compensated for the improvements. Over the next two years 3,000 to 4,000 additional Cherokee moved to the West, bringing the total population to around 6,000. Fort Smith, on the Arkansas River where the present boundary between the states of Arkansas and Oklahoma is, was established in 1817.

The census which, by the treaty, was scheduled for June 1818 was postponed so that the numbers could include happenings in the spring of 1819 — a postponement likely to increase the number attributed to the Western Cherokee. As it developed the need for a census was avoided when a delegation of Eastern Cherokee went to Washington in 1819 and offered to cede to the United States land "at least as extensive" as that which the United States would have been entitled to under the 1817 treaty. The offer was accepted and a treaty dated February 27, 1819,[11] executed. The land ceded was around the western, northern, and eastern periphery of the land retained by the Cherokee in the East and was 3 to 4 million acres. The large acreage retained by the Eastern Cherokee was mostly in Georgia with smaller amounts in Alabama, Tennessee, and North Carolina, and in total was 6 to 7 million acres.

On the ceded land thirty-one 640-acre reservations were made for "persons of industry ... capable of managing their property [most of whom had] made considerable improvements on the tracts reserved." Furthermore "each head of any Indian family" who would become a citizen of the United States would receive 640 acres. The cessions were to satisfy "all claims which the United States have ... on account of the cession to a part of their nation who have or may hereafter emigrate to the Arkansas." Unless objected to by the Cherokee west of the Mississippi, the annuity for the Cherokee would be divided, one-third to those west of the Mississippi and two-thirds to those in the East and no census taken.

The Eastern Cherokee had reason to believe that the treaty, signed by Secretary of War John C. Calhoun, agreed to their remaining in the East. It opens with the statement that "a greater part of the Cherokee nation" wanted to remain east of the Mississippi River and wanted "to commence ... measures ... necessary to the civilization and preservation of their nation." The United States was obligated to remove "all white people who [had] intruded, or may [thereafter] intrude, on the lands reserved for the Cherokees." It was a sound foundation for the Cherokee vow thereafter to not give up one foot more of land. An early step toward the requisite civilization was the Cherokee decision in 1820 to divide "their country into eight districts" and to appoint "circuit judges, sheriffs, constables, and justices" and to establish "a tax on the people to build a courthouse in each district."[12]

The Western Cherokee were without definite boundaries for their Arkansas land in 1816 and were in conflict with whites moving to the area. In 1821 the Western Cherokee advised the Secretary of War that "many ... whites [had] settled on [their] land."[13]

The Cherokee had their eyes on a rich section of land called Lovely's Purchase — a "triangular piece of territory north of the Arkansas River" starting near Fort Smith and going to the mouth of the Verdigri River. The United States had acquired the land from the Osage and it was also eyed by whites. Since the western boundary for the Western Cherokee had not been set, there was uncertainty as to whether Lovely's Purchase would be included as Cherokee land and whites were not allowed to settle there. The purchase was by William L. Lovely, the agent for the Cherokee in Arkansas, but the legal acquisition was between the United States and the Osage.

In 1824 a westerly boundary was set for the Arkansas Territory 40 miles west of where it eventually was established and Lovely's Purchase was within the Arkansas Territory. The United States relaxed its policy of not allowing whites to settle in the Purchase and by 1828 it had 3,000 whites.

The whites were undone in 1828 when another treaty[14] was made with the Western Cherokee. The treaty moved the western boundary of Arkansas to where it is today — that is, 40 miles eastward of where it had previously been located — and most of Lovely's Purchase, and millions more acres, were ceded to the Cherokee for their land further east in Arkansas. A result of ejecting the whites was strongly supported by Thomas McKenney from the Office of Indian Affairs on grounds of equity. Francis Paul Prucha in his book *American Policy in the Formative Years* speculated the clinching argument was the "chances of getting the remnants of the five Civilized Tribes to move west could not be jeopardized by a new example of failure to live up to pledges made to Indians."[15]

In 1817 when the Western Cherokee were to get Arkansas land President Monroe told them:

> ... [Y]ou are now in a country where you can be happy; no other white man shall ever again disturb you; the Arkansas will protect your southern boundary when you get there. You will be protected on either side; the white man shall never again encroach upon you, and you will have a great outlet to the West. As long as water flows, or grass grows upon the earth, or the sun rises to show your pathway, or you kindle your camp fires, so long shall you be protected by this Government, and never again removed from your present habitations.[16]

The 1828 treaty guaranteed forever seven million acres and specified the land boundaries. And further guaranteed "the Cherokee Nation a perpetual outlet, West, and a free and unmolested use of all the Country lying West of the Western boundary of the [described 7 million acres] and as far West as the sovereignty of the United States, and their right of soil extend." This was land in Indian Territory and later Oklahoma.

24

The Chickasaw and Choctaw
(1816–1820)

Although the Chickasaw ceded millions of acres to the United States in 1816, Jackson, Isaac Shelby, and the government were back for more in 1818. During the early 1800s the government had a forceful weapon to use against the Chickasaw. They both delayed and refused to pay annuities. The annuities were substantial. The first was in 1795 for $3,000. This increased to $3,100 for the period 1806–1816 and reached $35,100 in 1819. Full advantage of this weapon was taken in 1818. In addition to bribes the Chickasaw were to receive $20,000 a year for 15 years. The cession made on October 19, 1818, was immense — about "one-third of the state of Tennessee and one-tenth of the state of Kentucky"[1]— there were no more Chickasaw, nor any other Indian land within either of these states to be ceded. Left to the Chickasaw east of the Mississippi were about 6 million acres in northern Mississippi and 495,936 acres in northwest Alabama. Between 1801 and 1818 the Chickasaw ceded about 20 million acres to the United States.

Secretary of War John C. Calhoun told Congress in December 1818 that the Indians east of the Mississippi were no longer a terror and should be approached with commiseration. He agreed with Jackson that they should be controlled the same as others in the United States and that it was in their best interest to move to the West so as to avoid white interference in their development. But he differed from Jackson as to how this should be achieved. Force should not be used. He wanted to teach the Indians the white idea of land ownership. This could be done by giving individual Indians a limited number of acres. Important to implementing his ideas was educating Indian children in "agricultural techniques, home-making, Christianity, and citizenship."[2] The Choctaws were not against education and contributed funds for schools. Missionaries who opened schools were welcomed. But as to their land, they preferred no interference.

Calhoun tried to apply his policies by sending three commissioners to meet with the Choctaw, hoping for a cession of land in southern Mississippi. They were instructed to never demand anything but to suggest possibilities. A meeting was held in October 1818. Once a suggestion of removal was made, the Choctaw broke off discussions. Whites living in Mississippi wanted action not talks. Under pressure from them Calhoun appointed another set of commissioners to meet with the Choctaw — two commissioners were carried over from the earlier talks and Jackson was made the third commissioner. In an August 1819 meeting, at which Jackson harangued the Indians for three days, Choctaw chief Pushmataha said, "We wish to remain here, ... and do not wish to be transplanted into another soil."[3] Not rejecting completely the idea of removal, Pushmataha complained of the western land:

"I am well acquainted with the country contemplated for us. I have often had my feet sorely bruised there by the roughness of its surface."[4] Jackson was not for the conciliatory approach. He wrote to Calhoun that it was satisfactory to negotiate with Indians "so long as the arm of government was insufficient [but it was] high time the legislature should control the Indian tribes."[5]

Calhoun was swamped by letters from Mississippi wanting immediate removal of the Choctaws. Calhoun appointed two Mississippians together with Jackson to meet with them again. Jackson assured Calhoun that he would not force the Indians to remove — he would use diplomacy to persuade them. Calhoun agreed to a Jackson suggestion that specific western land be offered.

In the past Jackson got the results he wanted by intimidation and bribes. Giving chiefs some presents was not something he liked to do. He told Calhoun, on August 25, 1820:

> ... it is now discovered that nothing can be done without corrupting their Chiefs. This is so inconsistent with the principles of our Government that it is high time the Legislature should exercise its function and pass all laws for the regulation of the Indians. If they have too much land circumscribe them. Furnish them with the means of agriculture, and you will thereby lay the foundation of their civilization by making them husbandmen. Treat them humanely and Liberally but put an end to treating with them, and obtaining their Country by corrupting their Chiefs which is the only *way* by which a Treaty can be obtained.[6]

Pushmataha was the greatest of all Choctaw chiefs who fought in the War of 1812 on the side of the United States. This 1837 lithograph is after an 1824 painting by Charles Bird King (McKenney-Hall Collection, courtesy of the Oklahoma Historical Society, negative number 20516.1.6).

The Choctaw nation with a population of around 20,000 had to be dealt with. The Choctaw were friendly to the Americans through the Revolution and the War of 1812 and had traits consistent with the object of civilization. The English botanist, William Bartram, who traveled in the Gulf Coast of Mississippi in 1777, described the Choctaws he saw as "most ingenious and industrious husbandmen, having large plantations, or country farms, where they employ much of their time in agricultural improvements."[7]

The problem they posed was a claim to over 15 million acres, roughly two-thirds of the new state of Mississippi. Jackson gathered more than 500 Choctaw chiefs, headmen, and warriors near Doak's Stand on the Natchez road on October 10 and told them of whites putting pressure on the president for land in Mississippi.

The promise to the Choctaws at the time of the October 1816 treaty that "never again would the United States allow them to be mistreated"[8] did not stop Jackson. He said the president wanted "to perpetuate [the Choctaw as a] Nation" and this could be done by their moving west to "a country of tall trees, many water courses, rich lands and high grass abounding in game of all kinds — buffalo, bear, elk, deer, antelope, beaver, turkeys, honey and fruits of many kinds."[9] This description of the land was disputed by Pushmataha who said he knew "the country well.... The grass is everywhere very short, and for the game it is not plenty, except buffalo and deer.... There are but few beavers, and the honey and fruit are rare things"[10]; furthermore, it was already occupied by many white men.

Pushmataha had a right to speak candidly. He led the Choctaw in support of the United States in the War of 1812. As they considered what to do in 1812 Pushmataha cautioned the nation: "Reflect ... on the great uncertainty of war with the American people.... Be not deceived with illusive hopes.... Listen to the voice of prudence, ere you rashly act. But do as you may.... I shall join our friends, the Americans, in this war."[11] The support was real. In the Creek War about 700 Choctaw joined with the Mississippi militia and white volunteers in fighting the Red Sticks. An even larger number supported Jackson at the battle for New Orleans and the Choctaws received accolades from the Mississippi territorial legislature and thanks from Jackson on behalf of the United States.

After three days of debate among the Choctaw chiefs, on October 18, 1820, they agreed to a treaty following Jackson's angry warning that to refuse would lead to the destruction of the Choctaw nation. A contemporary paper described the ceded land "as fine as any in the United States."[12] According to the treaty[13] for 5 million acres the Choctaw received 13 million acres in southern Oklahoma and southwestern Arkansas. The 13 million acres were to be populated by those "who live by hunting and will not work." As for the Indians moving to the 13 million acres "each warrior [was to be given] a blanket, kettle, rifle gun, bullet moulds and nippers, and ammunition sufficient for hunting and defence, for one year. Said warrior ... also [to] be supplied with corn to support him and his family [for one year] and whilst traveling to the country ... ceded to the Choctaw nation." The Choctaw remaining east of the Mississippi who had settlements would "be secured in a tract or parcel one mile square."

Mississippians were elated and later named their capital, located within the ceded land, Jackson. Many Choctaw were dejected — "the government had sold them out to satisfy settlers in the old Southwest."[14] Militantly upset were white residents in the Arkansas Territory whose land was ceded to the Choctaw. The *Mississippi Gazette* thought the damage to Arkansas was temporary — once Arkansas became a state "the Indians [could] then be removed from her soil."[15] The answer, always the easy one for the whites, was another treaty with the Choctaw.

In November 1821 Calhoun stated that there was "great reason to believe that very few, if any of [the Choctaw] nation are inclined at present to emigrate west of the Mississippi."[16] Finally in January 1823 Calhoun convinced the president and Congress of the need to change the boundary line specified in the 1820 treaty "to avoid hardships for both Indians and whites."[17] After the Choctaw agent sabotaged a proposed meeting with commissioners, one of whom he knew the Choctaw would not talk to, Calhoun invited Choctaw chiefs to Washington.

Steps toward the whites' conception of civilization such as passing a law "organizing a corps of Light-Horse [with an] imperative duty to close all the dram-shops that were dealing in the miserable traffic in opposition to law and treaty stipulations"[18] and using nation funds to establish "a Choctaw Academy"[19] did not relieve the pressure for emigration.

The Choctaws arrived on November 1, 1824. Chiefs and subchiefs from each of the three districts into which the Choctaw nation was organized were in the party. Addressing Calhoun the great Choctaw chief Pushmataha said, "As a Nation of people, we have always been friendly, and ever listened to the applications of the American people. We have given of our country to them until it has become very small. I came here years ago when a young man to see my Father Jefferson. He then told me if ever we got into trouble we must come and tell him, and he would help us. We are in trouble, and have come...."[20] There was in fact give and take in the negotiations resulting in the Treaty of 1825 signed on January 20. Pushmataha did not have an opportunity to expand on his earlier remarks, he died shortly before the treaty was signed. Jackson said he was "the greatest and bravest Indian [he] ever knew."[21] The 60-year-old chief wanted to have "the big guns fired over [him]"[22] and they were at a military funeral attended by 2,000 in Washington. Because it was not possible to prepare bodies for burial at distant places the graves of Indians at this time were usually where they died — in Pushmataha's case in the Congressional Cemetery in Washington.

The treaty[23] changed the Choctaws' acquired western land's eastern boundary to be the western boundary of the Arkansas Territory in exchange for additional annuities. The reason given in the treaty for this retro-cession was that "the cession embrace[d] a large number of settlers." The Arkansas land also had the only salt springs in the area. In addition to paying money the United States agreed "to remove such citizens as may be settled on the west side, to the east side of said line, and prevent future settlements from being made on the west thereof." An agent and blacksmith provided for in the 1820 treaty were to be settled among them. This treaty was made and proclaimed in the last days of the Monroe administration. The Choctaw still had about 10 million acres in Mississippi and they refused to move to the West. Furthermore, when approached about a further adjustment in the western lands ceded to them in 1820 because it still included white settlers, the Choctaw adamantly told the Secretary of War they would "*sell no more land* on any terms."[24] Contemporary estimates of how many Choctaw migrated before Jackson was elected president in 1828 ranged from one to fifty.

Herman J. Viola in *Diplomats in Buckskins* says the Choctaw, who insisted in 1824 on meeting with the president in Washington to rectify the fact that the Treaty of Doak's Stand gave them land in Arkansas which was already occupied by 5,000 whites, "left the capital confident [they] had skinned the government."[25] Such a feeling might have been induced by the hard bargaining they engaged in through the efforts of a half-blooded Choctaw lawyer but could well be attributed to their stay in Washington. The delegation, originally 10 in number but reduced to 8 by deaths, stayed in Washington negotiating for three months, at the government's expense. Thomas J. McKenney, then head of the Bureau of Indian Affairs, was incensed when the bill for their living expenses was totaled. It came to almost $7,500 and included about $1,800 for liquor and $400 for oysters and brandy. McKenney refused to pay the total bills for the bar and refectory. When the time came for the delegation to leave one member was ill and got permission to stay with two others until he was able to travel. Neither he nor his companions were anxious to leave. After their stay extended into months McKenney was again outraged over their hotel bill. It was $1,500 of which

$935 was for liquor. Focusing his anger on Joshua Tennison, the hotel owner, he fumed that he had warned Tennison about allowing the Indians extravagance but admitted that as "[e]normous as the bar bill is, I am quite sure ... that you have charged no more than you actually furnished."[26] Considering that room and board at a Washington hotel only cost $1.25 per day and that a gallon of whiskey could be bought for $1.25, McKenney's surprise is understandable.

An exchange during the negotiations showed Choctaw movement toward civilization. Pushmataha stressed that to give up the Arkansas land would take all their valuable land. When Calhoun accused him of contradicting himself by noting that in 1820 Pushmataha had insisted the land was "all rocks and hills, and that the waters were only fit to overflow the crops, put out fires, and float canoes," Pushmataha responded: "I am imitating the white man. In 1820 we want to buy; now we are anxious to sell."[27]

25

The Creek (1818–1829)

In a treaty[1] with the Creek negotiated by David Brydie Mitchell, agent of Indian affairs for the Creek nation, on January 22, 1818, substantial acreage was ceded in north and south Georgia for a total of $120,000 to be paid over a 10-year period.

Around this time a significant organizational change was made in the Creek Confederacy. To manage their own affairs a centrally controlled law enforcement agency, called the "law menders,"[2] was established under Chief McIntosh. William McIntosh, the son of a Scotch trader and a Creek woman, also had a connection with the Cherokee. One of his three wives was a Cherokee. McIntosh, although considered the fifth most important chief in the Creek Confederacy, came to the front in dealing with whites. He had unusual assets. He spoke and wrote English, his cousin became Georgia's governor in 1823, one of his daughters married a son of Hawkins and another of Agent Mitchell, and within the confederacy he was the head warrior.

Mitchell found him to be an important link to the Creek nation and paid him $400 a year; he was paid the same amount by the Creek nation. Mitchell explained the governing arrangements to the Secretary of War on June 27, 1820. The governments of the Upper and Lower Creeks were separate. Big Warrior headed that for the Upper Creeks and Little Prince had done the same for the Lower Creeks until the year before when McIntosh became the chief executive. Because of Big Warrior's age Mitchell predicted that in time McIntosh would become chief executive of both groups.

Whites were entering the former Indian land at such a pace that Georgia wanted more land. Any further cession was opposed by Big Warrior and Little Prince; nonetheless, a meeting was held at Indian Springs with commissioners dominated by Georgians — the commissioner for the United States, General Thomas Flournoy, refused to participate. A treaty signed on January 8, 1821,[3] made a four-million-acre cession without participation by the Upper Creeks unless the presence of Chief McIntosh could be considered as their representative. Thirty-six chiefs present at the negotiations refused to sign and told the commissioners that those signing only represented a tenth of the nation. Georgia's western boundary with the Creeks moved from the Ocmulgee River to the Flint. McIntosh received "a handsome douceur" and 640 acres on the bank of the Ocmulgee River on which he had improvements and was allowed to keep.[4] Payments to the Creek nation totaling $176,000 were spread over 14 years. In addition, Georgia was to be paid up to $250,000 for claims against the Creek nation "for property taken or destroyed prior to the act of Congress" of 1802.

The relationship between McIntosh and Mitchell ended on February 16, 1821, thirty-nine days after the Indian Springs treaty, when Mitchell was discharged because of a charge of smuggling Africans into the United States in 1818. He was replaced by John Crowell of Georgia. In 1825 Little Prince said, "McIntosh and Mitchell [were able] to steal all our money, because they could write."[5]

An outgrowth of McIntosh's attendance at a council meeting of Cherokee in 1823 was a letter from the Cherokee to Big Warrior and Little Prince dated October 24, 1823. The letter[6] concluded that McIntosh's visit was motivated "entirely [for] speculative designs" since he urged some Cherokee chiefs "to yield their land" to the United States and promised large sums of money for them. He told others "that he had offered his whole country to the [United States] for two dollars per acre, and suggested [that] the Cherokees, Creeks, Choctaws, and Chickasaws, all ... surrender ... their country and emigrate West." The letter included an admonition that the Creeks "keep a

This chief, also known as General William McIntosh, was a Creek who often dealt with whites. He was put to death by his people for ceding land without consent of the nation (J.B. Milan Collection, courtesy of the Oklahoma Historical Society, negative number 20462.1.23).

strict watch over his conduct." When the United States appointed commissioners in July 1824 to buy more land from the Creek, Creek chiefs published a manifesto in newspapers: "it [is] contrary to the true interest of this nation to dispose of any more of our country; and any authority heretofore given to any individual ... has long since been revoked and done away ... it may be known to the world, that the Creek people are not disposed to sell one foot more of their lands."[7]

After meetings with Creeks in November and December 1824 the commissioners were told "the proposal to remove beyond the Mississippi, we cannot for a moment listen to."[8] Rejected was a proposal that negotiations be conducted by a number of chiefs without the presence of many other Creeks. After a recess the commissioners were told "to obtain an arrangement with General McIntosh, with the consent of the nation, for the cession of the country in question."[9]

At a new meeting at Indian Springs in February 1825 the commissioners were told "McIntosh knows that no part of the land can be sold without a full council, and without the consent of all the nation."[10] Notwithstanding, the Treaty of Indian Springs was signed on February 12, 1825,[11] by McIntosh and others representing 8 towns out of 56 in the nation.

Under the treaty all Creek towns except for Tokaubatchee ceded their land in Georgia and agreed to move west of the Mississippi to land in Arkansas. Special consideration was provided for McIntosh, the head chief of Cowetaus.

John Crowell alerted the Secretary of War that the "treaty was signed by McIntosh and his adherents alone" and if ratified might "produce a horrid state of things among these unfortunate Indians."[12] Anticipating trouble McIntosh and followers hurried to Milledgeville, Georgia's capital near Fort Wilkinson, and asked McIntosh's cousin, Governor Troup, for help. Troup proclaimed the ceded land to be owned by Georgia and declared "McIntosh and his people [to be] under [his] protection."[13] Wisely McIntosh did not attend the Creek annual meeting on April 19 but this did not save him. At the meeting the chiefs "determined to put him to death for a violation of [a Creek] law first proposed by [McIntosh]."[14] On April 30 his home was set on fire and he was shot as he ran from it.

Although on the third day of the new John Quincy Adams administration the treaty was proclaimed, it was declared null and void by a treaty of January 24, 1826.[15] The new treaty recited the protest of "a great majority of the chiefs and warriors" to the earlier treaty. The new treaty stated the United States was "unwilling that any cessions of land should be made to them, unless with the fair understanding and full assent of the Tribe making such cession, and for a just and adequate consideration, it being the policy of the United States, in all their intercourse with the Indians to treat them justly and liberally, as becomes the relative situation of the parties."

The new treaty provided for land west of the Mississippi for those wanting to emigrate and for the payment of money. The intention was for all Creek land in Georgia to be ceded. Roughly one-sixth of Georgia was transferred. As far as remaining Creek land east of the Mississippi was concerned, that is, its land in Alabama, it was "guarantee[d] to the Creeks." Adams' Secretary of War told Congress that even though he had been advised "to approach the influential chiefs with secret gratuities, justified ... by the usages of the Government" the full price was included in the treaty.[16]

When it was discovered that not quite all the Georgia land was ceded, the remaining sliver on Georgia's west boundary was surrendered on November 15, 1827: Cash was paid ($27,491) without conditions and a lesser sum ($5,000) "in blankets, and other necessary articles of cloathing." Another $15,000 was to be used "toward[] the education and support of Creek children," for two schools in the Creek nation, "erection of four horse mills," "purchase of cards and wheels," and "blankets and other necessary and useful goods."[17]

Some Creeks who had been McIntosh followers decided to go west. The exploratory party for these returned with a favorable report and during the period 1827–1829 about 2,400, perhaps half of whom were from the majority of the Creeks, emigrated. Those emigrating had complaints — aggressions by wild Indians and the failure of the United States to carry out the pledges of the treaty an all-too-common situation. Some whites in Alabama were reported as seeing any Indian movement to the West as a windfall: "We may now confidently look forward to the speedy acquisition of the delightful and valuable territory possessed by this miserable race."[18]

26

Jackson and Florida
(1816–1829)

Florida posed a unique danger to the United States and an area of opportunity for expansionists. When a force of 80 men captured Baton Rouge in September 1810 and sent the Spanish government a list of grievances, and a request for annexation to the United States, Madison ignored them. But by presidential proclamation of October 21, 1810, he took possession of that part of West Florida between the Mississippi and Perdido rivers pending a settlement with Spain. In part he relied on doubts as to the boundaries of the Louisiana Purchase. Some in Congress claimed he was making war on Spain without Congress's approval. This was cured when Congress approved his action on January 15, 1811. Control of the river routes to Mobile and the Gulf through the area seized was an aim of those in Tennessee.

Fearing that England might use Spanish Florida in case of war, Congress passed a secret law on January 15, 1811, giving the president authority to seize Florida or any part of it if "the local authority ... deliver[ed] up ... possession ... or in the event of any attempt to occupy [it] or any part [of it], by any foreign government."[1] It wasn't until the end of the War of 1812 that England used part of Florida as a staging area but early in 1812 some Georgia volunteers calling themselves "Patriots" invaded East Florida at St. Mary's and marched on St. Augustine. As they proceeded southward they acted as the "local authority" and surrendered land taken to American forces following them. St. Augustine was never occupied but it was not until May 1813 that American troops were withdrawn. In the interim blacks and Indians attacked Americans in Florida and Americans burned Seminole houses and bushels of corn and took away horses and cattle. The invasion turned a prosperous area into one of desolation.

As commander of the U.S. Army's southern division in 1815 Jackson had the responsibility of guarding the southern boundary with Florida. One problem for him was Spain's presence in Florida which created a haven for hostile Creeks and for slaves escaping from Georgia. In February 1816 Hawkins told the Secretary of War that Georgia slaves "were being invited to go to the Seminoles and be free."[2] The native Florida Indians were a cross-border threat. They opposed Georgia settlers moving on to land north of the Florida border that was ceded by the Fort Jackson treaty — this was hunting ground for them.

A thorn in Jackson's side was Negro Fort near the mouth of the Apalachicola River in Spanish Florida. The fort, built by Colonel Edward Nicholls on Prospect Point when the British were in Florida, was turned over to the Indians together with a stockpile of arms and ammunition and food when Nicholls returned to England in the summer of 1815. After

137

As a military commander, Andrew Jackson demanded large land cessions. As president, he favored removal to Indian Territory. This ca. 1860 engraving by A.H. Ritchie was made from a painting by Dennis M. Carter (Library of Congress, LC-USZ62–5099).

a short time escaped slaves took control of the fort from the Indians. In the spring of 1816 Jackson asked Spain to "destroy or remove from [the] frontier"[3] the banditti of blacks and Indians operating out of the fort. The Spanish governor at Pensacola told Jackson he was not failing to act "from a want of inclination"[4]— the Spanish were weak in Florida since troops had been taken elsewhere to deal with South American insurgencies. Without authority from Washington, in fact, in the face of instructions from the Secretary of War that only the governor of West Florida or the president could determine what to do about Negro Fort, Jackson ordered General Edmund Pendleton Gaines, in charge of army units in the Florida area, to move against the Indians in Florida. Gaines mounted a ground and water attack on the fort. A naval gunboat ignited a fort powder magazine with a ball heated red-hot and the fort, flying a British flag, was destroyed on July 27, 1816. Up to 300, mostly blacks in the fort, men, women, and children, were killed.

In December 1816, presumably having in mind the Negro Fort action, Gaines was told: "The state of our negotiations with Spain, and the temper manifested by the principal European Powers, make it impolitic, in the opinion of the President, to move a force ... into the Spanish possessions for the mere purpose of chastizing the Seminoles."[5]

In March 1817 Indian agent David Mitchell reported to a new president, James Monroe, on the unstable conditions along the Georgia-Florida line. He later said the "peace of the frontier of Georgia has always been exposed and disturbed, more or less, by acts of violence, committed as well by the whites as the Indians; and a spirit of retaliation has mutually prevailed."[6] The Indians were being armed by a Scottish trader, Alexander Arbuthnot, who thought this necessary for their self-defense and an opportunity for profits. An Englishman active in Florida was Robert C. Ambrister. The Indians in Florida, referred to here as Seminoles, were a mixture of Indians born in Florida, Red Sticks who fled to Florida, and friendly Indians who went to Florida as a consequence of the Fort Jackson treaty. The Creek Confederacy saw the Seminoles as "a set of outlaws."[7]

Following the Creek treaty at Fort Jackson, the race to stake claims to ceded land was on and the Alabama Territory established on March 3, 1817, was the destination of many. In August 1817 a letter written by a North Carolinian described what was happening: "The *Alabama Feaver* rages here with great violence and has carried off vast numbers of our Citizens.... There is no question that this *feaver* is contagious ... for as soon as one neighbor visits another who has just returned from Alabama he immediately discovers the same symptoms which are exhibited by the one who has seen alluring Alabama."[8] The Creek nation was compressed between settlers in Alabama and those in Georgia pressing to move westward. The white population in Alabama went from virtually zero before the treaty to 127,901 at the time of the first Alabama census in 1820 after it became a state on December 14, 1819.

In the fall of 1817 Mitchell reported on Indians killing a Mrs. Garrett and two children, and that the Indians attributed this to a belief that Mr. Garrett had attacked a Seminole party on its way to Georgia to trade and killed one of them. Seminoles and Gaines traded accusations at a meeting in which Gaines called the Seminoles "bad people." Ill feelings turned into organized confrontations in November when Chief Neamathla of Fowltown, a hold-over Creek village in south Georgia, warned Americans not to cut wood on their land. Neamathla refused to go to Fort Scott to talk about this and Gaines sent 250 men to arrest him. They did not succeed but did kill four warriors and a woman. With evidence of friendship between Neamathla and the British, Gaines ordered the town to be burnt and it was. Mitchell was upset since the Fowltown Indians had never been belligerent and were neutral in the Creek War.

On November 30 a party of Fowltown Indians, who had fled to Florida, with some black allies, struck back. An army barge carrying forty or so soldiers and some wives and children up the Apalachicola River was attacked. Most of those on board were killed. The acting Secretary of War, long-time chief clerk in the War Department, George Graham, told Gaines that the "honor of the United States [required a] war with the Seminoles should be terminated speedily." Jackson was the man to do this — he said "the protection of our citizens will require that the Wolf be struck in his den" and he wasn't concerned about where the "den" was located.[9] In April 1817 he had told Graham that he would "enforce Justice from [U.S.] neighbors, whether Indian, British, or Spanish."[10]

On December 26 Jackson was told to take personal command. He was at Prospect Bluff, the site of the former Negro Fort, in March 1818. In April he went on offense with an overwhelming force — 3,300 troops and 1,500 Creek warriors. His character was such

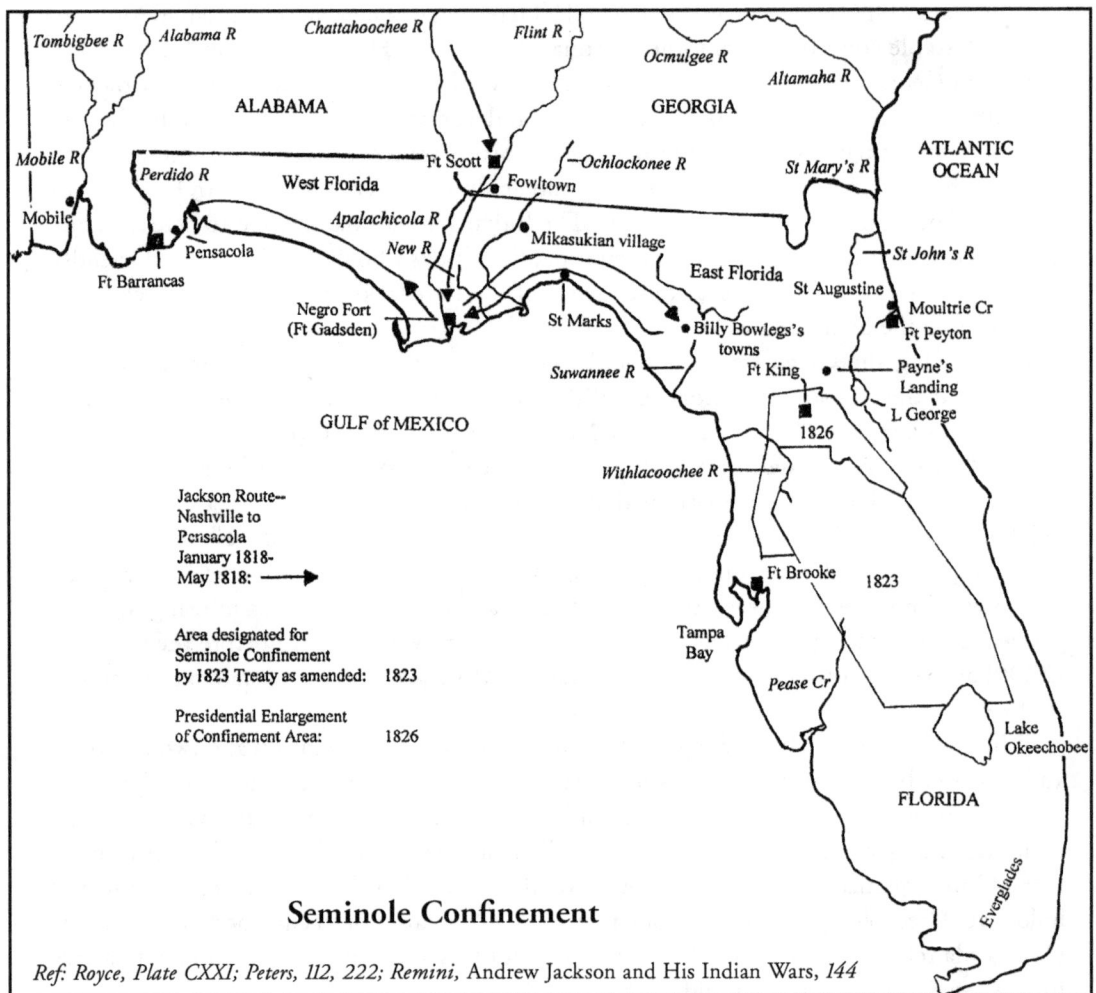

Seminole Confinement

Ref: Royce, Plate CXXI; Peters, 112, 222; Remini, Andrew Jackson and His Indian Wars, *144*

that he wouldn't hesitate to trample any Spanish opposition. The "mantle of glory" Jackson had from his New Orleans victory gave him a degree of independence.

With little fighting the Seminoles retreated back through the Mikasuki towns located just below the Georgia–Florida boundary; 300 houses were burnt and large stores of grain taken. Resistance was expected from Seminoles at St. Marks, where Jackson next went, destroying Indian villages in his path. The illusive Indians were not found at St. Marks but Jackson, to have a depot for his operation, commandeered the fortress there, replacing the Spanish flag with U. S. colors. Jackson lowered the Spanish flag with his own hands and handed it to the humiliated Spanish governor Luengo. Without delay he set out for the towns of Chief Billy Bowlegs, an important Seminole leader, located east of St. Marks on the Suwannee River. When he arrived on April 16 there were no Seminole warriors. After burning 300 houses he headed back to St. Marks considering the war against the Seminole over since he could not find a force to oppose his army.

From St. Marks he headed west to Fort Gadsden, which Americans had built on the site of the demolished Negro Fort and advised Secretary of War John C. Calhoun that he intended to take Pensacola from the Spanish. To him this was necessary to cut off an Indian source of "ammunition and munitions of war" and also a place where 400 to 500 warriors were preparing to continue the war. To take Pensacola had larger international implications than what had gone before. It was an important location of the Spanish government in Florida. With about 1,200 men he captured Pensacola without any significant resistance at the end of May 1818. However, it wasn't until he exchanged artillery fire with the Spanish garrison which had retreated to nearby Fort Barrancas that Governor Jose Masot, who Jackson bullied, agreed to surrender the fort. In leaving Pensacola Jackson proclaimed that it would be returned when "Spain demonstrated it could protect West Florida."[11] No significant number of warriors were at Pensacola.

Another international crisis was created when British citizens Alexander Arbuthnot, a guest of the Spanish at St. Marks, and Robert Ambrister, who wandered into an American camp mistaking it for one of the Seminoles, were captured and court-martialed. Arbuthnot was found guilty of "exciting and stirring up the Creek Indians to war against the United States" and Ambrister of "aiding, abetting, and comforting the enemy, supplying them with the means of war ... and leading [them] against the United States."[12] Both were put to death. Seventy-year-old Arbuthnot was hung from the yardarm of his own schooner, and twenty-year-old Ambrister executed by firing squad. Ambrister's court-martial sentence was 50 lashes on the back and 12 months in prison but Jackson changed it to death. In their book *Old Hickory's War* David S. and Jeanne T. Heidler assert that Arbuthnot had worked for peace between the United States and the Seminoles and his critical conduct may have been an accusation that Jackson and Gaines had manufactured a border crisis so they could grab Indian land.

Jackson did not hesitate to mete out capital punishment. Earlier in 1818 he ordered that two Red Sticks captured by subterfuge be hanged. Homathlemico, a chief, and Josiah Francis, a prophet, mistakenly went aboard a U. S. Navy ship flying the British Union Jack.

Jackson was ready to do more. On June 2 he told Monroe that what he had done was "essential to the peace and security of [the American] frontier."[13] If Monroe would give him more men, guns, and a frigate, he would take possession of Fort Augustine in East Florida, where Spain had a small force, and Cuba. Monroe had enough. Jackson's actions had created an atmosphere in which either England or Spain or both might declare war on the United States. Within Monroe's cabinet Calhoun thought Jackson had gone too far, but the Secretary of State, John Quincy Adams, thought his action was justified. Calhoun accepted the reality that it was "inexpedient to punish"[14] Jackson.

Politically Monroe, unable to severely censure Jackson for acts so popular with the general population of the West, tried to have it both ways, that is, acting to mollify the Spaniards without enraging Jackson. He wrote him on July 19, 1818, that "[i]n transcending the limit prescribed by [your] orders, you acted on your own responsibility, on facts and circumstances, which were unknown to the government, when the orders were given, many of which occurred afterwards, and which you thought imposed on you the measure, as an act of patriotism, essential to the honour and interests of your country."[15] During a hailstorm of criticism by outraged congressmen accusing him of going to war without congressional approval, Jackson always declared that he acted within his orders.

Privately, in a letter of November 28, 1818, John Quincy Adams hailed Jackson's destructive actions against a motley tribe of black, white, and Indian combatants. Adams had the task of dealing with the irate Spanish who wanted St. Marks and Pensacola returned. Adams gave no quarter; he told them "Spain must immediately make her election, either to place a force in Florida adequate at once to the protection of her territory, and to the fulfillment of her engagements, or cede to the United States a province, of which she retains nothing but ... nominal possession."[16] Spain accepted the suggestion of a cession and discussions began. On February 22, 1819, representatives of the two countries signed the Adams-Onis treaty ceding Florida to the United States and defining the boundaries of the Louisiana Purchase, and the United States took responsibility for 5 million dollars in claims against Spain.

Even though Spain did not ratify the treaty for two years Calhoun proceeded as if it were a fait accompli. On March 11, 1819, he directed the Creek agent, Mitchell, to move the Seminole Indians "up into the body of the Creek Nation ... in the most expeditious and economical manner."[17] About the same time the Creek Confederacy claimed title to the Indian land in Florida and the right to dispose of it. Calhoun disagreed. The United States had the right to dictate the terms under which the Seminoles could have peace and rebuked Mitchell when he suggested the United States would buy the Florida land; however, Calhoun held out the possibility of "liberal and suitable compensation" if the Creek Confederacy would "cooperate with the government in removing [the Seminoles] from Florida" and would "assign a portion of their country to the Seminoles."[18]

If Adams, Jackson, and Monroe had had their way, Spain would have been prodded into action on the treaty. Monroe asked Congress in his Annual Message in December 1819 for authority to invade Florida. Congress was not receptive and Monroe withdrew the request.

The Seminoles became subjects of the United States when both Spain and the United States ratified the Adams-Onis treaty in February 1821. They were not allowed much leeway. Jackson was appointed governor of Florida and was ready to move them into the Creek nation north of the boundary established in the Fort Jackson treaty but faced opposition from Georgia, which didn't want the Creek nation in that area strengthened. Although Jackson continued to think removal was most desirable, absent that, he wanted to consolidate the Florida Indians. Jackson ceased to be primarily responsible for working with the Florida Indians when he moved back to Tennessee in October 1821 and a temporary agent was appointed for the Florida Indians, Captain Bell. Bell studied the Seminole's relationship with the Spanish and concluded that Spain had recognized the boundary of Indian lands to be that which the English established, that is, virtually all of the non-coastal part of Florida. Calhoun accepted this.

The Seminole, a word meaning "separatist" or "runaway," consisted of a mix of Creeks who migrated to Florida over the years as well as remnants of other tribes, the Hichiti, Yamasee, and Yuchi, and, to the chagrin and anger of neighboring Americans, a large number of blacks who were either runaway slaves or blacks captured by the Seminole. To the extent that the Seminole were considered as slave owners, it was "a form of benevolent bondage, exacting only their fealty and a small amount of corn, stock or peltries."[19] The Seminole were mistakenly assumed to be a part of the Creek nation. A premise in the 1821 Treaty of Indian Springs with the Creeks was that the Creeks were responsible for the actions of the Seminole. The Seminole never agreed that the Creek had any control over them.

After a new governor for Florida, William P. Duval, was appointed, he wrote to Calhoun on July 18, 1822, stressing the need "to locate the Indians speedily" since "settlers [were] crowding in their claims to the lands promiscuously, and fixing their habitations where they choose."[20] With the object of consolidating the Indians within Florida, treaty commissioners were appointed in April 1823. Jackson recommended to the Secretary of War that "[a] movement of troops to Tampas bay, previous to the *Talks* being held with them, would have a powerful influence upon their minds, and give *great effect* to the Talks of the commissioners."[21] Calhoun agreed but there wasn't time to move the soldiers. On September 6 talks began at Moultrie Creek just south of St. Augustine.

A treaty was signed on September 18[22] by Duval and two other commissioners, and 32 chiefs and warriors. Many influential chiefs did not sign because it gave up the good land on which their villages were located. The chiefs said the Seminole population was 4,883, occupying 37 towns. All of Florida except for land in the middle of the peninsula was ceded to the United States. The Seminoles were not to retain any land closer than 15 miles to the Gulf of Mexico or 20 miles to the Atlantic Ocean. Six principal chiefs who signed did not have to move into the land set aside for the Seminoles. An additional Article signed the same day as the treaty allowed them to stay on specified land in northern Florida and promised them a share of the $6,000 to be spent on "implements of husbandry, and stock of cattle and hogs" and a share of $5,000 to be paid annually for 20 years. The relative strengths of the parties are demonstrated in Article I: "The undersigned chiefs and warriors ... have appealed to the humanity, and thrown themselves on, and have promised to continue under, the protection of the United States."

Commissioner James Gadsden predicted the Indians' future: "Your father the President ... will not permit you to be scattered all over Florida; he will place you by yourselves, mark your boundaries, protect your property, prevent his white men and the Creeks from disturbing you, separate you from your false prophets and bad men from across the water."[23] Neamathla, who spoke for the Indians, was appropriately contrite: "We are ... poor and needy; we do not come here to murmur or complain; we want advice and assistance; we rely upon your justice and humanity."[24] After the fact, Gadsden wrote: "It is not necessary to disguise the fact ... that the treaty effected was in a degree a treaty of imposition — The Indians would never have voluntarily assented to its terms had they not believed that we had both the power & disposition to compel obedience."[25]

The Indians signing were, as stated in the treaty,[26] "under the impression that [the land set aside] did not contain a sufficient quantity of good land to subsist them." In the treaty the United States agreed to "take the Florida Indians under their care and patronage." To make them leave good land in north Florida, which was rapidly settled by whites, and go on to land not good enough for them to subsist on did not speak well of their patron. When Duval toured the land set aside for the Seminoles he concluded no part of it was worth cultivating—to him "it was by far the poorest and most miserable region he had ever beheld."[27] In 1825 Acting Governor George Walton wrote to Thomas McKenney, head of the Office of Indian Affairs established in March 1824, that the "situation of these unfortunate human beings is miserable in the extreme, and requires prompt and effectual relief from the humanity, if not the justice of the Government."[28] Two executive orders, one in 1824 and another in 1826, added tillable land.

A favorable development for the Seminoles was the appointment on June 14, 1825, of Colonel Gad Humphreys as their agent. He faced problems of squatters settling illegally on public land and of avaricious whites selling liquor to the Indians. Humphreys noted a shortcoming in the judicial system which compelled Indians to seek redress in some other way: "The great disadvantage under which the almost proscribed children of the forest labor for want of credibility as witnesses in our courts of law, destroys everything like equality of rights; forbids the idea of their success in legal controversy, in opposition to their white neighbours, and thus virtually excludes them from our halls of justice."[29] A source of heated differences between the Seminoles and the whites was over blacks living with the Seminoles. Slaves, a valuable property to whites, found their way into the Seminole land by purchase or by fleeing. They were hidden in the swamps and hummocks.

Duval told McKenney of the problem in March 1826: "The justice which the Indians are entitled to they cannot obtain, while they surrender to our citizens the slaves claimed by them, their own negroes that have been taken from them are held by white people who refuse to deliver them up. I have felt ashamed [in] urging the Indians to surrender their ... property held by our citizens. The Government should have their property restored to them, or pay the Indians the value of it. To tell one of these people that he must go to law for his property, in our courts, with a white man, is only adding insult to injury."[30]

Even more fundamental was the lack of food. Humphreys wrote to Duval in March 1827 that there was not at the "moment ... in the whole nation, a bushel of corn or any adequate substitute for it."[31] Humphreys, in the same letter, said "any man who reads the history of this inglorious *war* and its effects, will learn and see much which, as an American, a member of a nation calling itself *Christian*, he must blush at."[32]

Another indignity imposed by the territorial legislature was "An Act to Prevent the Indians from roaming at large, throughout the Territory" under which adult Indians found outside their reservation without a pass could be punished "by inflicting not more than thirty-nine stripes on the bare back and to take his gun from him."[33] The only action that would satisfy the whites was to have the Indians removed. Duval tried to persuade them to go to the West but reported on March 2, 1826, that they would not do so "unless the Creek nation should also emigrate."[34]

In January 1829 Chief John Hicks, recognized leader of the Seminoles, sent a speech to the president outlining grievances: "He asked why the Indians must always pay for the death of a white man while whites rarely were held accountable for that of an Indian. He said that white men constantly took away Negroes which the Indians had captured in war or raised from children. He pointed out that although his people were destitute, their annuity was being withheld because they would not give up their property to citizens who claimed it. He said they were always being called upon to make reparations for lost cattle, hogs, or horses but had never been able to recover those taken from them."[35] The situation became worse on March 21, 1830, when Humphreys was discharged as Indian agent. His replacement, Major John Phagan, syphoned off Indian funds to himself. Some action was expected when Andrew Jackson became president in 1829 and the Indian Removal Act became law in 1830.

27

Removal to
the West — Choctaw

Before the Indian Removal Act became a law on May 28, 1830, steps were taken within the Choctaw nation to get a treaty of removal. One of the chiefs, a shrewd half-blooded Choctaw, Greenwood LeFlore, maneuvered to have himself appointed as chief of the whole nation. Shortly thereafter he sponsored a treaty providing for removal which purported to represent the desires of the tribe and delivered it to the president's representative. Before it was acted on a protest from chiefs and leading men was sent to Washington. After the Senate considered both documents it rejected the proposed treaty. The tribe, in particular the full-blooded Choctaws, rejected LeFlore as a single chief. It may have been in part a result of an injunction given by their beloved chief Pushmataha who died in 1824. He advised that the people should never "permit to participate in the government of the nation any one having a drop of white blood in his veins. The inherent avarice of the white blood, he said, would prompt its owner to favor sale of their land."[1]

Accepting that there were legitimate arguments for removal, except for those Cherokee who were as civilized, if not more so, than those trying to take their land, the Removal Act of May 28, 1830, was fair in its terms.[2] Land west of the Mississippi River was available "for the reception of such tribes or nations of Indians as may choose to exchange the lands where they now reside, and remove there." Payment was to be made for improvements on the land ceded. The land provided in the West was to be free of any prior Indian title, and the United States would protect the moving tribe from "interruption or disturbance from any other tribe or nation of Indians, or from any other person or persons whatever." What wasn't fair was how the Act was implemented.

Jackson's election fed expectations for a rapid solution of Indian problems. The Choctaw claimed 10 million acres of land in Mississippi and the Chickasaw 6 million acres. A menacing Mississippi legislature passed a law on February 4, 1829, extending "legal process into that part of the state now occupied by the Chickasaw and Choctaw tribes of Indians."[3] Whites eager to take over the Indian lands may have been surprised at Jackson's moderate stance in his first inaugural address: "It will be my sincere and constant desire to observe toward the Indian tribes within our limits a just and liberal policy, and to give ... humane and considerate attention to their rights and their wants."[4] Nonetheless, in his first annual message to Congress in December 1829 he stated his conviction that to not separate the Indians from the whites would lead to their disintegration as nations.

Evidence supporting Jackson's conviction is the act of the Mississippi legislature passing a law in January 1830 to extend Mississippi law "over the persons and property of the Indians resident within its limits."[5] By eliminating the authority of the Choctaw nation over its land, Mississippi opened it to "rivers of whiskey."[6]

After the Indian Removal Act became law Jackson hastened to arrange a meeting with the Choctaw and other tribes considered favorable for removal while he was vacationing in Franklin, Tennessee. The Chickasaw met with him but no one from the Choctaw did. Differences within the tribe precluded the appointment of anyone to represent the tribe. After a provisional agreement was reached with the Chickasaw, Secretary of War John H. Eaton and John Coffee, two dedicated Westerners and Jackson intimates, went to Mississippi to confer with the Choctaw. Without a single chief, the Choctaw being organized into three districts with a chief for each district were difficult to deal with. Mushulatubbe, a full-blooded Choctaw and one of the district chiefs, opposed the treaty LeFlore had fashioned and refused to be intimidated into resigning when LeFlore demanded that he do so. Their differences almost came to an armed struggle at a July council meeting at which annuities were distributed and each had hundreds of armed supporters. In league with LeFlore was David Folsom, a mixed-blood Choctaw, who was a rival of Mushulatubbe.

According to the Choctaw agent, William Ward, after LeFlore was rejected as a "King for life"[7] over the Choctaw he took a tack against any treaty. The rejected one he had proposed had "reserved to himself, Folsom, and others, large and valuable tracts."[8] Ward described LeFlore as "a greater Tyrent and coward"[9] than any he had seen.

Eaton and Coffee started discussions with the Choctaw on September 15. The meeting was held at Dancing Rabbit Creek within the nation with 6,000 or so Indians and many scoundrels, "[g]amblers, saloonkeepers, frontier rowdies, and prostitutes,"[10] trying to take advantage of them. They outlined the reality of the Choctaw situation. If they remained in Mississippi the United States would not be able to protect them from the Mississippi laws and armed white men would compel them to submit. The best that Eaton could achieve, and only after many had left thinking it had been decided not to sign a treaty, was an agreement for the Choctaw to examine the land in the West and to remove if they found it satisfactory. Important to the agreement was the understanding that a respected merchant, George S. Gaines, would lead a party to examine the western land and, if it was found satisfactory, he would manage the removal. In the treaty[11] the Choctaw ceded "the entire country they own[ed] ... east of the Mississippi River" and agreed to remove beyond the river. The treaty was detailed as to the respective obligations.

The pressure on the Choctaw is exposed in the introductory paragraph which the Senate refused to ratify: "the General Assembly of the State of Mississippi has extended the laws of said State to persons and property within the chartered limits of the same, and the President of the United States has said that he cannot protect the Choctaw people from the operation of these laws; Now therefore that the Choctaw may live under their own laws in peace with the United States and the State of Mississippi they have determined to sell their lands east of the Mississippi."[12]

In his annual report of December 1830 Eaton stated, "We sought through persuasion only, to satisfy them that their situation called for serious reflection.... No secret meetings were held, no bribes were offered, no promises made."[13] If by bribes Eaton meant payments outside the framework of the treaty, the statement may have been true. However, the special treatment of the three chiefs (LeFlore; Nitakechi, a nephew of Pushmataha; and Mushulatubbe) signing the Treaty of Dancing Rabbit Creek on September 27, 1830, and for possibly

500 others was undoubtedly important to the agreement, which was opposed by a majority of the tribe. Each chief received four sections of land in addition to $250 annually so long as they were in office. Captains, sub-captains, and principal men were to receive smaller parcels of land. Maybe even more important was Article 14, which allowed Choctaws to stay in Mississippi, become state citizens, and, for each head of family staying, have at least 640 acres of land. The largess provided to individuals was so extensive that a supplement to the main treaty was signed by the three chiefs and a small number of others on September 28. Roughly 180 signed, mostly by marks subjoining their names, the treaty and 18 the next day supplement.

The treaty was ratified on February 24, 1831, and Jackson proclaimed the grant to the western land on May 26. Considering that the advancing horde of whites might continue to threaten the Choctaw west of the Mississippi, the treaty had some good features, including provisions that "[a]ll intruders shall be removed from the Choctaw Nation and kept without it" and "that no part of the land granted them shall ever be embraced in any Territory or State" and the United States would protect them from state and territorial laws. In cases of "violence committed upon persons and property of the people of the Choctaw Nation," the President of the United States would "see that every possible degree of justice is done to said Indian party." Their movement, to land in present-day Oklahoma, was to take place over three falls, those of 1831, 1832, and 1833. No land which they ceded was to be settled on until they had left, but surveyors were permitted immediate entry.

The exploration party led by Gaines crossed into the Indian Territory on November 28, 1830. It only had two of the Choctaw chiefs, Nitakechi and Mushulatubbe. LeFlore decided not to go either because he was too busy "negotiating with Indians whom he could induce to remove at once for the sale of their improvements to white men, whom he immediately put in possession of the land and improvements,"[14] or fearing that in his absence he would be replaced as chief. If the latter, he failed; he was replaced as were the two chiefs that accompanied Gaines. Jackson was not phased by the Choctaw decision to replace the chiefs who signed the treaty, and he refused to recognize the new chiefs. As Gaines wrote to Eaton, discontents were "appear[ing] in portions of all the districts."[15]

LeFlore's activities putting whites on the land was contrary to the as yet not ratified treaty. Washington did not object. LeFlore excused his actions by asserting the Choctaw needed to move as fast as possible "to escape the evils of intemperance which are flowing upon the country on all sides and have caused the death of a considerable number since the administration of the Choctaw law was arrested"[16] by the state of Mississippi.

The Gaines exploration party returned in February 1831 and was pleased with land north of the Red River. Under the treaty the Choctaw were given land between the Arkansas and the Red rivers. With the treaty ratified, plans were made for the removal. A census taken in September 1830 showed there to be 19,554 Choctaws. Even before the removal was well underway, Jackson asked Eaton and Coffee to see if the Choctaw would be willing to sell 4.5 million acres of their western lands to the Chickasaw. The Choctaw took a sensible stance: they should be allowed to "put their feet on their new land before they [were] asked for it."[17] When the removal under the treaty was declared to be complete as of November 22, 1833, there were still around 7,000 in the East who had exercised their right to become Mississippi citizens.

LeFlore's machinations resulted in 427 emigrants being in the new nation by October

1831, at which time the first large group to be moved by the government was being gathered east of the Mississippi for the move. In anticipation of this movement wagons, oxen, and horses were ordered for placement at Little Rock for use of the emigrants. At the same time Fort Smith, which had been abandoned, was repaired as a reception point.

Four thousand were at Vicksburg on November 25, 1831. These were split into a party to go to the Red River area by way of the Arkansas River to Little Rock and then over land to Fort Towson, the end point near the Red River, and another party to go down the Mississippi to the Red River and then up the Red to a point about 160 miles from Fort Towson, which was reached over land.

An eyewitness to an assembly of Choctaw preparing to migrate from Hebron, Mississippi, was a nine-year-or-so-old H. B. Cushman, the son of a missionary. He wrote of what he saw and heard: "[T]he wailing of the Choctaw women.... The venerable old men ... expressed the majesty of silent grief.... [T]he young and middle-aged warriors, now subdued and standing around in silence profound...."[18] A sympathetic George Gaines wrote: "The feeling which many of them evince in parting, never to return again, from their own long cherished hills, poor as they are in this section of country, is truly painful to witness; and would be more so to me, but for the conviction that the removal is absolutely necessary for their welfare."[19]

Another group of 406, mostly full-blooded Choctaws who were followers of Mushulatubbe, marched to Memphis, wanting to settle near Fort Smith. They did not want anything to do with missionaries. Alexis de Tocqueville saw migrants at Memphis in 1831:

> It was ... in the depths of winter.... The Indians brought their families with them; there were among them the wounded, the sick, newborn babies, and old men on the point of death. They had neither tents nor wagons, but only some provisions and weapons. I saw them embark to cross the great river, and the sign will never fade from my memory. Neither sob nor complaint rose from that silent assembly. Their afflictions were of long standing, and they felt them to be irremediable.[20]

Those traveling during the winter of 1831–1832 struggled with bad roads, swamps, and cold weather. The road from Little Rock to the Red River, a distance of 230 miles, was described as being "through a country little settled, and literally impassable to any thing but wild beasts."[21] Captain Jacob Brown who was in charge of the trip from Little Rock to the Red River said, "This unexpected cold weather must produce much suffering. Our poor emigrants, many of them quite naked, and without much shelter, must suffer: it is impossible to be otherwise."[22] With these obstacles surmounted and some deaths, rations were being furnished to over 3,700 in the Red River area in April 1832, and for 541 near Fort Smith. LeFlore traveled with a party that went up the Red River but soon went back to Mississippi.

Before the start of the 1832 migration season, a decision was made to construct a road from Fort Smith to Fort Towson to facilitate getting supplies to the Red River area. In three months 147 miles were completed. In the spring of 1832 many squatters were settling on Choctaw land in Mississippi. Disregarding the provisions of the Dancing Rabbit Creek treaty, Mississippi passed a law "granting permission to the whites to settle in the Choctaw Nation"[23] and there were squatters in all directions. When Mushulatubbe asked for federal troops to remove the intruders, they were ordered to the area only to have the orders canceled after Representative F. E. Plummer of Mississippi lodged a complaint with the Secretary of

War. The Choctaw agent William Ward, who was conniving with the whites went to Washington and said the Indians had invited the whites into the country. This was true insofar as LeFlore was concerned but probably not so respecting the full-bloods.

Facing the experience of 1831–1832 it was decided to start the trip earlier to avoid winter weather and some started on October 3. It was decided to drop the Red River route and to take all from either Memphis or Vicksburg to Rock Roe (near modern Clarendon, Arkansas), a point on the White River, and then all would proceed to Little Rock and from there some would go over land to Fort Towson and some go up the Arkansas River as far as possible to reach Fort Smith. A new specter appeared almost immediately. Cholera was spreading down the Mississippi from Louisville and St. Louis.

Fear of cholera kept many from boarding a steamboat to go from Memphis to Rock Roe, a trip of 4 or 5 days. Those deciding to go by land took two weeks to travel 90 miles. At Rock Roe many teamsters waiting to take them another 60 miles to Little Rock disappeared after the group traveling by steamboat had two cholera deaths aboard the boat and 10 shortly after arriving. Before the trip to Little Rock started, additional Indians came to Rock Roe from Vicksburg. The total leaving for Little Rock on November 14 was 1,400.

Without too much difficulty the 1,400 reached Little Rock on November 19 and most were across the Arkansas River by the 21st. By December 2 some were at Washington, Arkansas, about 50 miles from the Arkansas-Indian Territory boundary and some reached Choctaw country on December 9. Others numbering 648, called Nail's party, was at destination end on December 18.

Another large number left Memphis for Rock Roe on November 3 by land, which turned out to be largely a swamp, and suffered a number of deaths from cholera. There were 1,300 at Rock Roe and by December 6 they were at Little Rock and by December 14 1,000 reached Fort Smith. A separate 500 traveled on their own so as to be able to claim a $10 per capita commutation payment when they reached their destination. They bogged down in the swamp and decided to stay there but were found by Captain William Armstrong, who organized the trips out of Rock Roe, and sent them on their way. They reached Fort Smith on January 20, 1833.

A large group of about 1,800 under Chief Nitakechi left Vicksburg *en route* to Rock Roe and arrived on November 21. Before reaching Vicksburg on November 4, learning of cholera there, they camped north of it for a wet and cold week. The trip from the mouth of the White River, which they reached on November 18, to Rock Roe, about 50 miles, took 4 days. They immediately left Rock Roe for Little Rock.

There was no delay leaving Fort Smith for Fort Towson. But it was difficult to get the Indians to leave their fires in the mornings. The Choctaw in this group were described as arriving at the rendezvous place for enrollment to go west of the Mississippi with "nothing under heaven to protect their naked bodies from the pitiless storm but a share of their parents' blanket, which served as a mantle by day and as a bed by night."[24] Cholera was a terrible presence. Armstrong wrote that "[n]o man but one who was present can form any idea of the difficulties that we have encountered owing to the cholera, and the influence occasioned by its dreadful effects.... death was hourly among us, and the road lined with the sick. The extra wagons hired to haul the sick are about five to the 1,000; fortunately they are a people that will walk to the last, or I do not know how we could get on."[25] They reached the end of their journey in mid–December.

Settlements in the Red River area were increased by 3,333 over the winter of 1832–1833, and 2,000 more settled around the Choctaw agency near Fort Smith. Overall about 7,000 had emigrated since the Treaty of Dancing Rabbit Creek. Others went to Texas, and during the winter of 1833–1834 emigrants made the trip without government help. Overall after November 1832, a total of 3,215 claimed the $10 commutation payment.

Marring generally honest efforts to make the moves easy for the Choctaw was the conduct of their Mississippi agent, William Ward. Under the treaty Choctaws wanting to stay in Mississippi had to register within a six-month period. Ward made this difficult by being unavailable or placing other obstacles in the way of their registering. An investigation of complaints resulted in an 1838 report finding Ward unfit to be an agent and that his conduct was "marked by a degree of hostility ... he was often arbitrary, tyrannical, and insulting, and intended to drive [the Choctaw] west."[26]

Angie Debo concluded in her book *The Rise and Fall of the Choctaw Republic* that after reaching Indian Territory the Choctaws proceeded over the next thirty years to make an "orderly development almost unprecedented in the history of any people."[27] The development was without the presence of LeFlore who stayed in Mississippi, became a United States citizen and, over the next 30 years, developed a 15,000-acre plantation employing 400 slaves and served for a time in the Mississippi House and Senate. The compassion of the Choctaw was observed in 1847 when "many full-blooded Choctaw" made a substantial contribution to a fund to help "famishing Ireland."[28]

28

Removal to
the West — Chickasaw

Over half of Mississippi was legally in the hands of the Chickasaw and Choctaw when it became a state in 1817. The Constitutional Convention prepared a memorial for Congress: "The quantity of Land to which the Indian title is extinguished is very small, and it is to be feared that many years will elapse before the [tribes] can be induced to dispose of it to the Government. This circumstance alone will confine the growth and population of the State, until it shall be overcome by some exercise of executive authority, which will lead to the extinguishment of Indian title over this Tract of Country."[1] The danger from this situation was not lost on the mixed-blooded leadership of the Chickasaw. In reality mere title could not protect the Indians — in 1810 Governor Holmes reported to the Secretary of War that four to five thousand white persons were on Indian land and were "determined to remain there in Opposition to the laws of the United States until removed by force."[2] In this case a threat by the Chickasaw to run the squatters off was enough to prompt the United States to remove them.

The Chickasaw lifestyle was changing. The game east of the Mississippi was not sufficient for the full-blooded Chickasaw, who preferred the hunting life, to adequately sustain themselves. One solution was for bands of Chickasaw to move west of the river. Those staying in Mississippi, encouraged by the federal agent, turned to agriculture. The mixed-blooded members of the tribe went beyond subsistence farming; they engaged in commercial farming and rather than living in towns built homes on farms and plantations. By 1827 cotton gins and grain mills were available, and grain, livestock, and cotton were exported mostly through Cotton Gin Port, the head of navigation of the Tombigbee River, to the Gulf markets. Chickasaw exposure to outsiders was a result of the Natchez Trace through their land and a road, called Gaines' Trace, running from Muscle Shoals to Cotton Gin Port. Enterprising Chickasaw operated ferries and public inns and sold necessities to travelers who in 1815 numbered in the thousands. The 1816 treaty provision limiting white tradesmen in the nation allowed commercial development within the tribe.

To conform to their new situation the Chickasaw in 1824 divided the nation into four districts to facilitate a judicial system and government administration. In 1829 a code of laws was adopted which dealt with civil and criminal wrongs and protected private property. Whiskey was banned. A mounted police force of 125 men from each district was formed. None of this satisfied Mississippi or Alabama. Between 1819 and 1830 laws were enacted by each which "abolished tribal government and incorporated the Chickasaw Nation into state jurisdiction."[3] State pressure coupled with a federal attitude expressed by Monroe just before he left office in 1825 convinced the Chickasaw that they would have to move. Monroe had a plan for removal which he said was "of very high importance to [the] Union, and [could] be accomplished on conditions and in a manner to promote the interest and happiness of those tribes, the attention of the Government has been long drawn with great solicitude to that object."[4]

With John Quincy Adams in the White House, Congress appropriated funds for a council with the Choctaw and Chickasaw. In October 1826 a council with the Chickasaw was fruitless. Levi Colbert, an important leader, said they feared that to move would be like "transplanting an old tree, which would wither and die away." Furthermore, they were "a people ... not enlightened [and could not] consent to be under [the white] Government."[5]

Thomas L. McKenney, the superintendent of Indian affairs, attributed the failures to the "enlightened half-breeds [who] read in the history of the past the effect of this mode of acquiring lands. They see the entire country of the east ... swept of their brethren who once inhabited there; and that, as the chiefs in the middle and northern States have listened to proposals to treat with them, they also have disappeared, until only a remnant of their once mighty race is left."[6] With a softer approach McKenney in 1827 got agreement from the Chickasaw to go and look at the western land with the assumption that McKenney "would not wish [them] to move away into a Country where [they] could not live as well as [at present]."[7]

In 1828 a delegation of Chickasaws, Choctaws, and Creeks went west — the Chickasaws to look at the land and the others to visit tribesmen already settled there. When the Chickasaw were back home they told the tribal council the land did not equal that they presently had. The federals were told the Chickasaw could not "consent to remove to a country destitute of a single corresponding feature of the one in which [they presently resided]."[8]

After the Indian Removal Act was passed in 1830 and with an imperious Andrew Jackson as president, the Chickasaw were convinced to move. Mississippi and Alabama passed laws stripping the Indians of any powers different from those of others resident in the states. When they complained to Jackson he told them he wanted them "perpetuated and preserved as a nation" and this could only be achieved by their "consent to remove to a country beyond the Mississippi."[9] The state laws which "must operate upon [them]"[10] made it difficult to keep intruding white men off their land.

In August 1830 the Chickasaw were summoned to meet with United States commissioners John H. Eaton and John Coffee at Franklin, Tennessee, at a time when Jackson would be there. A treaty was signed which would only go forward if the Chickasaw found in the West "a country suitable to their wants."[11] When they didn't, the treaty died but conditions were so bad with the elimination of tribal law that the Indians were ready to negotiate another treaty. In December 1832 the Chickasaw agent reported to the Secretary of War that "whiskey traders and pedlers — with other intruders upon the Indian land [were] over running the Country."[12] An example of the state law in application is found in Grant Foreman's book *Indian Removal*:

Two white peddlers ... entered the Chickasaw country in violation of the law and opened a trading store; on the complaint of old Chief Tishomingo [the] United States sub-agent seized the [peddlers'] goods and sold them, turning half the proceeds over to [the Chickasaw.] The white men then went into the ... Mississippi [court and] Tishomingo and [the sub-agent were] thrown into jail and [a judgment was entered] against them for $493.09.[13]

The United States appealed to the Mississippi supreme court, which affirmed the lower court decision. To increase pressure for a new treaty Chickasaw annuity payments were withheld. At Pontotoc Creek, Coffee negotiated a treaty dated October 20, 1832, and supplemented on October 22, 1832, which at the outset says the "Chickasaw Nation find themselves oppressed in their present situation; by being made subject to the laws of the States in which they reside."[14] The treaty was much fairer than those previously ceding land for one or two cents per acre. Basically the price was for what the United States was selling the public domain. The sophistication of the Chickasaw negotiators is obvious.

This show of generosity on the part of the United States can be traced back to 1805 when the Colberts told American commissioners that if the Chickasaw "were disposed to sell ... land [they] would not sell it by wholesale. [They would] have it surveyed and have so much an acre for it, the same as the white people does to one another with these lands."[15] To actually get the United States to agree to such an even-handed arrangement was an amazing accomplishment when the terms of contemporaneous Choctaw and Creek cessions are considered, as well as the earlier Chickasaw cessions totaling about 20 million acres. The 1832 cession had a finality to it—with some reservations it took all Chickasaw land east of the Mississippi.

The ceded land was to be sold at public auction with most of the proceeds going to the Chickasaw. No right of preference was to be given to anyone and the United States was to guard against schemes that would prevent land selling for its full value. Until suitable land was found in the West, adult Chickasaws, 17 or older, were assigned a "comfortable settlement" to live on. When the nation moved, the "comfortable settlements" would be given up and sold for the benefit of the tribe. A prohibition against leasing the "comfortable settlements" was included.

Since the money to be received by the nation would be large, a perpetual fund was to be created of at least three-fourths of the proceeds the interest from which would be available for tribe use. Fifty years hence, the fund would be turned over to the Chickasaw if they had become so enlightened as to be capable of managing so large a sum of money. A federal agent was to stay with the Chickasaw. The tribe asked that the United States establish two mail routes across the nation so they could carry out the business of the nation.

Two provisions in the treaty sounded good but turned out to be worthless. The United States guaranteed "to the Chickasaw nation, the quiet possession and uninterrupted use of the [comfortable settlements] so long as they may live on and occupy the same." Another provision expressed a request of the Chickasaw: "no persons be permitted to move in and settle on their country before the land is sold." Eager whites were not deterred. There were squatters aplenty, and when the United States marshal posted notices warning them to remove, no one obeyed and the government did nothing. The inaction can be understood in the face of a decision of the Mississippi circuit court in late 1832 "that the laws of the United States regulating intercourse and trade with the Indians had been nullified in that state by the extension of the laws of Mississippi over the Indians."[16] To disregard treaty language, although not new, was a stain on the United States. It ignored the Constitution provision (art. I, sec. 8) giving Congress the power "To regulate commerce ... with the Indian Tribes." On December 9, 1832, the Secretary of War was told that "whiskey traders and peddlers with other intruders [were] overrunning the country to the manifest injury of the Chickasaw tribe."[17]

Some prominent Chickasaws, including Levi Colbert and Tishomingo, a revered old chief who under the October treaty was to receive $100 per year for life, did not approve of it. They prepared a memorial detailing their complaints, mainly asserting the mixed-blooded men and white men married into the tribe were favored to the detriment of the full-blooded Chickasaws. They accused Coffee of browbeating and abusing them. The memorial was taken to Washington but they were not able to get any change in the treaty.

The year 1833 passed without any agreement as to land in the West. The year 1834 brought on another treaty[18] which added provisions to those in the 1832 treaty and made several significant changes. Those negotiating the May 24, 1834, treaty in Washington were primarily successful mixed-blooded Chickasaws (Colberts) and a well-to-do Benjamin Love. Under the treaty these men had a veto over the sale of land by any Chickasaw who they considered incompetent to handle a "comfortable settlement." A major change was made in the 1834 treaty in that those assigned "comfortable settlements" had title "in fee," which meant they had the option to sell the land and improvements.

To fight the onslaught of Mississippians using Mississippi laws to wrest land and money from the Chickasaws, an Article III in the 1834 treaty was included. In it the Chickasaws said they would forebear requesting military force to protect their rights but wanted help to get legal civil remedies. The United States agreed that its agent would pursue all lawful civil means, which the laws of the state permit to get justice and if he failed a claim would be made against the United States. Those negotiating for the Chickasaw were surely realists enough to not put too much faith in this article. In Article X the negotiators reverted to what had been common in earlier treaties — sections of land were granted to them in consideration of their efforts to come to Washington to negotiate and the effort they would make respecting Chickasaws not competent to handle their "comfortable settlements." Others were also provided for, including Benjamin Reynolds, their long tried and faithful agent.

Grant Foreman in *Indian Removal* relates the consequences of making land available for purchase from the Chickasaws: "After the survey had been completed so that the Indians' lands could be described and conveyances made, the customary campaign of larceny of their holdings was soon launched by the conscienceless horde of whites who invaded the country."[19] The impact on the Chickasaw was devastating. James Colbert wrote to the Secretary of War in June 1835:

> A host of Speculators are going over the country and have hired all the half breeds to interpret for them and give them five or ten dollars for each contract they make; they use every strategem they can devise and practice every imposition on their ignorance; these half-breeds tell them the agent says you must sell and they believe every thing the agent tells them must be done....[20]

Much of the money the Chickasaws received was squandered. A land office was set up at Pontotoc and the register and receiver described what was happening. Adjacent to the land office "a number of Shops [were] established whither the Indians resort, and drink Spirits to an intoxication of almost unparalleled extent."[21]

The delay in arranging for land in the West was not caused by a lack of suitable land, but rather with working out an agreement with the Choctaw for the Chickasaw to occupy the western half of the Choctaw reservation. The Choctaw in the 1820 Doak's Stand treaty traded 5 million acres in Mississippi for 13 million acres between the Arkansas and Canadian rivers and the Red River. Later, in 1825, when Arkansas complained the eastern boundary to the 13 million acres needed to be changed, it was, to the current western boundary of

Arkansas. In the 1830 Choctaw treaty (Dancing Rabbit Creek) the Choctaw were given fee-simple title to the 13 million acres in what was known as Indian Territory, although it never became a territory in a legal sense, and later became Oklahoma. In 1837 the Seminole also paid the Choctaw to settle on Choctaw land.[22]

In December 1833 the Choctaw were not willing to sell any of their land but would let the Chickasaw make their home there. The Chickasaw refused. A meeting was held in January 1836 without any agreement, but in January 1837, at Doaksville, near Fort Towson in the Choctaw country, agreement[23] was reached. The Chickasaw agreed to a less than clear title to the land and an unfettered right to control their own affairs and the Choctaw were to be paid, with conditions, $530,000. The need to emigrate was obvious. "[M]uch of their nation had been occupied by settlers."[24]

In the West the Chickasaw could not sell any of the land and were to be subject to the same laws to which the Choctaw were. The Chickasaw retained control over their funds. Any differences between the two tribes were to be referred to the Choctaw agent with a right to appeal to the president. Choctaws and Chickasaws could settle in the country of the other and Chickasaws were eligible to all the different offices of the Choctaw Nation. Except for $30,000 the Choctaw would only benefit from the interest of the remaining $500,000 for the next 20 years.

The Chickasaw planned for the first migration to start on May 1. The superintendent of the removal, A. M. M. Upshaw, sounded a note of urgency, saying that "an average of 50 to 100 are drunk each day" and "as long as they have a cent" the tavern keepers and "petty merchants will use all exertions to keep them here."[25]

A party of 500 went through Memphis *en route* to their new home on July 4, 1837, and were described as "present[ing] a handsome appearance, being nearly all mounted, and, with few exceptions, well dressed in their national costume."[26] Half of this group reached Fort Coffee on the Arkansas River in Indian Territory on August 2 but the other half insisted on going by an overland route to the Red River instead of by water up the Arkansas River to Fort Coffee, and did not arrive at Fort Towson until September after some hardship.

In November another 4,000 were at Memphis and those willing to go by water, roughly 2,000, made the trip to Fort Coffee in less than two weeks. Those traveling by land who were frightened by news that a steamboat with Creek emigrants had sunk, resulting in the death of 300 Creeks, took longer and had much difficulty. A complication in moving the Chickasaw was the amount of baggage and livestock they took with them. Upshaw said the "Chickasaws have an immense quantity of baggage. A great many of them have fine wagons and teams. They have also some four or five thousand ponies. I have used all the influence that I had to get them to sell off their horses, but they would about as lieve part with their lives as part with a horse."[27]

Out of 5,338 Chickasaws starting for Indian Territory in the fall of 1837 only 3,001 traveled by water. Accepting a census taken before the emigration started, of 6,070 (comprised of 4,914 Chickasaws and 1,156 slaves), most of the nation was west of the river in 1838. Mistakenly, Upshaw reported in 1839 that except for a few families capable of moving on their own, the movement was complete. In fact it wasn't until 1850 that all of the Chickasaw had migrated.

An observer of the large group going by land described what he saw:

[An] immense column of moving Indians ... with the train of Govt. waggons, the multitude of horses; it is said three to each Indian & besides at least six dogs and cats to an Indian. They were all most comfortably clad — the men in complete Indian dress with showy shawls tied in turban fashion round their heads — dashing about on their horses ... many of them presenting the finest countenances & figures that I ever saw. The women also very decently clothed like white women, in calico gowns — but much tidier and better put on than common white-people — and how beautifully they managed their horses, how proud & calm & erect, they sat in full gallop.[28]

The Chickasaw treaty with the United States specified the Chickasaw were to pay the costs of emigration. They had the funds. Of the 6,422,400 acres they ceded east of the Mississippi, 4 million acres had not been allotted and were sold at auction, bringing $3.3 million to the Chickasaw, who could use one-fourth of that amount for tribal matters. Many Chickasaws, up to 1,000, went to the Indian Territory on their own. Overall the movement went well but after they arrived they were threatened by Kickapoos and Shawnees who had villages on their land and Kiowas and Comanches roaming in the area. Federal Fort Washita was located to give them some protection in 1842. A smallpox epidemic in 1838 caused the death of over 500 Chickasaws and Choctaws and fraud and incompetency left them short of rations when they arrived in Indian Territory.

Too late to help, the Secretary of War sent Major Ethan Allen Hitchcock to Indian Territory to investigate what happened in 1841 and 1842. Among his findings was evidence of "worn-out oxen and bulls [being] forced upon the half-starving people at an exorbitant price" and of "spoiled rations to the value of $200,000 [being] sold to the Chickasaws." He said the "air is full of scandals."[29] For a time the Secretary of War was able to keep the report hidden but eventually Congress was able to see it and 50 years later the Chickasaws were somewhat compensated.

On August 1, 1838, Upshaw explained why it had been expensive to move the Chickasaw:

... [T]hey had a great deal of money, that is, their own private funds which they spent very freely. They bought a great many valuable articles for themselves to take west, believing that their wants could not be supplied after getting to their homes.... Besides the waggons that they brought loaded, they brought about seven thousand ponies and horses, all packed as long as an Indian can pack them, and they can pack more on a horse than other people I ever saw. Well sir, all this came to Memphis. What had I to do? I complained ... [T]he reply of the chiefs and head men ... was this: "We are moved out of our own money. This is our property. We want it.... Were we to attempt to sell it, we could not for a hundred dollars worth get five dollars. Will you make us burn or throw our property in the River? ... In our treaty with our Great Father, it does not say that we shall not carry our baggage with us." Under these circumstances what could I say? I tell you what I did say: "Put your baggage in the boat."[30]

29

The Betrayal of the Creeks

Jackson's first term as president was due to expire in March 1833 and a rush was on in 1832 to complete removal treaties with the Creek, Chickasaw, and Seminole. Jackson could not act fast enough for Alabama and Mississippi, each having already enacted anti–Indian laws. An ultimate in anti–Indian bias was found in the Alabama "law prohibiting the word of an Indian from being received in court against that of a white man."[1] With whites settling on their land of 5 million acres in Alabama, the Creeks sent a message to Washington in April 1831 reading in part:

> ... Murders have already taken place, both by the reds and whites. We have caused the red men to be brought to justice, the whites go unpunished. We are weak and our words and oaths go for naught; justice we don't expect, nor can we get.... [The whites] daily rob us of our property; they bring white officers among us, and take our property from us for debts that were never contracted.... We are made subject to laws we have no means of comprehending; we never know when we are doing right.[2]

By December 1831 the Creeks counted 1,500 whites "including horsethieves and other criminals"[3] squatting on their land and marking out situations they designed occupying. The Indian situation was not only bad legally; many Creeks were starving. Despite the justice in their requests for federal protection, well founded in prior treaty provisions, the Jackson administration never wavered from its position that it could not interfere with what the states were doing.

The determined Jackson administration received an outright cession of 3 million acres of Creek land in a treaty signed March 24, 1832,[4] in Washington. However, notwithstanding the desire of the United States for the Creeks to move west, at the expense of the United States, under the treaty none would be compelled to emigrate — "they [were] free to go or stay, as they please[d]." Ninety chiefs were each to retain a section of land, heads of a family could select a half section, and 29 sections could be assigned to such Creeks as the Creek tribe selected. Furthermore, 20 sections were to be set aside "for the orphan children of the Creeks." These Creek reservations totaled 2 million acres. In due course the Creeks were to get a patent or grant of land west of the Mississippi in accord with the Act of Congress dated May 1830 titled "An Act to provide for an exchange of lands with the Indians residing in any of the States, or Territories, and for their removal West of the Mississippi."

Enticements for going west of the Mississippi were removal "at the expense of the United States" and sustenance for one year. Triggered after half the Creeks emigrated was a blacksmith for 20 years and steel. Perhaps more important was a guarantee of freedom from any laws by a State or Territory. A census taken in 1833 showed the Creeks numbered 14,142, including 445 Negro slaves, in the Upper Towns and 8,552, including 457 Negro slaves, in the Lower Towns.

As to Creek land east of the Mississippi, the treaty invited fraud. Reserved land could "be conveyed by the persons selecting the same, to any other persons for a fair consideration, in such manner as the President may direct." Sales were not valid until "the President approve[d]" them. With whiskey as a lubricator unscrupulous whites could buy land from unsophisticated Creeks at little cost. Since the United States paid the Creeks roughly 10 cents per acre for the 3 million acres, the "fair consideration" constraint to protect Creeks could be expected to be low.

Not only was the land something whites schemed to take from the Creeks, under the treaty $100,000 was to be paid "[f]or the purpose of paying certain debts due by the Creeks" and whatever was left would be used for "their own relief." Grasping whites were not likely to leave much of this sum for relief of the Creeks. Additional money was an initial annuity of $12,000 to be paid for 5 years, and then an annuity of $10,000 for 15 years.

The treaty outlined what could have been an orderly progression. All intruders in the "country ... ceded [were to] be removed by law ... until the country [was] surveyed ... and the [Creek] selections made." Once Creek selections were made, intruders would be removed for a term of five years "or until the [land was] conveyed to white persons." The plan was for surveys to be completed in 1833 and for selections to then be made.

The Creeks made the mistake of believing the United States would fulfill its treaty commitments. Orders to the United States marshal for the southern district of Alabama were far from forceful. The marshal was "to be as conciliatory as may be compatible with the object to be obtained" and force applied "only when absolutely necessary."[5] In the fall of 1832 the Creeks wrote to the Secretary of War: "we are surrounded by the whites with their fields and fences, our lives are in jeopardy, we are daily threatened.... We are prevented from building new houses, or clearing new fields."[6]

When the U.S. marshal ejected trespassers, as soon as he left the "whites returned in force and ran the Indians away."[7] Alabamans were not intimidated by any show of federal authority. Some intruders ejected by the marshal sued the Indians for trespass in the state courts and were legally reinstated. In January 1833 General Enoch Parsons wrote to the Secretary of War that the Creeks had "very little corn, and scarcely any stock" and that "[n]othing can preserve their property, or their existence, other than their immediate removal to the country designed for them."[8]

The situation was out of control. On March 14, 1833, Secretary of War Lewis Cass ordered the office of Indian affairs to "put an end to this lawless and disgraceful practice of intrusion."[9] By this time the number of intruders had risen to 3,000. In July Deputy Marshal Jeremiah Austill met resistance from intruders who were organizing to thwart his efforts. The marshal was frustrated by claims of whites against the Indians and threats to take the issue to Alabama courts where the outcome was sure to be against the Indians. Marshal Robert L. Crawford wanted to take action and described the intruders as "some of the most lawless and uncouth men I have ever seen; some of them refugees from the State of Georgia, and for whom rewards are offered."[10] Contributing to the general unrest was "the sale of whiskey upon the Creek lands ... to the utter ruin of the Indians."[11] Austill saw no solution but for the Indians to surrender — he told the Secretary of War: "The officers of the State have in some cases issued false precepts, and executed them upon the Indians. False accounts are made out; the Indians seized and put in jail, and compelled to surrender all they have, either their land claims or their property.... how this species of fraud and villainy is to be obviated I am unable to say, unless the Indians leave the country."[12]

In May 1833 Cass asked Col. John J. Abert and General Enoch Parsons to approach the Creek with the offer of another treaty under which they would immediately move to the West at government expense and under their own management. Abert told Cass the Creeks were not capable of organizing such a move. Their deterioration over the preceding "two or three years [saw them go from] a state of comparative plenty to that of unqualified wretchedness and want."[13] Abert explained what had happened:

> The free egress into the nation by the whites; encroachments upon their lands, even upon their cultivated fields; abuses of their persons and property; hosts of traders who, like locusts, have devoured their substance and inundated their homes with whiskey, have destroyed what little disposition to cultivation the Indians may have once had ... [and] the corn crop of this season ... will not be sufficient to feed more than a quarter of them.... They are brow beat, and cowed, and imposed upon, and depressed with the feeling that they have no adequate protection in the United States, and no capacity of self-protection in themselves.[14]

Abert and Parsons were dismayed, saying, "Their helpless ignorance, their generally good character, (for they are a well disposed people) their honesty of purpose, and general honesty of conduct, instead of establishing claims upon good feelings, seems rather to expose them to injuries."[15]

Uncontrolled whites poured into the Indian lands and Francis Scott Key, who went to Alabama to help defend indicted federal officers and soldiers in the Alabama courts, estimated their numbers to be 10,000 in the winter of 1833. If there are degrees of cheats, a higher class of cheats surfaced when the Indians were able to sell their land. Prosperous citizens committed many frauds. Reacting to an investigative report, the commissioner of Indian affairs said in 1838: "Persons, heretofore deemed respectable, are implicated in the most disgraceful attempts to defraud those who were incapacitated from protecting their own interests.... [The report related] acts that make the blood of a just man mount to his cheeks for shame that he and the perpetrators of them belong to the same community."[16] A legal form of stealing was an Alabama law allowing whites to administer Indian estates and to be well paid from the estate, mostly in land.[17]

The ways around the "fair consideration," federal certification, and presidential approval safeguards were numerous. Certification agents were appointed in November 1833 and the job of locating Indian reservations was completed in January 1834. Almost immediately the certifying agents reported "manifold instances of fraud and injustices." Cass washed his hands of the allegations and told the certifying agents that the frauds "were clearly beyond [their] reach as they [were] beyond the reach of [his] office."[18] The frauds were so egregious and disgusting that in May 1835 white Alabamans prepared resolutions to the president asking that he withhold his approval of certificates without a re-examination of the facts. The resolutions read in part:

> great fraud has been recently committed in obtaining title to lands, belonging to Indians without their knowledge or consent in any way whatever; the person committing such frauds or rather stealing the lands of the Indians has some other Indian who he has drilled with the description of locations and other matters in relation to the land; the Indian when thus drilled ... goes before the certifying agent and passes his land by certificate as being the real Indian owning that tract of land to the stealer or white man, who immediately sends such certificate to Washington City for the approval of the President; the Indians who are the rightful owners of the lands knowing nothing of this foul and dishonest transaction until nearly all their lands have been swept from under them.[19]

Land stealers crowded into the land office in droves.

Washington was persuaded to stop certification of sales and in April 1835 assigned one of the certifying agents, J.W.A. Sanford, to investigate the charges of fraud. Sanford was a poor choice. He was not trusted by the Indians and committed a colossal injustice in requiring complaining Indians to come to Columbus, Georgia, to make their complaints. Columbus was home to many of the land thieves, and when the rumor was spread among the Indians that they would be arrested if they went to Georgia and forced to emigrate, the result was that no Indians appeared to complain. Sanford refused a request to meet those complaining on the Alabama side of the Chattahoochee River.

The situation was so bad that the president was told by a group of Upper Creeks that they were ready to emigrate but couldn't do so without money from the sale of their land. The president then sent a friend of the Indians, John B. Hogan, to investigate. Hogan verified what had happened in reports of January and February 1836: "A greater mass of corruption perhaps, has never been congregated in any part of the world, than has been engendered by the Creek treaty in the grant of reservations of lands."[20] With a belief that emigration would be under the supervision of Hogan, the Lower Creeks reluctantly agreed to move. Then a tremendous error was made by the federal government. A contract for their removal "was let to a company made up principally of the men who had been most active in stealing [the Creek] lands, and for whom the Indians cherished implacable hatred."

Even this development did not stop some of the Creeks from continuing to plan to move. However, they were discouraged by threats from whites who filed suits against Indians with the object of taking their blacks, horses, and other property. Around the first of January in 1836 a familiar pattern developed which was disastrous for the Indians. Hungry Creeks moved into Cherokee country in Alabama and Georgia, and Georgia militia attacked those camped within Georgia. Later 1,000 Georgia militia assaulted the Creeks in Alabama. Thus started what historian Grant Foreman labels the Creek War of 1836. The war escalated when some Lower Creeks started attacking whites and destroying property in the vicinity of Columbus which braced for an onslaught which never came. Speculation was that the raids were encouraged by whites fearful of the ongoing investigation and hoping to deflect it. Whites in the area were murdered and others, frightened, abandoned their property.

The federal government did not act with dispatch to protect the Indians but when it came to protecting the whites, whether in the right or wrong, they acted promptly. On May 19 Cass ordered a stop to the investigation into fraud and directed the removal of all Creeks as a military measure. The terms of the treaty were cast aside. General Thomas S. Jesup was to carry out the removal. To locate and capture hostile Creeks, other Creeks were urged to seek them out and did so. Jesup had an armed force of about 11,000, of whom 1,806 were Creeks. The reward for the friendly Creeks, as was true in the earlier Creek War, was to be treated much the same as those who were hostile — they were also forced to migrate.

Governor Clement C. Clay of Alabama told federal commissioners appointed to determine the cause of the hostilities that "the opinion prevails extensively ... that the frauds and forgeries practiced upon the Indians to deprive them of their lands, were amongst the principal causes which excited them to hostilities. [Other explanations are] the vice and intemperance introduced amongst them by a class of white men; and to the destitute, and almost starving condition to which they were reduced."[21]

The difficulty of moving destitute men, women, and children was signaled when near 600 émigrés willingly started for Indian Territory in December 1834. They traveled during an unusually severe winter, and only 469 lived to reach their destination in April 1835. In addition to traveling in rain, snow and freezing conditions, it was a time when many were dying in Arkansas from influenza.

With Cass's order in place, 2,500 hostiles were marched to Montgomery, Alabama, and loaded on boats starting to the West. A Montgomery newspaper reported in July 1836 that the "spectacle ... was truly melancholy. To see the remnant of a once mighty people fettered and chained together forced to depart from the land of their fathers into a country unknown to them, is of itself sufficient to move the stoutest heart."[22] After about two months and 81 deaths the hostile Creeks reached Fort Gibson in Indian Territory on September 3, 1836. Under a threat that they would receive no annuity unless they accepted the government already established by the McIntosh Creeks who had emigrated in 1829, they took up residence with the Western Creeks. A smaller group of hostiles, 165 out of the 210 who started the trip, arrived a month later. Of those failing to reach Indian Territory 17 were seized by Alabama authorities and 19 died.

The next large group to start for the West was comprised of 2,700 friendly Creeks. They faced whites who wanted to take more of their property. On August 30, 1836, Jesup wrote to Cass that "[s]uits were multiplied against the Indians — their negroes, horses, and other property taken ... [and there] seemed to be no means of getting them out of the country peaceably, but by enabling them to pay the just demands against them and defending them against those which were doubtful or unjust."[23] The Indians wanted money for the land they were leaving and an advance payment of their 1837 annuity. They had little leverage over the United States and only escaped by agreeing to Jackson's plans for using a force of Creeks to fight the Seminoles in Florida. They received a $31,900 advance of the 1837 annuity to be applied to alleged debts and could keep any plunder (slaves) they captured in Florida.

On December 7 about 1,200 arrived at Fort Gibson. Coming behind them were many others. The *Memphis Enquirer* said in November that "8,000 [emigrating Creek Indians] have crossed the Mississippi ... and 5,000 more are around us. In about two weeks the whole tribe, about 15,000, will be west of the Mississippi."[24] Of the 15,000 new Creek émigrés in the West in the spring of 1837, a total of 2,495 were considered as hostile.

The trip from Memphis to Fort Gibson was arduous. Overall one group starting from Chambers County, Alabama, near Columbus, Georgia, traveled 800 miles by land and 425 by water in 96 days. Out of 2,000 there were 29 deaths —14 children and 15 "aged, feeble and intemperate."[25] These friendly Indians wrote a letter complimentary to the lieutenant who conducted them but excoriated those ordering the march:

> You have been with us many moons.... you have heard the cries of our women and children.... our road has been a long one.... and on it we have laid the bones of our men, women and children. When we left our homes the great General Jesup told us that we could get to our country as we wanted to. We wanted to gather our crops, and we wanted to go in peace and friendship. Did we? No! We were drove off like wolves ... lost our crops ... and our peoples' feet were bleeding with long marches.... Tell General Jackson if the white man will let us we will live in peace and friendship ... But tell him [the emigrating contractors] came not to treat us well, but [to] make money and tell our people behind not to be drove off like dogs. We are men ... we have women and children, and why should we come like wild horses?[26]

A breach of faith was the treatment of the Creek warriors in Florida fighting the Seminole and the Creek families. On the assurance that they would be discharged on February

1, 1837, 776 Creek warriors, under pressure, enlisted to serve in Florida. The date was one which would allow the warriors to proceed to the West with their families so as to be there in time to plant a crop. Jesup decided, against the Indian will, to keep them in Florida for another 7 months. To at least in part compensate for the delay, Jesup agreed that they would be subsisted for a year after they reached the West. While the warriors were in Florida, their families were to stay in Alabama in concentration camps under the protection of the United States.

The protection, which was mainly the presence of a federal agent and a few subordinates in the camps, was only protection in name. When citizen groups from Alabama and Georgia burned houses and made prisoners of 253 males, planning to take them away, the best the agent could do was to get agreement that the men would not be taken if the Indians left for the West. The Indians agreed and within 36 hours a party of 1,000 marched away. Another camp was surrounded and the Indians' horses, mules and ponies taken. The agent was told to have the Indians ready to move and within a half-hour the camp was moving toward Tuskegee. Georgia militia hunted for Indians who fled to the swamps and killed at least 40.

Alabama's Governor Clay got permission from the Secretary of War to remove these friendly Indians and by March 8, 1837, roughly 4,000 were in the Montgomery vicinity ready to be sent down the river to Mobile on their way to the West. The *Montgomery Advertiser* recognized the injustice being done — it reported on the situation: "The spectacle exhibited ... is truly heart rending; with all their cruelties, they are human beings and no man of feeling can look upon their present destitute condition.... while our citizens are rolling in ease and luxury, those who are natives of the country are in the most abject poverty, dependent for their sustenance on the charity of the government."[27]

With indignation the returning warriors were angered that their families had been moved before they returned and had a chance to assist and to preserve their property. Most of the displaced families were held at Mobile Point, near the entrance to Mobile Bay, and Pass Christian, between Biloxi, Mississippi, and New Orleans, to be joined by the warriors in Florida who returned in September 1837. It was a time of much illness and many died. Another tragedy befell them after the men returned and they were put on boats to take them up the Mississippi. The steamboat *Monmouth* collided with another ship and sank immediately, taking 311 of the 611 Indians aboard to a watery death. The *New Orleans Free American* blamed the removal contractors whose "avaricious disposition to increase the profits [chartered an] unseaworthy boat[]" and then packed the Indians "in such crowds that not the slightest regard [was] paid to their safety, comfort, or even decency."[28]

With a show of zeal never displayed in upholding the Indians rights, the army hunted for Creeks who had fled to the Cherokee and Chickasaw and packed them off to the West. By December 1837 the Creek emigration was essentially complete.

30

Seminole Saga

It didn't take long after the Indian Removal Act of 1830 for the Seminoles to be disabused of the belief that they had a commitment to stay in Florida for 20 years according to the Moultrie Creek treaty in 1823. The first sentence of a treaty signed at Payne's Landing on May 9, 1832,[1] is so unctuous as to cast a doubt on the Seminole willingness to sign; it reads: "The Seminole Indians, regarding with just respect the solicitude manifested by the President ... for the improvement of their condition, by recommending a removal to country more suitable to their habits and wants than the one they at present occupy" were willing to examine land west of the Mississippi. Recognizing the de facto situation, the treaty specified that those Indians "at present occupying the Big swamp, and other parts of the country beyond the [boundaries]" set in the 1823 treaty would be the first to move.

After a delegation visited the proposed western land, another treaty was signed at Fort Gibson in the Indian Territory on March 28, 1833. It described the western land going to the Seminole and declared the treaty of May 9, 1832, to be applicable. Most Seminole made no effort to comply with the three-year emigration period specified in the 1832 treaty. Major Ethan Allen Hitchcock, who in later years participated in the war against the Seminole, wrote in his diary: "The treaty of Payne's Landing in 1832 ... was a fraud upon [the Seminole] and they have in fact never agreed to emigrate. I say therefore that the Indians are in the right to defend themselves in the country to the best of their ability."[2]

Trouble quickly boiled to the surface when the new Indian agent, Wiley Thompson, who replaced Major Phagan (who had discrepancies in money accounts), called the chiefs together on April 3, 1835. Only eight minor chiefs signed a paper agreeing to the move. Others refused even though Jackson had conveyed that they would be destroyed if they did not comply. Thompson's answer was to strip those chiefs not signing of their chiefdoms; he was finally able to get 400 Indians to agree to emigrate. Blocking their emigration were Osceola and Jumper. Osceola, a half-blooded Seminole, "drew his knife and stabbed down savagely on the treaty"[3] in refusing to sign.

Micanopy, the legal hereditary chief of the Seminoles, was firmly against moving. Charley Emathla, a chief willing to discuss emigration, asserted that "[a]t Payne's Landing the white people forced us into the treaty."[4] Any doubts as to the depth of the resistance were resolved when Charley Emathla was killed after agreeing to move. Osceola's dislike of Agent Thompson, first prompted by "his young wife [being] carried off into slavery," became hatred when Thompson had him placed in irons for raging at Thompson, who refused to sell him arms. Predicting the future, Osceola shouted, "I shall remember the hour! The agent has his day. I will have mine!"[5] Sensing the resisters' determination, Thompson asked the government to reconsider a policy of forced emigration but was told to proceed.

Osceola was a Seminole chief who opposed removal vocally and by his actions. This painting by George Catlin is titled "Os-ce-o-la, The Black Drink, a Warrior of Great Distinction" (Smithsonian American Art Museum, gift of Mrs. Joseph Harrison, Jr., accession number 1985.66.301).

Strong supporters of the resistance to emigration, the Seminole blacks, moved deep into the Florida swamps. Records are not definitive on the relationship between the blacks and the Indians. To protect the blacks "the Indians ... insist[ed] to white authorities that the blacks were all slaves which they intended to defend from the depredation and claims of Americans."[6] Thompson's analysis in 1833 was that the blacks "always had a great influence over the Indians," and that they "live[d] in villages separate, and, in many cases, remote from their owners, and enjoy[ed] equal liberty with their owners, with the single exception [of supplying some product from their fields.] Many ... slaves have stocks of horses, cows, and hogs, with which the Indian owner never assumes the right to intermeddle."[7] As time approached for armed confrontations, the Seminole women and children went into the swamps and the settlers to forts.

War broke out on December 18, 1835, when Osceola, chosen to be the head war chief, with 80 warriors stopped a wagon train escorted by thirty mounted militia, eight of whom were killed and six wounded. Ten days later 110 soldiers marching from Fort Brooke to Fort King were ambushed — only one lived. Osceola did not participate in the second fight; he was near the Seminole agency waiting for a chance to take revenge against Thompson. He caught him outside the fort and Thompson died with 14 bullets in his body. At the Seminole camp scalps from the ambush of the 110 were placed on a tall pole around which a victory dance was performed. Osceola challenged General Duncan L. Clinch in a January letter: "You have guns, and so have we — you have powder and lead, and so have we — you have men, and so have we — your men will fight, and so will ours, till the last drop of the Seminole's blood has moistened the dust of his hunting ground."[8]

A northern newspaper described Osceola as "about 6 feet high [with] a 'lean and hungry look' [who in] salutations ... is full of smiles, exceedingly courteous, and hearty in the shake of the hand.... [but who could exhibit] a mixture of hate and unconquerable resolution." Osceola was about 35, and Jumper "[who was] exceedingly intelligent, and [perhaps] the most influential Chief in the nation" was about 55.[9]

It wasn't only in Osceola's area that Indians and blacks attacked. Night raids were made against plantations along the St. John's River. More American forces, 1,800, arrived at Tampa

Bay on February 9, 1836, under the leadership of General Edmund Pendleton Gaines. Nothing came of an Indian-proposed truce which would let them stay south of the Withlacoochee and the troops wouldn't pursue them. While Gaines was trying to cross the Withlacoochee River he was attacked by Osceola and several hundred Indians. Gaines' 200 men fortified themselves and did not move for several days. Then Clinch appeared with reinforcements and, not knowing about the truce offer, fired on the Indians who fled. The terms of the interrupted truce offer were not followed for long—homes of the whites were burned and Indians were killed.

During this same period, on April 11 and 12, a total of 407 willing Indians left Tampa Bay for the West. It took them two months to reach Seminole land near the Canadian River. There were 87 deaths. Lt. Joseph W. Harris, who led the group part of the way, wrote to the Secretary of War after the trip was completed: "They have lost everything.... 'Many' or 'few' are terms sufficiently definite to [their] thinking to indicate the extent of [their] riches or poverty.... The loss to which [they] attached the greatest importance was that of their ponies."[10]

Jackson was anxious to resolve the insurrection and called upon the hero of the War of 1812, Winfield Scott, to take charge. Known as "Old Fuss and Feathers" he arrived in March 1836 with "a fine military band and three wagons full of furniture [and] a good supply of fine wines."[11] An authority on infantry tactics, he planned a three-prong attack on Osceola. With 4,650 men Scott was unable to capture 1,200 Seminoles. The Seminole strategy was simple. Let the enemy struggle through the swamps—"dark and murky [water], filled with rotted tree stumps, tangled vines, and nameless living creatures"[12] and periodically shoot at them from an advantageous position. American forces suffered during summer months with illness transmitted by fever-bearing insects.

At the end of 1836, in the view of John T. Sprague, who was in Florida for part of the war and wrote the book *The Origin, Progress, and Conclusion of the Florida Wars*, 1836 was a year of large expenditures of money and serious embarrassments.

In December 1836 General Thomas Sidney Jesup took over from Scott, hoping to end the war early by having plenty of troops. With 8,000 men he had some immediate success in surprising groups of Seminoles, burning towns and villages, and capturing livestock. Jesup agreed, in writing, "that the Seminoles and their allies who came in to emigrate should be secure in their lives and property; that their Negroes should accompany them West and that their cattle should be paid for by the United States government."[13]

Signs for emigration were good and two large camps of Seminoles were situated near Tampa Bay. Then two events sent the Seminoles and blacks into the swamps. There was an outbreak of measles which killed 20 and Jesup gave in to pressure from whites for whites to go among the Seminoles looking for missing slaves. Some chiefs, including Micanopy and Jumper, did not want to return to the swamps. Those in opposition were carried off with their families by warriors, including Osceola, opposed to emigration. The differences with the Seminole hardened when Jesup wrote on September 9, 1837, that the "Seminole negro prisoners are now all the property of the public."[14]

An important development was the capture in the fall of King Philip, the principal Seminole chief on the east coast. Hoping to have him released, Coacoochee, his son, and Osceola came to talk. They were also hopeful of an agreement that would allow the Seminole some land in Florida. Osceola, standing under a white flag of truce, was taken prisoner and was never free again to lead the Seminoles. Coacoochee was also made a prisoner. Thereafter Jesup made prisoners of several leading chiefs, many of whom were captured under flags of truce, and organized another campaign which successfully forced most of the Seminole south of Tampa Bay.

In the winter of 1837 the Cherokee were anxious to relieve the Seminole of their suffering and offered to mediate between them and Jesup. Micanopy and other chiefs agreed to go to Jesup's headquarters under a flag of truce. When Micanopy said they were ready to emigrate and asked for time to assemble his people, Jesup had Micanopy and his whole party held hostage and demanded that all of his people come in within ten days. The Cherokees were outraged that they had been a party to Jesup's trickery and complained to the Secretary of War, but this did nothing to deter Jesup's determination to end the warfare. Jesup offered the Seminoles land south of Tampa Bay if they would return runaway slaves entering it and would defend it from foreign invasion. The Seminoles were willing to accept the offer but it turned out to not have Washington approval.

The year 1837 ended with a thousand troops having a three-hour battle with Seminoles, which caused the Seminoles to retreat. The year was not a good one for the Seminoles. Jumper and about 64 others surrendered in December and were on their way to New Orleans in January. Osceola and other leaders were in Jesup's hands and their loss of homes, crops, and livestock left the Seminoles in dire straits. As it developed over the next five years there were no more large battles but it took that time to essentially tame most of the Seminoles.

In 1838 the Seminoles regained a recognized leader. Coacoochee escaped together with a black, John Cavallo also known as Gopher John. To prevent further escapes Osceola, Micanopy, King Philip, and other Seminoles were moved from St. Augustine to Fort Moultrie at Charleston. They, without Osceola, were taken to New Orleans a month later. The shining light of Osceola was extinguished on January 30, 1838. On his death bed in full dress he "covered one half his face, neck and throat with vermillion, 'a custom practiced when the irrevocable oath of war is taken.'"[15] George Catlin, who painted Osceola while he was a prisoner, succinctly stated what had happened and was to happen:

> With this tribe the government have been engaged in deadly and disastrous warfare for four or five years; endeavoring to remove them from their lands.... [M]uch more [in money and lives] will doubtless be yet spent before they can be removed from their almost impenetrable swamps and hiding places ... from which they will be enabled in their exasperated state, to make continual sallies upon the unsuspecting and defenceless inhabitants of the country....[16]

Early in 1838 Jesup contacted the Seminole to explore a peaceful conclusion of the war and was asked for a guarantee of some land. Jesup passed this condition on to the president, Martin Van Buren, and ventured into the national policy realm in a letter to the Secretary of War dated February 11, 1838:

> ... [W]e have committed the error of attempting to remove [the Seminoles] when their lands were not required for agricultural purposes; when they were not in the way of the white inhabitants; and when the greater portion of their country was an unexplored wilderness, of the interior of which we were as ignorant as of the interior of China....
>
> ... [T]he prospect of terminating the war in any reasonable time is anything but flattering. My decided opinion is, that unless *immediate* emigration be abandoned, the war will continue for years to come, and at constantly accumulating expense.[17]

Secretary of War Joel R. Poinsett told him that government policy was to ship all Indians west of the Mississippi but if it helped to make a "temporary" agreement for the Seminoles to have land in Florida that would be acceptable.

In 1838 Jesup was replaced by General Zachary Taylor. Jesup claimed that between December 1836 and the summer of 1838 about 2,400 Indians and blacks were captured or killed. Of these were about 700 capable of bearing arms. A substantial number of Seminoles, over a thousand, were shipped to the West in the spring and summer of 1838. Another 700 or so arrived in the West during 1838 and early in 1839.

All did not go well for the Seminoles who emigrated. An important provision in the March 28, 1833, treaty signed at Fort Gibson specified Seminole land between the Canadian River and the north fork of the river would be separate from the Creek land. However, when the Seminole started arriving in the West they found that this land was already occupied by Creeks and many settled in the Fort Gibson area.

The U.S.-Creek treaty of February 14, 1833, provided that the Creek land in Indian Territory was to provide a "permanent and comfortable home" for the Seminoles, and that the Seminoles would be "a constituent part of [the Creek] nation." This conflict in the 1833 treaties was not resolved until a 1845 treaty with the Creeks and Seminoles recited that a large portion of the Seminoles had refused to settle on Creek land and they could settle either separately or as a body on Creek land and could make their own regulations under the general control of the Creek council on which they would be represented. The wedge on recalcitrants was loss of treaty benefits if they didn't move.

Taylor didn't have any great success in 1838 and 1839. He reported in 1840 that if "the enemy [could] be brought to battle ... the war would soon be closed.... Fortunately for them ... concealment is found to be more efficacious than opposition, and they leave the climate to fight their battles, which certainly has proven more destructive to our troops than the rifle or scalping knife.... Should the war be renewed, (which I sincerely hope may never be the case) the only way to bring it to a successful issue ... is to cover the whole country so as to prevent the enemy from hunting and fishing."[18] Unhappy Floridians thought they knew how to find the enemy. They purchased bloodhounds and in December 1839, with the approval of the Secretary of War, who wanted the dogs muzzled, turned them loose. The dogs, trained to track slaves, had no luck finding Indians.

Van Buren wanted the head of the army, General Alexander Macomb, to negotiate with the Seminoles and he proceeded to meet with several chiefs in May 1839 and promised land on the peninsula: "Lay down the scalping knife, rifle and tomahawk; go south of Little Pease Creek, and your Great Father will see that you are left tranquil and undisturbed."[19] What he didn't tell the chiefs was that this was to only be a temporary arrangement. Agreement was reached, Macomb declared the war over and left Florida, but, within a month, peace vanished when a group of Indians not party to the agreement raided trains and travelers, overran plantations, and attacked some troops.

A new general, W. K. Armistead, took over in May 1840. He had close to 5,000 men, of whom 1,000 were mounted. Even though over 500 were ill it was still a sizeable force to search for the Seminoles, who were less than 1,000 men, women, and children.

A change in leadership in May 1841 put Colonel W. J. Worth in command with a charge from the new government of President John Tyler "to terminate as speedily as possible the protracted hostilities in Florida."[20] He determined to destroy the Indians' crops and villages. He ordered that Coacoochee be brought back from New Orleans so that he could convince Seminoles to come in. He was blunt with Coacoochee — either he and his warriors would convince others to emigrate or they would be hung from the yardarm. Coacoochee spoke:

> We know but little; we have no books which tell us things; but we have the Great Spirit, moon, and stars; these told me last night, you would be our friend. I give you my word ... I wish now to have my band around me and go to Arkansas. You say I *must* end the war! Look at these irons! Can I go to my warriors? Coacoochee chained! No ... I never wish to tread upon my land unless I am free. If I can go to them *unchained* they will follow me in; but I fear they will not obey me when I walk to them in irons.[21]

Undoubtedly fearful that Coacoochee might lead his band someplace else, he was only allowed to choose five men to go to his band. He gave them a message:

> Have I not led the war dance and sung the song of the Seminole? ... Has not my scalping knife been red with blood, and the scalps of our enemy been drying in our camps? Have I not made the war path red with blood, and has not the Seminole always found a home in my camp? Then will the warriors of Coacoochee desert him?

* * *

> ... The Great White Chief will be kind to us.... He has given us forty days to [surrender].... Take these sticks; here are thirty-nine, one for each day; this much larger than the rest, with blood upon it, is the fortieth. When the others are thrown away, and this only remains, say to my people, that with the setting sun Coacoochee hangs like a dog, with none but white men to hear his last words.... Come for the voice of Coacoochee speaks to you![22]

Coacoochee lived — 78 warriors, 64 women, and 47 children came in, and he gained his freedom by working thereafter to convince Seminoles to emigrate. In October 1841 he left with 290 others for the West. On leaving Coacoochee, then 30 years old, said, "I have thrown away my rifle; have taken the hand of the white man, and now say to him, take care of me."[23]

Army service in Florida exposed soldiers to nature. No building could "keep out sand flies, mosquitoes, immense spiders, chiggers, black fleas, and other pests."[24] Dysentery from drinking stagnant water was common. At the end of 1841 the soldiers were not fighting large groups of warriors. Their efforts were compared to "men harpooning minnows and shooting sand pipers with artillery."[25]

Worth continued to ship Seminoles west. On February 5 and April 10, 1842, a total of about 340 were on their way. Worth told the Adjutant General in February that there were no more than 301 Indians left in Florida. As to those left, he suggested that groups in the West be allowed to circulate in Florida to persuade them to emigrate. And those who did not emigrate should be left alone as long as they peacefully stayed south of Pease Creek. A smaller number of troops would be used to protect white settlements. He wanted to declare the war over. Those remaining were spread out in small groups. Before he was allowed to declare the war over he set a goal of capturing Halleck-Tustenuggee who had been attacking travelers on their way to St. Augustine. Halleck made the mistake of agreeing to go to Fort King to meet with Worth; he was made a prisoner and his band surrounded and captured after he left.

With the approval of President John Tyler in May 1842, Worth was allowed to tell those still in the swamps that if they peacefully stayed south of Pease Creek they would be allowed, for the present, to stay. On May 11, 1842, Adjutant General Winfield Scott advised Worth that he could in his discretion declare the war was over. He did this and over the summer of 1842 Worth turned over the job of advising the Seminoles of the offer and of withdrawing the army to Col. J. H. Vose.

Worth was able to remove 602 Indians and blacks during his time in command. Only a small number had not been removed but among those were several formidable chiefs. Even though the Secretary of War ordered the war to continue, Vose took the route of negotiation and a message to the Indians that "inevitable disaster ... must attend [any] hostile demonstrations."[26] When this had only partial success he asked Worth, who had been promoted to a Brevet Brigadier General, to resume command. Worth took steps to capture several of the remaining chiefs, and then decided to resort to putting a bounty on each chief ($300) and warrior ($100) that troopers captured.

Worth ordered Colonel Ethan Allen Hitchcock on November 28 to reopen the war. Hitchcock, with a philosophical bent, decided to seek removal without any blood being shed. His target was a band of Creeks whose chief was Pascofa. When contact was made he found the band was destitute and willing to talk peace. In January 1843 the band came aboard a ship as the first step towards the Indian Territory. The number of Seminoles in Florida had been reduced to such a small number that Worth was agreeable to those left not being pursued. So long as they stayed in the Everglades and did not bother the whites, they could stay. Governor Call was ecstatic, saying, "The last war whoop has been heard on our southwestern border and peace and security are permanently restored in that quarter."[27] This peaceful coexistence lasted until 1848, during which time the Seminole numbers grew to between 400 and 500, 120 of whom were warriors.

The Seminoles were living well. They had game and seafood, horses, cattle, hogs, and poultry and grew vegetables on the higher hummocks. Then the peace was broken by an attack on a New River plantation located between the Apalachicola and Ochlockonee rivers in the Florida panhandle. Next was the murder of two at a store on Pease Creek and the burning and looting of the store. When the Indians agreed to deliver those responsible, and followed through, peace was restored.

Although there was some disturbance in 1850 the Secretary of War's annual report claimed peace in Florida. The possibility of emigration was discussed intermittently and in 1852 Holatter Micco (Billy Bowlegs) and some sub-chiefs went to Washington to talk with the Secretary of War. While there, Bowlegs marked a paper agreeing to move west, but after the group left Washington with clothing and presents, they disappeared into the Florida hinterland. In December 1853 Bowlegs sent word to the army that there was no intention to emigrate but they would remain peaceful if not molested. All went well until December 1855.

A surveying crew, for the sport of it, hacked down Bowlegs' banana plants and laughed at him when he complained. The survey crew was attacked; Secretary of War Jefferson Davis authorized mobilization of volunteers and three minor skirmishes occurred between January and April 1856. In 1857 the Seminoles were harassed and attacked but few agreed to emigrate. Destruction of their lodges and fields created hardship. When a group came from the West to talk about emigration in 1858 and money was offered for those willing to do so, Billy Bowlegs agreed. Off to New Orleans went 164, and the Florida wars passed into history, soon to be overshadowed by a war of monumental dimensions. An editorial in the *Boston*

Herald glamorized what happened: "The agonizing struggle [of 23 years] has at last terminated in the ruin and destruction of the gallant Seminole.... The Seminoles as a nation [in Florida] have been destroyed, but what an array of glory, faith, horrors, and anguish does this retrospect present!"[28] By one measure the Seminoles prevailed. Today there are five Seminole reservations in south Florida.

31

The Cherokee versus Georgia

Early in the Monroe administration (1817–1825) Cherokee territory had gone from 40,000 square miles, which the Cherokee claimed when they first traded with the white colonists in the 1700s, to 10,000,000 acres, or 15,625 square miles, mostly in northwest Georgia, where two-thirds of the Cherokee lived. Pressure by Secretary of War John C. Calhoun for the Cherokee to move west of the Mississippi River brought a Cherokee observation: "The Indians say they don't know how to understand their Father, the President. A few years ago he sent them a plough & a hoe — said it was not good for his red children to hunt — they must cultivate the earth. Now he tells them there is good hunting at the Arkansas: if they go there he will give them rifles."[1]

During the Monroe presidency the Eastern Cherokee made progress in changing their culture towards agriculture. They accepted mission schools, with 18 in operation in 1826. In 1821 a Cherokee alphabet, called a syllabary, was designed by Sequoyah, whose creation was prompted by a discussion of whether the power of a white man's document, called by the Cherokee *the talking leaf,* was a gift of the Great Spirit to the white man or something discovered by the white man. Sequoyah proved it was the latter. In 1828 a newspaper, *Phoenix,* using both English and the Cherokee language, was started by a Cherokee, Elias Boudinot. His Indian name was Buck Waite and his adopted name was that of an elderly theologian he visited in New Jersey who asked him to use the name. Together with his cousin, John Ridge, he attended school in Cornwall, Connecticut, and, as did his cousin, married a white New Englander. English was the official language of the Cherokee. Sequoyah's syllabary was so successful that half of the Cherokee households were literate by 1835.

In 1824–1825 the Eastern Cherokee had "22,000 cattle, 7,600 horses; 46,000 swine; 2,500 sheep; 762 looms; 2,488 spinning wheels; 172 wagons; 2,943 plows; 10 sawmills; 31 gristmills; 61 blacksmith shops; 8 cotton machines; 18 schools; 18 ferries; and a number of public roads."[2] In December 1825 Thomas J. McKenney, who headed a Bureau of Indian Affairs in the War Department starting in 1824, told the Secretary of War, "The Cherokees on this side of the Mississippi are in advance of all other tribes. They may be considered as a civilized people."[3] Scholars differ on how extensive these changes were but it is undeniable that great strides were made to conform to what the presidents from Washington through John Quincy Adams advocated.

For the Indians to become civilized wasn't enough for Monroe. He told Congress:

It would promote essentially the security and happiness of the tribes within our limits if they could be prevailed on to retire west and north of our States and Territories on lands to be procured for them by the United States in exchange for those on which they now reside. Surrounded as they are, and pressed as they will be on every side by the white population, it will be difficult if not impossible for them with their kind of government to sustain order among them. Their interior will be exposed to frequent disturbances, to remedy which the interposition of the United States will be indispensable, and thus their government will gradually lose its authority until it is annihilated. In this process the moral character of the tribes will also be lost.... All these evils may be avoided if these tribes will consent to remove beyond the limits of our present States and Territories. Lands equally good and perhaps more fertile may be procured for them in those quarters. The relations between the United States and such Indians would still be the same.[4]

When the Bureau of Indian Affairs was established in 1824, as a division of the War Department, the bureau's official business was described as the making of treaties to expedite exile.

The Eastern Cherokee had a zealous enemy, the state of Georgia. With the Cherokee nation looking more and more like a state, the state of Georgia was afraid the Cherokee might obtain citizenship in which case the 1802 pact made between the United States and Georgia might prove no mightier than a piece of paper. Under that pact the United States guaranteed Georgia the elimination of Indian title within the state.

Georgia harangued the federal government to act. In 1822 Calhoun told the Cherokee that commissioners would be appointed to negotiate a treaty of land cession with them. The Cherokee weren't interested. They "unanimously with one voice [expressed] their determination to hold no treaties with any Commissioners of the U.S.... being resolved not to dispose of even one foot of ground."[5] An effort to bribe high Cherokee officials in 1823 didn't succeed.

An 1824 Cherokee delegation to Washington was accused by Georgians of presenting letters to the president and Secretary of War written by someone other than the Cherokee, who were not capable of writing such letters. In a message to a Washington newspaper, the *National Intelligencer,* the Cherokee said:

> ... Indians can think and write for themselves....
> [And turning to their conflict with Georgia,] We are not ignorant of the Convention of 1802.... If [its promises] are to be violated and the ... war whoop ... be raised against us to dispossess us of our lands we will gratify the delegation of Georgia in their present earnestness to see us removed or destroyed by adding additional fertility to our lands by a deposit of our bodies and our bones — *For we are resolved never to leave them but by a parting from them and our lives together.* How the Christians of America and the world will [justify] their attempts upon our rights ... it is not for us Indians to say — but our cause is with God and good men, and there we are willing to leave it.[6]

Monroe reported to the governor of Georgia that he had been unable to get a cession and the governor charged him with not keeping his word with the Georgia delegation and of being weak. Monroe reacted by telling Congress that, even though removal would be in the best interest of the Indians, the Compact of 1802 did not provide for the Cherokees' removal by the employment of force. He thought forceful removal of the Cherokee would be "revolting to humanity, and utterly unjustifiable."[7]

To block a past favorite American technique of getting one part of the Cherokee nation to agree to a cession, in 1825 the Cherokee Legislative Council specified that the "Principal Chiefs of the nation shall in no wise hold any treaties or dispose of public property in any manner without the express authority of the Legislative Council in session."[8] In the 1820s the Council decided on a new permanent capital first called New Town and later New Echota in recognition of Chota which was the Overhill Towns' capital for many years on the Little Tennessee River. New Echota was located in northwest Georgia.

Georgia still tried through the federal government to force the Cherokee into a cession and a new president, John Quincy Adams, sent a representative to discuss a removal of the nation from lands within Georgia's boundary. The Cherokee were adamant and Adams so reported to Georgia. To more conform to the white man's ways, the Cherokee nation had a court system with a National Superior Court and a government similar to that used by the states. Making it even closer on July 26, 1827, a new constitution was adopted based on three departments, legislative, executive, and judicial. John Ross, a 38-year-old, one-eighth-blood Cherokee who fought under Andrew Jackson in the Creek Wars, was elected as the principal chief in October 1828 and continued as a Cherokee leader until his death in 1866. He married a full-blooded Cherokee but was never fluent in Cherokee. Assertions in the constitution that the Cherokee nation was "one of the sovereign and independent nations of the earth with complete jurisdiction over their own territory" was not conceptually in tune with the American government. A sympathetic John Quincy Adams in his final message to Congress in December 1828 cited a need for "a remedy which, while it shall do justice to those unfortunate children of nature, may secure to the members of our confederation their rights of sovereignty and of soil."[9] This was consistent with an Adams speech in 1802:

> Their cultivated fields; their constructed habitations; a space ... for their subsistence ... was undoubtedly by the laws of nature theirs. But what is the right of the huntsman to the forest of a thousand miles over which he has accidentally ranged in quest of prey? ... Shall the exuberant bosom of the common mother, amply adequate to the nourishment of millions, be claimed exclusively by a few hundreds of her offspring? Shall the lordly savage not only disdain the virtues and enjoyments of civilization himself, but shall he control the civilization of the world?[10]

There was a dark cloud on the horizon. Andrew Jackson became president of the United States and in his first annual message to Congress on December 8, 1829, stated he would introduce a bill for moving the Indians across the Mississippi. Jackson was not acting out of malice if his words expressed in private correspondence in his first year as president showed his true feelings: "You may rest assured that I shall adhere to the just and humane policy towards the Indians which I have commenced. In this spirit I have recommended them to quit their possessions on this side the Mississippi, and go to a country to the west where there is every probability that they will always be free from the

John Ross was a Cherokee who argued against moving to Indian Territory. He reigned in the Indian Territory until his death in 1868. This 1837 lithograph was made after an updated painting by Charles Bird King (courtesy of the Oklahoma Historical Society, negative number 20516.3.23).

mercenary influence of White men, and undisturbed by the local authority of the states: Under such circumstances the General Government can exercise a parental control over their interests and possibly perpetuate their race."[11]

Secretary of War for most of Jackson's administration was Lewis Cass. His attitude about the morality of forcing the Indians to surrender land was that "the Creator intended the earth should be reclaimed from a state of nature and cultivated; that ... a tribe of wandering hunters ... have a very imperfect possession of the country over which they roam."[12] Cass undoubtedly expressed a sentiment held by many in an expanding American population, which reached 13 million in 1830, an increase of 33.5 percent over the count made in the 1820 census. This was a population that could penetrate the land west of the Appalachians by steamboat and railroads. Some railroads were in place by 1827. The practicality of using steamboats on western rivers was first proven in 1811 when a partner of Robert Fulton, Nicholas Roosevelt, and his pregnant wife took the steamboat *New Orleans* from Pittsburgh to New Orleans and in the process survived the New Madrid earthquake, which many Indians thought to be the result of Tecumseh stamping his foot.

To head off any Cherokee willing to emigrate who might have been willing to sell Cherokee land, a so-called Blood Law was put in place by the National Council on October 24, 1829. In part it read: "if any citizen ... of this nation should treat and dispose of any lands belonging to this nation without special permission from the national authorities, he or they shall suffer death."[13] The Ridge, also called Major Ridge, after fighting with Jackson against the Creeks in 1814, and his son John diligently worked among the Cherokees to bolster anti-immigration sentiments. The Ridge, who did not converse in English and was prosperous and well respected, spoke often. One speech given in February 1829, the essence of which was written by John, had the following thoughts:

> We have noticed the ancient ground of complaint, founded on the ignorance of our ancestors and their fondness for the chase, and for the purpose of agriculture as having in possession too much land for their numbers. What is the language of objection this time?
>
> The case is reversed, and we are now assaulted with menaces of expulsion, because we have unexpectedly become civilized, and because we have formed and organized a constituted government. It is too much for us now to be

Major Ridge was a respected Cherokee who reluctantly concluded that relocating to Indian Territory was required. This 1837 lithograph was made by I.T. Bowen (McKenney-Hall Collection, courtesy of the Oklahoma Historical Society, negative number 20462.1.35).

honest, and virtuous, and industrious, because then are we capable to aspiring to the rank of Christians and Politicians, which renders our attachment to the soil more strong, and therefore more difficult to defraud us of the possession....

 If the country, to which we are directed to go is desirable and well watered, why is it so long a wilderness and a waste, and uninhabited by respectable white people, whose enterprise ere this would have induced them to monopolize it from the poor and unfortunate of their fellow citizens as they have hitherto done?[14]

Georgia worked as assiduously to bring about removal. After the Cherokee adopted its U.S.-like constitution on July 26, 1827, the Georgia legislature in December 1827 stated the Indians were only tenants at will and Georgia could take the lands and make them subject to Georgia laws. In 1828 it included Cherokee land in Georgia counties. The Cherokee complained in a letter of February 17, 1829, to the Secretary of War. Jackson, who was sworn in on March 3, 1829, gave Georgia a green light when his Secretary of War, John H. Eaton, told the Cherokee in a letter of April 18, 1829, "they had no hope of succor from the federal government." According to Eaton the Treaty of Hopewell, and those following, only gave the Cherokee a "possessory [right].... The soil, and the use of it, were suffered to remain with [them], while the Sovereignty abided precisely where it did before, in those states within whose limits you were situated."[15]

Following Jackson's message to Congress on December 8, 1829, stating he would initiate an act to remove Indians to the West, Georgia acted quickly. On December 19, 1829, it passed laws to confiscate Cherokee land and for the arrest of any Cherokee advocating against removal. Alabama and Mississippi enacted similar laws. Georgia did not want the Cherokees to benefit from newly discovered gold deposits near Dahlonega and Dalton, Georgia, and made it illegal for them to mine the gold. Word of the discovery spread in the summer of 1829 and "men came from every state ... acting more like crazy men than anything else."[16] On June 3, 1830, Georgia's governor claimed "all the Cherokee lands including the gold mines, belonged to the State."[17] When fighting broke out between Cherokees ordered to leave the gold fields and Georgians, Jackson offered to send federal troops, but Governor John Forsyth let it be known that the Georgia Guard could handle the situation. From that time forward the Georgia Guard acted aggressively. The Georgia courts gave the Cherokee no protection.

The Cherokee could not expect any help from Jackson, who told Congress in December 1829 that some of the southern Indians had "attempted to erect an independent government within the limits of Georgia and Alabama"[18] and that to permit this would violate the Constitution, which forbade the erection of a new state within the territory of an existing state without that state's permission. To Jackson, to permit enclaves of Indians within Georgia and the new states of Alabama, admitted in 1819, and Mississippi, admitted in 1817, would lead to the degradation and destruction of the Indians and "[h]umanity and national honor demand[ed] that every effort should be made to avert so great a calamity."[19] This reasoning had some truth in it, but failed to recognize the progress the Cherokee had made in adapting to the ways of the whites. At that time Jackson denied an intention to use force, stating that "emigration should be voluntary, for it would be as cruel as unjust to compel the aborigines to abandon the graves of their fathers and seek a home in a distant land."[20] Jackson was forthright in saying that if the Indians remained they would lose much of their land and that they should not hope to retain land "merely because they [had] seen [it] from the mountain or passed [it] in the chase."[21]

The Cherokee were barred from protecting themselves from whites in the Georgia courts. A December 1829 proclamation by Georgia governor George R. Gilmer specified that "no Indian ... residing within the Creek or Cherokee nations of Indians, shall be deemed a competent witness in any court of [Georgia] to which a white person may be a party."[22] At the same time Georgia demanded that the federal government act on its 1802 promise to remove Indians from the state. About 500 Cherokee migrated in 1829 and 1830.

Relying on the sanctity of prior treaty language, John Ross wrote in 1830: "Don't let the Talk of the President and Secretary of War that is going about scare you. Their say so does not effect our rights to the soil.... The Treatys entered into between us and the General Govt. are very strong and will protect us in our right of soil."[23]

On May 23, 1830, Jackson's Indian Removal Bill became the law of the land. Those in Congress opposing the law were strident. Congressman Horace Everett from Vermont, on the floor of the House, denied that the bill would elevate the Indians; to the contrary he saw the bill as "unmingled, unmitigated evil."[24] Equally strident were those supporting removal. Governor Gilmer scorned any rights that might be claimed under past treaties: "treaties were expedients by which ignorant, intractable, and savage people were induced without bloodshed to yield up what civilized peoples had a right to possess by virtue of that command of the Creator delivered to man upon his formation — be fruitful, multiply, and replenish the earth, and subdue it."[25] The House Committee on Indian Affairs, which reported the removal bill reached the same conclusion as did Gilmer: "[money payments were a] substitute which humanity and expediency have imposed, in place of the sword, in arriving at the actual enjoyment of property claimed by the right of discovery, and sanctioned by the natural superiority allowed to the claims of civilized communities over those of savage tribes."[26] The vote in the House was close, 102 for and 97 against.[27]

32

Cherokee Intransigence

The Cherokee were neither humble nor cooperative when Jackson wanted them to move. Their Legislative Council resolved in July 1830 that they did not desire to meet with the president to discuss an exchange of land and that there was no "[i]nclination to remove from [their] land."[1] The Jackson administration brought pressure by changing how the annual annuity was paid. In the past it was paid into the Cherokee treasury, but it was decided to make payments to Cherokee individuals, thereby keeping the money out of the hands of the Cherokee leadership.

The Cherokee used the American method of conflict resolution by hiring lawyers to take their case to court. Their principal attorney was William Wirt, attorney-general in the Monroe presidency. Wirt was one of many lawyers offering to represent the Cherokee. Georgia was not impressed with the judicial efforts. It ignored a December 12, 1830, summons to appear in Washington City signed by John Marshall, chief justice of the United States Supreme Court. The Cherokee were challenging a Georgia murder conviction of a Cherokee scheduled to be hanged. By ignoring the summons and executing the man, Georgia evaded the court decision. Georgia's governor, Wilson Lumpkin, told Jackson that Georgia was not going to be dictated to by the United States Supreme Court, writing that "[t]he Supreme Court has as much right to grant a citation to cite the King of Great Britain for any assignable cause as to cite the govt. of Georgia for the manner in which the state chooses to exercise her jurisdiction."[2]

At the Cherokees' October 1830 council meeting, they were told by a representative of the Secretary of War, then John Henry Eaton, that the federal government would not interfere with Georgia entering Cherokee territory to survey it. To see if this was true the Cherokee decided to send a delegation, including John Ridge, to Washington. On their arrival a correspondent for the *New York Observer* reported they "were well-dressed gentlemen of good manners — themselves good society for any sensible man — sitting at the publick tables throughout the City — undistinguished from the common mass except it be in superior delicacy of feeling."[3] With educated representatives the Cherokee were able to deal with whites in the white man's arena. It was not like the observation in 1751 of the Cherokee Skiagunsta to the governor of South Carolina: "My tongue is my pen and mouth my paper. When I look upon writing I am as if I were blind and in the dark."[4]

In December Ridge was able to put the question directly to Eaton as to what the United States would do if Georgia moved to take the Indian lands away from the Cherokee but was not able to get a direct answer. Ridge had to settle for presenting a five-page memorial to Congress detailing the oppression the Cherokee were suffering from white intruders and the Georgia Guard. The Cherokee found supporters, most prominently Henry Clay and his followers, and anticipated they would get relief when there was a new president. An Indian champion in the House was Massachusetts congressman Edward Everett who spoke for two days on Cherokee affairs including the failure to pay the annuity in the usual way. He stressed the failure of the United States to honor past treaties, some of which had been signed by President Jackson. His oratory did not convince the House to take action.

Ridge witnessed another setback. The Cherokee lawyers argued in the Supreme Court in March 1831 about Georgia's denial of the court's jurisdiction. Although the court's decision, made in July, read by Chief Justice Marshall, was sympathetic to the Cherokee plight, it refused to give any relief on the grounds that the Cherokee suit was brought as that of a foreign nation which they were not. The court described their status as that of "a domestic, dependent nation ... in a state of pupilage."[5]

John Ridge was the well-educated son of Major Ridge. He argued forcefully against removal, only to decide there was no alternative. This 1837 lithograph was based on an 1825 painting by Charles Bird King (McKenney-Hall Collection, courtesy of the Oklahoma Historical Society, negative number 20699).

The delegation was seen by Jackson after the court decision and he told one member as they left that the Cherokee could continue to live on their Georgia lands but that he could not "interfere with the laws of that state to protect [them]."[6] After the delegation returned to the nation the Cherokee leaders, including Major Ridge and John Ross, decided to stay the course until Jackson was out of office and Henry Clay was president.

Georgia was very aggressive after the removal act was passed. Its laws were extended over Cherokee land in June 1830 and declared that any application of Cherokee law could bring a sentence to a penitentiary. The Cherokee lands were being overrun by whites in 1831 and Cherokee resolve was weakened by the introduction of barrels of whiskey. Georgia acted against the white missionary supporters of the Cherokee. No white man could be on Cherokee land unless he swore an oath of allegiance to Georgia and to break that requirement could result in imprisonment.

The refusal of some missionaries to comply led to the historic Supreme Court decision in *Worcester v. Georgia*. Samuel A. Worcester had worked with the Cherokee since 1825 and, when tried by the Supreme Court of Georgia in July 1831 on a charge of violating the oath requirement, he refused to comply and was sentenced to four years of hard labor.

When the October 1831 Cherokee council met, it decided to send a delegation to Washington to renew their grievances. John Ridge and two others were appointed. They communicated with a new Secretary of War, Lewis Cass, who assured them in writing that Jackson wanted to work with them; however, he saw "no remedy but in a removal beyond the immediate contact of the white people."[7] They were told no coercion would be applied.

To marshal public support for a time Ridge abandoned his position with the Washington delegation and joined with Elias Boudinot in a lecture tour of the North. Boudinot was trying to raise money for the newspaper *Phoenix* which no longer could rely on the depleted Cherokee treasury. They were well received and felt vindicated when the United States Supreme Court decision in the *Worcester* case came down. The court decided in March 1832 that the "Cherokee Nation [was] a distinct community occupying its own territory ... in which the laws of Georgia can have no right to enter but with the assent of the Cherokees."[8] Boudinot saw a shift in the battleground: "It is not now before the great state of Georgia & the poor Cherokees, but between the U.S. & the State of Georgia, or between the friends of the judiciary and the enemies of the judiciary."[9]

Boudinot was wrong. The U.S. elected not to challenge Georgia. If it were true that, as rumored, Jackson said, "John Marshall has rendered his decision; now let him enforce it,"[10] the Cherokee had not gained much in a real sense. Ridge hurried to the White House and was told that Jackson would not oppose Georgia. In Washington there was a suspicion that the Cherokee delegation had changed its mind and, in fact, two members of the delegation indicated a willingness to negotiate.

Cass met with the delegation on April 6, 1832, and offered terms for removal; there would be no reservations of land within the territory ceded. The delegates refused to carry terms for removal back to the nation when they left Washington on May 15, 1832, and Cass sent them by a special emissary. On April 7, 1832, Jackson said, "[T]he decision of the supreme court has fell still born, and they find that it cannot coerce Georgia to yield to its mandate."[11] A confrontation was avoided when Jackson asked Georgia to pardon the men who were the subject of the Supreme Court case and Georgia did.

For a time John Ridge maintained the anti-treaty position he had energetically espoused, but he soon embraced with equal zeal the belief that it was best for the Cherokee to move. Ridge was told in May 1832 by David Greene of the American Board of Commissioners for Foreign Missions that the political parties in Washington thought it impossible to protect the Cherokees further where they then lived. It must have been a relief to John Ridge upon his return to the nation to find that his father, The Ridge, had reached the same conclusion.

During 1832 about 400 Cherokee migrated but only after, as reported by Benjamin F. Currey, who was supervising removals, they were "decoyed by the irrisistible influence of ardent spirits, and ... induced to create debts without the prospect of advantage to themselves or families."[12]

A split in the leadership surfaced at a special council meeting convened on July 23, 1832, at Red Clay, near modern Chattanooga, to consider the treaty offered by Cass. The council decided to avoid the wrath of Georgia and not to hold an election of a new government. John Ross would continue as the principal chief. The Ridges were not pleased. John Ridge had wanted to run for the office. They were further frustrated when Ross and the majority at the council refused to consider the proposed treaty. After the council meeting

Boudinot resigned as editor of the *Phoenix* when Ross refused to let the paper fully print the substance of the report of the delegation which returned from Washington. Boudinot told Ross that the Cherokee needed to be told the danger in refusing to remove. Ross replaced Boudinot with his (Ross's) own brother-in-law, Elijah Hicks.

A letter dated August 6 was sent to Cass rejecting the proposed treaty. The breach between the Ridges and Ross was not complete — the Ridges signed the letter. Georgians were not waiting for a treaty nor paying any attention to the Supreme Court decision in *Worcester v. Georgia*. Their legislature designated Cherokee land west of the Chattahoochee River and north of Carroll County to be Cherokee County and made plans to divide it into lots which would be distributed in a huge lottery for those who had lived in Georgia for four years. This was essentially all of the Cherokee land remaining in Georgia, that is, the northwest corner of the state. Boudinot sounded an alarm which was not heeded by most of the Cherokees — he wrote "our lands, or a large part of them, are about to be seized and taken from us."[13]

At the regular council meeting held in October, the pro-treaty advocates were in the minority. The decision was for Ross and others to go to Washington. Ross encouraged those against the treaty to hold firm and perhaps Jackson would be defeated by Henry Clay in the upcoming 1832 presidential election. In Washington Ross rejected Jackson's offer of 3 million dollars for the Cherokee land, saying the gold fields alone were worth more than that. While Ross was in Washington, those winning lottery plots fanned out over the Cherokee nation. John Ridge wrote to Ross that the Cherokee were being "robbed & whipped by the whites almost every day."[14] When Ross returned in April 1833 he found that his house and farm had been taken over by lottery winners and he moved his family into Tennessee. Others suffered loss of their property as well. Early plots drawn included land on which the homes of the two Ridges were located. They were allowed to stay in their homes for the time being because of their pro-treaty beliefs.

After Jackson was re-elected Ross gave in somewhat to the pro-treaty Cherokee at a council meeting in May 1833. If a pro-treaty faction petition of protest against the Ross leadership could be put over to the regular October council meeting, Ross would give a full answer then, and be governed by what was then decided. At the October meeting Ross refused to budge on the treaty and the best the pro-treaty faction could get was agreement for another delegation to go to Washington. This was a meaningless accomplishment since Ross refused to give the delegation authority to make a treaty. Major Ridge was disgusted with Ross's conduct. He said, "Past experience has shown that Ross and his party hold no pledge sacred."[15]

Early in 1834 Lt. Joseph W. Harris took about 700 Cherokee to the Indian Territory mostly by water. According to Stanley W. Hoig's book *The Cherokee and Their Chiefs* those agreeing to move were convinced by "bribery, the use of whiskey, beatings, and even the threat of death."[16] It took less than a month to reach Little Rock but the remainder of the trip was slower when they were forced to walk because of low water. At that point deaths started from cholera. And the illness plus a shortage of food and wagons required the emigrants to abandon "bedding, household utensils, looms, ovens, pot-hooks, spinning-wheels, farming implements, plows, hoes, and harness."[17] They reached Cherokee country on May 8. During the trip 81 died, most from cholera, 45 of whom were children under 10 years.

Pressure was put on Ross to talk with Secretary Cass about emigration when a small group of Cherokee wanting to emigrate, including John Ross's brother, Major Ridge and Boudinot, went to Washington around April 1834 to try to make arrangements for their emigration. Earlier in 1834 a pro-treaty delegation went to Washington instructed to try to join with Ross's representatives already there to get agreement for a treaty and only if unsuccessful, on their own "to effect a treaty for the present Emigrants & followers & those Emigrants who [had] preceded them."[18] The Ross group was not interested in unity, but the government received the pro-treaty men warmly. However, the War Department wanted to deal with someone with prestige with the Cherokee people. This led to Major Ridge and others coming to Washington.

This activity brought Ross to Washington and he explored an agreement whereby the Cherokee would cede some of its land and the government would guarantee them protection on the retained land. Jackson's position was that all must emigrate.

Major Ridge resolved that a partial cession would not be in the best interest of the Cherokee; to do so would cause the common Indian to "be perpetually made drunk by the whites, cheated, oppressed, reduced to beggary, [and to] become miserable outcasts, and as a body dwindle to nothing," a fate of the Virginia Powhatan. John Ridge saw himself and others as embarked on a crusade to "induce the Indians to abandon this land of whiskey kegs & bottles, the vile corruption of the whites, where ... poor women [were] contaminated to become wretches."[19]

At an August 1834 council meeting called by Ross, it was decided to impeach both Ridges and David Vann for "maintaining opinions and a policy to terminate the existence of the Cherokee community on the lands of [their] fathers."[20] Another pro-treaty man, John Walker, Jr., was assassinated on his way home. Jackson was incensed and declared that "[t]he Government of the U.S. [had promised those pro-immigration] protection [and] *it will perform its obligations* to a tittle."[21]

At an October council meeting Ross and others refused to try the Ridges and Vann but refused to dismiss the charges. By vote the government's offer of $5 million for all Cherokee land east of the Mississippi River in exchange for 13 million acres in the West already guaranteed to the Western Cherokee plus an additional 800,000 acres was rejected. The breach within the Cherokee nation was complete and the three accused left and called a council of their own to meet in November. Eighty-three Indians attended the pro-treaty council and it was decided to send a delegation to Washington.

Memorials from both the Ross and Ridge factions were before Congress and the administration in 1835. Ross's proposal for the U.S. to buy the Cherokee land from Georgia did not meet Jackson's terms and the War Department appointed a retired preacher from New York, John F. Schermerhorn, to work with the Ridge group. Schermerhorn was said to be a "crafty and subtle individual."[22] Seeing the lay of the land Ross changed his proposal to be a cession of all Cherokee land for 20 million dollars, which was scoffed at by Jackson. Nonetheless, at Ross's insistence, the proposal was sent to the Senate whose determination of the price Ross agreed to "recommend" to the nation. When the Senate proposed a payment of $5,000,000 Ross was in no hurry to lay the proposed amount before the nation. He hoped to leave the final decision to the presidential administration that would follow that of Jackson.

After the Senate action Schermerhorn, in negotiations with the Ridge group, offered $4.5 million and additional land in the West worth $500,000. John Ridge considered the offer and other terms proposed as reasonable and thought if it could be laid before the Cherokee nation it would be accepted. A treaty was signed on March 14, 1835, but it was only to be effective if ratified by the tribe in full council. To gain support for the treaty John Ridge suggested that Jackson send a talk to the Cherokee saying "they should have a home, a country which, in no future time, should be encroached upon by State intrusion." Jackson complied.[23]

When John Ridge returned home he called for a council of those favoring a treaty but did not get many to assemble in either April or May. Ross was busy talking against the treaty. Ross agreed to a meeting at Running Water in July 1835 which would deal with the annual annuity and provide an opportunity for discussion of the proposed treaty. Earlier in May John Ridge asked the governor of Georgia for help:

> The President has assured me that he will stand by this treaty as the Ultimatum of the Government and no other shall be offered to the Cherokee people. But, Sir, the Ross party disbelieve it, & this party composed as it is of Half breed Nullifiers wish to change it and suit themselves.... [Y]ou have ... all the time until the Indians are removed the most important part to act. The last hold & retreat of this unholy Indian Aristocracy is the *banded outlaws* who are harbored by the Ross party for the purposes of intimidation or assassination.... You must break up this incubus or nightmare which sets so heavily upon the breasts of the ignorant Indians.... John Ross is unhorsed at Washington and you must unhorse him here.[24]

Governor Lumpkin promised protection to persons and property.

The meeting held at Running Water, attended by 4,000, was monitored by a detachment of the Georgia Guard. Both Ross and John Ridge spoke. Ridge said he was ready to acknowledge Ross as the principal chief if he came forth with a better plan than that proposed by the Ridges. Schermerhorn spoke about the treaty at length and proposed that another meeting be scheduled for July 30 at the Cherokee agency to make plans for a treaty convention. Only the Ridge faction went to the agency at the end of July; Ross sent a letter saying he was ill and proposed a future meeting of only Cherokee. The Ridges delivered their agreement to such a meeting to Ross at Ross's home.

Tempers were at high pitch. Pro-Ridge Indians were beaten and three murdered. A showdown occurred at the October council meeting held at Red Clay on the Tennessee border. The meeting, restricted to only the Cherokee, was, at first, able to apparently resolve the differences between the two Cherokee factions, but it then became apparent that Ross was not willing to give up the Cherokee land for 5 million dollars. Agreement was reached for a delegation to go to Washington. The Schermerhorn treaty was rejected, even by John Ridge and Boudinot, who hoped for its adoption with minor changes in Washington.

Schermerhorn was not satisfied and scheduled a meeting of the federal commissioners with a General Council at New Echota on December 21 on the assumption that Jackson would not meet with the delegation. In giving the Cherokee notice of the New Echota meeting, Schermerhorn used a questionable technique — any Cherokee not attending would be considered as approving what was done at the meeting.

A heavy-handed arrest of John Ross on November 7 by the Georgia Guard, which crossed over into Tennessee, aroused passions. John Ridge, who only learned of the arrest after the fact, met with Ross and his captors and without explanation Ross was released on November 16. The Cherokee delegation which left for Washington around December 1 included Ross, John Ridge, and Stand Watie, a brother of Elias Boudinot. At Washington

Jackson told the Ross delegation that not more than 5 million dollars would be paid, no reservations would be made for individuals, and the money would only be paid to individuals.

John Ridge broke with Ross after this. Boudinot later wrote to Ross that it was Ross's "continued evasive and non-committal policy, and the refusal of the Government to negotiate [sic] with you at Washington" that led to the break and for Ridge "to do the best the times and circumstances presented."[25] About the same time of the Ross delegation's meeting in Washington, Schermerhorn was active. He held the meeting at New Echota, attended by a small number of Indians, between 300 and 400 and no principal officers of the nation. Schermerhorn spoke to those present on December 23 and the next day the proposed treaty was read to those gathered. Major Ridge and Boudinot each spoke in favor of the treaty. Ridge explained the situation: "The Georgians have shown a grasping spirit lately; they have extended their laws, to which we are unaccustomed, which harass our braves and make the children suffer and cry; but I can do them justice in my heart. They think the Great Father, the President, is bound by the compact of 1802 to purchase this country for them, and they justify their conduct by the end in view.... There is but one path of safety, one road to future existence as a Nation. That path is open before you. Make a treaty of cession. Give up these lands and go over beyond the great Father of Waters."[26]

When Boudinot spoke he acknowledged that those opposing the treaty were not present and that by signing the treaty he anticipated the opponents would "put us across the dread river of death!"[27] A committee of 20 was appointed to meet with Schermerhorn and on December 29 signed the treaty. The next day their action was approved by a council and representatives appointed to go with Schermerhorn to Washington. Major Ridge was reported to have said that he expected to die for his action.

When a delegation from New Echota arrived in Washington on January 23, 1836, John Ridge and Stand Watie joined them and signed the treaty. Notwithstanding a demonstration by Ross and others that thousands of Cherokee opposed the treaty, the Senate approved it by one vote. On May 23, 1836, Jackson proclaimed its completion. Ross's 15,000 or so Cherokee had until May 23, 1838, to move. Ross was notified that Jackson no longer "recognize[d] any existing government among the eastern Cherokee, and any further effort by [Ross] to prevent the consummation of the treaty would be suppressed."[28] John Quincy Adams who was then a House member called the Senate's ratification as an "eternal disgrace upon the country."[29]

Many councils were held in the Cherokee nation and resolutions renouncing the treaty and the methods used were prepared and given to General John Ellis Wool who was in command of the federal troops in the nation. He made the mistake of thinking these were important to Washington and sent them there. Jackson castigated him for sending "a paper so disrespectful to the Executive, the Senate and the American people [and] declared his settled determination that the treaty should be carried out without modification and with all consistent dispatch."[30] A copy of Jackson's letter was to be delivered to Ross and "no further communication, by mouth or writing, should be held with him concerning the treaty."[31] Another official who would not listen was Governor Wilson Lumpkin of Georgia. He wrote Jackson on September 24, 1836, that "statements of Ross and others that the late treaty was made contrary to the will of a majority of the Cherokee people is entitled to no respect or consideration whatever. Nineteen-twentieths of the Cherokees are too ignorant and depraved to entitle their opinions to any weight or consideration in such matters."[32] Boudinot justified the action of the minority pro-treaty faction similarly: "If one hundred persons are ignorant of their true situation and are so completely blinded as not to see the destruction that awaits them, we can see strong reasons to justify the actions of a minority of fifty persons to do what the majority *would* do if they understood their condition, to save a *nation* from political thralldom and degradation."[33]

Another voice speaking out was that of Maj. W. M. Davis who was to enroll the Cherokee for removal. He wrote the Secretary of War: "that paper ... called a treaty, is no treaty at all, because not sanctioned by the great body of the Cherokee and made without their participation or assent. I solemnly declare ... that upon its reference to the Cherokee people it would be instantly rejected by nine-tenths of them.... The delegation taken to Washington by Mr. Schermerhorn had no more authority to make a treaty than any other dozen Cherokee accidentally picked up for the purpose."[34]

Jackson's second term was coming to an end and Wool was not to be quieted as to what was happening. On February 18, 1837, he reported that the Cherokee as a "people almost universally opposed ... the treaty and ... maintain that they never made such a treaty."[35] A group he had addressed "however poor or destitute, would [not] receive either rations or clothing from the United States lest they might compromise themselves in regard to the treaty.... Many [had] said they will die before they will leave the country."[36]

In the face of charges of acting ambitiously, John Ridge wrote that "sooner or later he will have to yield his life as the penalty for signing." John Ridge, Boudinot, and Stand Watie sent a letter to Schermerhorn expressing the consequences of emigration: "thousands ... will be relieved from the lowest state of wretchedness and who, now reduced almost to nakedness and starvation; buffeted and lacerated by the settlers among them; driven, with their women and little ones, from their cabins and their fields, to the woods and mountains, stripped of the little property they once possessed; wandering outcasts, and dependent on the cold charity of their new oppressors."[37]

33

The Trail of Tears

Under the New Echota treaty representatives from both Cherokee factions were to serve on a committee arranging for emigration. Ross and his followers refused to serve. Ross called for a council, which convened at Red Clay in September 1836. Three thousand Cherokee gathered and General Wool and federal troops were camped nearby. Ross used the gathering to harden resistance to the treaty.

Major Ridge called to the president's attention the need for federal troops: "[The white] people ... have got our lands and now they are preparing to fleece us of the money accruing from the treaty.... [O]ur plantations [have been] taken either in whole or in part by the Georgians [and] suits instituted against us for back rents for our own farms.... Thus our funds will be filched from our people, and we shall be compelled to leave our country as beggars and in want.... [T]he lowest classes of the white people are flogging the Cherokees with cowhides, hickories, and clubs.... Send regular troops to protect us from these lawless assaults.... If it is not done, we shall carry off nothing but the scars of the lash on our backs, and our oppressors will get all the money."[1]

A difficulty in controlling the whites was the conflict between the states and the federal government. Wool acted in the summer of 1837 to expel whites from expropriated property and to stop sales of whiskey in Alabama. Notwithstanding that this was sanctioned by the treaty, Alabama complained to the Secretary of War of Wool "usurp[ing] the powers of the civil tribunals, disturb[ing] the peace of the community, and trampl[ing] upon the rights of citizens."[2] When Alabama made no showing at a court of inquiry convened in September, Wool was found blameless. Similar conduct was happening in Georgia. On December 8, 1837, the governor asked the legislature to pass a law banning licenses to sell whiskey to the Cherokee.

First to emigrate were 600, primarily pro-treaty, early in 1837. Most of these had carriages and wagons and traveled with slaves, saddle horses, and droves of oxen. They went by land. The next group of about 470, including the Ridge and his family, was transported by the government. They went to Ross's Landing (now Chattanooga, Tennessee), so named because of a trading post and warehouse established there in 1813 by John Ross and another, and were loaded on to 11 flatboats, later transferred to a steamer and, at Muscle Shoals, put on a train — one of the first west of the Appalachians. At Tuscumbia, Alabama, they were embarked on a steamboat towing two 60-ton keelboats and were able to go down the Tennessee, Ohio, and Mississippi rivers to the mouth of the Arkansas. The steamboat made it to Little Rock where a transfer was made to a lighter draft steamboat, which made it to Fort Smith where some Indians went ashore, and the remainder went by boat to Fort Coffee. The trip took the month of March. Unusual for removals, there were no deaths.

Indian Removal 1830–1839

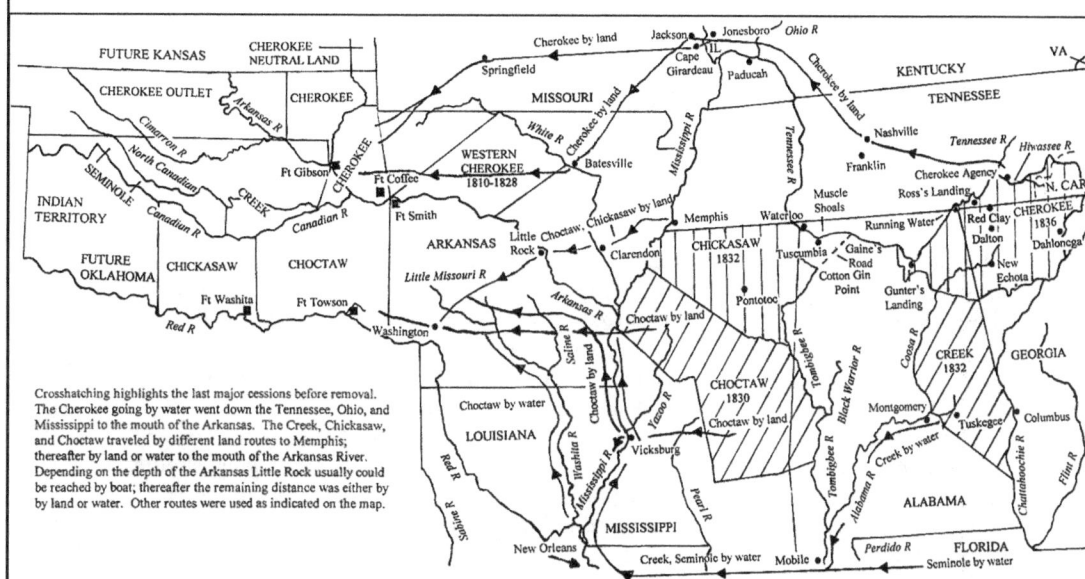

Crosshatching highlights the last major cessions before removal. The Cherokee going by water went down the Tennessee, Ohio, and Mississippi to the mouth of the Arkansas. The Creek, Chickasaw, and Choctaw traveled by different land routes to Memphis; thereafter by land or water to the mouth of the Arkansas River. Depending on the depth of the Arkansas Little Rock usually could be reached by boat; thereafter the remaining distance was either by by land or water. Other routes were used as indicated on the map.

Ref: Royce, Plates CVIII, CXIII, CXXII, CXXIX, CXXX, CXLIII, CLXI;
Foreman Indian Removal; Prucha, Great Father, 275; Hoig, 206

In the fall of 1837 two groups of willing émigrés numbering about 700 made the trip. As a foretaste of what was to come there was much illness *en route* and at least 15 died. During the same period the John Ridge and Boudinot families, one other family, and a lone woman, safely traveled on their own. John Ridge settled in the northeast corner of what is now Oklahoma, near where his father was located. A final willing group of 250 made the trip with two deaths in April 1838. Lt. Edward Deas, who was in charge, noted that there was "never any difficulty in managing Indians when sober, provided they are properly treated; but when under the effects of liquor (in the use of which they have no moderation) they are unmanageable."[3]

Time was running out on those Cherokee who refused to go west. Only about 2,000 had made the trip; 15,000 to 17,000, including 500 of those favoring the treaty, remained in the East. In the spring of 1838 Ross presented a protest and memorial to Congress signed by more than 15,000 Cherokee but President Van Buren refused to act and in the Senate the document was tabled. When Van Buren was inclined to extend the May 23, 1838, deadline, the governor of Georgia threatened a collision with the state and no extension was given. The Van Buren administration proceeded to apply force. General Winfield Scott arrived on May 8, 1838, to relieve General Wool. Wool saw Cherokee removal under the circumstances as an act of kindness; they needed to be placed "beyond the reach of the white men, who, like vultures, are watching, ready to pounce upon their prey and strip them of everything they have or expect from the government of the United States."[4]

Scott, who had command of 7,000 federal and state troops, called on May 10, 1838, for the Cherokee to be submissive:

Chiefs, head-men, warriors! Will you then, by resistance, compel us to resort to arms? God forbid! Or will you, by flight, seek to hide yourselves in mountains and forests, and thus oblige us to hunt you down? Remember that, in pursuit, it may be impossible to avoid conflicts. The blood of the white man or the blood of the red man may be spilt and, if spilt, however accidentally, it may be impossible for the discreet and humane among you, or among us, to prevent a general war and carnage. Think of this my Cherokee brethren! I am an old warrior, and I have been present at many a scene of slaughter; but spare me, I beseech you, the horror of witnessing the destruction of the Cherokees.[5]

Scott's orders to his troops a week later showed an intention to treat the Cherokee with dignity:

The Cherokees, by the advances they have made in Christianity and civilization, are by far the most interesting tribe of Indians in the territorial limits of the United States. Of the 15,000 of those people who are now to be removed ... it is understood that about four fifths are opposed ... to distant emigration; and ... the troops will probably be obliged to cover the whole country they inhabit, in order to make prisoners and to march or to transport prisoners, by families ... to be delivered over to the Superintendent of Cherokee Emigration.

Considering the number and temper of the mass to be removed ... [e]very possible kindness ... must ... be shown by the troops, and, if, in the ranks, a despicable individual should be found, capable of inflicting a wanton injury or insult on any Cherokee man, woman or child, it is hereby made the special duty of the nearest good officer or man, instantly to interpose, and to seize and consign the guilty wretch to the severest penalty of the laws.[6]

However, much of what followed did not meet the spirit of Scott's orders. There were plenty of "despicable individuals" and too few "good officers or men." As described by a soldier who was there:

"The Trail of Tears," a painting by Robert Lindneux (Woolaroc Museum, Bartlesville, Oklahoma).

Men working in the fields were arrested and driven to the stockades. Women were dragged from their homes by soldiers whose language they could not understand. Children were often separated from their parents and driven into the stockades with the sky for a blanket and the earth for a pillow. And often the old and infirm were prodded with bayonets to hasten them to the stockades.

In one home death had come during the night, a little sad faced child had died and was lying on a bear skin couch and some women were preparing the little body for burial. All were arrested and driven out leaving the child in the cabin. I don't know who buried the body.[7]

The *Niles' National Register* reported in 1838 that the "captors sometimes drove the people with whooping and bellowing, like cattle through rivers, allowing them no time even to take off their shoes and stockings. Many, when arrested, were not so much as permitted to gather up their clothes."[8] Grace Steele Woodward, in her book *The Cherokees*, says that some of Scott's soldiers carried out "rape, robbery, murder, and acts of bestiality."[9]

Grant Foreman in *Indian Removal* recites other terrible conduct[10]: "Systematic hunts were made ... for Indian graves, to rob them of the silver pendants and other valuables deposited with the dead." "Well-furnished houses were left a prey to plunderers, who, like hungry wolves, follow in the train of the captors. These wretches rifle the houses, and strip the helpless, unoffending owners of all they have on earth;" "Many of the Cherokees, who, a few days ago, were in comfortable circumstances, are now victims of abject poverty." Once the prisoners were in the stockades, at least in some, they were treated "with great respect and indulgence." One estimate is that 2,500 died in the process of being rounded up and forced into the stockades.

Stockades were used to hold the Cherokee in Georgia, North Carolina, Tennessee, and Alabama. In 1835 the approximate Cherokee populations were 2,500 in Tennessee, 3,600 in North Carolina, 9,000 in Georgia, and 1,500 in Alabama. After about 17,000 had been placed in the stockades, the forced removal began. Some 5,000 were taken to three different embarkation points: one on the Hiwassee River, at present Calhoun, Tennessee, and two on the Tennessee River, Ross's Landing and Gunter's Landing (now Guntersville, Alabama).

The *Niles' National Register* described scenes of distress exhibited at Ross's Landing[11]: "On the arrival there of the Indians, the horses brought by some of them were demanded by the commissioners of Indian property, to be given up for the purpose of being sold. The owners refusing to give them up,—men, women, children *and horses* were driven promiscuously into one large pen, and the horses taken out by force, and cried off to the highest bidder, *and sold for almost nothing.*" In loading steamboats at times no regard was given to keeping families together.

On June 6 about 800 left Ross's Landing guided by Lt. Deas and, using the same water route used the year before, arrived after two weeks with close to 500. There were no deaths after leaving Ross's Landing and the reduced number is in part explained by an accurate count not being made at the start and some Indians escaping.

A group of 875 leaving Ross's Landing on June 13, following the water route, did not fare so well. Before they reached Little Rock there were 10 deaths and about 150 escaped. After Little Rock they were not able to continue up the Arkansas River and had to go by land. Conditions were not good. The land was dry, water scarce, and the temperature hot. It took about a month to go from Little Rock to the Cherokee nation. Deaths of three to five per day were not uncommon and overall the party suffered 70 deaths. Of the original party 602 arrived.

On June 17 Scott discharged volunteer troops who had been part of the Cherokee roundup. On the same date 1,070 Cherokee in poor condition left by land from Ross's Landing for Waterloo, which was on the Tennessee River beyond Muscle Shoals. They were to get on boats at that point. Even though Scott agreed on June 19 with a Cherokee request that further trips be delayed until the fall, which would be a healthier time of year, he refused to stop the travel of this group, which suffered five deaths before it reached Waterloo. A refusal of the party to proceed to Waterloo was overcome by force and, except for the escape of 200 or so, arrived some 65 miles below Little Rock around July 20, where they had to shift to another steamboat of less draft. After Scott's agreement another 2,000 were removed with 219 deaths *en route*.

Scott's agreement to a hiatus followed a resolution of the Cherokee national council for the Cherokee to take over the responsibility of the movement in the fall. In addition to the sickly season, another factor in favor of a delay was the effect of a drought on the Tennessee River; it almost ceased to be navigable. Scott was pleased, writing that "the great body of the Cherokees remaining east for the first time consented to emigrate, or to do any act tending to their emigration."[12] Washington also reacted affirmatively and in July directed Scott to put further movements into the hands of John Ross.

When Jackson, who was out of office, learned that Scott had let John Ross assume the position of Superintendent of Cherokee Removal and Subsistence, in which capacity he could requisition money from time to time as "necessary for the Cherokee emigration,"[13] he exploded. Writing from the Hermitage to the attorney general of the United States on August 23, 1838, he asserted the cost would double under Ross's administration: "Ross *must be arrested*, and General Smith left to superintend the removal. The time and circumstances under which Gen'l Scott made this contract shows that he was no economist, or is, sub rosa, in league with Clay and Co. to bring disgrace on the administration."[14] In the context of the communication, "arrested" meant taken off the contract not physically arrested. Ross was not arrested and the costs increased to over $500,000 but Scott did not attempt to pare this amount down by the elimination of soap, sugar, or coffee — all of which were considered useless luxuries by the War Department.

The plight of the Cherokee kept in camps under military guard over the summer was terrible. Disease was rampant: measles, whooping cough, pleurisy, and bilious fever. An estimate was of 500 deaths during the summer.

Ross's direction of the removal of the remaining 13,000 or so was organized into detachments of 1,000 with the requisite number of wagons and horses. Something outside Ross's control precluded a safe and speedy travel over land. Scott had specified that the movement should start by September 1 and an effort was made to do so. But it was found that the creeks in the Cumberland Mountains had dried up and water for more than a small number was not there. Consequently it wasn't until October, after some late September rains, that the first group left. Unfortunately this meant winter weather prevailed for much of the trip.

Separate from those under Ross's direction were 700 pro-treaty Cherokee who refused to be under Ross's command. This group, described by Lt. Deas, who was leading them, as "composed for the most part of highly respectable and intelligent families [most of whom] have ... made considerable advancement in civilization,"[15] accomplished the movement between October 11 and January 7, 1839, without any significant problems.

Ross's detachments were scheduled to leave three or so days apart. The first left on

October 1, followed three days later by the next. When Nashville was reached about 16 days later a number were sick. This route, suggested by Scott, was considerably longer than that followed by Deas, who marched directly to Memphis, and also roughly 200 miles to the north, a difference important during winter months. Grace Steele Woodward covers what happened: "the thirteen groups under native conductors encountered accidents, disease, death, and discomfort from winter weather. Laboriously, horses, oxen, and footsore emigrants struggled over the Cumberland Range of Mountains, crossed their ancestors' hunting grounds [Tennessee], and upon, reaching the icy Ohio, ferried across it into Illinois."[16] At the Mississippi River they suffered from an early and severe winter. Some detachments went due west through southern Missouri and then southwest into Indian Territory and others headed south earlier into the middle of Arkansas and then due west to Indian Territory. The last detachment didn't leave until November 4. Mistreatment did not stop once they were on the trail. One of the groups found that "since [they had] been on [their] march many [had] been stopped and [their] horses taken from [their] teams for the payment of unjust ... debts."[17]

Ross was not free of tragedy. His wife was in a frail condition when his detachment reached Paducah, Kentucky, and it continued from there by boat. When the winter weather made travel up the Arkansas by boat too dangerous, they stopped and camped near Little Rock where his wife Quatie died.

The last arrival in Indian Territory was on March 24, 1839. On average it took the detachments under Ross's management 116 days to reach Indian Country. The journey routes are called the Trail of Tears; tears from being uprooted from their many farms and homes and for the deaths and suffering occurring during the emigration. The numbers leaving and arriving have been the subject of considerable study but data showing the number in each of the 13 groups leaving and arriving give the general magnitude of what happened —13,149 left and 11,504 arrived, or a loss of 12.5 percent from start to end. If the deaths in the detention centers before the trips began are counted, one estimate is that there were 4,000 deaths.

Two contemporaneous descriptions illustrate what happened between November 1838 and March 24 when the last group reached the Indian country. A Maine traveler saw a

detachment of the poor Cherokee Indians ... about eleven hundred Indians — sixty waggons — six hundred horses, and perhaps forty pairs of oxen. We found them in the forest camped for the night by the road side ... under a severe fall of rain accompanied by heavy wind. With their canvas for a shield from the inclemency of the weather, and the cold wet ground for a resting place, after the fatigue of the day, they spent the night.... Many of the aged Indians were suffering extremely from the fatigue of the journey, and the ill health consequent upon it ... several were then quite ill, and one aged man we were informed was then in the last struggles of death....

... We met several detachments in the southern part of Kentucky on the 4th, 5th, and 6th of December.... The last detachment which we passed on the 7th [comprised nearly] two thousand Indians with horses and mules in proportion. The forward part of the train we found just pitching their tents for the night, and notwithstanding some thirty or forty waggons were already stationed, we found the road literally filled with the procession for about three miles in length. The sick and feeble were carried in waggons ... a great many ride on horseback and multitudes go on foot — even aged females, apparently nearly ready to drop into the grave, were traveling with heavy burdens attached to the back — on the sometimes frozen ground, and sometimes muddy streets, with no covering for the feet except what nature had given them.... We learned from the inhabitants on the road where the Indians passed, that they buried fourteen or fifteen at every stopping place, and they made a journey of ten miles per day only on an average.[18]

A Cherokee who made the trip and whose parents and five brothers and sisters died on the road described what happened: "Long time we travel on way to new land. People feel bad when they leave Old Nation. Womens cry and make sad wails. Children cry and many men cry, and all look sad like when friends die, but they say nothing and just put heads down and keep on go towards West. Many days pass and people die very much."[19]

The hard feelings between the Ridge and Ross factions continued in Indian Territory with the arrival in 1839 of those forced to move. Revenge was taken on Major Ridge, John Ridge, and Elias Boudinot on one fateful day, June 22, 1839. Each was murdered—John Ridge was dragged from his bed and repeatedly stabbed, Boudinot was stabbed in the back and had his skull shattered by repeated tomahawk blows, and Major Ridge was ambushed by riflemen. This was done without prior approval by John Ross. To most Cherokee these were not murders; they were executions under the Blood Law adopted in 1829 at a time when Major Ridge and John Ridge were part of those leading the nation. None of the executioners were ever punished.

In the outstanding book by Thurman Wilkins, *Cherokee Tragedy*, which focuses in large part on the Ridges and Boudinot, he likens the decades following the removal as a Corsican vendetta. Each side killed without judicial process and property was not safe. Stand Watie, who had been targeted for execution but was warned in time to flee, assumed leadership of the Ridge faction. To address the internecine warfare, President Polk suggested giving each group its own territory and government. This so alarmed John Ross, who had assumed the presidency of the whole nation, that he made some accommodations with the Watie group. When he arrived in Indian Territory John Ross prevailed in getting a constitution for the united Cherokee nation that put the reigns of government in the hands of the majority, which was by far the Ross faction. When the Civil War broke out the Watie followers went with the South and Ross's with the North. Watie is thought to have been the last Confederate general to surrender his sword. The death of Ross after the war brought on a full-blooded chief who was able to reunify the two factions.

34

After the Exodus

Although tribal lands in most states have been reduced from millions of acres to thousands, or less, the Indian population has increased in recent years at a greater rate than the overall population. Over the period 1970–2005 the population of all races, for the United States, went from 203,000,000 to 296,000,000, an increase of 46 percent. The American Indian population, for this same period, went from 827,000 to 2,960,000 (the 2005 number includes those identified as "American Indian and Alaska Native persons"), reflecting a 257 percent change. The change in the Indian population for the states south of the Ohio River and the Mason-Dixon line (mainly the southern border of Pennsylvania), 1970–2005 is even larger: 72,172 to 483,873, an increase of 670 percent. According to a National Geographic map titled *Indian Country* prepared in 2004, 127,248 of the 483,873 lived in states without any federally recognized Indian land or tribe. In Oklahoma the increase was from 97,731 to 391,949, a 301 percent increase.

The historic relationship between the government and the Native Americans was addressed in September 8, 2000, at a ceremony commemorating the 175th anniversary of the Bureau of Indian Affairs (BIA). Kevin Gover, Assistant Secretary-Indian Affairs, Department of the Interior, characterized it as causing "[p]overty, ignorance, and disease." He vowed that BIA would "[n]ever again ... be complicit in the theft of Indian property. Never again [would it] appoint false leaders who serve purposes other than those of the tribes.... Never again [would they] attack [Indian] religions, ... languages, ...rituals, or any of [the] tribal ways."[1]

Legal efforts to right wrongs inflicted on American Indians have changed over the years. In 1863 a United States Court of Claims was established to handle legal suits against the United States but excluded from the court's jurisdiction were those based "on any treaty entered into ... with Indian tribes."[2] Tribal grievances had to be presented to Congress in the hope of getting legislation referring the complaint to the Court of Claims. The first congressional referral was in 1881 and between then and 1946, 142 Indian claims were litigated. An example of a pre–1946 claim was an award to the Creek Nation for Creek land erroneously sold by the United States in 1891. The case went to the Supreme Court, which allowed not only the value of the land in 1891 but added to that the lost value of the use of the money after then and 1926, when the lawsuit was brought.

In 1946 the *Indian Claims Commission Act*[3] was passed and an open period of time for the filing of claims until August 1951 was in effect — during that time 850 claims were filed. The *Indian Claims Commission Act* created an administrative agency (Indian Claims Commission) to decide all claims made with jurisdiction in the Court of Claims to review the Commission's decisions. Questions of law decided by the Court of Claims could be appealed directly to the Supreme Court. The Act provided that any Indian claims arising after August 13, 1946, could be pursued in the Court of Claims.

Between 1778 and 1871 the federal government dealt with tribes by treaties consistent with the 1831 holding by the U.S. Supreme Court in *Cherokee Nation v. Georgia* that tribes were "domestic dependent nation[s]." The fairness of those treaties and their implementation has often been a basis for Indian claims.

The Indians were the subject of changing goals adopted by the federal government. The *General Allotment Act* of 1887 authorized but didn't require the president to survey reservations or parts of them with good agricultural and grazing land and to make allotments to individual Indians. Those supporting the Act thought this was a way to civilize the Indians. But it fell afoul of those anxious to take advantage of the Indian individuals. A number of tribes were not subject to the Act, including the Five Civilized Tribes.[4] Senator Henry L. Dawes, who introduced the bill in the Senate, was worried about the "thirst of the white man for the Indians land [which was] almost equal to his 'hunger and thirst for rightouness.'"[5]

What had been 155,632,312 acres of Indian land in 1881 was down to 77,865,373 acres in 1900, with 5,409,530 acres which had been allotted. Legislation in 1871 provided that no Indian tribe would be recognized as an independent nation with whom the United States would contract with by treaty. The first Oklahoma land rush, called "Harrison's Hoss Race" after President Benjamin Harrison, aimed at 2 million acres (the Oklahoma District) purchased from the Cherokee, Creek, and Seminole earlier, was in 1889. Shortly thereafter a territorial government was formed for the Oklahoma District to which the Oklahoma Panhandle was added in 1890.

Pressure was put on the Cherokee to sell part of the Cherokee Outlet (6 million acres) and that land was opened in 1893 by way of 100,000 homesteaders rushing in to locate homes.[6] In 1895 a major blow was delivered to Indian independence in the Indian Territory by the abolition of tribal laws and courts — United States courts were to be used. The Five Civilized Tribes did not escape from the allocation fever for long. Congress, in 1896, provided for a roll of Indian citizens preparatory for allocations. Between 1897 and 1902 an agreement was made with each of the tribes. In 1901 every Indian in the Indian Territory was made a U.S. citizen. Although there were some who wanted a separate Indian state, Congress voted for one state, Oklahoma, with a population of 1.4 million, about half of whom lived in the old Indian Territory.

In 1906 Congress passed an act "to provide for the final disposition of the affairs of the Five Civilized Tribes," a result never achieved. When Oklahoma became a state in 1907 Congress retained its prior relationship with the Indians and preserved the Indians' "rights of person or property." Allocations of land were made and any surplus sold.

The Merriam Report of 1928 found assimilation for all Indians to be a failed policy and one with the wrong goal — the correct goal was for the Indians to use their land and maintain their culture. What followed was the Indian Reorganization Act of 1934, which encouraged the formation of or strengthening of tribal governments. The tribes' organization under the Act often resembled that of other local governments.

Congress changed its policy between 1954 and 1962 and voted to end the special relationship between the federal government and about 70 tribes and bands. Affected were 13,263 tribal members and 1.4 million acres. An about-face occurred in 1970 when President

Nixon sent a message to Congress saying the special relationship between the federal government and the Indians is the result of "solemn obligation" and "[t]o terminate [the] relationship would be no more appropriate than to terminate the citizenship rights of any other American."[7] Congress agreed in 1975 when it passed the Indian Self-Determination Act. In short, under the self-determination policy, up to 50 percent of the funds voted for programs operated by BIA are transferred to tribes for administration. Most of the terminated tribes have been again given federal status. Some Indians see the BIA programs as "attempt[s] ... to live up to thousands of treaty obligations incurred when establishing the land base for this Nation."[8]

Through these policy changes the Five Civilized Tribes remained, in different degrees, extant as organizations. In 1949 the Cherokee elected W. W. Keeler, then president of Phillips Petroleum Company, as their chief pursuant to an act of Congress. The Choctaw had its first popular election of a president in 1971 and adopted a new constitution in 1979. The Chickasaw adopted a new constitution in 1985. The Creek are organized into eight administrative districts and recently had a $106 million budget. The Seminole in Florida entered into agreements with the United States in 1957 and 1962, confirming their sovereignty over tribal lands.

A series of federal lawsuits thrust Indians into what may be called the "gaming" stage of their relationship with others. Initiatives for making gambling a profit center for Indian tribes were made by the Seminoles living in South Florida. In 1978 the tribe reached an agreement with a management organization for a high-stakes bingo operation on its reservation. Bingo was allowed by Florida law but jackpots were limited to $100 per night. The Seminole did not think the jackpot limit applicable to them. The final word came from the U.S. Supreme Court in 1987 which said only the federal government had "authority to forbid Indian gambling enterprises on Indian Reservations."

Some 10 years later the 2,200 Seminoles were earning $100 million per year and had opened other bingo halls around the state and had investments in other businesses. In the *Washington Post* for December 8, 2006, is a report of the Seminole Tribe of Florida buying "the famed Hard Rock business, including its casinos, restaurants, hotels and huge collection of rock memorabilia."

Recognizing a need for regulation the U.S. Congress passed the *Indian Gaming Regulation Act* (IGRA) on October 17, 1988. Congress said the existing situation was that the "Indian tribes [had] the exclusive right to regulate gaming activity on Indian lands if the gaming activity [was] not specifically prohibited by Federal law and [was] conducted within a State which [did] not, as a matter of criminal law and public policy, prohibit such gaming activity."

Specified objects of IGRA were to "promot[e] tribal economic development," and "to ensure that the Indian tribe is the primary beneficiary of the gaming operation." There was to be an "independent Federal regulatory authority" and a "National Indian Gambling Commission." Indian tribes within the context of the law are those recognized by the Secretary of Interior as "possessing powers of self-government" and being eligible for federal programs and services. "Indian lands" are those within reservations or those held in trust for Indians by the United States or held by Indian tribes or individuals "subject to restriction by the United States against alienation and over which an Indian tribe exercises governmental power."

The Act established three different classes of gaming. Broadly speaking, Class I, is social games, with prizes of minimal value; II includes bingo and card games not explicitly forbidden by the state; and III anything else, including slot machines. The tribes have complete control over Class I gaming and over Class II if the state "permits such gaming." However, the proceeds from Class II gaming must be used for specified purposes such as "the general welfare of the Indian tribe and its members." Per capita payments can be made to tribe members if approved by the Secretary of Interior. Under specified conditions Class II gaming can be licensed to non–Indian persons or entities.

Class III gaming can only be in a state "that permits such gaming for any purpose by any person, organization, or entity" and shall be conducted "in conformance with a Tribal-State compact" approved by the Secretary of Interior. If a tribe asks a state for the needed compact "the State shall negotiate ... in good faith." If the state is thought to have not negotiated in good faith, the tribe could bring a suit in a U.S. district court.

The supporters of Indian gaming overreached by getting in the Act authority for a state to be sued by an Indian tribe in a United States district court. In 1996 in *Seminole Tribe v. Florida* the U.S. Supreme Court held that when Florida refused to enter into a compact with the Seminole it could not be sued by the Seminole and forced to proceed under IGRA. This decision gives the states leverage over tribes wanting to have a Class III operation since a compact is required. Also the state has an ultimate weapon in its right to close down all or certain types of gambling including the profitable Class III on Indian lands by doing the same for the entire state.

IGRA is detailed enough and long enough that considerable litigation of what it allows and doesn't allow could be expected and an examination of cases brought under its terms verifies this to have been the case.

The stampede to have Indian gaming operations resulted in "350 tribal gaming facilities located in 30 states" in 2003. However, the Class III gross revenue created in 2003 came mostly from five states: California's 56 sites, two casinos in Connecticut, Minnesota's 19, Wisconsin's 22, and Arizona's 22 locations.

With about 80 gaming sites in Oklahoma in 2010 it appears that IGRA has given tribal members additional income and presumably jobs. Large casinos in the Southeast are those of the Mississippi Choctaw at Pearl River Resort (Silver Star Casino and Golden Moon Casino) in Mississippi and Harrah's Cherokee Casino and Hotel in Cherokee, North Carolina. The Seminole in Florida with seven sites have been able to expand into other business ventures—in 2005 they had $22.6 billion in revenue. The Catawba have a high-stakes bingo operation in South Carolina and in Alabama there is a Creek Entertainment Center and a Creek Bingo Palace.

As the success of Indian gaming facilities has advanced, so have questions concerning what is happening. A common assertion is "that tribes get rich at the expense of nontribal communities without paying their fair share." This is responded to by statistics showing that new jobs and businesses are created. Also there are compacts that provide for payments to state and local governments.

A troubling fact is that tribes without gaming operations do not benefit from IGRA, which shelters gaming profits from federal, state, and local taxes. Is it a worthwhile federal program which primarily benefits tribes located where suitable profits can be expected from a gambling operation? California has taken one approach to spreading the IGRA benefits by including in its compacts with gaming tribes a requirement that the tribes share their profits with non-gaming tribes in California. Another question, one of many that needs to be considered, is whether tribes nationwide with gaming casinos should be required to share with the 350,000 Navajo who have elected to not have gaming because of traditional Navajo beliefs.

Answers to such questions are not easy. The pros and cons are considered extensively in the book *Indian Gaming and Tribal Sovereignty* by Steven Andrew Light and Kathryn R.L. Rand. In practice the Act has only partly met its objectives of "promoting tribal economic development, tribal self-sufficiency, and strong tribal governments."

Chapter Notes

The following abbreviations are used in the notes: **Annals**— *The Annals of America*, Vols. 1–4 (1493–1820). Mortimer J. Adler, ed. in chief. Chicago: Encyclopaedia Britannica, Inc., 1968; **ANB**—*American National Biography*. John A. Garraty and Mark C. Carnes, general editors. New York: Oxford University Press, 1999; **ASP IA**—*American State Papers. Indian Affairs*. 2 vols. Buffalo, NY: William S. Hein, 1998; **ASP MA**—*American State Papers. Military Affairs*. 7 vols. Buffalo, NY: William S. Hein, 1998; **ASP FA**—*American State Papers. Foreign Affairs*. 6 vols. Buffalo, NY: William S. Hein, 1998; **Congress Annals**—*Annals of the Congress of the United States*. 42 vols. (1st–18th Cong. 1st Session). Printed by Gales and Seaton, 1834–1856. Buffalo, New York: William S. Hein, 2003; **DAB**—*Dictionary of American Biography*. Allen Johnson and Dumas Malone, editors. New York: Scribner's, 1927; **Documents (Commager)**—*Documents of American History*, 9th edition. Henry Steele Commager, editor. 2 vols. Englewood Cliffs, NJ: Prentice Hall, 1973; **Early Treaties**—*Early American Indian Documents: Treaties and Laws 1607–1789*. Alden T. Vaughan, general editor. Vols. I–V. Frederick, MD, and Washington, D.C.: University Publications of America, Inc., 1979, 1984; **Handbook**—*Handbook of North American Indians*. William C. Sturtevant, general editor, vol. 4. Wilcomb E. Washburn, editor, vol. 15. Bruce G. Trigger, editor, vol. 15. Washington: Smithsonian Institution, 1988; **Jefferson**— Jefferson, Thomas, and William Peden, ed., introduction, notes. *Notes on the State of Virginia*. New York: W. W. Norton, 1972; **Jefferson Writings (Boyd)**— *The Papers of Thomas Jefferson*. Julian P. Boyd et al., editors. Princeton, NJ: Princeton University Press, 1950; **Jefferson Writings (Lipscomb)**—*The Writings of Thomas Jefferson*. Andrew A. Lipscomb, editor in chief. Washington, D.C.: Thomas Jefferson Memorial Association, 1905; **Remini**—Remini, Robert V. *Andrew Jackson and the Course of American Empire 1767–1821*. New York: Harper & Row, 1977; **Royce**—Royce, Charles C. *Indian Land Cessions in the United States*. Smithsonian Institution. Bureau of American Ethnology. Eighteenth Annual Report, 1896–1897. Washington: GPO, 1899; **TP**—*The Territorial Papers of the United States, Colonial Times*. 28 vols. Clarence E. Carter, ed. Washington, D.C.: 1934–1975; **Virginia Calendar**—*Calendar of Virginia State Papers*. 11 vols. William P. Palmer, ed., 1884. Reprint. New York: Kraus Reprint Corp., 1968; **Virginia Encyclopedia**—*The Encyclopedia of Virginia*. New York: Somerset Publishers, 1992; **Washington Diaries**—*The Diaries of George Washington, 1748–1799*. Regents' edition. 4 vols. John C. Fitzpatrick, ed. Cambridge, MA: Riverside Press, 1925; **Washington Writings (Fitzpatrick)**—*George Washington's Writings*. 39 vols. John C. Fitzpatrick, ed. Washington, D.C.: GPO, 1938.

Chapter 1

1. Kirkpatrick Sale, *The Conquest of Paradise* (New York: Alfred A. Knopf, 1990), 304.

2. Thomas Jefferson and William Peden (ed., intro., notes). *Notes on the State of Virginia* (New York: W. W. Norton, 1972), 98.

3. Herman J. Viola, *After Columbus* (New York: Orion Books, 1990), 56–57.

4. Ronald Wright, *Stolen Continents* (Boston: Houghton Mifflin, 1992), 87–88.

Chapter 2

1. Warren M. Billings (ed.), *The Old Dominion in the Seventeenth Century: A Documentary History of Virginia, 1606–1689* (Chapel Hill: University of North Carolina Press, 1975), 25.

2. Ibid., 20.

3. Warren M. Billings, John E. Selby, and Thad W. Tate, *Colonial Virginia* (White Plains, NY: KTO Press, 1986), 32.

4. Billings, *The Old Dominion*, 26.

5. Billings, *Colonial Virginia*, 32–33.

6. *Early American Indian Documents: Treaties and Laws, 1607–1789*, vol. IV, edited by Alden T. Vaughan (Frederick, MD, and Washington, DC: University Publications of America, 1979, 1984), 3–4.

7. Kirkpatrick Sale, *The Conquest of Paradise* (New York: Alfred A. Knopf, 1990), 287.

8. Billings, *The Old Dominion*, 215.

9. Sale, *The Conquest of Paradise*, 276–277.

10. Ibid., 269, 303.

11. Angie Debo, *The History of the Indians of the United States* (Norman, OK: University of Oklahoma Press, 1970), 40–41.

12. Bil , *God Gave Us This Country* (New York: Anchor Books, 1989), 22.

13. William Byrd, "Surveying the Frontier," in *The Annals of American*, Vol. 1, edited by Mortimer J. Adler (Chicago: Encyclopædia Britannica, 1968), 382.

14. Benjamin Franklin letter of May 9, 1753, to Peter Collinson.

15. Benjamin Franklin, circa 1783, "Remarks Concerning the Savages of North America."

16. Ibid.

17. Robert F. Berkhofer, Jr. *The White Man's Indian* (New York: Alfred A. Knopf, 1978), 116.

18. Billings, *The Old Dominion*, 217–18.

19. Samuel Eliot Morison, *The Oxford History of the American People* (New York: Oxford University Press, 1965), 51.

20. Sale, *The Conquest of Paradise*, 274.

21. John Pory, "The Work of the Colonial Legislature," *Annals*, Vol. 1, 42–45.

22. John R. Sparke, "The Attraction of Florida," *Annals*, Vol. 1, 8.

23. Billings, *Colonial Virginia*, 40, note.

24. Sale, *The Conquest of Paradise*, 282.

25. Ibid., 286.

26. Pory, "The Work of a Colonial Legislature," 42–45.

27. "Pocahontas," *American National Biography*, edited by John A. Garraty and Mark C. Carnes, (New York: Oxford University Press, 1999), 607.

28. Robert M. Utley and Wilcomb E. Washburn, *The Indian Wars* (New York: American Heritage Publishing / Bonanza Books, 1982), 25.

29. John Winthrop, *Life and Letters of John Winthrop*, Wikipedia, 314.

Chapter 3

1. Warren M. Billings (ed.), *The Old Dominion in the Seventeenth Century: A Documentary History of Virginia, 1606–1689* (Chapel Hill: University of North Carolina Press, 1975), 226–28.

2. Ibid., 228.

3. Wesley Frank Craven, *The Southern Colonies in the Seventeenth Century 1607–1689*, Vol. 1 (Baton Rouge: Louisiana State University Press, 1949), 367–368.

4. Ibid., 368.

5. Douglas Edward Leach, *The Northern Colonial Frontier 1607–1763* (New York: Holt, Rinehart and Winston, 1966), 185.

6. William Walker Hening, *A Collection of all the Laws of Virginia from 1619 to 1808*, Vol. III (Charlottesville: University of Virginia Press, 1969), 204–205.

7. Robert L. Kincaid, *The Wilderness Road* (1947; reprint, Middlesboro, KY: Bobbs-Merrill, 1966), 24–26.

8. Martin Ridge and Ray A. Billington (eds.). *America's Frontier Story: A Documentary History of Western Expansion* (New York: Holt, Rinehart and Winston, 1969), 82–84.

9. Thomas Jefferson and William Peden (ed., intro., notes). *Notes on the State of Virginia* (New York: W. W. Norton, 1972), 96, 281.

10. Wilcomb E. Washburn, *Handbook of North American Indians*, vol. 4 (Washington: Smithsonian Institution, 1988), 9.

Chapter 4

1. William Byrd, "Surveying the Frontier," *The Annals of American*, Vol. 1, edited by Mortimer J. Adler (Chicago: Encyclopædia Britannica, 1968), 382.

2. David H. Corkran, *The Creek Frontier 1540–1783* (Norman: University of Oklahoma Press, 1967), 31–32.

3. William R. Nester, *The First Global War* (Westport, CT: Praeger, 2000), 26.

4. Francis D. Pastorius, "German Settlers in Pennsylvania," *The Annals of American*, Vol. 1, edited by Mortimer J. Adler (Chicago: Encyclopædia Britannica, 1968), 313.

Chapter 5

1. Russell Thornton, *The Cherokees: A Population Study* (Lincoln: University of Nebraska Press, 1990), 29.

2. Stanley W. Hoig, *The Cherokees and Their Chiefs* (Fayetteville: University of Arkansas Press, 1998), 11; see Duane H. King (ed.), *Memoirs of Lieut. Henry Timberlake 1756–1765* (Cherokee, NC: Museum of the Cherokee Press; distributed by the University of North Carolina, c. 2007).

3. Louis De Vorsey, Jr., *The Indian Boundary in the Southern Colonies, 1763–1775* (Chapel Hill: University of North Carolina Press, 1966), 49–51.

4. Ibid., 51.

5. Hoig, *The Cherokees and Their Chiefs*, 36.

6. Ibid., 38.

7. Ibid., 39.

8. J. Russell Snapp, *John Stuart and the Struggle for Empire on the Southern Frontier* (Baton Rouge: Louisiana State University Press, 1996), 56.

9. Grace Steele Woodward, *The Cherokees* (Norman: University of Oklahoma Press, 1963), 77.

10. Hoig, *The Cherokees and Their Chiefs*, 43.

11. Ibid., 45.

12. Ronald Wright, *Stolen Continents* (Boston: Houghton Mifflin, 1992), 110.

Chapter 6

1. "Opportunities for Settlers in Carolina," *The Annals of American*, Vol. 1, edited by Mortimer J. Adler (Chicago: Encyclopædia Britannica, 1968), 240–242.

2. W. Stitt Robinson, *The Southern Colonial Frontier, 1607–1763* (Albuquerque: University of New Mexico, 1979), 84.

3. Ibid., 107.

4. Ibid., 108.

5. Ibid., 88.

6. Louis B. Wright, *The Colonial Civilization of North America 1607–1763* (London: Eyre & Spottiswoode, 1949), 222.

7. Francis Paul Prucha, *American Indian Policy in the Formative Years* (Lincoln: University of Nebraska, 1962), 8–9.

8. Robinson, *The Southern Colonial Frontier*, 112.

9. Ibid., 119.

10. Ibid., 146.

11. Prucha, *American Indian Policy in the Formative Years*, 6.

12. De Vorsey, *The Indian Boundary in the Southern Colonies*, 137.

13. David H. Corkran, *The Creek Frontier 1540–1783* (Norman: University of Oklahoma Press, 1967), 91.

14. James F. Doster, *The Creek Indians and Their Florida Lands 1740–1823*, vol. 1 (New York: Garland Publishing, 1974), 37.

15. Corkran, *The Creek Frontier*, 101.

16. De Vorsey, *The Indian Boundary in the Southern Colonies*, 146.

17. Robinson, *The Southern Colonial Frontier*, 216.

18. Ibid.

19. Corkran, *The Creek Frontier*, 233.

20. Ibid., 233–234.

21. De Vorsey, *The Indian Boundary in the Southern Colonies*, 28.

22. Ibid.

23. Ibid.

24. Henry Steele Commager (ed.), *Documents of Amer-*

ican History, 9th ed. (Englewood Cliffs, NJ: Prentice Hall, 1973), 47.

Chapter 7

1. Douglas Summers Brown, *The Catawba Indians* (Columbia: University of South Carolina Press, 1966), 135.
2. Ibid., 230.
3. Ibid., 250–251.
4. Louis De Vorsey, Jr., *The Indian Boundary in the Southern Colonies, 1763–1775* (Chapel Hill: University of North Carolina Press, 1966), 151.
5. David H. Corkran, *The Creek Frontier 1540–1783* (Norman: University of Oklahoma Press, 1967), 238–239.
6. Ibid., 265.
7. Ibid., 270–271.
8. Ibid., 271.
9. Corkran, *The Creek Frontier*, 230.
10. De Vorsey, *The Indian Boundary in the Southern Colonies*, 124.
11. Ibid., 127.
12. Ibid., 127–128.
13. Ibid., 129.
14. Ibid., 131–132.
15. Ibid., 133.
16. Ibid., 99.
17. Ibid., 100.
18. Grace Steele Woodward, *The Cherokees* (Norman: University of Oklahoma Press, 1963), 86.
19. J. Russell Snapp, *John Stuart and the Struggle for Empire on the Southern Frontier* (Baton Rouge: Louisiana State University Press, 1996), 71.
20. Ibid., 58–59.
21. De Vorsey, *The Indian Boundary in the Southern Colonies*, 191.
22. Ibid., 192.
23. Ibid., 207.
24. Ibid., 209.
25. Ibid., 213.
26. Ibid.
27. Snapp, *John Stuart and the Struggle for Empire on the Southern Frontier*, 57.
28. Ibid., 119–120.
29. Ibid., 126.
30. Ibid., 140.

Chapter 8

1. Grace Steele Woodward, *The Cherokees* (Norman: University of Oklahoma Press, 1963), 79.
2. Louis De Vorsey, Jr., *The Indian Boundary in the Southern Colonies, 1763–1775* (Chapel Hill: University of North Carolina Press, 1966), 60.
3. Ibid., 19.
4. Ibid., 12.
5. Hard Labor treaty, *Early American Indian Documents: Treaties and Laws, 1607–1789*, vol. V, edited by Alden T. Vaughan (Frederick, MD, and Washington, DC: University Publications of America, 1979, 1984), 328.
6. De Vorsey, *The Indian Boundary in the Southern Colonies*, 102.
7. Ibid., 49.
8. Ibid., 64.
9. Ibid., 71–72.
10. Ibid., 77.
11. Ibid., 78.

12. Ibid.
13. Ibid., 88.
14. Ibid.
15. Ibid., 83.
16. Ibid., 84–85.
17. Lochaber treaty, *Early American Indian Documents: Treaties and Laws, 1607–1789*, vol. V, edited by Alden T. Vaughan (Frederick, MD, and Washington, DC: University Publications of America, 1979, 1984), Vol. V, 368.
18. Ronald Wright, *Stolen Continents* (Boston: Houghton Mifflin, 1992), 111.
19. Ibid.
20. Woodward, *The Cherokees*, 85.
21. Walter H. Mohr, *Federal Indian Relations 1774–1788* (Philadelphia: University of Pennsylvania Press, 1933), 21.
22. Ibid., 6.

Chapter 9

1. Henry Steele Commager (ed.), *Documents of American History*, 9th ed. (Englewood Cliffs, NJ: Prentice Hall, 1973), 49.
2. Quoted from Thomas Perkins Abernethy, *Western Lands and the American Revolution* (New York: Russell & Russell, 1959), 20–21; Commager (ed.), *Documents of American History*, 49.
3. Commager, *Documents of American History*, 49.
4. Ibid.
5. Abernethy, *Western Lands and the American Revolution*, 69.
6. Ibid., 29.
7. A. Gwynn Henderson, "Dispelling the Myth: Seventeenth- and Eighteenth-Century Indian Life in Kentucky," *Bicentennial Issue of the Register of the Kentucky Historical Society*, vol. 90, no. 1 (1992): 3, 6–8, 17, 22, 24.
8. Abernethy, *Western Lands and the American Revolution*, 54.
9. Solon J. Buck and Elizabeth Hawthorn Buck, *The Planting of Civilization in Western Pennsylvania* (Pittsburgh: University of Pittsburgh, 1939), 159; Nicholas B. Wainwright, *George Croghan, Wilderness Diplomat* (Chapel Hill: University of North Carolina, 1959), 286–287.
10. Thomas Jefferson and William Peden (ed., intro., notes). *Notes on the State of Virginia* (New York: W. W. Norton, 1972), 71–72.
11. Anthony F. C. Wallace, *Jefferson and the Indians* (Cambridge, MA: Belknap Press, 1999), 7.
12. Thomas Jefferson and William Peden (ed., intro., notes), *Notes on the State of Virginia* (New York: W. W. Norton, 1972), 250–251.
13. Ibid., 252.
14. Reuben Gold Thwaites and Louise Phelps Kellogg (eds.), *Documentary History of Dunmore's War, Bicentennial Edition, 1774–1974* (Harrisonburg, VA: C. J. Carter, 1974), 386.
15. Ibid., 386–387.
16. Robert L. Kincaid, *The Wilderness Road* (1947; reprint, Middlesboro, KY: Bobbs-Merrill, 1966), 94.
17. John Mack Faragher, *Daniel Boone* (New York: Henry Holt, 1992), 108.
18. Ibid., 109.
19. Ibid.
20. Ronald Wright, *Stolen Continents* (Boston: Houghton Mifflin, 1992), 113.
21. Ibid.
22. Kincaid, *The Wilderness Road*, 99.
23. Ibid., 105.

24. Ibid., 205.

25. Ibid.

26. Parke Rouse, Jr. *The Great Wagon Road* (New York: McGraw-Hill, 1973), 111–112.

27. Walter H. Mohr, *Federal Indian Relations 1774–1788* (Philadelphia: University of Pennsylvania Press, 1933), 16.

Chapter 10

1. Stanley W. Hoig, *The Cherokees and Their Chiefs* (Fayetteville: University of Arkansas Press, 1998), 34.

2. John E. Selby, *The Revolution in Virginia, 1775–1783* (Williamsburg, VA: Colonial Williamsburg Foundation, 1988), 186.

3. Billington, 176.

4. Grace Steele Woodward, *The Cherokees* (Norman: University of Oklahoma Press, 1963), 93.

5. Julian P. Boyd et al. (eds.), *The Papers of Thomas Jefferson* (Princeton, NJ: Princeton University Press, 1950) 1:494.

6. Andrew A. Lipscomb (ed.), *The Writings of Thomas Jefferson* (Washington, D.C.: Thomas Jefferson Memorial Association, 1905), 18:141.

7. Robert F. Berkhofer, Jr. *The White Man's Indian* (New York: Alfred A. Knopf, 1978), 42.

8. J. Russell Snapp, *John Stuart and the Struggle for Empire on the Southern Frontier* (Baton Rouge: Louisiana State University Press, 1996), 197.

9. Woodward, *The Cherokees*, 99.

10. Ibid., 100.

11. Selby, *The Revolution in Virginia*, 200.

12. Hoig, *The Cherokees and Their Chiefs*, 63.

13. David H. Corkran, *The Creek Frontier 1540–1783* (Norman: University of Oklahoma Press, 1967), 291.

14. Ibid., 323.

Chapter 11

1. John Walton Caughey, *McGillivray of the Creeks* (Norman: University of Oklahoma Press, 1938), 22.

2. Ibid., 17.

3. Walter H. Mohr, *Federal Indian Relations 1774–1788* (Philadelphia: University of Pennsylvania Press, 1933), 144–46.

4. Colin G. Calloway (ed. and intro.), *The World Turned Upside Down* (New York: Bedford Books of St. Martin's Press, 1994), 172–173.

5. James F. Doster, *The Creek Indians and Their Florida Lands 1740–1823*, vol. 1 (New York: Garland Publishing, 1974), 71.

6. Florette Henri, *The Southern Indians and Benjamin Hawkins 1796–1816* (Norman: University of Oklahoma Press, 1986), 42.

7. Doster, *The Creek Indians and Their Florida Lands*, vol. 1, 86.

8. Ibid., 91.

9. Ibid., 90.

10. Ibid., 92.

11. Ibid., 94.

12. Caughey, *McGillivray of the Creeks*, 30.

13. Doster, *The Creek Indians and Their Florida Lands*, vol. 1, 100.

14. Ibid., 97.

15. Ibid., 98.

16. Ibid., 103–104.

17. Henri, *The Southern Indians and Benjamin Hawkins*, 80.

18. Thomas A. Bailey, *A Diplomatic History of the American People*, 8th ed. (New York: Appleton-Century-Crofts, 1979), 62.

19. Ibid., 63.

20. Caughey, *McGillivray of the Creeks*, 27.

21. Doster, *The Creek Indians and Their Florida Lands*, vol. 1, 110.

22. Ibid., 120.

Chapter 12

1. John Walton Caughey, *McGillivray of the Creeks* (Norman: University of Oklahoma Press, 1938), 38.

2. Florette Henri, *The Southern Indians and Benjamin Hawkins 1796–1816* (Norman: University of Oklahoma Press, 1986), 49.

3. Merritt B. Pound, *Benjamin Hawkins — Indian Agent* (Athens: University of Georgia Press, 1951), 57.

4. United States, *Statutes at Large*, vol. 7, 35–38.

5. Caughey, *McGillivray of the Creeks*, 273–274.

6. James F. Doster, *The Creek Indians and Their Florida Lands 1740–1823*, vol. 1 (New York: Garland Publishing, 1974), 140–142.

7. Ibid., 141–142.

8. Henri, *The Southern Indians and Benjamin Hawkins*, 74–75.

9. Pound, *Benjamin Hawkins — Indian Agent*, 191.

10. Henri, *The Southern Indians and Benjamin Hawkins*, 4–5, 18–19.

11. Ibid., 76.

12. Ibid., 77–78.

13. Doster, *The Creek Indians and Their Florida Lands*, vol. 1, 152–153.

14. Ibid., 166.

15. Ibid., 171.

16. Henri, *The Southern Indians and Benjamin Hawkins*, 53–54; John C. Fitzpatrick, *George Washington's Writings* (Washington, D.C.: U.S. GPO, 1938), 32:108.

17. Doster, *The Creek Indians and Their Florida Lands*, vol. 1, 184.

18. Ibid., 176.

19. Henri, *The Southern Indians and Benjamin Hawkins*, 99–100.

20. Doster, *The Creek Indians and Their Florida Lands*, vol. 1, 186.

21. Ibid., 188.

22. Ibid., 198.

23. Ibid., 204.

24. Ibid., 206.

25. Ibid., 209–210.

26. Henri, *The Southern Indians and Benjamin Hawkins*, 101.

Chapter 13

1. Walter H. Mohr, *Federal Indian Relations 1774–1788* (Philadelphia: University of Pennsylvania Press, 1933), 140.

2. Ibid., 141 n. 7.

3. Colin G. Calloway (ed. and intro.), *The World Turned Upside Down* (New York: Bedford Books of St. Martin's Press, 1994), 163.

4. Ibid., 164–166.

5. Ibid, 170

6. Arell M. Gibson, *The Chickasaws* (Norman: University of Oklahoma Press, 1971), 77.

7. United States, *Statutes at Large*, vol. 7, 24–26.

8. Gibson, *The Chickasaws*, 87.
9. United States, *Statutes at Large*, vol. 7, 21–22.
10. *American State Papers: Indian Affairs* (Buffalo, NY: William S. Hein, 1998), 1:49.

Chapter 14

1. *American State Papers: Indian Affairs* (Buffalo, NY: William S. Hein, 1998), 1:604.
2. Florette Henri, *The Southern Indians and Benjamin Hawkins 1796–1816* (Norman: University of Oklahoma Press, 1986), 56.
3. Ibid., 58.
4. United States, *Statutes at Large,* vol. 7, 56–60; Merritt B. Pound, *Benjamin Hawkins–Indian Agent* (Athens: University of Georgia Press, 1951), 97.
5. Henri, *The Southern Indians and Benjamin Hawkins,* 112.
6. Ibid., 114.
7. Ibid., 93.
8. Pound, *Benjamin Hawkins—Indian Agent*, 103.
9. Ibid., 105.
10. Ibid., 110.
11. Ibid., 111.
12. Ibid., 114.
13. James F. Doster, *The Creek Indians and Their Florida Lands 1740–1823*, vol. 1 (New York: Garland Publishing, 1974), 224.
14. Ibid., 221.
15. Pound, *Benjamin Hawkins—Indian Agent*, 108.
16. Henri, *The Southern Indians and Benjamin Hawkins,* 68.
17. Ibid.
18. Ibid., 96.
19. Ibid., 110.
20. Ibid., 104.
21. United States, *Statutes at Large*, vol. 7, 18–26.
22. Henri, *The Southern Indians and Benjamin Hawkins,* 60.
23. Doster, *The Creek Indians and Their Florida Lands,* vol. 1, 248.

Chapter 15

1. Samuel Cole Williams, *The Memoirs of Lieut. Henry Timberlake 1756–1765* (Marietta, GA: Continental, 1948), 20–21.
2. Ibid., 22.
3. Ibid., 20.
4. William H. Masterson, *William Blount* (Baton Rouge: Louisiana State University Press, 1954), 90.
5. Williams, *History of the Lost State of Franklin*, 1.
6. Ibid., 30, 41.
7. Ibid., 41.
8. *Wikipedia,* "Battle of Kings Mountain," citing John Buchanan, *The Road to Guilford Court House: The American Revolution in the Carolinas* (New York: John Wiley & Sons, 1997), 219.
9. Williams, *History of the Lost State of Franklin*, 63–64.
10. Ibid., 74–76.
11. Ibid., 82–83.
12. Ibid., 77–79.
13. Florette Henri, *The Southern Indians and Benjamin Hawkins 1796–1816* (Norman: University of Oklahoma Press, 1986), 85.
14. Williams, *History of the Lost State of Franklin*, 92.
15. Ibid., 93.

16. United States, *Statutes at Large*, vol. 7, 18–21; Francis Paul Prucha, *Documents of United States Indian Policy*, 2nd ed., expanded (Lincoln: University of Nebraska Press, 1975), 6–8.
17. Masterson, *William Blount*, 106.
18. Ibid.
19. Williams, *History of the Lost State of Franklin*, 102.
20. Ibid.
21. Masterson, *William Blount*, 90.
22. John Donelson. *Dictionary of American Biography*, edited by Allen Johnson and Dumas Malone (New York: Scribner's, 1927, 720–21.
23. Williams, *History of the Lost State of Franklin*, 142.
24. Ibid.
25. Ibid., 141–142; William P. Palmer (ed.), *Calendar of Virginia State Papers* (1884; reprint, New York: Kraus Reprint Corp., 1968), 4:241–242.
26. Merritt B. Pound, *Benjamin Hawkins–Indian Agent* (Athens: University of Georgia Press, 1951), 54.
27. Stanley W. Hoig, *The Cherokees and Their Chiefs* (Fayetteville: University of Arkansas Press, 1998), 3.
28. Prucha, *American Indian Policy in the Formative Years*,148.
29. Julian P. Boyd et al. (eds.), *The Papers of Thomas Jefferson* (Princeton, NJ: Princeton University Press, 1950), 9:640–642.
30. Andrew A. Lipscomb (ed.), *The Writings of Thomas Jefferson* (Washington, D.C.: Thomas Jefferson Memorial Association, 1905), 5: 390.
31. Williams, *History of the Lost State of Franklin*, 103.
32. Ibid., 262.
33. Ibid., 266.
34. Hoig, *The Cherokees and Their Chiefs*, 71.
35. Williams, *History of the Lost State of Franklin*, 213 n. 9.
36. Hoig, *The Cherokees and Their Chiefs*, 73.
37. Williams, *History of the Lost State of Franklin*, 224.
38. Ibid.
39. Ibid.
40. Grace Steele Woodward, *The Cherokees* (Norman: University of Oklahoma Press, 1963), 109.
41. Williams, *History of the Lost State of Franklin*, 226.
42. Ibid., 251 n. 7.

Chapter 16

1. Grace Steele Woodward, *The Cherokees* (Norman: University of Oklahoma Press, 1963), 110–112.
2. Francis Paul Prucha, *American Indian Policy in the Formative Years* (Lincoln: University of Nebraska, 1962), 28.
3. William H. Masterson, *William Blount* (Baton Rouge: Louisiana State University Press, 1954), 177; Clarence E. Carter (ed.), *The Territorial Papers of the United States, Colonial Times*, vol. 4 (Washington, DC: Government Printing Office, 1934–1975), 19–20.
4. Masterson, *William Blount*, 187.
5. Ibid., 196.
6. Ibid., 198
7. Florette Henri, *The Southern Indians and Benjamin Hawkins 1796–1816* (Norman: University of Oklahoma Press, 1986), 192.
8. United States, *Statutes at Large*, vol. 7, 39–42.
9. Masterson, *William Blount*, 206–207.
10. *American State Papers: Indian Affairs* (Buffalo, NY: William S. Hein, 1998), 1:205.
11. Prucha, *American Indian Policy in the Formative Years*, 139.

12. Henri, *The Southern Indians and Benjamin Hawkins*, 195.

13. Masterson, *William Blount*, 252–253, Stanley W. Hoig, *The Cherokees and Their Chiefs* (Fayetteville: University of Arkansas Press, 1998), 85–86.

14. Hoig, 81.

15. Masterson, *William Blount*, 228.

16. Henri, *The Southern Indians and Benjamin Hawkins*, 194.

17. Ibid.

18. Masterson, *William Blount*, 241.

19. Carter, *The Territorial Papers of the United States*, vol. 4, 274–275.

20. Ibid., 299–300.

21. United States, *Statutes at Large*, vol. 7, 43–44.

22. Masterson, *William Blount*, 265.

23. Woodward, *The Cherokees*, 116.

24. Ibid.

25. Carter, *The Territorial Papers of the United States*, vol. 4, 370.

26. Masterson, *William Blount*, 272.

27. Joseph S. Lucas, "Civilization or Extinction: Citizens and Indians in the Early United States," *Journal of the Historical Society*, VI, no. 2 (June 2006): 243.

Chapter 17

1. William H. Masterson, *William Blount* (Baton Rouge: Louisiana State University Press, 1954), 312–313; *Annals of the Congress of the United States*, 5th Congress (repr. Buffalo, NY: William S. Hein, 2003), 2349–2350.

2. Masterson, *William Blount*, 313.

3. Florette Henri, *The Southern Indians and Benjamin Hawkins 1796–1816* (Norman: University of Oklahoma Press, 1986), 203.

4. Masterson, *William Blount*, 319.

5. Ibid., 321.

6. Ibid., 327–328.

7. Merritt B. Pound, *Benjamin Hawkins–Indian Agent* (Athens: University of Georgia Press, 1951), 123.

8. Ibid.

9. Ibid., 125.

10. Ibid.

11. Henri, *The Southern Indians and Benjamin Hawkins*, 207.

12. United States, *Statutes at Large*, vol. 7, 62–65; Charles C. Royce, "Indian Land Cessions in the United States." *Smithsonian Institution. Bureau of American Ethnology.* Eighteenth Annual Report, 1896–1897 (Washington, D.C.: U.S. GPO, 1899), Plate CXLIII, Parcel 42.

13. Grace Steele Woodward, *The Cherokees* (Norman: University of Oklahoma Press, 1963), 119.

14. Ibid., 121.

15. Ibid., 122.

Chapter 18

1. Anthony F. C. Wallace, *Jefferson and the Indians* (Cambridge, MA: Belknap Press, 1999), 206.

2. Ibid.

3. Dumas Malone, *Jefferson the President, First Term, 1801–1805* (Boston: Little, Brown, 1970), 146.

4. *American State Papers: Indian Affairs* (Buffalo, NY: William S. Hein, 1998), 1:650.

5. Wallace, *Jefferson and the Indians*, 282.

6. United States, *Statutes at Large*, vol. 7, 65–66.

7. William C. Davis, *A Way Through the Wilderness* (New York: HarperCollins, 1995), 17.

8. Ibid., 24.

9. United States, *Statutes at Large*, vol. 7, 66–68.

10. Florette Henri, *The Southern Indians and Benjamin Hawkins 1796–1816* (Norman: University of Oklahoma Press, 1986), 227–228.

11. Ibid., 223.

12. Ibid., 226.

13. H. B. Cushman and Angie Debo (eds.), *History of the Choctaw, Chickasaw, and Natchez Indians* (1899; reprint, Norman: University of Oklahoma Press, 1999), 109, 111.

14. Henri, *The Southern Indians and Benjamin Hawkins*, 81.

15. Ibid., 142.

16. Ibid., 220.

17. James F. Doster, *The Creek Indians and Their Florida Lands 1740–1823*, vol. 1 (New York: Garland Publishing, 1974), 244.

18. William Augustus Bowles, *Dictionary of American Biography*, edited by Allen Johnson and Dumas Malone (New York: Scribner's, 1927), 519–20.

19. Henri, *The Southern Indians and Benjamin Hawkins*, 237.

20. Malone, *Jefferson the President*, 246; Clarence E. Carter (ed.), *The Territorial Papers of the United States, Colonial Times*, vol. 5 (Washington, DC: Government Printing Office, 1934–1975), 144.

21. Henri, *The Southern Indians and Benjamin Hawkins*, 231.

22. Ibid., 233.

23. Statute at Large 7 (1802): 68–70.

24. Henri, *The Southern Indians and Benjamin Hawkins*, 230

25. "Andrew Pickens," *American National Biography*, edited by John A. Garraty and Mark C. Carnes, (New York: Oxford University Press, 1999), 469–70.

26. *American State Papers: Indian Affairs*, 1:680.

27. Malone, *Jefferson the President*, 240.

28. Ibid., 250.

29. Ibid., 249.

30. Ibid., 269–270.

31. Wallace, *Jefferson and the Indians*, 221.

32. Ibid., 222.

33. Andrew A. Lipscomb (ed.), *The Writings of Thomas Jefferson* (Washington, D.C.: Thomas Jefferson Memorial Association, 1905), 10: 357–359.

34. Statute at Large 7 (1802): 73–74.

35. Henri, *The Southern Indians and Benjamin Hawkins*, 254.

36. Ibid., 255.

37. Statute at Large 7 (1803): 80–81.

38. Henri, *The Southern Indians and Benjamin Hawkins*, 244; Garraty and Carnes, "James Wilkinson," 222–26.

39. Francis Paul Prucha, *The Great Father*, vol. I (Lincoln: University of Nebraska, 1984), 120.

40. Merritt B. Pound, *Benjamin Hawkins–Indian Agent* (Athens: University of Georgia Press, 1951), 207.

41. Cushman and Debo, *History of the Choctaw, Chickasaw, and Natchez Indians*, 431–432.

42. James F. Doster, *The Creek Indians and Their Florida Lands 1740–1823*, vol. 1 (New York: Garland Publishing, 1974), 263.

Chapter 19

1. Florette Henri, *The Southern Indians and Benjamin Hawkins 1796–1816* (Norman: University of Oklahoma Press, 1986), 239.

2. Ibid., 242.

3. Grant Foreman, *Indians and Pioneers*, revised ed. (Norman: University of Oklahoma Press, 1936), 11–12.

4. Henri, *The Southern Indians and Benjamin Hawkins*, 240.

5. Anthony F. C. Wallace, *Jefferson and the Indians* (Cambridge, MA: Belknap Press, 1999), 224.

6. Ibid.

7. Ibid.

8. Henri, *The Southern Indians and Benjamin Hawkins*, 242.

9. Andrew A. Lipscomb (ed.), *The Writings of Thomas Jefferson* (Washington, D.C.: Thomas Jefferson Memorial Association, 1905), 10: 363.

10. Henri, *The Southern Indians and Benjamin Hawkins*, 246.

11. Merritt B. Pound, *Benjamin Hawkins–Indian Agent* (Athens: University of Georgia Press, 1951), 186.

12. Lipscomb, *The Writings of Thomas Jefferson*, vol. 10, 358.

13. James F. Doster, *The Creek Indians and Their Florida Lands 1740–1823*, vol. 1 (New York: Garland Publishing, 1974), 272

14. United States, *Statutes at Large*, vol. 7, 96–98; Charles C. Royce, "Indian Land Cessions in the United States." *Smithsonian Institution. Bureau of American Ethnology*. Eighteenth Annual Report, 1896–1897 (Washington, D.C.: U.S. GPO, 1899), Plate CXXII, Parcel 60.

15. Pound, *Benjamin Hawkins — Indian Agent*, 186.

16. Ibid., 208.

17. United States, *Statutes at Large*, vol. 7, 97.

18. Henri, *The Southern Indians and Benjamin Hawkins*, 252.

19. United States, *Statutes at Large*, vol. 7, 228–229; Royce, "Indian Land Cessions in the United States," Plate CXXII, Parcel 52.

20. United States, *Statutes at Large*, vol. 7, 93–94; Royce, "Indian Land Cessions in the United States," Plate CLXI; Parcel 57.

21. Thurman Wilkins, *Cherokee Tragedy* (New York: Macmillan, 1970), 35–36.

22. United States, *Statutes at Large*, vol. 7, 93–96; Royce, "Indian Land Cessions in the United States," Plate CLXI, Parcels 58, 59.

23. United States, *Statutes at Large*, vol. 7, 101–103; Royce, "Indian Land Cessions in the United States," Plate CLXI, Parcel 64.

24. Grace Steele Woodward, *The Cherokees* (Norman: University of Oklahoma Press, 1963), 129.

25. James F. Doster, *The Creek Indians and Their Florida Lands 1740–1823*, vol. 2 (New York: Garland Publishing, 1974), 16.

26. Wilkins, *Cherokee Tragedy*, 38.

27. Stanley W. Hoig, *The Cherokees and Their Chiefs* (Fayetteville: University of Arkansas Press, 1998), 105.

28. Foreman, *Indians and Pioneers*, 34 n. 35.

29. United States, *Statutes at Large*, vol. 7, 103–104.

30. United States, *Statutes at Large*, vol. 7, 89–90; Royce, "Indian Land Cessions in the United States," Plate CLXIII, Parcel 55.

31. Doster, *The Creek Indians and Their Florida Lands 1740–1823*, vol. 2, 25.

32. *American State Papers: Indian Affairs* (Buffalo, NY: William S. Hein, 1998), 1:749.

33. Wallace, *Jefferson and the Indians*, 238.

34. Ibid., 263.

35. Francis Paul Prucha, *American Indian Policy in the Formative Years* (Lincoln: University of Nebraska, 1962), 140–141.

36. Julian P. Boyd et al. (eds.), *The Papers of Thomas Jefferson* (Princeton, NJ: Princeton University Press, 1950), 24:29–30.

37. Clarence E. Carter (ed.), *The Territorial Papers of the United States, Colonial Times*, vol. 5 (Washington, DC: Government Printing Office, 1934–1975), 739–740.

38. Henri, *The Southern Indians and Benjamin Hawkins*, 252.

39. Prucha, *American Indian Policy in the Formative Years*, 160.

40. Ibid., 161–162; Carter, *The Territorial Papers of the United States*, vol. 6, 108.

41. Prucha, *American Indian Policy in the Formative Years*, 162; Carter, *The Territorial Papers of the United States*, vol. 6, 107.

Chapter 20

1. James F. Doster, *The Creek Indians and Their Florida Lands 1740–1823*, vol. 2 (New York: Garland Publishing, 1974), 27.

2. Ibid., 32.

3. William Warren Rogers, Robert David Ward, Leah Rawls Atkins, and Wayne Flynt, *Alabama: The History of a Deep South State* (Tuscaloosa: University of Alabama Press, 1994), 45.

4. Doster, *The Creek Indians and Their Florida Lands*, vol. 2, 42–43.

5. Ibid., 46.

6. Ibid., 47.

7. Florette Henri, *The Southern Indians and Benjamin Hawkins 1796–1816* (Norman: University of Oklahoma Press, 1986), 268.

8. Arrell M. Gibson, *The Chickasaws* (Norman: University of Oklahoma Press, 1971), 96.

9. Henri, *The Southern Indians and Benjamin Hawkins*, 269.

10. Ibid.

11. Ibid., 270.

12. Ibid., 281.

13. Ibid., 269–270.

14. Ibid.

15. Ibid., 270.

16. Ibid., 275.

17. Doster, *The Creek Indians and Their Florida Lands*, vol. 2, 50.

18. Ibid., 51.

19. Ibid., 55.

20. Henri, *The Southern Indians and Benjamin Hawkins*, 273.

21. Doster, *The Creek Indians and Their Florida Lands*, vol. 2, 54–55.

22. Ibid., 80.

23. Ibid.

24. Ibid.

25. Ibid., 83.

26. Henri, *The Southern Indians and Benjamin Hawkins*, 281.

27. Ibid., 285.

28. Robert V. Remini, *Andrew Jackson and the Course of American Empire, 1767–1821* (New York: Harper & Row, 1977), 142–143.

29. Ibid., 192.

30. Henri, *The Southern Indians and Benjamin Hawkins*, 280.

31. David S. Heidler and Jeanne T. Heidler, *Old Hickory's War* (Mechanicsburg, PA: Stackpole Books, 1996), 18.

32. "Andrew Jackson," *American National Biography*,

edited by John A. Garraty and Mark C. Carnes, (New York: Oxford University Press, 1999).732–34.

33. Remini, *Andrew Jackson and the Course of American Empire*, 121–122.

34. Ibid., 146.

35. Henri, *The Southern Indians and Benjamin Hawkins*, 290.

36. Ibid., 291.

37. Remini, *Andrew Jackson and the Course of American Empire*, 203.

38. Ibid., 213.

39. Ibid., 214.

40. Rogers, Ward, Atkins, and Flynt, *Alabama*, 53.

41. Remini, *Andrew Jackson and the Course of American Empire*, 215.

42. Ibid., 218.

43. Henri, *The Southern Indians and Benjamin Hawkins*, 286.

Chapter 21

1. James F. Doster, *The Creek Indians and Their Florida Lands 1740–1823*, vol. 2 (New York: Garland Publishing, 1974), 126.

2. United States, *Statutes at Large*, vol. 7, 120–122.

3. Doster, *The Creek Indians and Their Florida Lands*, vol. 2, 111.

4. Florette Henri, *The Southern Indians and Benjamin Hawkins 1796–1816* (Norman: University of Oklahoma Press, 1986), 296.

5. Doster, *The Creek Indians and Their Florida Lands*, vol. 2, 112.

6. Ibid., 115–116.

7. Ibid., 119.

8. Ibid., 118.

9. Ibid., 120.

10. Ibid., 122.

11. Ibid., 124.

12. Arrell M. Gibson, *The Chickasaws* (Norman: University of Oklahoma Press, 1971), 98–99; Royce, "Indian Land Cessions in the United States," Plates CVIII and CXXII, Parcel 75.

13. Henri, *The Southern Indians and Benjamin Hawkins*, 299.

14. United States, *Statutes at Large*, vol. 7, 120.

15. Ibid., 121; Robert V. Remini, *Andrew Jackson and the Course of American Empire, 1767–1821* (New York: Harper & Row, 1977), 220.

16. Doster, *The Creek Indians and Their Florida Lands*, vol. 2, 131–132.

17. Remini, *Andrew Jackson and the Course of American Empire*, 286.

18. Ibid., 293.

Chapter 22

1. Robert V. Remini, *Andrew Jackson and the Course of American Empire, 1767–1821* (New York: Harper & Row, 1977), 300.

2. James F. Doster, *The Creek Indians and Their Florida Lands 1740–1823*, vol. 2 (New York: Garland Publishing, 1974), 156.

3. Ibid.

4. Ibid.

5. Ibid., 160.

6. Ibid.

7. Ibid., 162.

8. Ibid., 163.

9. Ibid., 166.

10. Ibid.

11. Ibid., 168.

12. Ibid., 170.

13. Ibid., 285.

14. Ibid., 223–224.

15. Thurman Wilkins, *Cherokee Tragedy* (New York: Macmillan, 1970), 80.

16. Ibid., 83–84.

17. Ibid., 84.

18. Ibid., 80.

19. Ibid., 87–88.

20. Ibid., 88.

21. Ibid., 90.

22. United States, *Statutes at Large*, vol. 7, 139–40.

23. Wilkins, *Cherokee Tragedy*, 91.

24. Ibid., 27.

25. Ibid., 38.

26. Ibid., 39.

27. Grace Steele Woodward, *The Cherokees* (Norman: University of Oklahoma Press, 1963), 135.

28. Remini, *Andrew Jackson and the Course of American Empire*, 326.

29. Wilkins, *Cherokee Tragedy*, 94.

30. United States, *Statutes at Large*, vol. 7, 148–149; Royce, "Indian Land Cessions in the United States," Plate CVIII, Parcel 79.

31. Ibid., 149.

32. Wilkins, *Cherokee Tragedy*, 95.

33. Arrell M. Gibson, *The Chickasaws* (Norman: University of Oklahoma Press, 1971), 65.

34. United States, *Statutes at Large*, vol. 7, 150–152; Royce, "Indian Land Cessions in the United States," Plates CVIII, CXLIII, and CLXIII, Parcels 79, 80.

35. *American State Papers: InAffairs* (Buffalo, NY: William S. Hein, 1998), 2:104–105.

36. United States, *Statutes at Large*, vol. 7, 152–153.

37. Florette Henri, *The Southern Indians and Benjamin Hawkins 1796–1816* (Norman: University of Oklahoma Press, 1986), 305–306.

38. Ibid., 313.

Chapter 23

1. Robert V. Remini, *Andrew Jackson and the Course of American Empire, 1767–1821* (New York: Harper & Row, 1977), 326.

2. Ibid.

3. Ibid., 338.

4. Francis Paul Prucha, *The Great Father*, vol. I (Lincoln: University of Nebraska, 1984), 184.

5. Fred L. Israel (ed.), *The State of the Union Messages of the Presidents 1790–1966*, vol. 1 (New York: Chelsen House-Robert Hector, Publishers, 1966), 152–153.

6. United States, *Statutes at Large*, vol. 7, 156–160; Royce, "Indian Land Cessions in the United States," Plates CVIII, CXXII, and CLXI, Parcels 83–86.

7. Remini, *Andrew Jackson and the Course of American Empire*, 335.

8. Grant Foreman, *Indians and Pioneers*, revised ed. (Norman: University of Oklahoma Press, 1936), 44.

9. Florette Henri, *The Southern Indians and Benjamin Hawkins 1796–1816* (Norman: University of Oklahoma Press, 1986), 315.

10. United States, *Statutes at Large*, vol. 7, 156–160.

11. United States, *Statutes at Large*, vol. 7, 195–198; Royce, "Indian Land Cessions in the United States," Plates CVIII, CXXII, and CLXI, Parcels 83–86.

12. Foreman, *Indians and Pioneers*, 79.

13. Francis Paul Prucha, *American Indian Policy in the Formative Years* (Lincoln: University of Nebraska, 1962), 174.

14. United States, *Statutes at Large*, vol. 7, 311.

15. Prucha, *American Indian Policy in the Formative Years*, 177.

16. Stanley W. Hoig, *The Cherokees and Their Chiefs* (Fayetteville: University of Arkansas Press, 1998), 110.

Chapter 24

1. Robert V. Remini, *Andrew Jackson and the Course of American Empire, 1767–1821* (New York: Harper & Row, 1977), 337.

2. Arthur H. DeRosier, Jr., *The Removal of the Choctaw Indians* (1970; reprint, New York: Harper & Row, 1972), 43.

3. Ibid., 51.

4. Ibid.

5. Ibid., 51–52.

6. Remini, *Andrew Jackson and the Course of American Empire*, 466–467 n. 24.

7. DeRosier, *The Removal of the Choctaw Indians*, 10.

8. Ibid., 37.

9. Remini, *Andrew Jackson and the Course of American Empire*, 394.

10. Ibid., 395.

11. DeRosier, *The Removal of the Choctaw Indians*, 34.

12. Remini, *Andrew Jackson and the Course of American Empire*, 395.

13. United States, *Statutes at Large*, vol. 7, 210–213.

14. DeRosier, *The Removal of the Choctaw Indians*, 60.

15. Ibid., 71.

16. Ibid., 75.

17. Ibid., 77.

18. H. B. Cushman and Angie Debo (eds.), *History of the Choctaw, Chickasaw, and Natchez Indians* (1899; reprint, Norman: University of Oklahoma Press, 1999), 335.

19. Ibid.

20. Ibid., 269.

21. DeRosier, *The Removal of the Choctaw Indians*, 83.

22. Herman J. Viola, *Diplomats in Buckskins* (1981; reprint, Bluffton, SC: Rivilo Books, 1995), 165 .

23. United States, *Statutes at Large*, vol. 7, 234–236.

24. DeRosier, *The Removal of Choctaw Indians*, 90.

25. Viola, *Diplomats in Buckskins*, 29.

26. Ibid., 33.

27. Ibid., 31.

Chapter 25

1. United States, *Statutes at Large*, vol. 7, 171–172.

2. James F. Doster, *The Creek Indians and Their Florida Lands 1740–1823*, vol. 2 (New York: Garland Publishing, 1974), 286.

3. United States, *Statutes at Large*, vol. 7, 215–218.

4. Ibid., 215; Doster, *The Creek Indians and Their Florida Lands*, vol. 2, 286.

5. Doster, *The Creek Indians and Their Florida Lands*, vol. 2, 285.

6. Ibid., 287.

7. Ibid., 287–288.

8. Ibid., 289.

9. Ibid., 291.

10. Ibid.

11. United States, *Statutes at Large*, vol. 7, 237–240.

12. Doster, *The Creek Indians and Their Florida Lands*, vol. 2, 292.

13. Ibid., 293.

14. Ibid.

15. United States, *Statutes at Large*, vol. 7, 286–290 ; Royce, "Indian Land Cessions in the United States," Plate CXXII, Parcels 127–131.

16. *American State Papers: Indian Affairs* (Buffalo, NY: William S. Hein, 1998), 2:665.

17. United States, *Statutes at Large*, vol. 7, 307–309 ; Royce, "Indian Land Cessions in the United States," Plate CXXII, Parcel 141.

18. Grant Foreman, *Indians and Pioneers*, revised ed. (Norman: University of Oklahoma Press, 1936), 259.

Chapter 26

1. Virginia Bergman Peters, *The Florida Wars* (Hamden, CT: Archon Books, 1979), 37.

2. Florette Henri, *The Southern Indians and Benjamin Hawkins 1796–1816* (Norman: University of Oklahoma Press, 1986), 308.

3. James F. Doster, *The Creek Indians and Their Florida Lands 1740–1823*, vol. 2 (New York: Garland Publishing, 1974), 181.

4. Ibid., 182.

5. Ibid., 212.

6. Ibid., 206.

7. Ibid., 201.

8. William Warren Rogers, Robert David Ward, Leah Rawls Atkins, and Wayne Flynt, *Alabama: The History of a Deep South State* (Tuscaloosa: University of Alabama Press, 1994), 54.

9. Doster, *The Creek Indians and Their Florida Lands*, vol. 2, 216.

10. David S. Heidler and Jeanne T. Heidler, *Old Hickory's War* (Mechanicsburg, PA: Stackpole Books, 1996), 92.

11. Ibid., 174.

12. *American State Papers: Military Affairs* (Buffalo, NY: William S. Hein, 1998), 1:721–734.

13. Robert V. Remini, *Andrew Jackson and the Course of American Empire, 1767–1821* (New York: Harper & Row, 1977), 364.

14. Heidler and Heidler, *Old Hickory's War*, 203.

15. Remini, *Andrew Jackson and the Course of American Empire*, 367.

16. Henri, *The Southern Indians and Benjamin Hawkins*, 314; Thomas A. Bailey, *A Diplomatic History of the American People*, 8th ed. (New York: Appleton-Century-Crofts, 1979), 172.

17. Doster, *The Creek Indians and Their Florida Lands*, vol. 2, 239.

18. Ibid., 241.

19. Foreman, *Indian Removal*, 315.

20. Doster, *The Creek Indians and Their Florida Lands*, vol. 2, 267.

21. Ibid., 271.

22. United States, *Statutes at Large*, vol. 7, 224–228.

23. Doster, *The Creek Indians and Their Florida Lands*, vol. 2, 272.

24. Ibid., 273.

25. Ibid., 276.

26. United States, *Statutes at Large*, vol. 7, 224–228.

27. Peters, *The Florida Wars*, 71.

28. Ibid.

29. Ibid., 77.

30. Ibid., 78.

31. Ibid., 79.

32. Ibid.
33. Ibid., 78.
34. Doster, *The Creek Indians and Their Florida Lands*, vol. 2, 277.
35. Peters, *The Florida Wars*, 83–84.

Chapter 27

1. Grant Foreman, *Indian Removal* (Norman: University of Oklahoma Press, 1953), 26 n. 12.
2. United States, Statutes at Large, vol. 4, 411–12.
3. Arthur H. DeRosier, Jr., *The Removal of the Choctaw Indians* (1970; reprint, New York: Harper & Row, 1972), 100.
4. Hunt, John Gabriel 89–90.
5. DeRosier, *The Removal of the Choctaw Indians*, 104.
6. Gloria Jahoda, *The Trail of Tears* (New York: Holt, Rinehart and Winston, 1975), 79.
7. Foreman, *Indian Removal*, 26.
8. Ibid., 25.
9. Ibid., 26.
10. DeRosier, *The Removal of the Choctaw Indians*, 120.
11. United States, *Statutes at Large*, vol. 7, 333–342 ; Francis Paul Prucha, *Documents of United States Indian Policy*, 2nd ed., expanded (Lincoln: University of Nebraska Press, 1975), 53–58.
12. Foreman, *Indian Removal*, 28, note 18.
13. DeRosier, *The Removal of the Choctaw Indians*, 127–128.
14. Foreman, *Indian Removal*, 38.
15. Ibid.
16. Ibid., 39.
17. Ibid., 49.
18. H. B. Cushman and Angie Debo (eds.), *History of the Choctaw, Chickasaw, and Natchez Indians* (1899; reprint, Norman: University of Oklahoma Press, 1999), 114–115.
19. Foreman, *Indian Removal*, 56.
20. Francis Paul Prucha, *The Great Father*, vol. I (Lincoln: University of Nebraska, 1984), 218.
21. Foreman, *Indian Removal*, 54.
22. Ibid., 53.
23. Foreman, *Indian Removal*, 73.
24. Ibid., 91.
25. Ibid., 93.
26. DeRosier, *The Removal of the Choctaw Indians*, 136.
27. Debo, *The Rise and Fall of the Choctaw Republic*, 78.
28. "Greenwood LeFlore," *American National Biography*, edited by John A. Garraty and Mark C. Carnes (New York: Oxford University Press, 1999), 422–423;
Andrew Carroll (ed.), *Letters of a Nation* (New York: Broadway Books, 1997), 393.

Chapter 28

1. Arrell M. Gibson, *The Chickasaws* (Norman: University of Oklahoma Press, 1971), 155–156.
2. Clarence E. Carter (ed.), *The Territorial Papers of the United States, Colonial Times*, vol. 18 (Washington, DC: Government Printing Office, 1934–1975), 212.
3. Gibson, *The Chickasaws*, 156.
4. *American State Papers: Indian Affairs* (Buffalo, NY: William S. Hein, 1998), 2:541–542.
5. Gibson, *The Chickasaws*, 164.
6. Ibid., 166.
7. Ibid., 167.
8. Ibid., 169.

9. Ibid., 170.
10. Ibid., 171.
11. Ibid., 173.
12. Ibid., 174.
13. Grant Foreman, *Indian Removal* (Norman: University of Oklahoma Press, 1953), 199 n. 21.
14. United States, *Statutes at Large*, vol. 7, 381–391 ; Royce, "Indian Land Cessions in the United States," Plates CXLIII, CVIII, CLXI, Parcel 178.
15. Gibson, *The Chickasaws*, 176.
16. Foreman, *Indian Removal*, 201.
17. Ibid.
18. Statutes at Large 7 (1834): 450–457.
19. Foreman, *Indian Removal*, 201.
20. Ibid.
21. Ibid., 202.
22. Francis Paul Prucha, *The Great Father*, vol. I (Lincoln: University of Nebraska, 1984), 215–216; Angie Debo, *The History of the Indians of the United States* (Norman, OK: University of Oklahoma Press, 1970), 125, 127.
23. United States, *Statutes at Large*, vol. 11, 573–575.
24. Gibson, *The Chickasaws*, 182.
25. Ibid., 183.
26. Foreman, *Indian Removal*, 206.
27. Ibid., 214.
28. Gibson, *The Chickasaws*, 187.
29. Ibid., 213.
30. Foreman, *Indian Removal*, 217–218.

Chapter 29

1. Grant Foreman, *Indian Removal* (Norman: University of Oklahoma Press, 1953), 107 n. 4.
2. Ibid., 107–108.
3. Ibid., 109.
4. United States, *Statutes at Large*, vol. 7, 366–368.
5. Foreman, *Indian Removal*, 113.
6. Ibid., 113.
7. Ibid., 114.
8. Ibid., 115.
9. Ibid., 116.
10. Ibid., 117.
11. Ibid., 116.
12. Ibid., 117.
13. Ibid., 119.
14. Ibid., 119–120.
15. Ibid., 121.
16. Ibid., 131.
17. Gloria Jahoda, *The Trail of Tears* (New York: Holt, Rinehart and Winston, 1975), 149.
18. Foreman, *Indian Removal*, 129–130.
19. Ibid., 136.
20. Ibid., 134.
21. Ibid., 150.
22. Ibid., 154.
23. Ibid., 160–161.
24. Ibid., 163.
25. Ibid., 174.
26. Ibid., 176.
27. Ibid., 183–184.
28. Ibid., 187.

Chapter 30

1. United States, *Statutes at Large*, vol. 7, 368–370.
2. Grant Foreman, *Indian Removal* (Norman: University of Oklahoma Press, 1953), 321 n. 21.

3. Virginia Bergman Peters, *The Florida Wars* (Hamden, CT: Archon Books, 1979), 95.

4. *American State Papers: Military Affairs* (Buffalo, NY: William S. Hein, 1998), 6:67–68.

5. Peters, *The Florida Wars*, 98–99.

6. Peters, *The Florida Wars*, 98.

7. *American State Papers: Military Affairs*, 6:533–534.

8. Foreman, *Indian Removal*, 327.

9. Ibid., 328–329.

10. Ibid., 340.

11. Peters, *The Florida Wars*, 113.

12. Ibid., 117.

13. Ibid., 142.

14. Foreman, *Indian Removal*, 349.

15. Peters, *The Florida Wars*, 160.

16. Ibid., 159.

17. Foreman, *Indian Removal*, 360.

18. Peters, *The Florida Wars*, 183–184.

19. Ibid., 181.

20. Ibid., 206.

21. Ibid., 212.

22. Ibid., 213–214.

23. Ibid., 219.

24. Ibid., 227.

25. Ibid., 233.

26. Ibid., 252.

27. Ibid., 262.

28. Ibid., 283.

Chapter 31

1. Grace Steele Woodward, *The Cherokees* (Norman: University of Oklahoma Press, 1963), 136.

2. Thurman Wilkins, *Cherokee Tragedy* (New York: Macmillan, 1970), 189.

3. Woodward, *The Cherokees*, 185.

4. Gloria Jahoda, *The Trail of Tears* (New York: Holt, Rinehart and Winston, 1975), 31.

5. Woodward, *The Cherokees*, 147.

6. Ibid., 149.

7. Francis Paul Prucha, *The Great Father*, vol. I (Lincoln: University of Nebraska, 1984), 187.

8. Woodward, *The Cherokees*, 150.

9. Prucha, *The Great Father*, vol. I, 190.

10. Virginia Bergman Peters, *The Florida Wars* (Hamden, CT: Archon Books, 1979), 68.

11. Prucha, *The Great Father*, vol. I, 199.

12. Florette Henri, *The Southern Indians and Benjamin Hawkins 1796–1816* (Norman: University of Oklahoma Press, 1986), 10–11.

13. Wilkins, *Cherokee Tragedy*, 201.

14. Ibid., 199–200.

15. Prucha, *The Great Father*, vol. I, 193.

16. Wilkins, *Cherokee Tragedy*, 202.

17. Grant Foreman, *Indian Removal* (Norman: University of Oklahoma Press, 1953), 229.

18. Prucha, *The Great Father*, vol. I, 194.

19. Ibid., 194.

20. Ibid.

21. Ibid.

22. Foreman, *Indian Removal*, 229.

23. Stanley W. Hoig, *The Cherokees and Their Chiefs* (Fayetteville: University of Arkansas Press, 1998), 146.

24. Woodward, *The Cherokees*, 160.

25. Prucha, *The Great Father*, vol. I, 196.

26. Ibid.

27. Stephen G. Christianson, *Facts About the Congress* (New York: H. W. Wilson, 1996), 83–84 (1830 Congress).

Chapter 32

1. Grace Steele Woodward, *The Cherokees* (Norman: University of Oklahoma Press, 1963), 161.

2. Ibid., 165.

3. Thurman Wilkins, *Cherokee Tragedy* (New York: Macmillan, 1970), 211.

4. Stanley W. Hoig, *The Cherokees and Their Chiefs* (Fayetteville: University of Arkansas Press, 1998), 2.

5. Wilkins, *Cherokee Tragedy*, 215.

6. Ibid., 217.

7. Ibid., 225.

8. Ibid., 228.

9. Woodward, *The Cherokees*, 171.

10. Ibid.

11. Francis Paul Prucha, *The Great Father*, vol. I (Lincoln: University of Nebraska, 1984), 212.

12. Grant Foreman, *Indian Removal* (Norman: University of Oklahoma Press, 1953), 242.

13. Wilkins, *Cherokee Tragedy*, 239.

14. Ibid., 242.

15. Foreman, *Indian Removal*, 248.

16. Stanley W. Hoig, *The Cherokees and Their Chiefs* (Fayetteville: University of Arkansas Press, 1998), 149–150.

17. Foreman, *Indian Removal*, 261.

18. Wilkins, *Cherokee Tragedy*, 250.

19. Ibid., 251.

20. Ibid., 253.

21. Ibid., 254.

22. Ibid., 257.

23. Ibid., 259.

24. Ibid., 262–263.

25. Ibid., 275.

26. Ibid., 276–277.

27. Ibid., 277.

28. Woodward, *The Cherokees*, 193.

29. Hoig, *The Cherokees and Their Chiefs*, 156.

30. Foreman, *Indian Removal*, 269.

31. Ibid.

32. Ibid., 269, n.9.

33. Hoig, *The Cherokees and Their Chiefs*, 161–162.

34. Foreman, *Indian Removal*, 270.

35. Ibid., 271.

36. Wilkins, *Cherokee Tragedy*, 281.

Chapter 33

1. Grant Foreman, *Indian Removal* (Norman: University of Oklahoma Press, 1953), 272.

2. *American State Papers: Military Affairs* (Buffalo, NY: William S. Hein, 1998), 7:540–541.

3. Foreman, *Indian Removal*, 285.

4. Thurman Wilkins, *Cherokee Tragedy* (New York: Macmillan, 1970), 304.

5. Russell Thornton, *The Cherokees: A Population Study* (Lincoln: University of Nebraska Press, 1990), 65.

6. Grace Steele Woodward, *The Cherokees* (Norman: University of Oklahoma Press, 1963), 204.

7. Thornton, *The Cherokees*, 65–66.

8. Ibid., 66.

9. Woodward, *The Cherokees*, 205.

10. Foreman, *Indian Removal*, 287–89.

11. Quote from Thornton, *The Cherokees*, 67.

12. Wilkins, *Cherokee Tragedy*, 310.

13. Woodward, *The Cherokees*, 211.

14. Ibid.

15. Foreman, *Indian Removal*, 301.

16. Woodward, *The Cherokees*, 215.

17. Ibid., 217.
18. Wilkins, *Cherokee Tragedy*, 313–314.
19. Ibid.

Chapter 34

1. Bureau of Indian Affairs Press Release, September 2000; Washington Post, section A, page 2, September 9, 2000.

2. United States, *Statutes at Large*, vol. 12, 765–767 ; Glen A. Wilkinson, "Indian Tribal Claims Before the Court of Claims," *Georgetown Law Journal* 55 (1966): 511–512, 515.

3. United States, *Statutes at Large* vol. 60, 1052.
4. Francis Paul Prucha, *The Great Father*, vol. II (Lincoln: University of Nebraska, 1984), 669.
5. Ibid., 670.
6. Prucha, *The Great Father*, vol. II, 747.
7. Theodore W. Taylor, *The States and Their Indian Citizens* (Washington: United States Department of the Interior, Bureau of Indian Affairs, 1972), 199.
8. Steven Andrew Light and Kathryn R. L. Rand, *Indian Gaming and Tribal Sovereignty* (Lawrence: University of Kansas Press, 2005), 127–128.

Bibliography

Primary Source Material

Adler, Mortimer J., editor in chief. *The Annals of America*. Vols. 1–4 (1493–1820). Chicago: Encyclopædia Britannica, 1968.

American State Papers: Foreign Affairs. Buffalo, NY: William S. Hein, 1998.

American State Papers: Indian Affairs. Buffalo, NY: William S. Hein, 1998.

American State Papers: Military Affairs. Buffalo, NY: William S. Hein, 1998.

Annals of the Congress of the United States. Washington, DC: Gales and Seaton, 1834–1856. Buffalo, NY: William S. Hein, 2003.

Bassett, John Spencer, editor. *Correspondence of Andrew Jackson*. Washington, DC: Carnegie Institution of Washington, 1926–1935.

Billings, Warren M., editor. *The Old Dominion in the Seventeenth Century: A Documentary History of Virginia, 1606–1689*. Chapel Hill: University of North Carolina Press, 1975.

Boyd, Julian P., et al., editors. *The Papers of Thomas Jefferson*. Princeton, NJ: Princeton University Press, 1950.

Bureau of Census. *Historical Statistics of the United States, Colonial Times to 1970*. Bicentennial Edition. Washington: U.S. Bureau of Census, 1975.

_____. Census data for 2000, 2005.

Byrd, William. "Surveying the Frontier." *Annals*, Vol. 1, 375–84.

Calloway, Colin G., editor, and introduction. *The World Turned Upside Down*. New York: Bedford Books of St. Martin's Press, 1994.

Carroll, Andrew, editor. *Letters of a Nation*. New York: Broadway Books, 1997.

Carter, Clarence E., editor. *The Territorial Papers of the United States*. Washington, D.C.: U.S. Government Printing Office, 1934–1975.

Caughey, John Walton. *McGillivray of the Creeks*. Norman: University of Oklahoma Press, 1938.

Commager, Henry Steele, and Richard Morris, eds. *The Spirit of Seventy-Six*. 1958. Reprint, New York: Da Capo Press, 1995.

Commager, Henry Steele, editor. *Documents of American History*. 9th ed. Englewood Cliffs, NJ: Prentice Hall, 1973.

Cushman, H. B., and Angie Debo, editors. *History of the Choctaw, Chickasaw, and Natchez Indians*. 1899. Reprint, Norman: University of Oklahoma Press, 1999.

Donovan, Frank. *The Benjamin Franklin Papers*. New York: Dodd, Mead, 1962.

Filson, John. *The Discovery, Settlement of Kentucke*. 1784. Reprint, Fairfield, Washington: Ye Galleon Press, 2001.

Fitzpatrick, John C., editors. *The Diaries of George Washington, 1748–1799*. New York: Houghton Mifflin, 1925.

_____. *George Washington's Writings*. Washington, D.C.: U.S. GPO, 1938.

Franklin, Benjamin. *The Autobiography*. New York: Vintage Books, The Library of America, 1990.

Heart, Jonathan. *Journal of Capt. Jonathan Heart*. Albany, NY: Joel Mansell's Sons, 1885.

Hening, William Walker. *A Collection of all the Laws of Virginia from 1619 to 1808*. Charlottesville: University of Virginia Press, 1969.

Hunt, John Gabriel, editor. *The Inaugural Addresses of the Presidents*. New York: Gramercy Books, 1995.

Israel, Fred L., editor. *The State of the Union Messages of the Presidents 1790–1966*. New York: Chelsen House-Robert Hector, Publishers, 1966.

Jefferson, Thomas, and William Peden, editor, introduction, notes. *Notes on the State of Virginia*. New York: W. W. Norton, 1972.

Lipscomb, Andrew A., editor in chief. *The Writings of Thomas Jefferson*. Washington, D.C.: Thomas Jefferson Memorial Association, 1905.

"Opportunities for Settlers in Carolina." *Annals*, Vol. 1, 240–42.

Palmer, William P., editor. *Calendar of Virginia State Papers*, 11 vols. 1884. Reprint, New York: Kraus Reprint, 1968.

Pastorius, Francis D. "German Settlers in Pennsylvania." *Annals*, Vol. 1, 310–14.

Peterson, Merrill, editor. *Thomas Jefferson: Writings*. New York: Library of America, 1984.

Pory, John. "The Work of a Colonial Legislature." *Annals*, Vol. 1, 40–46.

Prucha, Francis Paul. *Documents of United States Indian Policy*. 2nd ed., Expanded. Lincoln: University of Nebraska Press, 1975.

_____. *American Indian Treaties*. Berkeley: University of California Press, 1994.

Richardson, James D. *A Compilation of the Messages and Papers of the Presidents*. New York: Bureau of National Literature, 1897.

Ridge, Martin, and Ray A. Billington, eds. *America's Frontier Story: A Documentary History of Western Expansion*. New York: Holt, Rinehart and Winston, 1969.

Royce, Charles C. "Indian Land Cessions in the United States." *Smithsonian Institution. Bureau of American Ethnology*. Eighteenth Annual Report, 1896–1897. Washington, D.C.: U.S. GPO, 1899.

Sparke, John R. "The Attraction of Florida." *Annals*, Vol. 1, 6–10.

Thwaites, Reuben Gold, and Louise Phelps Kellogg, eds. *Documentary History of Dunmore's War: Bicentennial Edition, 1774–1974*. Harrisonburg, VA: C. J. Carter, 1974.

Tocqueville, Alexis de, J. P. Mayer, and Max Lerner, editors. *Democracy in America*. New York: Harper & Row, 1966.

_____. Senate Document No. 512, 23rd Cong., 1st Session. Correspondence on Removal of Indians West of Mississippi River, 1831–1833, in five volumes.

_____. House Document No. 452, 25th Cong., 2nd Session. Alleged Frauds on Creek Indians.

Vanderwerth, W.C. *Indian Oratory*. Norman: University of Oklahoma Press, 1973.

Vaughan, Alden T., general editor. *Early American Indian Documents: Treaties and Laws 1607–1789*. Frederick, M.D., and Washington, D.C.: University Publications of America, 1979.

Virginia State Bar. *A Collection of All the Acts of Assembly of Virginia, 1733*. Baltimore: Gateway Press, 1976.

Williams, Samuel Cole. *The Memoirs of Lieut. Henry Timberlake 1756–1765*. Marietta, GA: Continental Book, 1948.

Books and Articles

Abernethy, Thomas Perkins. *Western Lands and the American Revolution*. New York: Russell & Russell, 1959.

_____. *South in the New Nation, 1789–1819*. Baton Rouge: Louisiana State University Press, 1961.

Adams, James Truslow, editor in chief, and R. V. Coleman, managing editor. *Atlas of American History*. New York: Scribner's, 1943.

Agnew, Brad. *Fort Gibson*. Norman: University of Oklahoma Press, 1980.

Andrews, Matthew Page. *Virginia, The Old Dominion*. Vol. 1. Richmond, VA: Dietz Press, 1949.

Bailey, Thomas A. *A Diplomatic History of the American People*. 8th ed. New York: Appleton-Century-Crofts, 1979.

Bailyn, Bernard. *The Peopling of British North America. An Introduction*. New York: Alfred A. Knopf, 1986.

Berkhofer, Robert F., Jr. *The White Man's Indian*. New York: Alfred A. Knopf, 1978.

Billings, Warren M., John E. Selby, and Thad W. Tate. *Colonial Virginia*. White Plains, NY: KTO Press, 1986.

Billings, Warren M., editor. *The Old Dominion in the Seventeenth Century*. Chapel Hill: University of North Carolina Press, 1975.

Billington, Ray Allen. *Westward Expansion: A History of the American Frontier*. 4th ed. New York: Macmillan, 1974.

Boorstin, Daniel J. *The Americans: The Colonial Experience*. New York: Random House, 1958. Third Printing.

Brandon, William. *Indians*. 1961. Reprint. *The American Heritage Book of Indians*. Boston: Houghton Mifflin, 1987.

Brown, Douglas Summers. *The Catawba Indians*. Columbia: University of South Carolina Press, 1966.

Brown, John P. *Old Frontiers*. New York: Arno Press, 1971.

Buck, Solon J., and Elizabeth Hawthorn Buck. *The Planting of Civilization in Western Pennsylvania*. Pittsburgh: University of Pittsburgh, 1939.

Burstein, Andrew. *The Passions of Andrew Jackson*. New York: Alfred A. Knopf, 2003.

Calloway, Colin G., editor, and introduction. *The World Turned Upside Down*. New York: Bedford Books of St. Martin's Press, 1994.

Cartwright, Frederick F. *Disease and History*. New York: Thomas Y. Crowell, 1973.

Caughey, John Walton. *McGillivray of the Creeks*. Norman: University of Oklahoma Press, 1938.

Christianson, Stephen G. *Facts About the Congress*. New York: H. W. Wilson, 1996.

Chitwood, Oliver Perry. *A History of Colonial America*. 3rd ed. New York: Harper, 1961.

Churchill, Winston S. *A History of the English Speaking People: The Age of Revolution*. Vol. 3. New York: Dodd, Mead, 1964.

Clark, Thomas D. *Historic Maps of Kentucky*. Lexington: University Press of Kentucky, 1979.

_____. *Frontier America*. New York: Scribner's, 1959.

_____. *Kentucky: Land of Contrast*. New York: Harper & Row, 1968.

Coleman, Kenneth, editor. *A History of Georgia*. Athens: University of Georgia Press, 1977.

Corkran, David H. *The Creek Frontier 1540–1783*. Norman: University of Oklahoma Press, 1967.

Craven, Wesley Frank. *The Southern Colonies in the Seventeenth Century 1607–1689*. Vol. 1.

Baton Rouge: Louisiana State University Press, 1949.

Davidson, Miles H. *Then and Now.* Norman: University of Oklahoma Press, 1997.

Davis, William C. *A Way Through the Wilderness.* New York: HarperCollins, 1995.

Debo, Angie. *The History of the Indians of the United States.* Norman, OK: University of Oklahoma Press, 1970.

_____. *The Rise and Fall of the Choctaw Republic.* 2d ed. 1934. Norman: University of Oklahoma Press, 1961.

DeRosier, Arthur H., Jr. *The Removal of the Choctaw Indians.* 1970. Reprint, New York: Harper & Row, 1972.

De Vorsey, Louis, Jr. *The Indian Boundary in the Southern Colonies, 1763–1775.* Chapel Hill: University of North Carolina Press, 1966.

Doster, James F. *The Creek Indians and Their Florida Lands 1740–1823.* 2 vols. New York: Garland Publishing, 1974.

Drinnon, Richard. *Facing West.* Minneapolis: University of Minnesota, 1980.

Egloff, Keith, and Deborah Woodward. *First People: The Early Indians of Virginia.* Richmond: Department of Historic Resources, 1992.

Faragher, John Mack. *Daniel Boone.* New York: Henry Holt, 1992.

Feldman, Jay. *When the Mississippi Ran Backwards.* New York: Free Press, 2005.

Folmsbee, Stanley J., Robert E. Corlew, and Enoch L. Mitchell. *Tennessee: A Short History.* Knoxville: University of Tennessee Press, 1969.

Foreman, Grant. *Indians and Pioneers.* Revised ed. Norman: University of Oklahoma Press, 1936.

_____. *Indian Removal.* Norman: University of Oklahoma Press, 1953.

Garraty, John A., and Mark C. Carnes, eds. *American National Biography.* New York: Oxford University Press, 1999.

Gates, Paul W. *History of Public Land Development.* Washington: U.S. Government Printing Office, 1968.

Gibson, Arrell M. *The Chickasaws.* Norman: University of Oklahoma Press, 1971.

Gilbert, Bil. *God Gave Us This Country.* New York: Anchor Books, 1989.

Goodrum, John C., and others. *Rivers of Alabama.* Huntsville, AL: Strode Publishers, 1967.

Graymont, Barbara. *The Iroquois in the American Revolution.* Syracuse, N.Y.: Syracuse University Press, 1972.

Grove, Noel. *National Geographic Atlas of World History.* Washington, D.C.: National Geographic Society, 1997.

Heidler, David S., and Jeanne T. Heidler. *Old Hickory's War.* Mechanicsburg, PA: Stackpole Books, 1996.

Henderson, A. Gwynn. "Dispelling the Myth: Seventeenth- and Eighteenth-Century Indian Life in Kentucky." *Bicentennial Issue of the Register of the Kentucky Historical Society,* vol. 90, no. 1 (1992).

Henderson, Archibald. *The Conquest of the Old Southwest.* New York: Century, 1920.

Henri, Florette. *The Southern Indians and Benjamin Hawkins 1796–1816.* Norman: University of Oklahoma Press, 1986.

Hoig, Stanley W. *The Cherokees and Their Chiefs.* Fayetteville: University of Arkansas Press, 1998.

Jahoda, Gloria. *The Trail of Tears.* New York: Holt, Rinehart and Winston, 1975.

Johnson, Allen, and Dumas Malone, editors. *Dictionary of American Biography.* New York: Scribner's, 1927.

Kincaid, Robert L. *The Wilderness Road.* 1947. Reprint, Middlesboro, KY: Bobbs-Merrill, 1966.

King, Duane H. editor. *Memoirs of Lieut. Henry Timberlake 1756–1765.* Cherokee, NC: Museum of the Cherokee Press; distributed by the University of North Carolina, c. 2007.

Leach, Douglas Edward. *The Northern Colonial Frontier 1607–1763.* New York: Holt, Rinehart and Winston, 1966.

Lebergott, Stanley. *The Americans, An Economic Record.* New York: W. W. Norton, 1984.

Lee, Wayne E. "Peace Chiefs and Blood Revenge: Patterns of Restraint in Native American Warfare, 1500–1800." *The Journal of Military History* 71, no. 3 (2007): 701–741.

_____. "Fortify, Fight, or Flee: Tuscarora and Cherokee Defensive Warfare and Military Culture Adaptation." *The Journal of Military History* 68, no. 3 (2004): 713–770.

Lefler, Hugh Talmage, and Albert Ray Newsome. *North Carolina.* Chapel Hill: University of North Carolina Press, 1954.

Light, Steven Andrew, and Kathryn R. L. Rand. *Indian Gaming and Tribal Sovereignty.* Lawrence: University of Kansas Press, 2005.

Lucas, Joseph S. "Civilization or Extinction: Citizens and Indians in the Early United States." *Journal of the Historical Society,* VI, no. 2 (2006): 235–250.

Malone, Dumas. *Jefferson the President, First Term, 1801–1805.* Boston: Little, Brown, 1970.

Masterson, William H. *William Blount.* Baton Rouge: Louisiana State University Press, 1954.

Mohr, Walter H. *Federal Indian Relations 1774–1788.* Philadelphia: University of Pennsylvania Press, 1933.

Morgan, H. Wayne, and Ann Hodges Morgan. *Oklahoma, A History.* New York: W. W. Norton, 1977.

Morison, Samuel Eliot. *The Oxford History of the American People.* New York: Oxford University Press, 1965.

Morison, Samuel Eliot, and Henry Steele Commager. *The Growth of the American Republic.* Vol. 1, 4th ed. New York: Oxford University Press, 1951.

Morris, Richard B., editor. *Encyclopedia of American History.* New York: Harper & Brothers, 1953.

National Geographic Map. *Indian Country, 2004.*

Nester, William R. *The First Global War.* Westport, CT: Praeger, 2000.

Peters, Virginia Bergman. *The Florida Wars.* Hamden, CT: Archon Books, 1979.

Pound, Merritt B. *Benjamin Hawkins — Indian Agent.* Athens: University of Georgia Press, 1951.

Powell, William S. *North Carolina.* 1977. Reprint, Chapel Hill: University of North Carolina Press, 1988.

Prucha, Francis Paul. *Documents of United States Indian Policy,* 2nd ed., expanded. Lincoln: University of Nebraska Press, 1975.

_____. *American Indian Treaties.* Berkeley: University of California Press, 1994.

_____. *American Indian Policy in the Formative Years.* Lincoln: University of Nebraska, 1962.

_____. *The Great Father.* Vols. I–II, Lincoln: University of Nebraska, 1984.

Remini, Robert V. *Andrew Jackson and the Course of American Empire, 1767–1821.* New York: Harper & Row, 1977.

Robinson, W. Stitt. *The Southern Colonial Frontier, 1607–1763.* Albuquerque: University of New Mexico, 1979.

Rogers, William Warren, Robert David Ward, Leah Rawls Atkins, and Wayne Flynt. *Alabama: The History of a Deep South State.* Tuscaloosa: University of Alabama Press, 1994.

Rohrbough, Malcolm J. *The Trans-Appalachian Frontier.* New York: Oxford University Press, 1978.

Rouse, Parke, Jr. *The Great Wagon Road.* New York: McGraw-Hill Book, 1973.

Sale, Kirkpatrick. *The Conquest of Paradise.* New York: Alfred A. Knopf, 1990.

Selby, John E. *The Revolution in Virginia, 1775–1783.* Williamsburg, VA: Colonial Williamsburg Foundation, 1988.

Simmons, R. C. *The American Colonies.* New York: W.W. Norton, 1976.

Smith, George, founder, and Sir Leslie Stephen and Sir Sidney Lee, editors. *The Dictionary of National Biography.* London: Oxford University Press, 1917.

Snapp, J. Russell. *John Stuart and the Struggle for Empire on the Southern Frontier.* Baton Rouge: Louisiana State University Press, 1996.

Southerland, Henry DeLeon, Jr., and Jerry Elijah Brown. *The Federal Road.* Tuscaloosa: University of Alabama Press, 1989.

Stilgoe, John R. *Common Landscape of America 1580 to 1845.* New Haven: Yale University Press, 1982.

Straus, Jerry C. "Remarks of Jerry C. Straus of Hobbs, Straus, Dean & Walker, LLP, on A History of Federal Indian Policy." Delivered at Osher Lifelong Learning Institute, George Mason University, September 2006.

Sturtevant, William C., general editor, Wilcomb E. Washburn, vol. 4 editor, and Bruce G. Trigger, vol. 15 editor. *Handbook of North American Indians.* Washington: Smithsonian Institution, 1988.

Somerset Publishers. *Encyclopedia of Virginia.* Encyclopedia of the United States. New York, N.Y.: Somersert Publishers, 1992.

Taylor, Theodore W. *The States and Their Indian Citizens.* Washington: United States Department of the Interior, Bureau of Indian Affairs, 1972.

Thomas, Cyrus. Introduction. "Indian Land Cessions in the United States." *Smithsonian Institution.* 18th Annual Report, Bureau of American Ethnology, Washington, D.C.: U.S. GPO, 1899.

Thornton, Russell. *The Cherokees: A Population Study.* Lincoln: University of Nebraska Press, 1990.

United States. *Biographical Directory of the United States Congress, 1774–1989.* Washington, D.C.: U.S. Government Printing Office, 1989.

United States. *United States Statutes at Large.* Washington: U.S. Government Printing Office, 1789.

Utley, Robert M., and Wilcomb E. Washburn. *The Indian Wars.* New York: American Heritage Publishing Co. / Bonanza Books, 1982.

Vaughan, Alden T., general editor. *Early American Indian Documents: Treaties and Laws 1607–1789.* Frederick, MD, and Washington, D.C.: University Publications of America, 1979.

Viola, Herman J. *After Columbus.* New York: Orion Books, 1990.

_____. *Diplomats in Buckskins.* 1981. Reprint, Blufflon, SC: Rivilo Books, 1995.

_____. *Thomas McKenny, Architect of America's Early Indian Policy: 1816–1830.* Chicago: Swallow Press, 1974.

Wainwright, Nicholas B. *George Croghan, Wilderness Diplomat.* Chapel Hill: University of North Carolina, 1959.

Wallace, Anthony F. C. *Jefferson and the Indians.* Cambridge, MA: Belknap Press, 1999.

Wikipedia. On-line encyclopedia.

Wilkins, Thurman. *Cherokee Tragedy.* New York: Macmillan, 1970.

Wilkinson, Glen A. "Indian Tribal Claims Before the Court of Claims." *Georgetown Law Journal* 55 (1966): 511–528.

Williams, Samuel Cole. *History of the Lost State of Franklin.* 1924. Revised, New York: Press of the Pioneers, 1933.

Willison, George F. *Saints and Strangers.* 1945.

Special Edition. New York: Time Incorporated, 1964.

Winthrop, John. *Life and Letters of John Winthrop.* Wikipedia.

Woodward, Grace Steele. *The Cherokees.* Norman: University of Oklahoma Press, 1963.

Wright, Louis B. *The Colonial Civilization of North America 1607–1763.* London: Eyre & Spottiswoode, 1949.

Wright, Ronald. *Stolen Continents.* Boston: Houghton Mifflin, 1992.

Index

Page numbers in **bold italic** indicate illustrations

www.ingramcontent.com/pod-product-compliance
Lightning Source LLC
Chambersburg PA
CBHW080553270326
41929CB00019B/3285